CHRISTOPHER BLAKE'S
# EASY ELEGANCE COOKBOOK

# CHRISTOPHER BLAKE'S
# EASY ELEGANCE COOKBOOK

1978
CHELSEA HOUSE PUBLISHERS
New York, London

Design:          Susan Lusk
Project Editor:  Ingrid Russell
Associate Editor: Joy Johannessen

Copyright © 1978. Christopher Blake and Chelsea House Publishers.

LC: 78-56874
ISBN: 0-87754-070-5

CHELSEA HOUSE PUBLISHERS

Harold Steinberg, Chairman & Publisher      Andrew E. Norman, President
Susan Lusk, Vice President
A Division of Chelsea House Educational Communications, Inc.
70 West 40th Street, New York, N.Y. 10018

# CONTENTS

# 2
# HOLIDAYS IN NEW ORLEANS

# 3
# FAVORITE NEW ORLEANS RESTAURANTS

# 4
# RECIPES OF FRIENDS

# 5
# THE INTERNATIONAL INFLUENCE

ITALIAN

JAPANESE

JEWISH

RUSSIAN

SCANDINAVIAN

SOUTH AMERICAN

SPANISH

PART TWO
# BLAKE'S BASICS

## 6
## SOUPS

# 7
# EGGS

# 8
# FISH & SHELLFISH

# 9
# POULTRY & GAME BIRDS

# 10
# MEATS

# 11
# VEGETABLES & SALADS

# 12
# DESSERTS

# 13
# SAUCES, ETC.

# Preface

I shall always remember the scene—Louis Armstrong and Chris Blake in deep conversation at the National Press Club in Washington. They were not talking jazz, as you might expect, but how to cook Red Beans and Rice. If you are not from New Orleans, you could never understand how Red Beans and Rice can be the subject of conversation. Red Beans and Rice, you see, is more than food that graces the table of poor and rich alike in Louisiana—it is a big part of our joie de vivre. In New Orleans, Red Beans and Rice is what makes the old city pulsate. It is an ingredient like Mardi Gras, the Sazerac cocktail, Basin Street and the French Quarter.

Louis Armstrong, Chris Blake and the writer of this preface were raised on Red Beans and Rice. On the occasion in question, however, old Satchmo, ailing from a heart condition that was to claim his life in less than six months, had to settle for reminiscences. A rigid diet, enforced by his wife Lucille, would not accommodate his favorite dish, but this culinary tête-à-tête led to the predictable. Satchmo begged to sample the Blake approach to Red Beans and Rice, and Lucille relented.

This was my introduction to Christopher Blake and the beginning of my association with one of the most fascinating people I have ever met. Chris had come to Washington to prepare a New Orleans dinner for the seven hundred fifty guests on hand for my inauguration as president of the National Press Club on January 29, 1971. Lindy Boggs, the wife of House Democratic leader Hale Boggs of New Orleans, whom she later succeeded in office when he died tragically in an Alaskan plane crash, had arranged for Chris to offer his talents for the affair. At the time he operated one of the more popular restaurants in New Orleans. Chris created a gustatorial extravaganza that ranged from Louisiana Caviar (made with eggplant) to Shrimp Mousse to Chicken Sir Malcolm (made with Scotch). The plaudits are still being heard seven years later. Among the diners were David Frost, Diahann Carroll, Admiral Arleigh Berke, Madame Anna Chennault and a large number of senators and congressmen. Louis Armstrong blew his horn with great love that evening.

The National Press Club developed a fondness for Christopher Blake and invited him back over the years to show off his unique cooking skills. At one of his appearances the master of ceremonies dubbed him "Gourmet Laureate of New Orleans," and the name stuck. His artistry in the kitchen knows no bound, whether he is entertaining at an intimate candlelight affair or preparing a multi-course meal for hundreds. Once, he supervised an al fresco feeding of four thousand delegates to an international convention in New Orleans, and the unmistakable Blake touch still shone through. Another time I watched him create a dinner with an assortment of unusual oysters, clams, fish and other seafood produced artificially by the Lummi Indians of the state of Washington.

Good food, as Chris Blake consistently demonstrates, can be prepared easily and without all the fuss of trying to bring together twenty or thirty spices, herbs, condiments and what have you into a single recipe. His creations are simple and to the point. I've seen Blake, in tuxedo, whip up a delicious spread for twelve without ever putting down his martini—and not in hours, but in a few minutes. Always, however, there is a flair and a style to his cooking. A simple egg dish is rendered with the élan of a Toscanini. Christopher Blake cooks only as long as it is fun. If it becomes work he walks out of the kitchen. That is one of the reasons why he always makes the distinction that he is a cook and not a chef.

This is a cookbook to be used, not stored on the shelf. It will add adventure and zest, whether you're cooking for the family or entertaining guests. Chris Blake will lead you gracefully through the culinary arts. He has set no traps for the amateur. And the most experienced cook will learn new tricks. Bon appétit.

*Vernon Louviere*
*Former President, National Press Club*

# Introduction

SIX FORMATIVE YEARS in Paris tend to orient one's interests toward sex or cuisine. From the Cordon Bleu to the bordellos of Montmartre, a man emerges with a taste for living. To document his impressions, he writes his memoirs first, and then a cookbook.

While in Paris, I never fried an egg; but I dined everywhere and spent hours shopping with great cooks in the marketplaces of that city.

Recipe books are perhaps the greatest examples of plagiarism in modern publishing. A true creation in cuisine today is rare indeed. And so, new cookbooks are really adaptations and variations.

The recipes found in this volume are among my favorites, those I have found most useful and practical from my years abroad as well as at home in New Orleans, where one has an excellent view of world cuisine. They represent the secrets of my long experience with good food and good cooks.

I am proud to have kept my eyes and ears open to the best culinary tunes played in New Orleans and the Bayou Country. No cuisine, with the possible exception of Mandarin Chinese, Hungarian and classical French, evokes as much excitement for the gourmet palate as Cajun and Creole. I am also proud to have tasted these recipes in some of the finest restaurants and at the homes of the greatest hosts and hostesses in Louisiana.

As I read over the galley proofs of this volume, more than twenty years of fun and games in the kitchen passed before my eyes. These recipes were not tested in the great testing kitchens. These recipes, some many times over, have been personally prepared by me for friends and family. They represent my personal repertoire, and they were prepared in the kinds of kitchens that you, the reader, are used to.

Sometimes I can't remember where I first tasted a dish or where I got the recipe. I do remember, however, that my constant aim was to entertain, and to do it with ease and elegance.

*Christopher Blake*
*New Orleans, 1978*

PART ONE
# A TOUCH OF NEW ORLEANS

# 1
# WAY DOWN YONDER

THE SPIRIT of Louis Armstrong hovers over this chapter. Many of these dishes were served when Louis played one of his final concerts, the night of Vernon Louviere's inauguration as president of the National Press Club in Washington, D.C. The great man of jazz regretted that his diet did not permit him to indulge, but the memory was there. To that memory, and in honor of the colorful spirit that was Louis Armstrong, I have added even more recipes of the good New Orleans food he loved best.

Had Satchmo been destined to be a cook, he would have created recipes and spread the fame of New Orleans in a different manner. Another muse called him, but he never forgot the delicious aromas of the kitchens of his native New Orleans. Some of the more sophisticated Cajun and Creole recipes may have been denied him as a boy, but he sounded the trumpet for this traditional cuisine just as he played his trumpet everywhere.

# COCKTAILS

## CHRIS BLAKE'S BLOODY MARY

1 Tbs. seasoned salt
1 Tbs. Worcestershire sauce
¼–½ Tbs. Tabasco pepper sauce
Juice of 3 lemons

Juice of 1 lime
2 cups good vodka
1 large can V-8 juice (48 oz.)

*Serves 8–10*

Put all seasonings in a blender and blend well. Add 1½ cups of the vodka. Add the V-8 juice and finish with the remaining ½ cup vodka.
Pour over ice in large glasses and garnish with a green onion or a celery stick.

## PAT O'BRIEN'S HURRICANE PUNCH

2 oz. Jero's Red Passion Fruit
  cocktail mix

2 oz. fresh lemon juice
4 oz. good dark rum

*Serves 1*

Mix all ingredients and pour into tall glasses filled with crushed ice. Decorate with an orange slice and a cherry.
This cocktail originated in New Orleans. The Hurricane as served at the famous Pat O'Brien's was created by the late Mrs. Charles (Jo) Cantrell.

## RAGIN' CAJIN

*Serves as many as you like*

Make ice cubes with 2 drops Tabasco pepper sauce in each cube. Unmold 2 or 3 cubes in each Old-Fashioned glass. Fill with good vodka. Allow to sit for a few minutes and just sip.

## RAMOS GIN FIZZ

1–2 cups crushed ice
1 egg white
2 tsp. heavy cream
1 heaping tsp. confectioners'
  sugar

Juice of 1 lemon
2 oz. gin
½ tsp. orange flower water
Dash of Pechaud bitters
Twist of lemon peel

*Serves 1*

Place crushed ice and all ingredients into shaker. Shake, shake and shake again until it is frothy all through . . . almost like whipped cream. It's all in the shaking.

Strain and pour into a highball glass.

## SAZERAC COCKTAIL

3 dashes Abisante
1 lump sugar
1 dash orange bitters

Dash of Pechaud bitters
2 jiggers 100-proof bourbon or rye

*Serves 1*

Coat a double Old-Fashioned glass with the Abisante. Muddle sugar with the bitters and just a dash of water in the glass and fill with cubed ice. Pour bourbon or rye over this.

Stir until cocktail is ice cold. Remove ice and garnish with a lemon twist.

# APPETIZERS

## CRAB MEAT IMPERIAL

1 small green pepper,
  finely minced
2 pimientos, finely diced
1 Tbs. Creole mustard
1 tsp. salt
½ tsp. white pepper

2 whole eggs
1 cup mayonnaise
¼ tsp. Tabasco pepper sauce
2 lbs. lump crab meat
Extra mayonnaise for topping
Paprika

*Serves 8*

Mix green pepper and pimientos. Add mustard, salt, white pepper, eggs, mayonnaise and Tabasco; mix well.

Add crab meat and mix with fingers so that lumps do not break.

Distribute mixture into 8 shells or ramekins, heaping mixture lightly. Top with a light coating of mayonnaise and sprinkle with paprika.

Bake in a moderate oven (350°) for 15 minutes until delicately browned on top. Serve hot.

## EGGS PORT SALUT

| | |
|---|---|
| 6 eggs | 1 Tbs. Worcestershire sauce |
| 4 Tbs. butter | ½ tsp. Tabasco pepper sauce |
| 4 Tbs. flour | ¼ tsp. seasoned salt |
| 2 cups milk | ½ lb. Port Salut cheese, diced |
| Dash of nutmeg | 6 slices bacon, fried, drained and |
| 1 tsp. Creole mustard | crumbled |

*Serves 6*

Hard-boil eggs, peel and slice them in half lengthwise. Set to one side, keeping them warm.

Combine butter and flour to make a light roux and cook, stirring for 5 minutes.

Add milk, nutmeg, mustard, Worcestershire, Tabasco and seasoned salt. Stir until smooth.

Add diced cheese and continue cooking until cheese has melted and sauce is rich and creamy—about 15 minutes. Add bacon pieces and mix well.

Serve 2 halves of hard-boiled eggs per person, pouring the sauce over each portion. Eggs may be placed on an English muffin or a slice of toast.

## LOUISIANA CAVIAR

| | |
|---|---|
| 6 small whole eggplants | 1 tsp. salt |
| 5 medium white onions, finely | ½ tsp. Tabasco pepper sauce |
| minced | 1 cup very good olive oil |
| 1 clove garlic, minced | ½ cup wine vinegar |

*Serves 25 for cocktails*

Place whole eggplants in a moderate oven (350°) and bake until skins are very dark and wrinkled—about 30 minutes.

Remove from oven and allow to cool long enough to handle. Peel away the skins with your fingers. Drain the eggplants of any excess liquid and mash with a potato masher or similar instrument until a fine mush is achieved.

Add the minced onion and garlic and mix well. Add the salt and Tabasco and then the olive oil a little at a time, blending well after each addition.

Finally add the vinegar in the same manner. Taste for seasonings and chill well.

This recipe makes enough to spread melba toast for a cocktail party for 25. It will also stuff about 12 medium tomatoes and is equally good to stuff celery for hors d'oeuvres.

## NEW ORLEANS BLUE CHEESE CANAPÉS

½ lb. blue cheese
½ lb. unsalted butter or
  margarine
½ tsp. Tabasco pepper sauce

Melba Toast (chap. 13)
Pieces of shelled walnuts or
  pecans

*Serves 6*

Cream blue cheese and butter together until the mixture reaches a spreadable consistency. Add Tabasco and combine well.

Spread each melba toast round with the cheese mixture, making a small mound. Top each mound with a piece of walnut or pecan.

Cover with plastic wrap and refrigerate until cold and firm.

## NEW ORLEANS PUSSY FINGERS

2 filets of catfish, cut up into
  finger-size pieces
1 cup flour, seasoned with salt
  and pepper
2 whole eggs
2 Tbs. water

1 Tbs. Worcestershire sauce
1 tsp. Tabasco pepper sauce
1 cup commercial fish-fry mix or
  bread crumbs
2 cups cooking oil

*Serves 4–6*

Wipe each piece of catfish. Dip each piece in seasoned flour.

Make an egg wash by beating the eggs with the water. Add Worcestershire sauce and Tabasco. Mix well.

Dip each piece of catfish in the egg wash and finally into the fish-fry mix or bread crumbs.

Arrange on a platter and refrigerate until ready to fry. I like to refrigerate them for at least 1-2 hours.

Heat, but do not boil, 1 cup of the oil in a heavy skillet, adding more as necessary. Dip catfish pieces in a few at a time and cook until they begin to float. Turn over and finish cooking—not more than 10 minutes in all.

Drain on paper toweling and serve with Chris's Cocktail Sauce (chap. 13).

## OYSTERS MARION

| | |
|---|---|
| 1 dozen large, fresh raw oysters in the shell | 1 cup diced celery |
| | 1 cup Béchamel Sauce (chap. 13) |
| 6 Tbs. water | ¼ cup Parmesan cheese, grated |
| ½ cup sherry | ¼ tsp. Tabasco pepper sauce |
| 1 stick butter | Paprika for garnish |

*Serves 3 as first course, 6 for cocktails*

Shell the oysters. Clean and reserve shells.

Mix oyster juices, water and sherry. Bring to a boil, reduce heat and poach oysters for about 3 minutes. Drain, set to one side and reserve liquid.

In a skillet, melt ⅔ stick of butter and sauté the diced celery until tender and transparent. Drain celery.

Place a tsp. of celery on the bottom of each oyster shell and place 1 large oyster on this bed.

Heat the béchamel sauce; add 1-2 Tbs. of the oyster-sherry liquor. Stir in the Parmesan cheese and Tabasco and blend well.

Cover each oyster with this mixture and dust with paprika. Put a pat of the remaining butter on each oyster and heat in a 350° oven for 10-15 minutes until piping hot.

This dish may be prepared in advance, kept refrigerated and reheated just before serving time. If used at cocktail time, be sure to furnish small plates and oyster forks.

## SHRIMP MOUSSE

6 cups shrimp, cooked (p. 247),          ½ cup chili sauce
   peeled and deveined                     ½ tsp. Tabasco pepper sauce
1 lb. Philadelphia cream cheese          1 tsp. salt
1 cup mayonnaise                         1 Tbs. Worcestershire sauce
2 cups sour cream                        2 Tbs. Knox gelatine
½ cup finely minced green pepper         Juice of 2 lemons
½ cup finely minced green onion          ¼ cup cold water
¼ cup finely minced pimiento

*Serves 8*

Chop cooked shrimp until very fine.

Cream together the cream cheese, mayonnaise and sour cream. Add the next 7 ingredients and blend well.

Dissolve gelatine in a mixture of the lemon juice and water. Heat in the top of a double boiler for 5–10 minutes. Gradually fold this into the cheese-and-seasonings mixture.

Add shrimp and blend well. Pour into a chilled 9″ ring mold and refrigerate overnight.

Unmold by running a sharp knife around the edge and placing in hot but not boiling water for a few seconds. Invert onto a chilled platter and garnish with watercress or parsley.

Serve as an hors d'oeuvre with melba toast or crackers or as a main course with a salad. It can even make an elegant picnic sandwich or a box lunch for a precocious, gourmet child.

*LEFTOVER VARIATION:* Melt shrimp mousse; add some cream and a little dry sherry. Heat thoroughly and serve as a quick shrimp bisque with some chopped shrimp or chopped almonds for garnish.

## SHRIMP REMOULADE CREOLE

2 Tbs. vinegar                           1 Tbs. finely chopped parsley
1 Tbs. lemon juice                       3 celery hearts with leaves,
8 Tbs. olive oil                            chopped
3 tsp. Creole mustard or a               2 tsp. salt
   horseradish mustard                   36 large or 48 small shrimp,
½ tsp. Tabasco pepper sauce                 cooked (p. 247), peeled,
6 Tbs. tomato ketchup                       cleaned and deveined
4 green onions, tops and
   bottoms, very finely chopped

*Serves 6*

Place all ingredients except the shrimp in a mason jar or the equivalent; blend well.

Pour this over the shrimp and store overnight in the refrigerator until ready to use. Serve on a bed of crisp lettuce.

If you wish to double or triple the sauce, it keeps well in the refrigerator for a week or so.

*VARIATION:* Instead of using shrimp, allow 2 hard-boiled eggs per person, cut lengthwise, and cover with the remoulade sauce.

*NOTE:* This Creole version of the classic French remoulade sauce always shocks the poor Frenchman who comes to New Orleans for the first time. However, by the time he has eaten 2 or 3 helpings, he agrees that a French gourmet dines pretty well in the colonies.

# SOUPS

## CHICKEN GUMBO
## WITH ANDOUILLE SAUSAGE AND OYSTERS

1½ cups cooking oil
1 4-lb. chicken, cut up
1 cup all-purpose flour
2 large stalks celery, chopped
3 large onions, chopped
1 green pepper, chopped
1 clove garlic, minced
4 quarts cold water
Salt and pepper to taste

1 Tbs. Worcestershire sauce
2 tsp. Tabasco pepper sauce
½ lb. andouille sausage, sliced*
1 pint large oysters, with liquid
½ cup parsley, chopped
½ cup green onions, tops and
   bottoms, chopped
Sprinkling of gumbo filé

*Serves 6*

In a heavy pot, heat 1 cup of the oil and brown the chicken pieces in this. Remove chicken pieces.

Add the flour and the remaining oil and stir constantly until you have a brown roux—about 20-25 minutes. Never stop stirring.

Add the celery, onions, green pepper and garlic. Sauté the vegetables, stirring occasionally, for about 15 minutes.

Add cold water all at once, as well as salt, pepper, Worcestershire sauce and Tabasco. Bring to a rapid boil and add chicken pieces and andouille sausage pieces. Reduce heat and simmer for about ½ hour or until chicken pieces are tender but not falling apart. Taste for salt and pepper again.

When chicken pieces are cooked, add shucked oysters (which have been previously cooked in their own liquid for about 5 minutes until they curl). Add the parsley and green onions. Cook for 10 minutes longer.

Serve with fluffy Louisiana rice. A sprinkling of gumbo filé may be used with each serving.

VARIATION: Turkey Gumbo is a good way to use leftover turkey. Simply substitute the turkey carcass and all the leftover turkey meat, dark and light, for the chicken. Since the turkey meat is already cooked, it should be cubed.

Omit the initial browning and cook the carcass in the liquid for at least 1 hour. Add the sausage halfway through.

Add turkey cubes just before the oysters and finish as above.

*Andouille sausage is very common in south Louisiana. In other parts of the country, where it may not be available, any good country sausage other than breakfast sausage may be used.

## OYSTER SOUP À LA CHRIS

| | |
|---|---|
| 1 pint fresh oysters | 1 tsp. Worcestershire sauce |
| 3 Tbs. butter | Salt and pepper to taste |
| 2 Tbs. flour | 1 lb. fresh spinach, cooked and |
| ½ cup red wine | coarsely chopped |
| 1 quart Chicken Stock | ½ cup Parmesan cheese, grated |
| (p. 183), hot | Half n' Half, if necessary |
| 1 tsp. Tabasco pepper sauce | |

*Serves 6*

Drain oysters and reserve any liquid. Chop raw oysters coarsely.

Melt butter in a saucepan and add flour. Stir for 5 minutes to make a light roux. Add oyster liquid and red wine and blend well.

Gradually add hot chicken stock and finally the seasonings. Cook until the sauce is rich and creamy—about 5-10 minutes.

Add chopped oysters, spinach and Parmesan cheese and stir.

If soup is too thick, it may be thinned with a little more chicken stock or Half n' Half.

Serve hot with crackers.

# PLANTATION PEANUT SOUP

¼ cup butter
1 cup thinly sliced celery
1 medium onion, finely chopped
1 Tbs. flour

2 quarts Chicken Stock (p. 183)
  or broth
1 cup creamy peanut butter
1 cup light cream
Fried Croutons (chap. 13)

*Serves 8*

Melt butter in large saucepan over low heat and add celery and onion. Cook until tender but not browned—about 10 minutes. Add flour and stir until mixture is smooth.

Gradually add chicken stock and bring to a boil. Blend in peanut butter and simmer for about 15 minutes.

Stir in cream just before serving.

Serve with Fried Croutons.

# SEAFOOD GUMBO

2 Tbs. cooking oil
2 Tbs. flour
4 cloves garlic, chopped
3 large onions, chopped
5 stalks celery, chopped
2 green peppers, chopped
1 Tbs. salt
½ tsp. black pepper
2 tsp. Tabasco pepper sauce (less,
  if desired)
1 Tbs. Worcestershire sauce

3 quarts boiling water
5 lbs. gumbo shrimp (small), raw
4 lbs. fresh crab meat
4 whole fresh crabs, cut up, shells
  and all (optional)
2 pints fresh oysters
½ cup chopped parsley
½ cup green onions, tops and
  bottoms, chopped
2 Tbs. gumbo filé

*Serves 25*

If you're going to make gumbo, you might as well make plenty of it, because it freezes well if you don't use it at once.

In a heavy pot, heat oil and add flour. Cook for about 20 minutes or until you have a dark roux. Stir constantly to prevent scorching, and when your roux is the color of brown wrapping paper, it is perfect.

Fry garlic in this roux. Add onions and cook for 10 minutes.

Add celery, green peppers, salt, black pepper, Tabasco and Worcestershire sauce.

Cook vegetables for another 10 minutes and then add the boiling water. Allow liquid to come to a boil and reduce heat.

Add the raw shrimp and cook for another 20 minutes.

Add the crab meat and the cut-up fresh crabs, shells and all, and cook for another 15 minutes.

If frozen seafoods are used, be sure they are thoroughly thawed out and individually heated for about 10 minutes before adding.

In a separate pan, bring oysters to a boil in their own liquid and cook until they just begin to curl—about 5-10 minutes. Add oysters and pan juices to the gumbo.

Add parsley and green onions and cook for another 15 minutes.

At the very last add the gumbo filé, blend well and remove from heat. Be very careful how you use the gumbo filé, because if you overdo it, the gumbo will become ropy. The filé is both a seasoning and a thickening agent, and some natives like to sprinkle more on top.

Place a large spoonful of fluffy white rice on the bottom of each individual bowl and ladle out gumbo servings.

If you have used whole crabs, you and your friends will enjoy picking up the shells and sucking out the meat.

NOTE: This gumbo is very close to the gumbo that Senator Ellender used to serve in Washington. I once served it at the National Press Club in Washington when he was present, and he loved it.

# SANDWICHES

## PO BOY SANDWICH #1

1 12" piece New Orleans Po Boy
  bread or the equivalent in
  French bread
¼ cup Basic Brown Sauce
  (chap. 13)
6–7 thin slices well-done
  roast beef

6 thin slices tomato
4 thin slices onion
Enough shredded lettuce
  to line bread
Slices of pickle
Dash of Tabasco pepper sauce
Mayonnaise

*Serves 1–2*

Heat the bread slightly and brush 1 side with enough basic brown sauce to make it soppy. Lay on the slices of roast beef. Top with the tomato and onion slices, lettuce, pickles and a few drops of Tabasco. Brush the other side of the bread with mayonnaise. Close sandwich and cut in half.

It is not a New Orleans Po Boy unless the juices drip down the sides of your chin.

## PO BOY SANDWICH #2

1 12″ piece New Orleans Po Boy
    bread or the equivalent in
    French bread
Mayonnaise
Creole mustard or a horseradish-
    type mustard

Enough shredded lettuce
    to line bread
6–7 slices tomato
Slices of pickle
6–7 slices hog's head cheese or
    souse
Dash of Tabasco pepper sauce

*Serves 1–2*

Spread bread with mayonnaise and mustard. Arrange lettuce, tomato and pickle slices on bread. Arrange slices of hog's head cheese or souse and sprinkle with a few drops of Tabasco pepper sauce.
Close sandwich and serve cold.

## PO BOY SANDWICH #3

1 dozen large raw oysters
1 package commercial fish-fry mix
    (or 1 cup flour, seasoned with
    salt and pepper)
1 cup cooking oil, more or less
1 12″ piece New Orleans Po Boy
    bread or the equivalent in
    French bread
2 Tbs. melted butter

1 Tbs. mayonnaise (optional)
Enough shredded lettuce to line
    bread
6–7 thin slices tomato
Slices of pickle
Juice of ½ lemon
Salt and pepper to taste
Dash of Tabasco pepper sauce

*Serves 1–2*

Drain oysters well. Dip them in the fish-fry mix or seasoned flour. Refrigerate.
When ready to make the sandwich, dip oysters once again in the fish-fry mix or flour.
Place the oysters a few at a time into a large skillet filled with 2″–3″ of hot cooking oil. Do not put them in all at once, and never crowd them. If the skillet is too small, fry the oysters in 2 batches.
After about 5 minutes, when the oysters float to the top, turn them over and cook for another 5 minutes or until golden brown and crisp. Drain them on paper toweling.
Scoop out the insides of the bread and brush with melted butter. Heat the bread. Spread with mayonnaise and arrange lettuce, tomato and pickles. Top with the fried oysters. Sprinkle with lemon juice. Season with salt and pepper and a few drops of Tabasco.
Close sandwich and serve hot.

# ENTRÉES AND ACCOMPANIMENTS

## BAKED CHICKEN WITH CORN BREAD DRESSING

1 9"-square pan cooked corn
   bread, your own recipe or a mix
2½ cups Chicken Stock (p. 183)
3 chicken gizzards
3 chicken livers
6 Tbs. butter
1 large onion, minced
1 clove garlic, minced

1 green pepper, minced
½ cup parsley, chopped
Salt and pepper to taste
1 Tbs. Worcestershire sauce
2 tsp. Tabasco pepper sauce
3 small broiler chickens
1 cup cooking oil
2 Tbs. paprika

*Serves 6*

In a mixing bowl, break up the cooked corn bread and moisten with half the chicken stock.

Sauté the gizzards and livers lightly in butter for about 5 minutes and cut them up fine. Sauté the onion, garlic, green pepper and parsley and add all of this to the corn bread mixture.

If more liquid is needed, add more chicken stock. Add salt, pepper, Worcestershire and Tabasco. Mix well. Divide dressing so that each broiler chicken has enough to fill its cavity. Truss the chickens.

Heat a little of the oil in a skillet and brown the chickens lightly on all sides. Sprinkle paprika generously over the chickens and bake in a moderate oven (350°) for 1–1½ hours or until chickens are tender and done.

Baste frequently with a mixture of the remaining oil, chicken stock and paprika so that the chickens are moist when finished.

Split the broilers and serve them hot. They may also be served cold.

## BRAISED SWEETBREADS

2 quarts water
1 whole lemon, cut in half
2 lbs. sweetbreads
1 stick butter
1 large onion, sliced
2 carrots, sliced
2 sprigs parsley

1 tsp. salt
½ tsp. white pepper
½ tsp. thyme
½ cup all-purpose flour
½ cup white wine
1 cup Chicken Stock (p. 183)
¼ cup dry sherry

*Serves 6*

Bring water and lemon to a boil; add the sweetbreads and parboil for 20 minutes. Remove to a bowl of ice and chill sweetbreads until firm. Remove membranes, tubes and excess fat from the sweetbreads, but keep the pieces as whole as possible.

In a heavy skillet, melt the butter and sauté the onion, carrots and parsley for about 15 minutes or until they turn color.

Lay the sweetbreads on this vegetable bed. Sprinkle the salt, pepper, thyme and flour over the sweetbreads and vegetables. Add the white wine and chicken stock. Bring to a boil.

Place the uncovered skillet in a moderate oven (325°). Cook for 1–1½ hours, basting the sweetbreads and turning them at 15-minute intervals. If sauce gets too thick and cooks away, add a little more chicken stock and wine. The sweetbreads are cooked if the edge of the meat falls apart when touched with a fork or knife.

When sweetbreads are cooked, remove them to a serving platter and strain vegetables from sauce. Correct seasonings. Mix sherry into the sauce and spoon over sweetbreads.

## CHARTRES STREET TROUT

| | |
|---|---|
| 6 filets of fresh trout | ¼ tsp. Tabasco pepper sauce |
| 1 stick butter | 4 Tbs. large capers |
| Juice of 2 lemons | Chopped parsley or chervil |
| Salt and white pepper to taste | |

*Serves 6*

Place trout in a buttered pan. Dot each trout with small pieces of butter and cover with buttered white butcher paper or waxed paper.

Bake in a moderate oven (350°) for 15–20 minutes, depending on the size of the trout. Do not overcook the fish.

When fish are done, immediately add the juice of the lemons to the butter in the pan, along with salt and pepper to taste and the Tabasco. Add the drained capers.

Serve immediately with chopped parsley or chervil and buttered wedges of toast.

## CHRIS'S SHRIMP NEWBURG

3 lbs. large shrimp, peeled and
   deveined while raw
1 stick butter
2 medium green peppers, sliced in
   slivers
4 large pimientos, sliced in slivers
½ cup all-purpose flour

3 cups Half n' Half
2 cups Cheddar cheese, grated or
   crumbled
½ tsp. Tabasco pepper sauce
1 tsp. salt
½ cup good dry sherry

*Serves 6*

Cook the shrimp in salted water to cover until firm and tender—about 20 minutes. Drain and reserve.

Meanwhile, in a saucepan, melt the butter and sauté the green pepper and pimiento slivers for about 20 minutes or until tender. Gradually add the flour and continue to cook until the roux is blended.

Slowly add the Half n' Half and continue cooking until sauce thickens slightly—about 5-10 minutes. Now add the Cheddar cheese a little at a time and continue to cook for another 5-10 minutes until sauce is well blended and thick.

Add the Tabasco, salt and sherry.

Do not combine the shrimp with the sauce until ready to serve. At the last minute, drop the reserved shrimp into boiling water for a few seconds and then drain.

Combine shrimp with the sauce and serve immediately with Green Rice (p. 22)

NOTE: Both shrimp and sauce may be prepared in advance. Just before serving, heat shrimp as directed above and heat sauce in the top of a double boiler.

## CHRISTOPHER BLAKE'S JAMBALAYA

3 Tbs. bacon or ham fat
1 lb. lean ham, cubed
3 cups finely chopped onions
3 cloves garlic, minced
2 large green peppers, cored,
   seeded and chopped
½ lb. country sausage, sliced
1 can (2 lb. 3 oz.) Italian tomatoes
6 ripe tomatoes, peeled, seeded
   and cut into wedges
1 small can (6 oz.) tomato paste
Salt and freshly ground
   pepper to taste
¼ tsp. thyme or 2 sprigs thyme

½ cup celery tops, chopped
½ cup parsley, chopped
½ cup green onions, tops and
   bottoms, chopped
1 or 2 bay leaves
2 lbs. raw shrimp, medium
1 quart water
1 Tbs. crab boil* (optional)
1 lemon, sliced
½ tsp. Tabasco pepper sauce
2 cups raw rice
2 dozen fresh oysters, shucked
   and drained

*Serves 6*

In a heavy skillet or dutch oven, heat the fat and add the ham cubes, onions, garlic and green peppers. Cook, stirring, until onions are lightly browned. Add the sliced sausage and cook for another 5 minutes.

Add canned tomatoes, fresh tomatoes and tomato paste. Add salt and pepper, thyme, celery tops, parsley, green onions and bay leaves. Cover and simmer for 2 hours.

Meanwhile, put the shrimp in a saucepan and add the water, crab boil, lemon slices and Tabasco. Add a little salt, bring to a boil and turn down heat. Cook for about 15 minutes.

Drain the shrimp, strain and reserve the cooking liquid. Peel and devein shrimp.

When tomato sauce has cooked, add the rice and the liquid in which the shrimp have been cooked. Cover and cook for about 20 minutes or until the rice is tender and has begun to absorb the liquid.

Add the shrimp and the oysters for the last 10 minutes and cook until rice completely absorbs the liquid and the dish is thoroughly heated.

Remove bay leaves and serve.

*Available in many gourmet shops.

# COQUILLES ST. JACQUES NEW ORLEANS

| | |
|---|---|
| 4 cups dry white wine | 2 Tbs. parsley, finely chopped |
| 1 Bouquet Garni (chap. 13) | 12 green onions, finely chopped |
| Salt and white pepper to taste | 2 Tbs. lemon juice |
| 4 lbs. scallops, preferably small | 4 Tbs. water |
| 2 lbs. shrimp, cooked (p. 247), | ½ cup all-purpose flour |
| peeled, deveined and chopped | 4 egg yolks lightly beaten with |
| 12 Tbs. butter | 2 Tbs. heavy cream |
| 1 lb. mushrooms, finely chopped | Buttered bread crumbs |

*Serves 15-20*

Put the white wine, bouquet garni, salt and pepper in a heavy pot. Bring to a boil.

Reduce heat and poach scallops in this wine for about 15 minutes or until tender. Discard bouquet garni, but reserve the liquid.

When the scallops are cool, slice thinly, combine with the finely chopped shrimp and reserve.

In a heavy skillet, melt 4 Tbs. of the butter; add mushrooms, parsley, green onions, lemon juice and water. Cover and simmer for about 10 minutes. Strain juices and reserve both juices and vegetables.

In the same skillet, melt the remaining 8 Tbs. butter, stirring in the flour to make a light roux. Slowly add the scallop-wine broth, stirring constantly until thick—about 10 minutes.

Remove from the heat and add slowly to the egg yolk-cream combination, stirring continuously so the eggs do not curdle.

Add the juices from the mushroom mixture and blend well. Then add the vegetables. Correct the seasonings for salt and white pepper.

Add the scallop-shrimp mixture and blend well. This dish should be thick and creamy.

Place in a casserole or in individual shells or ramekins. Top with buttered bread crumbs and heat in a 300° oven for 15 minutes.

This recipe may be used as an appetizer or an entrée. I like to make it in quantity because it freezes so well and is great to have around for any occasion.

# CREOLE MEAT LOAF

3 lbs. ground beef, lean
3 cups stale French bread,
  broken into pieces
1 cup milk
2 whole eggs
3 ripe tomatoes, peeled and diced
¼ cup parsley, chopped
1 clove garlic, minced
1 onion, minced
1 green pepper, cleaned and minced

½ tsp. Tabasco pepper sauce
1 Tbs. Worcestershire sauce
Salt to taste
2 or 3 bay leaves
¾ cup red wine
1½ cups Beef Stock (p. 183)
1 small can tomato sauce
2 Tbs. *Beurre Manié* (chap. 13),
  if necessary

*Serves 8*

In a mixing bowl, blend meat with bread that has been soaked in milk and squeezed of any excess liquid. Add the whole eggs, tomatoes, parsley, garlic, onion, pepper, Tabasco, Worcestershire sauce and salt and blend well.

Shape meat into a loaf and place on a greased baking sheet that is deep enough to hold the sauce; or place in a roasting pan. Top with 2 or 3 bay leaves.

Combine ½ cup red wine, 1 cup beef stock and the tomato sauce and pour some of this over the meat loaf. Bake in a moderate oven (350°) for about 1 hour.

Baste frequently with remaining sauce. When the meat loaf is cooked, remove from oven and allow to cool.

Strain sauce, correct seasonings and if more sauce is needed, add a mixture of the remaining red wine and beef stock. If sauce is not thick enough, work in 2 Tbs. *beurre manié*.

Meat loaf slices most easily and uniformly when cold. After slicing, heat by placing slices on a baking sheet in a moderate oven (350°) for 15-20 minutes. Heat sauce separately and pour over meat slices. Or lay meat slices in the sauce and heat at the same time.

Serve with whipped potatoes.

## DAUBE GLACÉ

5 lbs. boneless beef rump
¼ cup cooking oil
2 cans (10½ oz. each)
  condensed beef bouillon
1 onion, quartered
2 sprigs parsley
½ tsp. Tabasco pepper sauce
3 whole cloves
1 clove garlic, cut in half
1½ cups cold water
1½ cups red wine

2 stalks celery with leaves
2 carrots, whole
1 tsp. salt
1 tsp. dried thyme
¼ lb. salt pork
1 orange, cut in half
2 envelopes Knox gelatine
2 cans (1 lb. each) whole onions,
  drained and chilled
2 cans (1 lb. each) whole carrots,
  drained and chilled

*Serves 12*

Brown beef on all sides in oil in a dutch oven or kettle. Drain off oil. Add bouillon and the next 13 ingredients and cook for at least 2 hours or until meat is tender. Turn meat several times during the cooking.

Remove meat and chill. Strain stock and chill. Remove fat.

Sprinkle gelatine over 1 cup of the cold stock in a measuring cup or a small bowl. Boil remaining stock, uncovered, until it is reduced to 2½ cups. Add softened gelatine; stir until gelatine dissolves.

Pour about ⅛" of gelatine mixture into a serving platter; chill until firm. Chill remaining mixture until it is slightly thickened or syrupy.

Cut cold beef into thin slices. Arrange meat and cold vegetables on gelatine layer in platter. Spoon syrupy gelatine mixture over meat and vegetables; chill a few minutes and repeat with another layer of gelatine. Chill.

Chill remaining gelatine mixture, cut into small cubes and arrange around the platter.

No Mardi Gras party is complete without this poor man's elegant dish.

## DIRTY RICE

1 lb. chicken livers
½ lb. chicken gizzards
1 lb. ground beef
½ cup cooking oil
4 medium onions, chopped
4 stalks celery, chopped
2 cloves garlic, chopped
2 medium green peppers, chopped
½ cup chopped parsley

20 cups water
2 small cans mushrooms, caps
  and stems
Salt and black pepper to taste
1 Tbs. Worcestershire sauce
2 tsp. Tabasco pepper sauce
6 cups cooked rice
4 green onions, finely chopped
1 whole egg

*Serves 6-10*

Chop the livers and the gizzards together.

In a large, heavy pot, brown the chopped livers and gizzards with the ground beef in oil. Sauté the onions, celery, garlic, green peppers and parsley in this mixture for about 15 minutes.

Add about 20 cups water. Cover the pot and simmer this mixture for about 3 hours.

Add mushrooms, salt, pepper, Worcestershire sauce and Tabasco and simmer for 15 minutes.

Allow to cool and skim off all excess fat.

Toss this mixture with the 6 cups cooked rice, the green onions and the whole egg. Correct for salt and pepper. Mix well and reheat in a very low oven (200°–250°).

Serve with any meat or fowl.

SUGGESTION: Excellent as a stuffing for any fowl.

# FISH IN WHITE WINE SAUCE

½ lb. butter
¼ cup chopped parsley
½ cup chopped green onions
1 cup chopped carrots
1 clove garlic, chopped
¼ cup all-purpose flour
Salt and white pepper to taste

2 cups dry white wine
1½ cups Fish Stock (p. 184)
6 medium filets of fresh turbot,
   trout or any other firm fish
Extra chopped parsley
Lemon wedges

*Serves 6*

In a heavy skillet, melt butter. Add the parsley, green onions, carrots and garlic and sauté for 10 minutes or until vegetables are tender.

Add flour and stir until you have a light roux. Add salt and white pepper to taste. Gradually add the white wine and blend well.

Add half the fish stock and cook for another 10–20 minutes. Add more fish stock, if needed, until the sauce has the consistency of light cream.

In a shallow saucepan, bring sauce to a slow boil and poach the fish filets for 3–5 minutes on each side, depending on size of filet.

With a slotted spatula, remove fish filets to a platter and spoon sauce over each.

Garnish with chopped parsley and lemon wedges.

## GREEN RICE

| | |
|---|---|
| 4 cups cooked rice | ½ cup finely minced parsley |
| 1 stick softened butter | 1 cup finely minced green onions, |
| ½ tsp. salt | green parts only |
| ¼ tsp. Tabasco pepper sauce | 3 stiffly beaten egg whites |
| 3 lightly beaten egg yolks | |

*Serves 6–8*

In a mixing bowl, place 4 cups of hot rice that has not been overcooked. Add ¾ stick of the butter, reserving the remainder. Add salt and Tabasco and toss.

Blend in the egg yolks, then the parsley and green onions, mixing well until rice begins to acquire a rich green color.

Add the stiffly beaten egg whites and mix again.

Use remaining butter to grease a mold or casserole and line it with foil that has been buttered. Pour in the combined ingredients and bake in a moderate oven (325°) for 1 hour until firm.

Unmold* onto a platter or serve from the casserole.

Green Rice is the perfect accompaniment to Chris's Shrimp Newburg (p. 16).

*Unmold by inverting onto a platter and simply peeling off the foil.

## GRITS

| | |
|---|---|
| 2½ cups boiling water | 4 Tbs. Roc's Butter (chap. 13) |
| 2½ cups scalded milk | 1 cup grits |
| 1 tsp. salt | |

*Serves 6*

Mix water, milk, salt and seasoned butter in a heavy saucepan. Slowly stir in grits. Return to a boil. Reduce heat.

Cover and cook slowly for 25–30 minutes, stirring occasionally.

Serve piping hot as an accompaniment to Old-Fashioned Grillades (p. 23).

*LEFTOVERS:* Cut cold grits into squares and fry in butter.

## NEW ORLEANS EGGPLANT SOUFFLÉ

4 medium eggplants, peeled and cut into cubes
2 sticks butter
2 large white onions, thinly sliced
4 eggs, slightly beaten

1 lb. Cheddar cheese, grated
Salt to taste
½ tsp. Tabasco pepper sauce
1 cup Italian seasoned bread crumbs

*Serves 8*

Cook eggplant cubes in salted water until soft—about 10-15 minutes.

Reserve 3 Tbs. of the butter for later use. In a heavy skillet, melt the remaining butter and fry the onions until golden brown.

In a mixing bowl, combine the mashed eggplant with the fried onion rings; then add the beaten eggs, grated cheese, salt and Tabasco.

Mix thoroughly and correct seasonings. Turn this mixutre into a lightly buttered casserole. Top casserole with bread crumbs and dot with the reserved butter.

Bake in a very low oven (250°) for about 2 hours. The soufflé consistency should be on the dry side.

## OLD-FASHIONED GRILLADES

6 individual veal seven steaks (rib steaks)
1½ cups flour, seasoned with salt, pepper and a pinch of thyme
1–1½ sticks butter or margarine
8 medium gravy (overripe) tomatoes, quartered
2 large yellow onions, sliced
6 stalks celery, with leaves, cut into 3″ lengths
2 large green peppers, cleaned and quartered

½ cup parsley, coarsely chopped
2 bay leaves
1 clove garlic, minced
2 cups Beef Stock (p. 183)
1 cup red wine
½ tsp. Tabasco pepper sauce
1 tsp. Worcestershire sauce
1 can tomato sauce
1 Tbs. *Beurre Manié* (chap. 13), if necessary

*Serves 6*

Dredge the veal steaks in the seasoned flour. In a heavy pot, melt the butter or margarine and brown the floured veal steaks for about 3 minutes on each side.

Mix the vegetables, parsley, bay leaves and garlic together.

Remove the veal steaks to a dutch oven and make alternate layers of the veal steaks and the vegetable mixture.

Combine the beef stock with the red wine and add the Tabasco, the Worcestershire sauce, and the tomato sauce. Blend well. Pour this mixture over the veal and vegetables.

Cover and cook in a moderate oven (350°) for almost 1 hour or until the veal is tender but not falling apart.

Remove the veal gently from the vegetable mixture and keep warm. Strain the vegetable mixture to remove all the pulp,* using either a sieve or cheesecloth. The gravy should have the consistency of light cream. If it needs more thickening, simply add 1 Tbs. *beurre manié* to the gravy.

Pour the gravy over the hot veal steaks and serve with Grits (p. 22).

This dish may be prepared the night before and simply heated. Great for a Sunday brunch or after a football game.

*VARIATIONS:* Veal round is easier to manage for large buffets and may be used instead of the veal seven steaks. The ribs, however, give a lot of flavor. Beef rounds may also be used, but they will require a longer cooking time (1–1½ hours). In either case, allow ½ lb. meat per person.

*Don't throw away the vegetable pulp, as it makes an excellent Creole omelet.

# PERNOD CREAMED SPINACH

3 lbs. fresh spinach, washed
4 Tbs. butter
½ cup finely minced onion
½ cup finely minced celery
Salt and pepper to taste

½ cup sour cream or *Sauce Velouté* (chap. 13)
¼ cup Pernod or Abisante
1 cup bread crumbs
2 hard-boiled eggs, sliced
Paprika

*Serves 8*

Cook spinach in a small amount of salted water for 10 minutes. Drain and chop.

In a heavy skillet, melt butter and sauté the onion and celery until soft and tender—about 10 minutes

Add the spinach after pressing out as much liquid as possible. Stir in the salt and sour cream or *sauce velouté* and blend well. Finally, add the Pernod.

Place in a casserole; top with bread crumbs and the sliced hard-boiled eggs. Dust with paprika and pass under the broiler for 5 minutes or until well browned.

This dish may be prepared in advance and heated thoroughly for serving.

# RED BEANS AND RICE-LY YOURS

2 lbs. red beans
2 Tbs. bacon fat
½ lb. pickled pork, diced (or a
    commercial jar of pickled ham
    hocks, diced)
2 cloves garlic, minced
1 medium onion, chopped
1 cup tomato ketchup

1 Tbs. vinegar
Salt and pepper to taste
1 tsp. Tabasco pepper sauce
Sprig of fresh thyme or pinch
    of dried thyme
1 cup lean ham, diced
    (or 1 ham bone)

*Serves 6*

Pick over beans. Wash and soak them overnight in water to cover. When ready to cook, drain off all the water.

In a heavy pot, heat the bacon fat and brown the diced pickled pork or pickled ham hock. Add the garlic and onion and cook for about 10 minutes. Add the beans, tomato ketchup, vinegar, salt and pepper to taste, Tabasco and thyme.

Cover with fresh cold water, making sure that there is enough water, as the beans must cook thoroughly. After the water has come to a boil, reduce heat and simmer the beans until they are semicooked—about 1 hour.

Mash about a cupful of the beans and return them to the pot. Add the diced ham or the ham bone and cook slowly for 2 or 3 hours or until the beans are thoroughly cooked and the sauce is thick and creamy.

As they say in New Orleans, red beans need no thickening because they got it in themselves.

Serve with fluffy Louisiana boiled rice and garnish with fried ham, slices of fried country sausage or pork chops. Also serve chopped onions, vinegar and Tabasco pepper sauce on the side, and lots of New Orleans French bread.

*LEFTOVERS:* Place leftover beans in a blender and purée. Add ⅓ cup milk to the purée and blend well. Heat thoroughly. Add 1 Tbs. dry sherry and serve garnished with a slice of lemon and some chopped hard-boiled egg.

*NOTE:* Red Beans and Rice is a staple in New Orleans. It is served in the home, and most restaurants feature it on Monday. Louis Armstrong was raised on this dish, and he always signed his letters "Red beans and rice-ly yours." I have served my version of this dish on everything from paper plates to Georgian silver.

## REDFISH DANIEL

| | |
|---|---|
| 1 stick butter | Salt and white pepper to taste |
| 2 firm avocados, quartered | ½ tsp. lemon juice |
| 8 thick slices ripe tomato, | Chopped parsley |
|    just peeled | 6 lemon wedges |
| 2 filets of redfish,* ½ lb. each | |

*Serves 2*

You will need two skillets for this recipe.

Melt ½ stick butter in each pan. In one, sauté your avocado, first on one side and then on the other for a total of 5–8 minutes.

At the same time, sauté the fish filets in the other skillet for 3–5 minutes on each side. Add salt and pepper to taste and lemon juice.

Place each fish filet in the middle of an individual heated plate. On each side of the fish place an avocado quarter alternately with a tomato slice.

Correct seasonings of juices in both skillets, combine and pour over the fish filets.

Garnish with chopped parsley and lemon wedges.

*Other firm fish filets may be used.

## SHRIMP CREOLE

| | |
|---|---|
| 1 Tbs. lard or vegetable oil | Salt and pepper to taste |
| 1 Tbs. flour | 2 bay leaves |
| 2 onions, chopped | ¼ tsp. thyme |
| 2 cloves garlic, chopped | ¼ tsp. celery seed |
| 1 small green pepper, slivered | 2 lbs. large raw shrimp, shelled |
| 1 Tbs. chopped parsley |    and deveined |
| 1 large can tomatoes (or 1 lb. | 2 tsp. Worcestershire sauce |
|    fresh tomatoes, peeled and | ½ tsp. Tabasco pepper sauce |
|    quartered) | |

*Serves 4–5*

Heat lard or oil in a heavy pot. Stir in flour and cook for about 5 minutes to make a good roux.

Add onions, garlic, green pepper and parsley and stir until onions brown slightly.

Add the tomatoes. Season with salt and pepper, bay leaves, thyme and celery seed.

Now add the raw shrimp. Simmer very slowly for almost 1 hour. Be sure to keep pot covered. Do not add water, as shrimp and tomatoes will produce enough.

Add Worcestershire sauce and Tabasco about ½ hour before serving.

Serve with fluffy Louisiana rice.

## STUFFED CRABS

| | |
|---|---|
| 1 stick butter | 1 tsp. Tabasco pepper sauce |
| ½ cup minced onion or minced | Salt and white pepper to taste |
|    green onions, tops and bottoms | 2 beaten eggs |
| 2 cloves garlic, minced | 1 lb. claw crab meat, picked over |
| 1 large tomato, peeled, seeded | 1 lb. white crab meat, |
|    and chopped |    picked over |
| 1 Tbs. chopped parsley | 6–8 cleaned crab shells* |
| ¼ cup chopped celery and leaves | ½ cup commercial bread crumbs, |
| 1 small green pepper, chopped |    for topping |
| ¼–½ cup milk | Paprika |
| 2 cups stale bread cubes | ½ stick extra butter, for topping |
| 1 Tbs. Worcestershire sauce | |

*Serves 6–8*

Melt butter in a skillet. Sauté the onions, garlic, tomato, parsley, celery and green pepper for 5-10 minutes.

Pour the milk over the bread cubes. Allow to stand for ½ hour and then squeeze out all liquid. Combine sautéed vegetables with bread cubes.

Stir Worcestershire, Tabasco, salt and white pepper into the 2 beaten eggs and blend well. Add this mixture to the crab meats and combine with vegetable-bread mixture. Mix well and taste for salt and pepper.

Fill individual crab shells and pile high. Dust with bread crumbs and paprika and dot with the extra butter. Bake in a 350° oven until piping hot and golden brown—about 15 minutes.

These may be prepared in advance and even frozen until ready to use.

VARIATION: Roll crab mixture into bite-size balls, dip in seasoned flour, egg wash, and fish fry or bread crumbs and then fry in a deep fryer. Serve as hors d'oeuvres with a cocktail sauce.

*If fresh shells are not available, you can purchase shells made of plastic or foil, but these are not very elegant.

## STUFFED MIRLITON SQUASH
## WITH GROUND BEEF AND HAM

3 medium to large mirlitons*
¼ cup ham or bacon fat
1 lb. ground beef
½ lb. good country ham,
   chopped
Salt and pepper to taste
1 large onion, minced
1 clove garlic, minced
¼ cup minced parsley

Pinch of thyme
1 Tbs. Worcestershire sauce
1 tsp. Tabasco pepper sauce
2 cups stale bread, cubed and
   soaked in a little red wine
2 eggs, beaten
1 cup bread crumbs
Butter

*Serves 6*

Parboil the mirlitons in water to cover and cook until tender, about 20-25 minutes.

Remove from water. When cool enough to handle, cut off tops and scoop out pulp, leaving the shell to stuff later on. Remove all seeds. Mash pulp in a bowl.

Melt ham or bacon fat and brown ground beef and chopped ham. Add salt and pepper, onion, garlic, parsley, thyme, Worcestershire and Tabasco and fry together for 5-10 minutes.

Add bread cubes, eggs and mirliton pulp and blend thoroughly.

Stuff mirliton shells with this mixture when ready to use. Sprinkle with bread crumbs, dot with butter and bake in a moderate oven (350°) for 20-30 minutes.

*In New Orleans, mirlitons, or vegetable pears, grow everywhere and are available most of the year. For those who can't find mirlitons, white squash will do very nicely for this recipe.

## TROUT ALICE

*Sauce Alice:*
½ stick butter
6 ripe tomatoes
2 cucumbers, peeled, seeded and
   diced
1 clove garlic, minced
½ cup minced green onions
½ cup chopped green pepper

¼ cup chopped celery tops
¼ tsp. tarragon
4 Tbs. flour
1 small can tomato sauce
2 cups dry white wine
½ cup cold water
Salt and pepper to taste

*Trout:*
   6 medium filets of fresh trout

*Garnish:*
   24 large shrimp, cooked (p. 247),
      peeled and deveined
   6 lemon wedges

*Serves 6*

*To make sauce:* In a heavy saucepan, melt butter and sauté the vegetables, sprinkled with tarragon, for about 10 minutes. Add flour and combine well.

Add tomato sauce and cook for another few minutes until well blended. Add white wine and cold water. Mix well and simmer, covered, for almost 1 hour.

Correct for salt and pepper. If sauce is too thick, thin with a little white wine or water.

*To cook trout:* Bring the Sauce Alice to a boil in a large skillet. Reduce heat and poach trout filets in the sauce for about 5 minutes on each side.

*To serve:* With a slotted spatula, remove trout to individual plates, pour sauce over the servings and garnish each with 4 shrimp and a lemon wedge.

*The sauce may be made in advance and reheated when ready to poach fish.


## WHITE BEANS WITH HAM HOCKS

2 cups white beans
   (Great Northern)
6 cups cold water
1 large onion, chopped
½ cup chopped parsley
2 carrots, diced

3 Tbs. sugar
2 cloves garlic, chopped
3 ham hocks, trimmed
2 tsp. Tabasco pepper sauce
Salt to taste

*Serves 4*

Wash and pick over beans. Combine all ingredients in a large, covered pot. Bring to a boil. Reduce heat and simmer for 2–3 hours or until beans are tender.

Remove ham hocks from beans, cut away meat and dice. Return the diced meat to the beans.

You may prepare in advance up to this point and reheat when ready to serve. Serve with fluffly white rice.

# DESSERTS

## BLACK JAMAICAN

6 oz. (6 squares) Baker's
    semisweet chocolate
6 egg yolks, lightly beaten
    with a little salt

6 egg whites, stiffly beaten
½ cup Myers's Jamaican rum
Whipped cream

*Serves 6*

In the top of a double boiler, or over very low heat, melt the chocolate; remove from heat and then add the lightly beaten egg yolks.

Return to heat and cook slowly, stirring constantly, for about 5 minutes. Remove from heat and allow to cool slightly, but do not let the chocolate harden.

With a spatula, fold in the stiffly beaten egg whites until well blended. Gradually add the rum and pour immediately into small parfait glasses.

Refrigerate for 3-4 hours.

Garnish each serving with a dollop of whipped cream.

## CAFÉ BRÛLOT

1 cup cognac or brandy
30 cubes dot sugar
40 whole cloves
3 pieces cinnamon stick,
    broken into bits

½ orange peel, cut thin
Peelings from 1 lemon, cut thin
1 quart strong coffee, dripped
    New Orleans style
Extra brandy (optional)

*Serves 6-8*

Pour the cognac or brandy into a brûlot bowl (or any silver bowl). Add sugar, cloves, broken bits of cinnamon stick and the orange and lemon rinds.

The mixture should be set to steep for at least 6 hours in advance of serving time to allow the brandy, spices and citrus oils to blend.

Prepare coffee separately and do not mix with the spiced brandy until serving time.

Extra brandy may be heated, set aflame and added after coffee is stirred in.

This recipe will yield 20 demitasse or 8 large cups.

If a brûlot or silver bowl is not available, this may all be done in the kitchen and simply heated in a regular coffeepot without flaming.

## FLUFFY FROZEN PEANUT BUTTER PIE

4 oz. cream cheese
1 cup confectioners' sugar
⅓ cup peanut butter
½ cup milk
1 9-oz. can nondairy
   whipped topping

1 9" Basic Crumb Crust or Basic
   Pie Crust, bottom only
   (p. 382), baked and cooled
¼ cup finely chopped peanuts

*Serves 6*

Whip cheese until soft and fluffy. Beat in sugar and peanut butter. Slowly add milk, blending thoroughly into mixture.

Fold topping into mixture. Pour into baked pie shell. Sprinkle with chopped peanuts. Freeze for 2–3 hours until firm, and serve.

If not used the same day, wrap in plastic wrap after pie is frozen.

## PAIN PERDU
### Lost Bread

3 whole eggs
1 cup milk
1 tsp. vanilla

6 slices French-type bread,
   preferably a day or so old,
   sliced about 1" thick
1 cup vegetable oil or
   1 stick butter

*Serves 6*

Beat eggs, milk and vanilla. Soak bread slices in this mixture for a few minutes.

Heat oil or butter and place drained slices of bread in the pan. Cook on one side until golden brown—about 5 minutes—and then on the other.

Drain and serve immediately with powdered sugar and a bowl of your favorite jam or syrup.

# STRAWBERRIES DEVONSHIRE

2 pints fresh strawberries, hulled          ½ cup dark brown sugar
    and cleaned                             1 pint sour cream

*Serves 6- 8*

Slice the berries in half if they are too big. Reserve a whole berry to garnish each serving.

With a wire whisk, blend the brown sugar and sour cream until the mixture is thick and dark.

Chill berries and cream mixture separately until ready to serve. At the last minute, combine the berries and cream and serve in a wine glass topped with a whole berry.

*NOTE:* To achieve the right consistency, fresh strawberries must be used, as frozen berries bleed too much and tend to give a liquid consistency.

*VARIATION:* Use seeded grapes or fresh peaches in season.

# 2
# HOLIDAYS
# IN NEW ORLEANS

NEW ORLEANS is the only city I know where people give a party to prepare for another party. A tradition in New Orleans during Mardi Gras is to serve the king cake. It's a kind of oversized coffee cake or Danish pastry, all festive with the colors of Mardi Gras, purple, green and yellow, in sugar. Somewhere inside is buried a bean favor. The one who gets the slice of cake with the bean has to give the next party. I've never known any New Orleanian to swallow the bean just to get out of giving a party.

This feeling is contagious, and people who come to New Orleans, no matter what time of year, get into the mood. Everything necessary for a party is at one's fingertips—from food to decorations, and of course, guests. I've never known a city more polite to gate-crashers, and at Mardi Gras time we automatically invite houseguests of friends. About the only thing we don't do is pay celebrities to attend parties. Everyone is a celebrity at a party in New Orleans.

People down here like to use traditional recipes, create new recipes or borrow recipes for any special event. There are holidays and occasions for parties in New Orleans that exist in few other cities. I have even given Ash Wednesday parties.

Be it a wedding, a national holiday, a religious feast day or a wake, New Orleans entertaining carries a special meaning. The recipes and the spirit of New Orleans travel well, and I think you'll find it's easy to give a New Orleans party in your own home.

# SUGAR BOWL

**BLACK BEAN SOUP**    **PICKLED SHRIMP**
**CHILI CON CARNE**    **PECAN PIE**

With heads still reeling from New Year's Eve, the people of New Orleans and their guests are ready to take on Sugar Bowl on New Year's Day. This menu of what we call "sop-up food" is great for what ails you.

## BLACK BEAN SOUP

1 lb. black beans
2 oz. salt pork, diced
2 or 3 smoked ham hocks
1½ quarts cold water
1 pint white wine
1 large Spanish onion,
    finely chopped
1 clove garlic, minced

2 green peppers, chopped
1½ cups olive oil
1 bay leaf
½ tsp. salt
½ tsp. oregano
½ tsp. Tabasco pepper sauce
¼ cup vinegar

*Serves 6*

Wash beans and soak overnight. Drain and place in a large soup pot. Add salt pork and ham hocks; cover with water and wine. Simmer over low heat.

In a saucepan, sauté the onion, garlic and green peppers in the olive oil. Add all this to the beans. Season with bay leaf, salt and oregano. Simmer until the beans are tender and mixture has the consistency of a thick soup—about 1½–2 hours.

Correct seasonings with Tabasco. Just before serving, add the vinegar.

Serve hot with a little boiled white rice or Fried Croutons (chap. 13).

## PICKLED SHRIMP

36 large shrimp
2 cups red wine vinegar
$^2/_3$ cup olive oil
12 peppercorns, crushed
1 Tbs. salt
½ tsp. Tabasco pepper sauce
1 Tbs. pickling spices
1 tsp. allspice
Dash of nutmeg
2 cloves garlic, mashed

1 Tbs. chopped parsley
1 Tbs. chopped onion
1 Tbs. chopped tops of
   green onions
1 Tbs. chopped celery leaves
1 small carrot, finely chopped
Pinch of sugar
Juice of 1 lemon
2 small red onions, finely sliced

*Serves 6*

Cook shrimp with heads on in boiling water until they are just done—about 20 minutes. Drain, cool and remove heads, but leave shrimp in their shells.

Mix all the above ingredients, with the exception of the sliced red onions, to form a thick marinade. Add shrimp to this marinade and toss lightly, making sure that shrimp are well coated. Place in 1 or 2 mason jars. Cover tightly and marinate for at least 24 hours, unrefrigerated but in a cool place.

Chill before serving.

Serve shrimp in their shells with a little of the marinade. Garnish with some of the sliced red onions.

## CHILI CON CARNE

6 Tbs. rendered beef or bacon fat
3 lbs. top round, rump or chuck
   meat, cut into ¼" cubes
2 cups chopped onion
2 cloves garlic, chopped
2 Tbs. tomato paste

1 tsp. ground cumin
1 tsp. dried oregano
3–4 Tbs. good chili powder
1 tsp. salt
2 cups canned tomatoes, drained
2 cups hot Beef Stock (p. 183)

*Serves 6*

Heat the fat in a heavy pot and brown the beef cubes on all sides, a few at a time. They should sear, not stew. Remove the cubes as they are browned.

Add the onions and garlic and cook gently until the onions are limp—about 10–15 minutes. Mix in the tomato paste, cumin, oregano, chili powder, salt and tomatoes. Mix in the beef stock and stir over medium heat until it all comes to a boil.

Reduce heat, add meat and simmer, covered, for 2–3 hours, or until the beef is very tender and falling apart and the liquid has been reduced to a thick, soupy consistency.

Serve in bowls with crackers.

## PECAN PIE

| | |
|---|---|
| 2½ Tbs. sugar | 1¼ tsp. vanilla |
| 4 Tbs. flour | 3 Tbs. melted butter |
| 2 cups corn syrup | 1 9″ Basic Pie Crust bottom |
| 5 eggs, well beaten | (p. 382), unbaked |
| 1 tsp. salt | ¾ cup pecan halves |

*Serves 6*

Put sugar, flour and corn syrup into a mixing bowl and mix thoroughly. Beat in the eggs. Add salt, vanilla and the melted butter and mix thoroughly.

Pour the filling into the pie shell and cover with the pecan halves. Bake in a moderate oven (350°) for about 35 minutes or until set.

It will puff slightly around the edges, and if the filling seems to be about to boil over, reduce the heat a little for the remainder of the baking time.

*NOTE:* Pecan halves make a much better looking pie, but broken nut meats may be used.

In areas where pecan meal is obtainable you can try making the pie shell with it. This will probably result in a Pecan Brown Betty, as the crust will not slice, but it makes for a delicious, interesting dessert.

# BATTLE OF NEW ORLEANS

**REDFISH COURT BOUILLON        DRUNKEN PORK LOIN**
**SWEET POTATO AND TURNIP CASSEROLE**
**CRÊPE GÂTEAU BATTLE OF NEW ORLEANS**

On January 8, the people of New Orleans love to recall their romantic past, when such figures as General Andrew Jackson, Governor Claiborne and the pirate Jean Laffite joined together to beat the British at Chalmette and to break bread. This holiday always calls for gala balls and food.


## REDFISH COURT BOUILLON

3 Tbs. lard or butter
1 large onion, finely chopped
1 Tbs. flour
1 lb. Creole (or ripe) tomatoes,
  peeled, seeded and chopped
½ green pepper, chopped
3 green onions, white and green
  parts, chopped
Few sprigs of parsley, chopped

1 clove garlic, minced
Salt and pepper to taste
2 or 3 bay leaves
Dash of Creole seasonings
Dash of cayenne pepper
Juice of ½ lemon
²/₃ cup dry red wine
3 lbs. redfish, cut into small slices
Parsley and lemon slices

*Serves 6*

Melt the butter or lard in a deep frying pan and, when hot, add the onion and fry until golden—about 5 minutes. Sprinkle with the flour, mix well and brown.

Add the tomatoes, green pepper, green onions, parsley, garlic, salt, pepper, bay leaves, Creole seasonings and cayenne. Mix well.

Add the lemon juice and the red wine and just a bit of hot water, if needed, to thin down the sauce. It should be somewhat thin at this stage. Simmer gently for 10 minutes, mixing well.

Add the fish slices a few at a time and simmer until cooked—about 20 minutes. The fish is ready when it flakes to the fork. The sauce should have the consistency of light cream.

When done, place fish slices on a heated platter and cover with the sauce. Serve garnished with parsley and lemon slices.

# DRUNKEN PORK LOIN*

1 pork loin, 4–5 lbs.
Salt and black pepper to taste
2½ cups dry red wine
2 cloves garlic, finely minced

2 Tbs. chopped parsley
1–2 Tbs. *Beurre Manié*
(chap. 13), if necessary

*Serves 6*

Rub the loin with salt and pepper. Place in a dutch oven and roast, uncovered, at 400° for 30 minutes or until the meat is nicely browned.

Add the red wine, garlic and parsley. Cover, reduce the heat to moderate (350°) and continue to roast for another 1–2 hours, basting the loin frequently with the liquid in the pan. Remove the cover for the last 15 minutes of cooking.

Remove the meat to a heated platter. If the wine has not reduced to half its volume during the cooking time, reduce it over direct heat to about a cup.

The sauce may be thickened with a little *beurre manié* and poured over the meat slices.

* This amusing name comes from the fact that in the process of cooking, the red wine in which the pork is being cooked naturally reduces, and the pork is said to have drunk it and therefore to be intoxicated.

# SWEET POTATO AND TURNIP CASSEROLE

6 sweet potatoes
1 turnip, peeled and quartered
1 stick unsalted butter
1 tsp. Creole seasonings

Dash of nutmeg
Salt and pepper to taste
Dash of cayenne pepper
1 whole egg

*Serves 6*

Boil potatoes in water to cover for 30–40 minutes or until falling apart. Similarly, boil turnip in a separate saucepan for 30 minutes.

Peel and quarter sweet potatoes and mash, adding a little softened butter from time to time. Mash until smooth and creamy.

Mash in the turnip and mix well. Add all seasonings. Mix again. Add the whole egg and combine.

Butter a casserole and fill with the mixture. Bake in a moderate oven (350°) until thoroughly heated—about 20 minutes.

## CRÊPE GÂTEAU BATTLE OF NEW ORLEANS

*Crème patissière:*
   1½ cups milk
   1 3″ stick vanilla bean,
      cut in half

   ½ cup sugar
   4 egg yolks
   ¼ cup flour

*Crêpe Gâteau:*
   12 very thin Basic Beer Crêpes
      (p. 381)
   1 cup Louisiana
      strawberry preserves

   2 cups New Orleans Whipped
      Cream (chap. 13)

*Serves 6*

*To make the crème patissière:* Scald the milk with the vanilla bean. In a separate saucepan, mix the sugar and egg yolks until creamy and light-colored. Add the flour, mixing until just blended.

Add the scalded milk gradually, stirring vigorously until the mixture thickens. Do not boil.

Remove the vanilla bean, strain and cool until ready to use.

*To assemble the gâteau:* Prepare the crêpes and allow to cool.

Spread 1 crêpe thinly with *crème patissière* and then with a thin layer of strawberry preserves. Lay another crêpe on top and repeat the process, stacking the crêpes with their fillings until you are left with a plain crêpe on top.

Cover the entire *gâteau* with New Orleans Whipped Cream. Top with a whole strawberry preserve and dribble some of the strawberry syrup down the sides.

Refrigerate and slice as you would a layer cake.

# MARDI GRAS

**OYSTERS MCDOUGAL**            **SHRIMP EN GELÉE**
**CRESCENT CITY CORNUCOPIAS**   **BOILED BEEF CREOLE**
**RICE CALAS**

During the week of Mardi Gras in February or March, people are always dropping in to watch the many parades from the galleries. The following dishes are just a few that can be prepared in advance and brought out for a quick snack with drinks. In addition, if the party really goes on, Red Beans and Rice, Gumbos, Jambalaya, Red Bean Soup, Grillades, Grits and Daube Glacé, as well as a variety of Po Boy sandwiches, can be prepared for the big day of Mardi Gras itself. All of these recipes can be found in chapter 1.

## OYSTERS MCDOUGAL

3 Tbs. butter
3 Tbs. flour
1 cup chopped green onions
2 Tbs. minced green pepper
2 Tbs. minced celery
2 large tomatoes,
  peeled and chopped
4 dozen oysters,
  blanched for 2–3 minutes
  and chopped

2 cups chopped fresh mushrooms
Pinch of thyme
1 clove garlic, minced
2 Tbs. chopped parsley
Salt and white pepper to taste
½ tsp. Tabasco pepper sauce
½ cup dry white wine
24 large shrimp, cooked
  (p. 247), deveined and diced
3 dozen party-size patty shells

*Serves 12*

Heat butter and add flour, stirring for 5–10 minutes to make a golden roux. Add green onions, green pepper, celery and tomatoes. Cover and cook for 5 minutes. Add 1 cup water from the blanched oysters. Let come to a fast boil, then reduce heat and add mushrooms, thyme, garlic, parsley, salt, pepper and Tabasco. Simmer for about 10 minutes, until sauce thickens, before adding white wine.

Stir and add the shrimp and the oysters. Allow to cook for about 10–15 minutes. Do not overcook.

Heat patty shells in hot oven (400°) until they are crisp. Then fill them with the hot oyster-shrimp mixture. Do not fill and heat in advance, because the patty shells will become limp and moist.

## CRESCENT CITY CORNUCOPIAS

1 lb. Italian Genoa salami,          1½ sticks unsalted butter,
    thinly sliced                       softened
2 large bunches watercress           Salt and pepper to taste

*Serves 12*

Cut salami slices in half. Reserve 48 small watercress leaves with stems and finely chop the rest.

Blend the chopped watercress with the softened butter. Season with salt and pepper.

Spread this mixture on each half salami slice and roll. Insert one watercress leaf in each half as it is rolled, and press together to hold.

Refrigerate until butter hardens (2 hours or overnight), and serve.

## SHRIMP EN GELÉE

2 envelopes Knox gelatine           ½ cup finely chopped parsley
2 cans consommé madrilene           48 small shrimp, cooked
Juice of 1 large lemon                  (p. 247), cleaned and deveined
Salt and white pepper to taste      48 Melba Toast rounds
½ tsp. Tabasco pepper sauce             (chap. 13)

*Serves 12*

Dissolve the gelatine in the cold consommé. Add lemon juice, salt, pepper and Tabasco. Heat in a double boiler until mixture is well blended. Allow to cool.

Sprinkle a little of the chopped parsley in the bottom of 48 individual molds (use empty plastic egg cartons if you can't get anything else). Place 1 shrimp in each mold. Cover with the cooled consommé and place in the refrigerator to set.

When set and firm (2–3 hours or overnight), remove each molded shrimp with a sharp knife and serve on individual rounds of melba toast.

# BOILED BEEF CREOLE

*Boiled beef:*

1 brisket of beef, about 6 lbs.
2 Tbs. salt
1 Tbs. pepper

4 loaves French bread, cut into
12 sandwich servings

*Creole sauce:*

1 bottle tomato ketchup
2 Tbs. Creole mustard

2 Tbs. good horseradish
½ tsp. Tabasco pepper sauce

*Serves 12*

Place brisket of beef in a soup pot. Cover with water and add salt and pepper. Bring to a boil, reduce heat and cook for about 4 hours or until meat is tender but not falling apart.

Slice the meat when cool enough to handle and place the slices on individual sandwiches of French bread.

Make the Creole sauce by thoroughly blending all the ingredients.

Cover each sandwich with the Creole sauce and close.

# RICE CALAS

| | |
|---|---|
| 1 cup raw rice | 3 Tbs. flour |
| 6 cups boiling water | 1 tsp. nutmeg |
| 1 cake yeast | About 1 cup hot lard |
|    or the equivalent in dry yeast |    or vegetable oil |
| 6 eggs, well beaten | Powdered sugar |
| 1 cup sugar | |

*Serves 12*

Cook the rice in boiling water until it is mushy—about 30 minutes.

When cold, mash well and mix it into the yeast, which has been dissolved in a little water. Set aside to rise overnight.

Next morning, add the beaten eggs. Add the sugar and flour and beat into a thick batter.

Let it rise for 15 minutes and then add the nutmeg. Return the batter to the refrigerator and allow to chill thoroughly for better frying.

Heat the lard or vegetable oil in a skillet. Drop in the calas batter 1 Tbs. at a time and fry until golden brown—about 10–15 minutes—turning once. Do not overcrowd the pan.

Drain and wrap in a cloth to keep hot. Sprinkle with powdered sugar and serve with *café au lait* (equal parts strong, hot coffee and hot milk).

NOTE: These used to be sold on the streets of New Orleans by the old calas women crying, *"Belle calas tout chaud"* ("Good rice cakes piping hot").

# SAINT PATRICK'S DAY

**EGGS IN AMBUSH**     **GAELIC STEAK**
**PANCAKES COLLEEN**     **MINTED ANGEL FOOD CAKE**
**IRISH COFFEE**

Yes, we do have a Saint Patrick's Day in New Orleans, and it ranks with those of Boston and New York. We even have a section of the city called the Irish Channel. On Saint Patrick's Day, the paraders throw cabbages from the floats, drink green beer, eat corned beef and cabbage and green bread. However, if you're entertaining at home, why not try these authentic Irish recipes.

## EGGS IN AMBUSH

6 eggs
1 cup fresh green peas, cooked,
    or 1 cup frozen peas, blanched
½ cup Béchamel Sauce
    (chap. 13)

3 Tbs. Half n' Half
Salt and pepper to taste
1–1½ cups mashed potatoes, hot

*Serves 6*

Hard-boil the eggs and keep hot.

Rub ⅔ of the peas through a sieve, reserving the rest. Blend the sieved peas with the béchamel. Then add the Half n' Half and season with salt and pepper.

Shell the eggs and cut a thin slice from the bottom of each so they will stand up. Place an egg each in individual ramekins that have been warmed.

Coat eggs with sauce. Pipe some of the mashed potatoes around the edges of each egg, and then a ring of the remaining peas.

## PANCAKES COLLEEN

1 cup mushrooms, thinly sliced
28 shrimp, cooked (p. 247),
   peeled, deveined and finely
   chopped
1¾ sticks butter
1 cup Béchamel Sauce (chap. 13)

1 jigger good cognac
Salt and white pepper to taste
6 medium-size, very thin
   Basic Beer Crêpes (p. 381)
½ cup grated Gruyère cheese

*Serves 6*

Sauté the sliced mushrooms and 24 of the shrimp in half the butter. Add the béchamel sauce.

Pound the remaining 4 shrimp and 2 Tbs. of the butter into a paste and add. Add the cognac and blend well. Season to taste with salt and white pepper.

Fill the thin pancakes with this mixture and fold. Melt the rest of the butter and pour over the pancakes.

Sprinkle with the grated cheese and run under the broiler for 5 minutes to glaze.

## GAELIC STEAK

6 individual filets of steak
6–8 oz. unsalted butter
12 Tbs. heavy cream

12 Tbs. Irish whiskey
Watercress or parsley

*Serves 6*

Cook steak in melted butter until done to your liking. Remove from frying pan and drain.

Pour cream a little at a time into pan juices and beat slightly. Add Irish whiskey a little at a time and continue to beat until smooth and well blended. Pour this sauce over steaks.

Garnish with watercress or parsley and serve immediately.

## MINTED ANGEL FOOD CAKE

10 egg whites
1 tsp. cream of tartar
1¼ cups fine granulated sugar
1 cup cake flour
½ tsp. vanilla extract

1 Tbs. green crème de menthe
A few drops of green food
   coloring
Pistachio ice cream or
   whipped cream

*Serves 6*

Beat egg whites with 1 tsp. cream of tartar until stiff but not dry.

Sift 1 cup of the sugar 4 times and beat it into the egg whites 1 Tbs. at a time until thoroughly blended.

Sift the cake flour and the remaining ¼ cup sugar together and fold into the egg whites. Fold in the vanilla and crème de menthe. Color with the green food coloring.

When the batter is well blended, pour it into an unbuttered, lightly floured tube pan. Bake in a slow oven (250°) for 30 minutes. Increase the heat to 350° and bake for 30 minutes longer or until the angel food is delicately browned. Invert the pan on a wire rack and cool the cake for about 1 hour.

Place the pistachio ice cream in the center of the cake just before serving. Green-colored whipped cream may be used instead.

## IRISH COFFEE

6 good shots Irish whiskey,
   smooth as the wit of the land
12 tsp. sugar,
   sweet as the tongue of a rogue

6 goblets strong coffee,
   strong as a friendly hand
12 Tbs. whipped cream,
   rich as an Irish brogue

*Serves 6*

Heat 6 whiskey goblets. Into each, pour 1 good shot of Irish whiskey, the only whiskey with the smooth taste and full body to make this beverage satisfactorily.

Add 2 tsp. sugar. Fill each goblet with strong coffee to within 1″ of the brim. Stir to dissolve sugar. Top off with a floater of whipped cream.

NOTE: Do not stir after adding cream, as the true flavor is obtained by drinking the hot coffee and Irish whiskey through the coolness of the cream.

# SAINT JOSEPH'S DAY

**MUFALETTA SANDWICHES**
**VEAL WITH TUNA AND ANCHOVIES**
**RISOTTO WITH SHRIMP**
**NUT PUDDING**

There are probably more Italians living in the French Quarter than there are French. Saint Joseph's day, March 19, is a religious feast day for those of Italian heritage, but both natives and tourists love to join in and visit the Saint Joseph's Day altars that abound throughout the Quarter. Here are some of my Italian favorites, though they are not always found on Saint Joseph's Day altars.

## MUFALETTA SANDWICHES

3 loaves fresh Mufaletta Italian          12 slices mortadella
   bread                               12 slices Parma ham
1 quart Italian vegetable salad*          12 slices soft Italian salami
12 slices provolone cheese

*Serves 6*

Cut bread in half; rub salad juices on each half. Evenly distribute and arrange the meat and cheese on 6 of the halves. Cover sandwiches and cut each into 6 sections.

Arrange on a platter with a bowl of Italian vegetable salad in the middle.

*Italian vegetable salad is traditional in the French Quarter, and no Mufaletta sandwich is complete without it. It is a mixture of crisp celery, carrots, onions and black and green olives, all beautifully blended and marinated in spices, oil and vinegar. It is sold in Italian grocery stores in New Orleans.

## VEAL WITH TUNA AND ANCHOVIES

4 large anchovies in brine
¼ lb. tuna fish in oil
1 scant cup olive oil
Juice of 1 large lemon
2 Tbs. capers
1 young veal filet, about 2 lbs.

1 large onion stuck with
  2 whole cloves
1 carrot, sliced
1 stalk celery
1 bay leaf
1 Tbs. coarse salt
Lemon slices

*Serves 6*

A day or so before you plan to serve this dish, prepare the following sauce.

Bone 2 of the anchovies and pound them in a mortar with the tuna fish. Gradually add the olive oil, as if you were making a mayonnaise, and then the lemon juice a little at a time. The sauce should be somewhat liquid. Add the capers. Let the sauce stand in a cold place for a day or two. It should not be refrigerated during this time.

To prepare the meat, remove all fat and gristle. Take the remaining 2 anchovies, cut them in half and remove the bones. Cut them into 8 strips. Lard the veal filet with them and tie it up with a good string.

Put the veal in a heavy saucepan with water to cover. Add the onion, sliced carrot, celery, bay leaf and coarse salt. Bring to a boil. Simmer for 1½ hours.

Remove the meat from the saucepan and drain thoroughly. Carve into very thin slices.

When ready to serve, arrange the slices of meat on a cold platter, cover with the sauce and garnish with lemon slices.

## RISOTTO WITH SHRIMP

3 Tbs. olive oil
1 small onion, chopped
2 cups raw rice
2 cups Fish Stock made from the
  shrimp heads and shells (p. 184)
Salt and white pepper to taste
2 cloves garlic, chopped

3 dozen raw shrimp, shelled and
  deveined
1 cup flour, seasoned with salt
  and pepper
1 cup cooking oil, more or less
Parmesan cheese, freshly grated

*Serves 6*

In a heavy skillet, heat the olive oil and fry the chopped onion until golden brown—about 5 minutes. Add the rice and stir well.

Add the hot fish stock; season to taste with salt and pepper. Add the garlic. Stir well. Cover and cook for about 30 minutes or until the rice has absorbed all the stock.

While the rice is cooking, prepare the shrimp by dipping each in the seasoned flour and frying them a few at a time in hot oil until golden brown—about 8–10 minutes. Add them to the rice 10 minutes before cooking time is up.

Serve immediately with freshly grated Parmesan cheese.

# NUT PUDDING

6 oz. walnuts                    ¼ stick butter
¾ cup sugar                      1 cup plain bread crumbs
6 oz. grated chocolate           ½ pint heavy cream, stiffly
4 whole eggs, separated             whipped and flavored with
1 tsp. vanilla                      anisette
1 oz. candied orange or
   lemon peel, finely chopped

*Serves 6*

Pound the nuts in a mortar with the sugar, and when worked to a smooth paste, put in a bowl.

Mix with the chocolate and the egg yolks, and then flavor with the vanilla. Mix thoroughly. Finally add the egg whites, beaten very stiffly, and the finely chopped lemon or orange peel.

Butter a pie dish and sprinkle with the bread crumbs. Pour the mixture into this and bake in a moderate oven (350°) for about 30 minutes.

Serve when cool and garnish with the anisette-flavored whipped cream.

# EASTER

| POTAGE MONT ROUGE | GREEN GODDESS SALAD |
| RABBIT WITH PRUNES | EASTER PIE |

No matter how early or late Easter comes, the weather is always beautiful in New Orleans. There are parades, and Spring Fiesta is soon to begin. The restaurants prepare special Easter dinners, and there is much entertaining at home. Personally, I always feel I must have rabbit.

## POTAGE MONT ROUGE

1 stick butter
½ cup chopped red onion
¼ cup chopped celery
½ cup chopped parsley
2 large pimientos, chopped
½ tsp. salt
¼ tsp. white pepper
8 large Creole tomatoes, very
   ripe, peeled, seeded and
   quartered

2 Tbs. sugar
1 quart hot Chicken Stock
   (p. 183)
1 cup raw rice
1 pint light cream
Tabasco pepper sauce (optional)
Small Fried Croutons (chap. 13)

*Serves 8*

In a large, heavy soup kettle, melt half the butter and lightly sauté the onion, celery, parsley and pimientos. Add salt and pepper. Add the tomatoes and cook for 5 minutes.

Sprinkle sugar over the mixture. Add the hot chicken stock and then the rice. Bring to a boil and then simmer for a good hour.

Allow to cool. Purée a little at a time in a blender.

When ready to serve, heat, add cream a little at a time and then swirl in the rest of the butter. Correct seasonings, adding Tabasco if you like. Garnish with small fried croutons.

## RABBIT WITH PRUNES

2 good-size domestic rabbits,
   cut up into serving pieces
1 cup dry red wine
   (more if needed)
2/3 cup vinegar
1 Tbs. coarse salt
1 Tbs. crushed peppercorns
1/2 tsp. thyme
2 bay leaves, crushed
1/2 tsp. marjoram

1/2 tsp. fennel
1/2 tsp. allspice
1 stick plus 4 Tbs. butter
Salt and black pepper to taste
2 lbs. pitted prunes, soaked in
   water for 3–4 hours
4 Tbs. flour
2 Tbs. gooseberry jam or
   any similar tart jam or jelly

*Serves 8*

Place the rabbit pieces in a casserole and cover with a marinade made by blending the red wine, vinegar, salt, peppercorns, thyme, bay leaf, marjoram, fennel and allspice. Allow to stand for at least 24 hours, unrefrigerated.

Remove rabbit pieces from the marinade, drain and dry carefully. Brown the pieces a few at a time in the stick of butter, adding more butter if necessary. They should be just slightly brown.

Season highly with black pepper, but use salt discreetly. Return the rabbit pieces to the casserole so that they are barely covered with the marinade. Add more wine if needed.

Add the pitted prunes, bring to a boil and simmer until all the meat and prunes are quite tender—about 1–1½ hours.

Just before serving, mix the remaining 4 Tbs. butter with the flour and knead this into a *beurre manié*. Gradually add this to the hot sauce to thicken it a bit more. Finally add the gooseberry jam.

Serve from the casserole.

## GREEN GODDESS SALAD

*Salad:*

2 heads romaine lettuce,
   center leaves only

4 green tomatoes, thinly sliced
16 pitted green olives, halved

*Dressing:*

4 Tbs. lemon juice
8 Tbs. heavy cream
1 tsp. salt
1½ tsp. dry mustard

Dash of Tabasco pepper sauce
3 tsp. finely chopped capers
2 cups mashed, avocado,
   very ripe but still green

*Serves 8*

*To prepare the salad:* Wash, drain and dry the lettuce so that it will be crisp. Arrange all the salad ingredients in a large wooden bowl. Chill.

*To make the dressing:* Combine the lemon juice and cream and beat well. Add the salt, mustard, Tabasco and finally the chopped capers. Blend thoroughly. Add the avocado and heat over a low flame until well blended. Chill and use immediately.

Cover the salad with the dressing and serve.


# EASTER PIE

½ cup softened butter
1 cup granulated sugar
1 Tbs. cornstarch
3 egg yolks
1 cup Half n' Half

Juice and grated rind of 1 large
   or 2 small lemons
3 egg whites, stiffly beaten
1 9" Basic Crumb Crust (p. 382)
Whipped cream or
   powdered sugar (optional)

*Serves 8*

Cream together the softened butter, sugar and cornstarch. Add the egg yolks one at a time and whip until very fluffy.

Stir in the Half n' Half a little at a time until the mixture is well blended. Gradually add the lemon juice and lemon rind; then fold in the stiffly beaten egg whites.

Pour this mixture into the pie shell and bake in a moderate oven (350°) for about 45 minutes–1 hour.

This pie is a type of soufflé; and like all soufflés, when removed from the oven it will be puffy and golden brown on top. As it cools, it will deflate.

The pie may be served warm or cold, but it is tastier cold. However, after it has deflated, it is not as attractive. In order to improve its appearance, coat the top with whipped cream or sprinkle with powdered sugar.

# THE FOURTH OF JULY

**A COUNTRY HAM**          **CREOLE SALAD BOWL**
**RED, WHITE AND BLUE CABBAGE SALAD**
**WHITE COCONUT PRALINES**     **NEW ORLEANS ICED COFFEE**

Although New Orleans was not part of the 13 original colonies, she takes her patriotic enthusiasm for national holidays from her French heritage. Anything for a bang in New Orleans.

## A COUNTRY HAM

*Baked ham:*
　　1 good country ham, 15–19 lbs.*　　1 pint ginger ale
　　6–8 quarts buttermilk (optional)　　1 box cloves

*Ham glaze:*
　　Juice of 6 oranges,　　　　　　1½ boxes dark brown sugar
　　　　with the grated rind of 3　　1 Tbs. Dijon mustard
　　Juice of 2 lemons,　　　　　　2 cloves garlic, mashed
　　　　with the grated rind of 1　　1 can drained pineapple rings
　　1 pint ginger ale　　　　　　　1 small jar Maraschino cherries
　　1 cup dry white wine　　　　　　　with stems
　　1 cup canned pineapple juice

*Serves 12*

　　*To bake the ham:* Remove the cloth cover and any paper that comes off easily. Place the ham in a basin of hot water and with a good, stiff brush, scrub off any remaining paper. Continue scrubbing until all the green fungus is gone.

　　Wash ham thoroughly in cold water.

　　Place ham in a large basin and cover with clean, cold water mixed with a quart of buttermilk. Cover with a cloth and allow to stand 36–48 hours, changing the water-buttermilk mixture 6–8 times.

　　When ham is thoroughly clean, dry with towels. Place in a deep roasting pan (you'll have less mess with the disposable kind). Line the pan with heavy-duty foil. Pour ginger ale over the ham.

　　Cover tightly and bake in a moderate oven (350°) for ½ hour to the lb. There is no need to baste, but you may want to turn the ham 2 or 3 times during baking. Two-thirds of the way through baking time, remove pan from the oven, uncover and pour off any excess liquid and fat. With a sharp knife, remove the hard skin and the thick fat, leaving only a thin layer.

With the same knife, cut slits in the ham until you have covered it right down to the shank with diamond shapes. In each diamond, insert a whole clove. Recover the ham, return to the oven and continue baking.

Remove ham from its pan 2 hours before cooking time is up. Discard all juices and place ham in a fresh roasting pan.

*To make the glaze:* Mix all ingredients except pineapple rings and cherries. Ingredients must be well blended and on the thick side.

Spread glaze on the ham with a brush. Brush several times until the glzae begins to set. Then arrange the pineapple rings in a decorative pattern and secure with toothpicks. In the center of each ring place 2 or 3 Maraschino cherries, also secured. Then brush on the glaze 2 or 3 times more until it has all been used.

Finish baking. When ham is done, allow to cool slightly before carving into thin slices. If served hot, slices may be slightly thicker than when cold, but never serve ham too thick.

Serve hot with some of the sauce from the pan, skimmed of all excess fat. Or serve cold with mustard or mayonnaise.

*Georgia, Smithfield, Kentucky, North Carolina or West Virginia hams are all good country hams. I prefer this size to the smaller ones. You will have plenty left over, and it keeps well.

## CREOLE SALAD BOWL

Salt and pepper to taste
2 lbs. small shrimp, cooked
   (p. 247), peeled and deveined
1 1/3 cups Christopher Blake's
   French Dressing (chap. 13)
3 hard-boiled eggs, halved and
   separated
3 black olives, minced
1/2 sour pickle, minced

2 Tbs. minced hearts of celery
2 heads romaine lettuce
1 bunch watercress
2 Creole or garden-ripe tomatoes,
   peeled and seeded
1 green pepper, sliced
1 red onion, cut into rings
Extra olives, pickles and celery
Fried Croutons (chap. 13)

*Serves 12*

Salt and pepper the shrimp and saturate well with 1/2 cup of the French dressing.

Mash the 3 egg yolks and make a smooth paste with some more of the dressing. Add the minced olives and pickle, the minced white of 1 egg and the minced hearts of celery.

Alternate tender leaves of romaine with watercress in a deep platter or bowl. Cut the tomatoes in slices and place in the center of the platter with the green pepper slices and red onion rings.

Spread the shrimp around and spread the egg paste over them.

Decorate with the extra olives, pickles and celery and the remaining egg whites, sliced. Cover with plastic wrap and chill well before serving with the remaining French dressing.

Garnish with fried croutons.

## RED, WHITE AND BLUE CABBAGE SALAD

1 medium head white cabbage
3 tart apples, peeled,
   cored and cubed
1 cup cider vinegar
2 Tbs. sugar
Pinch of salt

1/2 cup vegetable oil
Salt and white pepper to taste
1 medium head red cabbage
1/2 lb. lean slab bacon,
   cut into very small cubes
1/4 lb. blue cheese, crumbled

*Serves 12*

Shred the white cabbage and cook in salted, boiling water for about 5 minutes. Drain thoroughly.

Soak the apples for about 1 hour in a mixture of ²/₃ cup vinegar, 1 Tbs. sugar and a pinch of salt. Drain the apples and mix with the white cabbage, reserving vinegar mixture.

Blend the vinegar mixture, oil, another ½ Tbs. sugar, salt and pepper. Toss this dressing with the white cabbage and apple mixture.

Shred the red cabbage and cook as for the white. Cook the bacon cubes in the remaining ¹/₃ cup vinegar for 10–15 minutes. Drain the bacon cubes (discarding vinegar) and sprinkle them with the remaining sugar. Toss with the red cabbage.

Now mix the 2 salads so that they are well blended. Sprinkle with crumbled blue cheese and toss once again.


# WHITE COCONUT PRALINES

2 lbs. powdered sugar                Meat of 1 medium coconut,
8 Tbs. water                         grated (or 2 cups packaged
2 dashes vanilla extract             grated coconut)

*Serves 12*

Place the sugar in an enameled saucepan with the water and cook until it begins to turn into syrup—about 15 minutes.

Add the vanilla and grated coconut, stirring continuously until the syrup can be drawn to a thread between fingers and thumb.

Remove mixture from the heat and put 1 Tbs. at a time on a well-buttered marble slab or large dish.

Shape each praline into a neat round cake about ¼" thick and 4"–5" in diameter. Let pralines sit for at least 1 hour.

When dry, remove from the slab or dish with a sharp knife. They should be light and crisp.

# NEW ORLEANS ICED COFFEE

8 cups good strong            2 cups New Orleans Whipped
   New Orleans coffee            Cream (chap. 13)
2 cups cold water             12 sprigs fresh mint

*Serves 12*

Mix 2 cups of the coffee with the cold water. Fill 2 or 3 ice-cube trays with this mixture and freeze.

When frozen hard, divide the cubes into 12 iced-coffee glasses and pour in the remaining 6 cups coffee, adding a little sugar if desired.

Top with the whipped cream and garnish with a sprig of fresh mint in each glass.

# BASTILLE DAY

**MOUSSE OF LUMMI SALMON          TOURNEDOS CREOLE**
**BAKED ALASKA NEW ORLEANS**

On July 14, after all the crazy French French and Louisiana French activities and fireworks down by the Mississippi River, I usually like to serve a late formal dinner.

## MOUSSE OF LUMMI SALMON

2 Lummi coho yearling salmon      ¼ cup grated celery
   (or 1–1½ lbs. other fresh       1 white onion, grated
   salmon)                         Juice of 1 lemon
4 oz. cream cheese                 1 cup poaching liquid
½ pint sour cream                     from salmon
1 cup mayonnaise                   2 Tbs. Knox gelatine
½ tsp. Tabasco pepper sauce        1 extra cucumber,
½ tsp. salt                           unpeeled and sliced
½ tsp. dried chives                Watercress or parsley
   (or 1 Tbs. fresh chives)        4 hard-boiled eggs, quartered
1 Tbs. horseradish                 Lemon wedges
1 whole cucumber,
   peeled, seeded and grated

*Serves 6*

Poach the salmon (p. 266), skin and allow to cool. Reserve 1 cup of the poaching liquid. Pick over the salmon meat, being careful to remove all fine bones.* Keep the salmon meat in a bowl in the refrigerator until ready to use.

In a large mixing bowl, cream together the cheese, sour cream and mayonnaise. Add all other ingredients except the lemon juice, poaching liquid, gelatine and garnishes. With a hand or electric beater, blend until thick and creamy.

Dissolve the gelatine in the lemon juice and poaching liquid. Heat but do not boil. Allow to cool for 5 minutes, and add this and the salmon pieces to the cream mixture. Beat until mixture is smooth and completely blended.

Fill a 9″ ring mold or a small loaf pan with the mixture and allow to set in refrigerator overnight.

To unmold, use a sharp knife or dip for a moment or two in a bath of hot but not boiling water. Invert onto a cold platter and garnish with sliced cucumber, watercress or parsley, hard-boiled egg quarters and lemon wedges.

* The Lummi tribe is now producing a variety of salmon that is boneless.

## TOURNEDOS CREOLE

*Tomato fondue:*
    1½ lbs. ripe tomatoes            1 Tbs. finely chopped tarragon
    6 oz. unsalted butter             (or ½ tsp. dry tarragon)
    Salt and white pepper to taste     ²/₃–1 cup Veal Stock (p. 185)
    Pinch of sugar                ½ cup dry white wine

*Tournedos Creole:*
    6 thick slices eggplant, unpeeled    1 stick unsalted butter
    ½–¾ cup olive oil             6 thick filet steaks

*Garnish:*
    6 whole pitted black olives

*Serves 6*

*To make tomato fondue:* Peel and seed tomatoes. You can peel them easily after placing them in boiling water for 3–4 minutes.

Slice the flesh very fine and cook in the butter for 3–4 minutes. Add salt, white pepper, sugar, tarragon, veal stock and white wine and continue to cook until tomatoes are soft but not puréed—about 15–20 minutes.

This may be made in advance and reserved.

*To cook Tournedos Creole:* Sauté eggplant in olive oil until tender—about 10 minutes. Reserve.

Heat butter in a heavy skillet and cook the filets to desired doneness.

*To assemble:* Place a filet on a slice of eggplant and garnish with the tomato fondue and the black olives.

# BAKED ALASKA NEW ORLEANS

1 Bogie's Pound Cake
  (p. 385), sliced
1 pint Louisiana strawberry
  preserves
½ cup finely chopped pecans

4 egg whites
¾ cup powdered sugar
1 quart hard-frozen French vanilla
  ice cream
½ cup granulated sugar

*Serves 6*

Cover an 11" x 16" wooden breadboard with white butcher paper. Arrange the pound cake slices down the center of the board. Spread the cake with the strawberry preserves and half the chopped pecans.

Make a meringue by beating the egg whites until stiff enough to form peaks; then gradually fold in the powdered sugar as you continue to beat until very stiff.

Using a sharp knife, carefully cut the carton off the hard-frozen ice cream. Slice the cylinder of ice cream in half lengthwise and arrange the 2 halves down the center of the board on top of the cake slices so that the cake extends ½"–1" beyond the ice cream all around. If it extends much more than that, trim it.

As quickly as possible, cover the entire surface of the ice cream and rim of the cake with the meringue. Dust the meringue with the granulated sugar and the rest of the pecans and place in a very hot oven (450°) for about 15 minutes—just long enough for the meringue to brown lightly on top.

Slip browned baked Alaska onto a platter and serve at once, or slice and serve directly from the board.

# ALL SAINTS' EVE

**YELLOW SPLIT PEA SOUP**　　**BAYOU PIE**
**FRIED SAUSAGE ASSORTMENT**　　**SOUFFLÉ FRITTERS**

On Halloween in New Orleans, there is always more to the menus than dunking for apples. Here are some suggestions to make "trick or treat" easier.

## YELLOW SPLIT PEA SOUP

14 oz. dried yellow split peas
2 pigs' feet
4 leeks, chopped
1 stick celery, cut up

Salt and black pepper to taste
½ lb. andouille sausage, cut into
　thick slices and then quartered
2 dozen very small fresh oysters

*Serves 6*

Soak the peas in cold water to cover for a few hours. Drain, put them in a large kettle and cover again with salted water. Bring to a boil and add the pigs' feet, leeks and celery. Season with salt and black pepper.

Simmer for 3–5 hours, until the pigs' feet are quite tender and the meat is detached from the bones. Remove the bones and any skin, leaving only whatever bits of meat remain.

Lightly sauté the sausage pieces. Add them to the soup ½ hour before it is finished and continue to cook.

In the meantime, poach the oysters in their own liquid for 2–3 minutes and add oysters and liquid to the soup 5 minutes before it is done.

Correct for seasonings and serve.

# FRIED SAUSAGE ASSORTMENT

½ lb. andouille sausage, thickly
  sliced but kept in casing
½ lb. mild Italian sausages,
  removed from casing but kept
  whole
½ lb. hot Italian sausages,
  removed from casing but kept
  whole

1½ cups flour, seasoned with
  salt and pepper
2 eggs beaten with
  2 Tbs. cold water
1½ cups bread crumbs
1–1½ cups cooking oil
2 dozen cold, freshly opened
  oysters in their shells

*Serves 6*

Roll each sausage slice and each whole sausage in seasoned flour, then in the egg wash and finally in bread crumbs. Refrigerate for at least 4 hours.

Fry in cooking oil until golden brown—about 20 minutes. Cut each sausage into bite-size pieces and arrange on a large platter. Fill another platter with the ice-cold oysters.

Eat an oyster and a piece of hot sausage at the same time, and try some good French bread with this.

# BAYOU PIE

*Crust:*
  1 Basic Pie Crust, bottom only
    (p. 382)
  2 Tbs. melted butter

*Filling:*
  2 cups fresh green peas, shelled
    (or about 1½ packages frozen
    peas)
  2 tsp. grated onion

4 Tbs. heavy cream
4 Tbs. melted butter
Salt and white pepper to taste

*Topping:*
  2 lbs. small shrimp, cooked
    (p. 247), peeled and deveined

1 cup Hollandaise Sauce
  (chap. 13)
Paprika

*Serves 6*

*To prepare the crust:* Line a 9″ pie pan with the crust, brush with the melted butter and refrigerate for 1 hour. Bake for 20 minutes, until almost done. Cool.

*To prepare the filling:* Cook the peas in water to cover until tender and then purée in a blender. Add the onion, cream and melted butter and correct for salt and pepper. Heat for 2–3 minutes and fill the pie shell with this mixture.

*To make the topping:* Reserve 10–15 shrimp and lay the rest on top of the purée so that the entire pie is covered. Finely mince the reserved shrimp and blend with the hollandaise. Spoon this mixture on top of the pie.

Run under the broiler for 1–2 minutes, dust with paprika and serve.

## SOUFFLÉ FRITTERS

A scant ½ cup cold water
4 Tbs. unsalted butter, divided
   into small pieces
Pinch of salt
1 Tbs. sugar
1–2 tsp. orange flower water

1 cup flour
3 large or 4 small eggs
1–1½ cups cooking oil
Powdered sugar
A bowl of syrup (optional)

*Serves 6*

Put the water in a saucepan along with the pieces of butter, the salt, sugar and the orange flower water. Bring to a boil on a quick fire, and as soon as the mixture bubbles remove from the fire.

Add the flour all at once and stir vigorously with a wooden spoon until the paste is perfectly smooth.

Return the saucepan to the fire and stir the paste with the spoon until it begins to dry and no longer clings to the bottom of the pan.

Remove the saucepan from the fire and stir in 1 egg at a time, making sure that each egg is well absorbed before adding the next. The paste should be well stirred and beaten in order to be light.

Shape into small balls no bigger than a walnut, either with your hands or a spoon, and drop them in a deep frying pan of hot oil a few at a time.

Cook until the fritters are a golden color and have swelled to 3 times their original size—about 5–8 minutes.

Drain, roll in powdered sugar and serve at once. A bowl of syrup may accompany the fritters.

Excellent for trick or treat.

# THANKSGIVING

**SHRIMP DE JONGHE**
**ROAST TURKEY WITH CHESTNUT DRESSING**
**HOMEMADE CRANBERRY SAUCE**
**PUMPKIN CAKE**

No matter how you look at it, we are still faced with the turkey. I prefer the French influence for the dressing, which has always made my Thanksgiving dinners somewhat different. This, of course, with all due respect to oyster or corn bread dressing.

## SHRIMP DE JONGHE

2 cloves garlic
½ cup finely chopped parsley
⅓ tsp. dried tarragon
  (or 1 Tbs. fresh, if available)
⅓ tsp. chervil
⅓ tsp. shallot, minced
⅓ large onion, finely minced

Dash of nutmeg, mace and thyme
1½ sticks unsalted butter
1 cup very fine bread crumbs
¼ tsp. Tabasco pepper sauce
½ cup very dry sherry
2 lbs. shrimp, cooked (p. 247), shelled and deveined

*Serves 6*

Mash the garlic and combine with the parsley, tarragon, chervil, shallot, onion, nutmeg, mace and thyme. Combine with 1 stick of the butter and the 1 cup bread crumbs and blend thoroughly.

Finally, add the Tabasco and moisten thoroughly with the dry sherry.

Butter 6 individual ramekins generously and arrange alternate layers of the bread-crumb mixture and the precooked shrimp, cut up into small pieces. You should finish with the bread-crumb mixture. Dot with the remaining butter and bake for 10–15 minutes in a 350° oven.

NOTE: This dish was created at the Hotel de Jonghe in Chicago and originally had lots of garlic. Add more if you like.

## ROAST TURKEY WITH CHESTNUT DRESSING

*Dressing:*

2 quarts chestnuts*
2 cups olive oil
8 cups Beef Stock (p. 183)
6 green onions, tops and
   bottoms, chopped
2 Tbs. butter
1 lb. breakfast sausage,
   removed from casing
Turkey liver, boiled for
   10 minutes and chopped
Turkey heart and gizzard, boiled
   for ½ hour and chopped

1 tsp. Creole seasonings
1 Tbs. chopped parsley
1 Tbs. chopped chives
½ tsp. each powdered thyme and
   marjoram
1 clove garlic, minced
½ loaf day-old French bread,
   broken into small pieces
1 cup milk
½ cup dry red wine
Salt and pepper to taste
2 jiggers good cognac

*Turkey:*

1 10–12-lb. turkey,
   prepared for roasting

Paprika
1 stick melted butter

*Gravy:*

Pan juices from turkey
2 Tbs. *Beurre Manié* (chap. 13)
½–1 cup light cream

*Serves 8*

*To make the dressing:* Make a gash in each chestnut with a sharp knife. Heat the olive oil, add the chestnuts and heat over a brisk flame for several minutes, shaking the pan constantly.

Drain the nuts, allow to stand until cool enough to handle and then peel them with a sharp knife. (This part is difficult and tedious and hard on the nails, but the results are worth it.) Remove shells and as much of the inner skins as possible.

Cook chestnuts in the beef stock for 2–3 hours or until they are tender. Chop about 1 cup very coarsely and mash the rest. Reserve any liquid.

Cook the green onions in a little butter until they turn golden. Stir in the sausage meat, liver, heart and gizzard and cook for another 20 minutes. Add all the seasonings and cook for another 5–10 minutes.

Soak the French bread in the milk and wine. Squeeze dry.

Combine both the mashed and the chopped chestnuts with the sausage-innards mixture and the bread. Mix well; moisten with a little of the reserved chestnut liquid. Correct for seasoning with salt and pepper and add the cognac.

Stuff the turkey with this dressing and truss well.

If there is any extra dressing, simply pack in some foil, add a little of the chestnut liquid and place near the bird.

*To roast the turkey:* Sprinkle turkey completely with paprika mixed with some of the melted butter. Roast in an open roasting pan for 4–5 hours at 350°, basting frequently with the remaining liquid from the chestnuts plus the juices from the pan. If turkey gets too brown, cover the breast with a cloth or a piece of brown paper that has been dipped in melted butter, and continue to cook.

*To make the gravy:* Allow turkey to cool slightly before carving. This will give you time to skim the pan juices and add 2 Tbs. *beurre manié* to thicken the gravy. Then add a little light cream.

*You should buy and cook some extra chestnuts, because when you peel them you may find that some are too old for use.

## HOMEMADE CRANBERRY SAUCE

3 cups sugar
4 cups water
2 lbs. fresh cranberries
2 red apples, peeled, cored and
    quartered
1 large orange,
    cut into quarters and seeded

2 small lemons,
    cut into quarters and seeded
1 tsp. cinnamon
Dash of nutmeg
2 jiggers cognac

*Serves 8*

Dissolve sugar in water and bring to a boil. Add cranberries, apples, orange, lemons and seasonings and cook until the cranberries are popping—about 15–20 minutes.

When thoroughly cooked, remove the orange, lemon and apple pieces. Stir in the cognac, which has been set aflame, and allow the mixture to cool.

Refrigerate until ready to serve.

# PUMPKIN CAKE

1 box spice cake mix
  (to make 2 layers)
½ tsp. baking soda
1 cup milk
1 cup canned or fresh-cooked
  pumpkin
½ cup chopped pecans

⅔ cup finely chopped dried dates
1½ cups cream, stiffly whipped
¼ cup powdered sugar
2 Tbs. honey
½ tsp. cinnamon
¼ cup finely chopped lemon peel

*Serves 8*

Blend cake mix with baking soda. Follow directions on package, using the milk in the place of water in the first addition of liquid, and pumpkin to replace the second addition of liquid.

Fold in the nuts and most of the dates, reserving about ¼ cup. Blend.

Pour into 2 greased and lightly floured 9″ round cake pans. Bake at 350° for 25–30 minutes or until a silver knife comes out clean when inserted. Allow cake to cool.

Flavor the whipped cream with the powdered sugar and blend in the honey and cinnamon. Add the lemon peel and the rest of the chopped dates. Spread between layers and then on top of the assembled cake.

Refrigerate, but serve at room temperature.

# CHRISTMAS

**ROAST SUCKLING PIG**          **CHRISTMAS ENDIVE SALAD**
**SWEET POTATO PUDDING**        **BÛCHE DE NOËL**

My Christmases in New Orleans are special because I always take time out to
make this version of the *Bûche de Noël*. I often make as many as a dozen and
give them to special friends for Christmas. They freeze beautifully—one friend
kept several slices so she could have Christmas in July. The head of the suckling
pig, surrounded with leftovers, makes for great hors d'oeuvres.

## ROAST SUCKLING PIG

*Dressing:*

3 cups French bread pieces
½ cup Louisiana orange wine (or
   a mixture of ⅛ cup Triple Sec
   and ³/₈ cup dry white wine)
2 Tbs. chopped parsley
2 Tbs. chopped green onions
1 clove garlic, mashed
1 Tbs. Creole seasonings

3 Tbs. grated onion
4 Italian sausages, cooked in
   simmering water for 20
   minutes, skinned and mashed
Salt and pepper to taste
Grating of nutmeg
2 whole eggs

*Roast Pig:*

1 young suckling pig,
   about 10 lbs.
3 cloves garlic, cut in half
Salt and pepper

1 cup Louisiana dry orange wine
   (or a mixture of ¼ cup Triple
   Sec and ¾ cup dry white wine)
1 stick melted butter

*Gravy:*

Heart of the pig
Liver of the pig
1 onion, grated
2 Tbs. chopped green onion

2 Tbs. chopped parsley
Pan gravy from the pig
2 Tbs. *Beurre Manié* (chap. 13)

*Garnish:*

1 orange
Cranberries
2 Maraschino cherries
2 Tbs. cold butter

Watercress
Parsley
Broiled tomatoes

*Serves 8*

*To make the dressing:* Soak the French bread in the wine and squeeze dry. Add all the other dressing ingredients and combine thoroughly.

*To prepare the pig:* Wash the pig in several changes of water and dry it well. Rub it inside with the garlic and discard garlic. Rub with salt and pepper inside and out. Brush with ½ cup of the orange wine or substitute.

Stuff the pig loosely with the dressing. Lace the openings. Rub the pig with melted butter. With a sharp knife, make a number of slits over the surface so that the fat can drip into the roasting pan.

Place a block of wood in the pig's mouth to brace it for the orange that will later garnish it. Cover the pig's ears with buttered brown paper, to keep them from burning.

Bake in a moderate oven (350°) for 3–3½ hours, basting frequently, adding a little white wine to the sauce from time to time. Cook until the meat is tender. If it browns too fast, cover the pig with buttered brown paper or a cloth dipped in fat.

*To make the gravy:* While the pig is roasting, boil the heart for ½ hour. Then add the liver, grated onion, green onion and parsley. Cook until the heart and liver are tender—about another 20 minutes. Drain, chop and reserve.

When the pig is done, skim off all the fat from the pan gravy. (An easy way to do this is to put the gravy in the freezer for an hour so the fat will congeal.)

Blend gravy with heart-liver mixture. Thicken gravy by reheating and working in the *beurre manié*. Taste for seasonings and add a little more wine if gravy is too thick.

While making gravy you may keep pig warm in a very low oven (200°).

*To garnish the pig:* Place an orange in the pig's mouth. Put a collar of strung cranberries around its neck and place a Maraschino cherry in each eye. Rub the skin thoroughly with the cold butter so that it melts. The skin should be shiny and crisp. Place on a platter surrounded with watercress and parsley. Garnish with broiled tomatoes and serve with Homemade Cranberry Sauce (p. 66).

NOTE: To serve at a cocktail party, cut off the pig's head and place it in the middle of a silver platter. Surround it with cut-up pieces of the meat on a bed of watercress and parsley and allow guests to use their hands.

## SWEET POTATO PUDDING

5 or 6 sweet potatoes          ½ pint milk
3 egg yolks                    3 egg whites, stiffly beaten
2 cups sugar                   Pinch of salt
3 Tbs. butter                  ½ tsp. white pepper

*Serves 8*

Scrub the sweet potatoes and bake in a 375° oven for about 50 minutes; or boil in salted water for about 20 minutes, until soft, and drain them.

Peel the sweet potatoes and rub them through a sieve into a bowl. Add the egg yolks one at a time and mix well. Then add the sugar, butter, milk and lastly the stiffly beaten egg whites. Season with a pinch of salt and the pepper.

Stir all the ingredients thoroughly until the mixture has the consistency of a smooth paste—light and almost liquid. Pour into a buttered pie dish and bake in a moderate oven (350°) for 1 hour, until well browned.

## CHRISTMAS ENDIVE SALAD

1 lb. beets                    Juice of 2 lemons
1 lb. carrots                  Salt and white pepper to taste
8 Belgian endives             2 tsp. chopped capers
1 pint sour cream             Watercress

*Serves 8*

Cook beets unpeeled and whole, without salt, in boiling water to cover for 30–60 minutes. Drain, plunge into cold water for a moment and slip off skins. Cut into julienne strips.

Cook the carrots, scraped and sliced, in boiling salted water for 10–25 minutes. Drain. Cut into julienne strips.

Wash and dry endives, reserving 4 or 5 of the large outer leaves per person. (Save the rest for another recipe.)

Divide the pint of sour cream in half into 2 separate bowls. Season each with the lemon juice, salt, pepper and capers. In 1 bowl, toss the julienne of beets; in the other, toss the julienne of carrots.

Fill half the endive leaves with beet mixture and the other half with carrot. Arrange the leaves alternately on a large platter and garnish the center with watercress.

## BÛCHE DE NOËL
### Christmas Log

*Cake:*

| | |
|---|---|
| 5 egg yolks | 5 egg whites, stiffly beaten |
| 1 cup powdered sugar | 2–3 Tbs. granulated sugar |
| 3 Tbs. cocoa | |

*Mocha butter filling:*

| | |
|---|---|
| 4 Tbs. unsalted butter | 5 Tbs. very strong coffee |
| 2 cups powdered sugar | 1 tsp. vanilla extract |
| 1 Tbs. dark cocoa | |

*Whipped cream filling:*

1 pint whipping cream
¼ cup powdered sugar

*Mocha butter-cream frosting:*

| | |
|---|---|
| 1 lb. butter | 3 tsp. very strong coffee |
| ½ cup powdered sugar | 2 Tbs. dark cocoa |

*Garnish:*

½ cup finely chopped
   pistachio nuts, unsalted
8–10 Maraschino cherries

*Serves 8*

*To make the cake:* Beat egg yolks until thick and pale yellow. Add the powdered sugar and cocoa and beat well again. Fold in the stiffly beaten egg whites and blend well.

Line a large rectangular pan (11" x 15½" x 1") with foil so that enough sticks out over the edges to lift later. Butter the foil and then lightly flour it, being careful that it is evenly distributed.

Pour the batter into this pan and spread evenly with a spatula. Bake in a moderate oven (350°) for 12–15 minutes or until a silver knife thrust into the cake comes out clean.

Grasping the edges of the foil, quickly turn the cake onto another sheet of foil that has been evenly sprinkled with granulated sugar. Peel off the first piece of foil. Fold the cake lengthwise in thirds, bringing one side to the center and folding the other over it. Reserve until ready to decorate.

This is really a rolled soufflé, and so very fragile to handle. You will want to bake 2 of these cakes, as you might break the original one, and you can always use the odd pieces to fill in. Nothing shows, as the cake is completely covered with frosting. In fact, I always lay a thin extra strip lengthwise down the center of the *bûche* because it makes it easier to decorate.

*To make the mocha butter filling:* Cream the butter until fluffy and lemon-colored. Gradually add the powdered sugar and then the cocoa. Blend thoroughly and beat in the coffee mixed with the vanilla. Beat until the filling is smooth, thick and creamy.

*To make the whipped cream filling:* Whip the cream until very stiff, adding the powdered sugar a little at a time.

*To make the mocha butter-cream frosting:* Cream the butter with the powdered sugar, adding a little at a time. Flavor with the coffee and cocoa, blending well.

*To assemble:* Unroll the cake and spread generously and evenly with the mocha butter filling. Then spread with the very stiff whipped cream. Fold, rather than roll, the cake from both sides towards the center.

Keep in the baking pan and place in the freezer until cream and cake are hard enough to work with—at least an hour.

Remove from the freezer. Cut off a small piece from each end on the diagonal so that you will have the effect of a log. Now spread the outside of the log with mocha butter-cream frosting, being very generous. Work it all with a knife so that you get the effect of rough bark.

Sprinkle pistachio nuts at the ends to give the effect of green moss. Garnish with Maraschino cherries.

Return to freezer and keep until ready to use. Remove from freezer and keep in refrigerator 2–3 hours before serving.

# NEW YEAR'S EVE

**CABBAGE SOUP**          **WHITE BEAN CHARCUTERIE**
**SWEDISH MEAT CROQUETTES**     **CREOLE BRANDY PUNCH**

Now we come to the end of the year, but just think—in New Orleans it's holiday time all year round.

## CABBAGE SOUP

2 medium heads white cabbage         6 quarts Veal Stock (p. 185)
6 Tbs. butter                        15 peppercorns
2 Tbs. light Karo syrup              Salt to taste

*Serves 10*

Remove the coarse outer leaves of the cabbages. Remove the ribs as well. Chop the cabbage and cook it in the butter until brown—about 20 minutes.
Add the syrup and stir constantly until the syrup is lightly browned, being careful not to let it get too dark. Add the veal stock, peppercorns and salt. Cover and simmer the soup for 2–3 hours.
This is a Swedish dish and is usually served with Frikadeller (Swedish Meat Croquettes).

## SWEDISH MEAT CROQUETTES

1 lb. veal                   1 cup milk
4 Tbs. butter                ½ tsp. salt
2 Tbs. bread crumbs          ½ tsp. pepper
1 tsp. potato flour          Salted water

*Serves 10*

Put the veal through a meat grinder 3 times. Mix the meat with the butter, bread crumbs, potato flour and milk. Season with salt and pepper. The mixture should be quite smooth. Refrigerate for a couple of hours.
Shape into very small balls and boil in salted water for about 10 minutes. Remove with a slotted spoon and serve with Cabbage Soup.

## WHITE BEAN CHARCUTERIE

2 lbs. Great Northern white beans,       1 lb. andouille sausage or Polish
  washed and soaked for 2 hours            kielbasa
Salt and pepper to taste                 ½ lb. hot Italian sausage
3 large carrots, peeled and sliced       ½ lb. mild Italian sausage
4 smoked ham hocks,*
  with plenty of meat

*Serves 10*

Place the beans in a large saucepan. Season with salt and pepper. Cover with water. Bring to a boil.

Skim if necessary and then add the carrots and ham hocks; bring to a boil once again. Skim again and then reduce heat and simmer, cooking very slowly until beans are tender but not falling apart—about 1–1½ hours. When they are done, there should be very little liquid.

In the meantime, slice and quarter the andouille or kielbasa sausage and fry lightly for about 10 minutes. In a separate pan, cook the Italian sausages in simmering water for about 20 minutes. When cool, slice and quarter them.

When beans are tender, about 15 minutes before cooking time is finished, remove ham bones and pick off the solid chunks of meat. Return these pieces to the beans. Add the sausages and continue cooking.

Correct seasonings and serve with crisp French bread.

*Use uncooked ham hocks if the smoked are not available.

## CREOLE BRANDY PUNCH

4 wineglasses good brandy                A good pinch of powdered
1 wineglass kirsch                         cinnamon
1 wineglass Maraschino liqueur           A good pinch of allspice
                                         20 small lumps of sugar

*Serves 10*

Pour 3 glasses of the brandy into a silver bowl. Add the kirsch, Maraschino liqueur, cinnamon and allspice. Put in the sugar lumps, and when they have absorbed the liqueurs, place some in a ladle or small saucepan.

Warm the ladle, add the remaining wineglass of brandy and as you're pouring it into the bowl, set it aflame. Burn for a few minutes, and when flame goes out, serve the punch in small glasses.

# 3
# FAVORITE
# NEW ORLEANS
# RESTAURANTS

NEW ORLEANS is known for fine cuisine, not only in its homes but in its many restaurants. Unlike restaurants in other major cities, there is a theme that flows throughout the restaurants in our city. That theme is Creole and Cajun. For this reason, you will find the same items on menus in different restaurants, each with its own interpretation.

While the famous restaurant Antoine's created Oysters Rockefeller (incidentally, the great John D. never tasted them), you will find Oysters Rockefeller on menus in almost every restaurant in New Orleans. The natives love to compare all the variations. You will find Crème Caramel, Red Beans and Rice and Shrimp Remoulade repeated again and again, and once more, the natives will argue for hours as to which chef serves the best. And, of course, you will find our famous New Orleans bread, in one form or another, and our chicory coffee on every menu in every restaurant.

Even our hotels boast excellent restaurants. For some reason, people seem to shy away from restaurants located in hotels. To shun a hotel restaurant in New Orleans is a mistake; they are among our best, and I have selected recipes from several for this book.

This chapter in no way intends to rate the restaurants of New Orleans, and the omission of certain restaurants in no way reflects on their reputations as fine eating places. These are simply the restaurants I have frequented over the years, the dishes I have ordered and reordered and enjoy when having lunch or dinner with friends.

I should like to share these recipes with my readers and extend my thanks to the wonderful restaurant owners and chefs for providing them.

# ANTOINE'S

**OYSTERS ROCKEFELLER**     **PIGEONNEAUX PARADIS**

You don't just eat at Antoine's. You dine. You grow up here and you see New Orleans's fun and history—and Mardi Gras before your very eyes. Of course, so much of this is changing, but it still can be had if you know how.

## OYSTERS ROCKEFELLER

| | |
|---|---|
| 6 Tbs. butter | Dash of Tabasco pepper sauce |
| 6 Tbs. finely minced raw spinach | ½ tsp. Herbsaint |
| 3 Tbs. minced onion | ½ tsp. salt |
| 3 Tbs. minced parsley | 1 lb. rock salt |
| 3 Tbs. minced celery | 36 freshly opened oysters |
| 5 Tbs. bread crumbs | on the half shell |

*Serves 6*

Melt butter in a saucepan. Add all ingredients except rock salt and oysters. Cook, stirring constantly, for 15 minutes or until soft. Press through sieve or food mill to make a sauce. Cool.

Place rock salt in 6 small pie tins. Set 6 oysters in their shells on each bed of rock salt. Place a spoonful of sauce on each oyster.

Broil oysters under medium heat until sauce begins to brown—about 3–5 minutes. Serve immediately in the pie tins.

*AUTHOR'S NOTE:* The exact recipe for Antoine's Oysters Rockefeller is a secret, but Roy Alciatore, grandson of the founder of Antoine's, used to tell me this was real close.

## PIGEONNEAUX PARADIS

*Roast squab:*
      6 squab
      Salt and pepper to taste
      ½ stick butter

      1 cup chopped celery
      1 cup chopped carrot
      ½ cup chopped onion

*Sauce Paradis:*
      ½ stick butter
      ¼ cup flour
      2 cups Veal Stock (p. 185)
        or Chicken Stock (p. 183)
      ½ cup Madeira wine

      2 Tbs. currant jelly
      2 cups seedless white grapes
      2 large truffles, sliced
      Salt and pepper to taste

*Serves 6*

To prepare squab: Sprinkle them inside and out with salt and pepper and rub with butter. Mix celery, carrot and onion and spread on the bottom of a roasting pan. Place squab on top.

Roast for about 30 minutes in a 325° oven. Remove squab from pan to a deep casserole.

To make sauce: Melt butter, blend in flour and stir until smooth. Add veal or chicken stock, stirring constantly until slightly thickened. Add wine and jelly, stirring until jelly is melted; then add grapes and truffles. Correct seasoning for salt and pepper.

Pour the Sauce Paradis over the squab, cover and bake for 15–20 minutes.

# BEGUE'S, ROYAL SONESTA HOTEL

**SEAFOOD NEWBURG**       **PRALINE ICE CREAM PIE**

For anyone who has seen *Saratoga Trunk* on the *Late Late Show,* that scene in New Orleans where Gary Cooper pours ketchup over his entrée before the horrified eyes of Ingrid Bergman was supposed to be in the very famous Mme. Begue's restaurant. Begue's has been recreated for today's gourmet, and you still don't need ketchup for the delicious dishes served.

## SEAFOOD NEWBURG

3 Tbs. melted butter
2½ cups shrimp, scallops
    and oysters combined
⅓ cup Madeira or sherry
4 large egg yolks
1 cup light cream

Dash of cayenne pepper
Dash of nutmeg
Salt to taste
1 Tbs. cognac or tomato paste
    (optional)

*Serves 6*

Place butter and seafood in the top of a double boiler and cook over low flame for 10 minutes or until the seafood meats are tender. Add the wine and cook until most of the liquid has evaporated.

Blend egg yolks with ¼ cup of the cream and add to the seafood. Stir in the remaining cream and cook over hot but not boiling water until the sauce is of medium thickness.

Remove from heat and add the seasonings. If desired, add cognac or tomato paste.

Serve on toast.

## PRALINE ICE CREAM PIE

1 pint vanilla ice cream
4 Tbs. praline paste
1 Basic Pie Crust,
    bottom only (p. 382)

1 cup cream, whipped
Crushed pralines

*Serves 6*

Combine ice cream and praline paste and mix together thoroughly with an electric beater. Place in prepared and baked pie shell.

Freeze until hard enough to slice with a knife—at least 2 hours.

Top with whipped cream. Sprinkle with crushed pralines and serve on a chilled plate.

# BRENNAN'S

### BRENNAN'S OYSTER SOUP          CHICKEN PONTALBA

It all started with Owen Brennan and his wonderful family. No one can ever forget those 25¢ martinis. The memory lingers, and the Brennans are still there on Royal Street.

## BRENNAN'S OYSTER SOUP

1 cup butter
2 cups finely chopped celery
2 cups finely chopped green onions
2 Tbs. flour
2 Tbs. finely chopped garlic
4 dozen large,
    freshly shucked oysters

12 cups oyster water
    (oyster liquor plus sufficient
    water to make 12 cups)
2 bay leaves
2 tsp. salt
1 tsp. white pepper

*Serves 8*

Melt butter over medium heat in a 6-quart heavy saucepan, and sauté the celery and green onions until tender but not browned, stirring frequently, for about 5–10 minutes.

Gradually stir in the flour and cook for 5 minutes longer, stirring constantly, over a low flame. Add the remaining ingredients and simmer for 20 minutes.

Remove the pan from the heat and scoop out the bay leaves with a slotted spoon or a long fork; discard. Serve immediately.

# CHICKEN PONTALBA

*Poached chicken:*

| | |
|---|---|
| 1 stick butter | Dash of pepper |
| 2 cups water | 8 chicken breasts |
| 1 tsp. salt | |

*Vegetables:*

| | |
|---|---|
| ½ cup butter | 1½ cups chopped boiled ham |
| 4 Tbs. finely chopped garlic | 1½ cups diced potato, |
| 2 cups chopped white onion |    deep fried for about 2 minutes |
| 2 cups chopped green onion | 3 Tbs. chopped parsley |
| 2 cups sliced mushrooms | ³/₄ cup dry white wine |

*Quick béarnaise sauce:*

| | |
|---|---|
| 4 Tbs. tarragon vinegar | 3 cups Hollandaise Sauce |
| 4 tsp. chopped parsley* |    (chap. 13), heated |
| 4 tsp. chopped tarragon* | Dash of cayenne pepper |
| 4 tsp. chopped chervil* | |

*Serves 8*

*To poach chicken breasts:* In a large skillet put the butter, about ¼" water, salt and pepper.

Place the chicken breasts in the pan and bring the water to a boil. Cover the pan and reduce the heat to low. Cook covered for about 15 minutes or until the chicken breasts are cooked through.

Remove from the pan with a fork or slotted spoon, allowing the liquid to drain back into the pan. Place on a platter and set in a 175° oven to keep warm.

*To prepare vegetables:* Melt the butter in a large skillet and add the garlic, onion, green onion and mushrooms. Sauté until browned—about 20 minutes. Then add the ham, fried potatoes, parsley and wine. Simmer for about 2 minutes more; then remove from the heat and set in the oven to keep warm.

*To make béarnaise sauce:* Blend vinegar and all herbs with the hot hollandaise sauce. Finish off with a dash of cayenne pepper.

*To serve:* On each of 8 heated plates, put first a layer of the sautéed vegetables, then a poached chicken breast. Cover with a generous layer of béarnaise sauce.

*If fresh herbs are not available, use 1 tsp. each of the dried herbs.

# BROUSSARD'S

### BREAST OF CHICKEN RATATOUILLE    SHRIMP ERNIE

A great Italian flair to what was once a very famous French restaurant. *Vive la différence!* However you look at it, the Italians and the French owe it all to Marco Polo and Catherine de Medici.

## BREAST OF CHICKEN RATATOUILLE

1 cup olive oil
2 eggplants, diced
3 zucchini, diced
1 medium onion, diced
10 fresh mushrooms, diced
4 cloves garlic, minced
1 tsp. each thyme, basil, oregano,
   sweet marjoram and fennel seed

4 ripe tomatoes, quartered
1 small can tomato paste
Salt and pepper to taste
6 chicken breasts, 8–10 oz. each
1 cup seasoned flour
1 cup Clarified Butter (chap. 13)

*Serves 6*

Heat olive oil in a saucepan and add diced vegetables. Cook until tender—about 10–15 minutes. Then add garlic and cook for another 5 minutes. Then add all the seasonings and finally the quartered tomatoes and tomato paste; correct with salt and pepper. Cook until well blended—about another 5–10 minutes.

Bone chicken breasts and dust with seasoned flour. Sauté in the clarified butter until tender—about 15 minutes.

Place chicken breasts on top of ratatouille and serve.

# SHRIMP ERNIE

*Remoulade sauce:*

1 pint mayonnaise
1 Tbs. Creole mustard
1 Tbs. horseradish

1 clove garlic, finely minced
2 green onions, finely chopped

*Fried shrimp:*

½ lb. medium shrimp (12–15)
1 egg mixed with 1 cup milk
2 cups yellow cornmeal

2 tsp. salt
1 tsp. black pepper
1 cup cooking oil

*Serves 2*

*To make remoulade sauce:* Combine all the ingredients in a bowl and blend well.

*To prepare shrimp:* Soak the shrimp in the egg and milk mixture. Season cornmeal with salt and pepper. Roll shrimp in cornmeal and deep fry for 3–4 minutes.

Serve hot with remoulade sauce.

*AUTHOR'S NOTE:* You will probably have some sauce left over, and it is delicious with crab meat.

# CAFÉ SBISA

### ROAST DUCK WITH GREEN PEPPER SAUCE

In French a *violon d'Ingres* means a hobby. Dr. Lawrence Hill has always had his hobby—cuisine. He is a doctor by profession, and now one of his dreams has come true—he has created his own restaurant.

## ROAST DUCK WITH GREEN PEPPER SAUCE

*Roast duck:*
    2 ducks, 4–4½ lbs. each
    Salt and pepper

    1 onion, halved
    2 carrots, halved

*Sauce:*
    4 Tbs. butter
    Giblets of the duck,
      coarsely chopped
    1 medium onion,
      coarsely chopped
    1 tomato, peeled,
      seeded and coarsely chopped

    1 clove garlic, crushed
    4 sprigs parsley
    2 bay leaves
    3–3½ cups Beef Stock (p. 183)
    3 Tbs. flour
    ⅓ cup Madeira
    1 Tbs. green peppercorns

*Serves 8*

*To roast ducks:* Rub the ducks with salt and pepper inside and out. Stuff each duck with an onion half and a carrot. Truss the ducks and place them on a rack in a roasting pan. Roast at 400° for 1½–2 hours, until done.

*To make sauce:* Melt 1 Tbs. of the butter in a saucepan and add the duck giblets. Sauté for 3 minutes. Add the vegetables and seasonings. Sauté for 5 more minutes. Add 3 cups of the beef stock. Simmer for 1 hour to reduce to 2 cups.

Strain the stock and discard the giblets and vegetables. Reserve stock.

Make a roux by melting the rest of the butter and adding the flour, allowing it to brown slightly.

Add the stock, Madeira and green peppercorns. Simmer for a few minutes. If sauce is too thick, add some of the remaining beef stock.

*To serve:* Carve the ducks or serve a quarter per person and pour sauce over the hot duck.

# CARIBBEAN ROOM, PONTCHARTRAIN HOTEL

### OYSTERS AND MUSHROOMS AU GRATIN
### TROUT VÉRONIQUE
### MILE HIGH ICE CREAM PIE

I always enjoy the true New Orleans elegance of this fine hotel restaurant. The Pontchartrain must certainly have created the "buffet" in New Orleans. The Trout Véronique is their own, and highly successful, adaptation of a classic.

## OYSTERS AND MUSHROOMS AU GRATIN

½ stick butter
1 quart fresh oysters, shucked
1½ dozen large mushrooms, chopped
1 small bunch green onions, chopped
2 cups Béchamel Sauce (chap. 13)

1 cup Hollandaise Sauce (chap. 13)
½ cup Pernod or Abisante
Gratings of cheese such as Romano, Parmesan or sharp Cheddar

*Serves 6*

In a heavy skillet, heat butter and sauté oysters, mushrooms and green onions for about 10 minutes. Do not brown. Once they are cooked, add the béchamel sauce and bring to a simmer.

Remove from the fire. Fold in the hot hollandaise sauce and the Pernod or Abisante a little at a time.

Place this mixture in a casserole and sprinkle grated cheese on top.

Bake in a 400° oven for about 10 minutes and serve immediately.

## TROUT VÉRONIQUE

1 trout filet from a 1½-lb. trout          ½ cup Hollandaise Sauce
½ pint dry white wine                          (chap. 13)
                                                          8 seedless white grapes

*Serves 1*

Poach trout in wine in a pan small enough so that wine covers trout. After poaching for about 7 minutes, remove trout, draining well, and place on an ovenproof serving plate.

Reduce remaining liquid. Add hollandaise sauce and stir briskly.

Place grapes on trout, cover with sauce, and glaze quickly in broiler.

## MILE HIGH ICE CREAM PIE

*Crust:*

1½ cups sifted flour                    2 cups shortening
½ tsp. salt                                   4–5 Tbs. cold water

*Pie:*

1 pint vanilla ice cream             ¼ tsp. cream of tartar
1 pint chocolate ice cream         ½ cup sugar
8 egg whites                               1 cup chocolate sauce
½ tsp. vanilla

*Serves 8–12*

*To make crust:* Sift together flour and salt. Cut in shortening until pieces are the size of small peas. Sprinkle 1 Tbs. cold water over flour mixture and gently toss with fork. Repeat until all is moistened.

Form into a ball with fingers and roll out to ⅛" thickness on a lightly floured surface. Fit loosely into a 9" pie pan, pricking well. Bake for 10–12 minutes at 450° degrees. Cool.

*To make pie:* Layer ice cream in pie shell. Beat egg whites with vanilla and cream of tartar until soft peaks form. Gradually add sugar, beating until stiff and glossy and sugar is dissolved. Spread the meringue over ice cream to edge of pastry.

Broil 30 seconds–1 minute to brown meringue. Freeze for at least several hours.

Drizzle chocolate sauce over each serving.

# CHINA TOWN CAFÉ

**CHEWEY PAY GUY**          **GUY LON GOW YOKE**
**(CRUNCHY SKIN CHICKEN)**   **(BEEF WITH BROCCOLI)**

China Town Café is the creation of Mr. and Mrs. Gee. Located in the heart of the French Quarter, it is what one could almost call Chinese-Creole. Mr. Gee, a native of China, was a genius in the kitchen, a master chef of the old Chinese tradition. His cookbook is a great Chinese cookbook. I love to pop in here and chat with Mrs. Gee, who is carrying on the tradition.

## CHEWEY PAY GUY
### Crunchy Skin Chicken

*Chicken:*
   ¼ small fryer
   1 tsp. baking soda
      diluted with 1 tsp. water

   1 Tbs. cornstarch
      or water chestnut flour
   ½ cup cooking oil

*Chinese Fruit Sauce:*
   1½ cups sugar
   ½ cup dark cider vinegar
   ½ cup water

   ½ cup crushed pineapple
   2 drops yellow food coloring
   1 tsp. diluted cornstarch

*Accompaniments:*
   Steamed rice
   Hot mustard

*Serves 1*

*To prepare chicken:* Clean both sides of chicken with clear water and then dry with a clean towel.

Brush the entire skin surface of the chicken with the baking soda and water mixture and allow to stand for 5 minutes. Wash soda from chicken with clear water. Do not dry.

Lay chicken flat, skin side up, and sprinkle with cornstarch or water chestnut flour until skin is well covered. Gently pat with a dry towel.

Fry chicken in deep oil until brown. Drain oil from chicken and cut into small pieces.

*To make Chinese Fruit Sauce:* Combine the sugar, vinegar, water, pineapple and food coloring. Bring to a boil, add diluted cornstarch and stir until smooth.

Serve the chicken with the Fruit Sauce, steamed rice and hot mustard.

## GUY LON GOW YOKE
### Beef with Broccoli

1 bunch fresh broccoli
1 lb. tenderloin of beef,
   cut into thin strips
2 drops sesame seed oil
1 clove garlic, minced
¼" piece ginger root, mashed

1 Tbs. sherry wine
1 Tbs. cornstarch
1½ cups water
¼ tsp. baking soda
2 Tbs. cooking oil
½ cup stock from broccoli

*Serves 2–3*

Remove flowers from broccoli. Peel stems and slice diagonally.

Marinate the tenderloin slices in a mixture of sesame seed oil, garlic, ginger root, sherry and cornstarch for just 1½ minutes.

Boil water and add baking soda. Add broccoli slices and flowers last. After about 5 minutes, when broccoli turns a vivid green in color, remove and wash well with cold water to remove all baking soda.

Heat the cooking oil over a high flame and add the tenderloin pieces. Stir and fry quickly for 1 minute. Add the broccoli, mix well but gently and continue to cook.

Pour the broccoli stock into the bowl where the beef has marinated, so as to collect all remaining residue of the marinade. Pour this over the meat and broccoli.

Cover with a lid and bring to a boil. Cook for about 5 minutes.

Serve with rice.

# COMMANDER'S PALACE

**TURTLE SOUP      EGGS HUSSARDE**
**FILET MIGNON STANLEY**

Ella Brennan, not to mention Adelaide, Dick and John, has turned a Garden District neighborhood restaurant into a Creole paradise. Here, I can always enjoy jazz music, friendship and great food.

## TURTLE SOUP

1 lb. turtle meat,
  cut into 1" cubes
1 cup butter
1 cup diced onions
1 cup diced celery
3 cloves garlic, minced
1 cup flour
16 oz. whole peeled tomatoes

3 quarts Beef Stock (p. 183)
4 bay leaves
½ cup Worcestershire sauce
Salt and pepper to taste
1 cup dry sherry
2 chopped hard-boiled eggs
½ cup chopped parsley

*Serves 8–10*

Sauté turtle meat in butter until very brown; add onions, celery and garlic and cook for 10 minutes. Blend in flour and cook 5 minutes longer.

Add tomatoes, stock and all other ingredients except sherry, hard-boiled eggs and parsley. Season for salt and pepper.

Simmer for about 1 hour or until meat is tender. Add sherry, chopped eggs and parsley and simmer for another 5 minutes.

Serve in bowls or cups with a thin slice of lemon and a carafe of sherry on the side.

# EGGS HUSSARDE

*Marchand de vin sauce:* *
    ¾ cup butter
    ⅓ cup finely chopped mushrooms
    ½ cup minced ham
    ⅓ cup finely chopped green onions
    ½ cup finely chopped onion
    2 Tbs. minced garlic

2 Tbs. flour
½ tsp. salt
⅛ tsp. pepper
Dash of cayenne
¾ cup Beef Stock (p. 183)
½ cup red wine

*Eggs:*
    2 large, thin slices ham, grilled
    2 Holland rusks or
      English muffins
    2 slices tomato, grilled

2 eggs, soft-poached
¾ cup Hollandaise Sauce
    (chap. 13)
Paprika

*Serves 1*

*To make marchand de vin sauce:* Melt butter in a 9″ skillet and lightly sauté the mushrooms, ham, green onions, onion and garlic.

When onion is golden brown, add the flour, salt, pepper and cayenne. Brown well for about 7–10 minutes. Blend in stock and wine and simmer over low heat for 35–40 minutes.

*To assemble eggs:* Lay a large slice of ham across each rusk and cover with *marchand de vin* sauce. Cover next with a tomato slice and then a poached egg. Top with hollandaise sauce and garnish with a sprinkling of paprika.

\* This recipe makes 2 cups, or enough for 8 servings of Eggs Hussarde. You may freeze any left over.

# FILET MIGNON STANLEY

2 filets (12 oz. each)
½ cup Béchamel Sauce (chap. 13)
Pinch of cayenne
Horseradish to taste

2 bananas, peeled
    and cut in half lengthwise
¼ cup flour
6 Tbs. unsalted butter

*Serves 2*

Grill filets medium or rare. Combine next 3 ingredients for sauce.
Dredge banana halves in the flour and sauté in butter for 3–5 minutes.

Place each filet in center of a warm plate. Arrange a banana half on either side of each filet and put a heaping spoonful of sauce on top of each banana. Spoon meat juices over all and serve.

# COURT OF TWO SISTERS

**EGGS CREOLE**          **REDFISH RECTOR**

The Court of Two Sisters has one of the most beautiful patios in the French Quarter. I enjoy these two dishes whenever I wander back to the courtyard from the huge bar up front to have brunch.

## EGGS CREOLE

*Shrimp Creole Sauce:*

2 Tbs. butter
2 cloves garlic, chopped
½ cup chopped onion
1 cup chopped celery
3 cups peeled, chopped tomatoes
1 bay leaf
½ tsp. thyme, crushed

¼ tsp. coarsely ground
   black pepper
¼ tsp. cayenne
½ tsp. salt
1 cup shrimp,
   cooked and deveined (p. 247)
¼ cup chopped fresh parsley

*Eggs:*

8 poached eggs
8 slices Canadian bacon

8 Holland rusks or
   English muffins or toast slices

*Serves 4*

*To make sauce:* Melt butter and sauté garlic, onion and celery for about 5 minutes or until tender. Add tomatoes and all other ingredients except shrimp and parsley. Cover and simmer for 5 minutes.

Add shrimp and cook 5 minutes longer. Add parsley.

*To assemble eggs:* Poach eggs the way you like them. Drain and lay each egg on a slice of fried Canadian bacon that has been placed on a rusk or toast slice. Cover the eggs with spoonfuls of the hot Creole Sauce.

If you wish, you can prepare the sauce in advance and preheat when ready to serve.

# REDFISH RECTOR

*Crab Meat Rector Sauce:*

¼ lb. butter
2 Tbs. diced green pepper
1 Tbs. finely chopped celery
½ cup chopped green onions
1 Tbs. diced pimiento
3 fresh mushrooms, sliced
1 lb. lump crab meat, picked

½ tsp. salt (garlic salt, if desired)
¼ tsp. white pepper
Pinch of cayenne
1 tsp. chopped parsley
Juice of 1 lemon
½ cup dry white wine

*Redfish:*

4 redfish steaks, 1″ thick

*Serves 4*

*To prepare the sauce:* Melt butter in skillet. Sauté green pepper, celery, green onions, pimiento and mushrooms until tender—about 10 minutes.

Then add the crab meat, salt, pepper, cayenne, parsley and lemon juice. Simmer for 20 minutes, stirring gently so crab meat will not break up.

Add the white wine and complete the sauce by cooking just long enough to blend all ingredients—about 5 minutes.

*To cook fish and serve:* Broil the redfish steaks for about 5 minutes on each side and keep warm.

Cover with the sauce and serve.

# ELMWOOD PLANTATION

### RED SNAPPER COURT BOUILLON
### VEAL ELMWOOD

The atmosphere here is that of an old Southern plantation. It is located under the Huey Long Bridge and is real old New Orleans.

## RED SNAPPER COURT BOUILLON

5 lbs. red snapper filet
1 bay leaf
1 tsp. oregano
1 tsp. crushed black pepper
1 tsp. salt
1 can (No. 2½) tomatoes
¼ cup sliced fresh mushrooms

3 cloves garlic, crushed
2 onions, chopped
½ green pepper, chopped
¼ cup olive oil
1 or 2 slices lemon
1 lb. lump crab meat, picked over
Salt and pepper to taste

*Serves 4*

Lay the fish on a bed of all the vegetables and seasonings in a deep pan; sprinkle with olive oil. Add a slice or two of lemon and sprinkle with crab meat. Add salt and pepper to taste.
Bake at 400° for 25–30 minutes.

## VEAL ELMWOOD

2 Tbs. olive oil
1 lb. filet of veal
  or tender veal cutlets,
  cut into small strips
1 2-oz. can button mushrooms
Pinch of coarse black pepper

Pinch of salt
Pinch of oregano
½ green pepper, sliced
½ onion, sliced
2 Tbs. white wine

*Serves 2*

Sauté all the ingredients except the wine in the olive oil for 15–20 minutes. Add the wine and simmer for 10 minutes longer.

# GALATOIRE'S

**CRAB MEAT YVONNE**          **TROUT MARGUERY**

The French like to think of a restaurant as an extension of their own homes, or a home away from home. No restaurant in New Orleans exemplifies this bourgeois tradition more than Galatoire's.

## CRAB MEAT YVONNE

| | |
|---|---|
| 1 stick butter | Salt and white pepper to taste |
| 1 cup sliced mushrooms | 1 lb. lump crab meat, picked |
| 3 fresh artichoke bottoms,* | Finely chopped parsley |
| precooked and sliced | |

*Serves 4*

In a large skillet melt butter and sauté mushrooms for about 10 minutes. Add artichoke bottoms and stir slightly. Season with salt and pepper.

Now add crab meat very gently and cook for about 5 minutes. Crab meat must remain lumpy but be well heated.

Serve immediately, sprinkled with finely chopped parsley.

*Either save the bottoms from 3 artichokes that you have cooked or use canned.

## TROUT MARGUERY

| | |
|---|---|
| 6 filets of trout | 1½ cups Hollandaise Sauce |
| (about 3 lbs. each) | (chap. 13) |
| Salt and pepper to taste | ½ cup boiled shrimp (p. 247), |
| 6 Tbs. olive oil | sliced |
| 1 cup water | ½ cup sliced mushrooms, |
| | sautéed in butter for 5 minutes |

*Serves 6*

Place the 6 filets of trout in a baking dish. Sprinkle with salt and pepper and spoon the olive oil over the fish. Add the water and bake in a 350° oven for about 15 minutes or until fish are tender.

Combine the hot hollandaise sauce with the shrimp and mushrooms. Correct seasonings.

Place fish on individual heated plates and cover each filet with some of the hollandaise mixture.

# JONATHAN

### CALVES' LIVER WITH ORANGE SAUCE

One of the newest and most elegant restaurants in the French Quarter. Its decor captures the art deco of Master Erté, and one dining room is named after him. Though the decor and music evoke the 1930s, the food captures the tradition of New Orleans with some very good new recipes like Tom Cowman's calves' liver.

## CALVES' LIVER WITH ORANGE SAUCE

*Orange Sauce:*
| | |
|---|---|
| 1½ cups orange marmalade | 1½ Tbs. beef base |
| 1 small can | ¼ tsp. powdered thyme |
| orange juice concentrate | ¼ cup Grand Marnier |
| 1 cup brandy | 2 Tbs. cornstarch |

*Calves' liver:* *
12 thin slices calves' liver
1 stick butter

*Serves 6*

*To make the sauce:* Heat the first 5 ingredients to boiling. Mix Grand Marnier and cornstarch and stir into the first 5 ingredients. Simmer, stirring occasionally, for at least 5 minutes or until clear and thick.

*To cook liver and serve:* Cook liver in melted butter very fast until it is the way you like it.

Divide onto individual hot plates and cover with the Orange Sauce.

* Dust liver with seasoned flour composed of the following: 1 cup flour, a pinch each of salt, pepper, powdered thyme and paprika, and a generous pinch each of white pepper, onion powder and dried mustard.

# KOLB'S

### KOLB'S SAUERBRATEN          POTATO PANCAKES

Believe it or not, there are German Creoles. For decades Kolb's has served the desires and appetites of New Orleanians for classic German cuisine.

## KOLB'S SAUERBRATEN

*Marinade:*

| | |
|---|---|
| 3 cups tarragon vinegar | ½ tsp. ground allspice |
| 4 cups water | 2 medium carrots, sliced |
| ½ cup sugar | 2 medium onions, sliced |
| ¼ cup salt | 1 green pepper, sliced |
| 4 bay leaves | 1 stalk celery, sliced |
| 12 whole cloves | ¼ bunch parsley, chopped |

*Meat and other ingredients:*

| | |
|---|---|
| 4 lbs. bottom beef round | 1 Tbs. ginger |
| 1–1½ cups cooking oil | Vinegar to taste |
| 1 Tbs. flour | Sugar to taste |

*Serves 8–10*

*To make marinade:* Combine all the ingredients.

*To prepare meat:* Cover meat with marinade and place in a covered bowl in your refrigerator. Allow to stand for a week, turning occasionally.

Remove from marinade and wipe dry with paper towels. Sear on all sides in hot oil in a dutch oven. Pour marinade back over meat, cover and cook slowly until tender—about 1–1½ hours.

*To serve:* Remove meat, strain liquid and thicken with a mixture of flour and ginger. Correct seasoning with vinegar and/or sugar to get just the right sweet 'n' sour gravy.

Slice meat and serve covered with the hot gravy.

## POTATO PANCAKES

| | |
|---|---|
| 3 medium potatoes, peeled | ½ tsp. salt |
| 1 egg yolk | 1 tsp. sugar |
| ½ cup sour cream | 1 cup chicken fat or cooking oil |
| ½ cup all-purpose flour | |

*Serves 4*

Grate potatoes, place in strainer and press out excess liquid.

Add all ingredients except oil and beat mixture well. Let stand for 10 minutes. Spoon off liquid, if any, from surface.

Shape and fry in hot chicken fat or cooking oil.

# MASSON'S

### LES MERVEILLES DE LA MER
### OYSTERS ALBERT

I remember their mother and father, and now there are the Masson boys and their families. I always enjoy being with my friends in this restaurant, where the food is good and the atmosphere authentic New Orleans.

## LES MERVEILLES DE LA MER EN CRÊPES

½ cup chopped green onions
½ cup sliced mushrooms
1½ lbs. butter
3 tsp. flour
½ cup white wine
1 quart light cream
3–4 egg yolks

½ lb. cooked lobster meat
 (p. 247), cut up
½ lb. cooked shrimp (p. 247),
 cut up
½ lb. cooked crab meat (p. 248)
2 tsp. cognac
8 savory crêpes
 (Basic Beer Crêpes, p. 381)

*Serves 8*

Sauté onions and mushrooms in ¾ lb. of the butter for 5 minutes. Add flour and cook for 2–3 minutes. Add wine slowly, then add cream and blend well. Simmer for 8–10 minutes.

Remove from fire and stir in egg yolks one at a time so that the sauce has a medium consistency.

Sauté seafoods in remainder of butter for 4–5 minutes. Warm the cognac in a ladle, pour into the pan and ignite. Let flame for several minutes.

Divide the sauce in half. To one half add the seafood pieces. Divide this among the 8 crêpes and roll up.

Use remainder of sauce to cover the crêpes.

## OYSTERS ALBERT

½ cup chopped green onions
¼ cup chopped cooked shrimp
  (p. 247)
½ lb. butter
Pinch of thyme, cayenne
  and garlic powder

½ cup bread crumbs
2 tsp. cognac
⅛ cup dry white wine
2 dozen raw oysters, shucked

*Serves 4*

Sauté green onions and shrimp in ¼ lb. of the butter for 10 minutes. Add thyme, cayenne and garlic powder. Allow to cool.

Add bread crumbs and cognac to half this mixture. Shape into a roll and refrigerate.

Heat the remaining shrimp mixture in the rest of the butter. Add the white wine and then the oysters. Cook until the edges curl—about 3–5 minutes.

Drain oysters and place 6 each in individual ramekins. Top with slices of the cold bread-crumb mixture. Bake 8–10 minutes in a 350° oven.

# MESSINA'S

### ITALIAN STUFFED ARTICHOKES
### STUFFED SHRIMP

Messina's Restaurant on Chartres Street in the French Quarter is one of *the* places with the natives. This is the first time any of Messina's famous recipes have ever been published.

## ITALIAN STUFFED ARTICHOKES

6 artichokes
6 cups bread crumbs
1 lb. American cheese, cubed
2 bunches green onions, chopped
½ cup chopped parsley
1 cup olives, chopped
1 tsp. garlic powder

1 tsp. oregano
¼ tsp. cayenne pepper
Salt and pepper to taste
1–1½ cups olive oil
½ cup grated Romano cheese
6 thin slices lemon

*Serves 6*

Wash artichokes thoroughly after cutting about ½" off the top (the object is to remove points from ends of leaves). Reserve until ready to use.

Mix all ingredients except oil, Romano cheese and lemon slices. After thoroughly mixing, pack tightly in a pan. Gradually pour olive oil over stuffing until oil can no longer be absorbed.

Open artichokes from center. Stuff every green leaf, packing tightly. Place a thin slice of lemon on top of each artichoke and sprinkle with Romano cheese. Wrap in foil.

Steam until tender—approximately 1½ hours.

## STUFFED SHRIMP

| | |
|---|---|
| 1 bunch green onions, finely chopped | Salt and pepper to taste |
| 1 stalk celery, finely chopped | 1½ cups cooking oil |
| 1 cup parsley, finely chopped | 1 lb. crab meat, white |
| 2 medium green peppers, finely chopped | 2–3 cups plain bread crumbs |
| 2 onions, finely chopped | 3 large eggs |
| 1 tsp. minced garlic | 1 lb. medium shrimp (30–36) |
| ½ tsp. cayenne pepper | 1 pint milk and 2 eggs, mixed |
| | 2 cups flour |
| | 2 cups seasoned bread crumbs |

*Serves 6*

Mix all vegetables and seasonings. Sauté in ½ cup oil until tender—about 10–15 minutes. Add crab meat and allow to cool. When cool, add bread crumbs and eggs and mix thoroughly.

Peel shrimp, leaving ¼" of shell plus tail. Form a ball by rolling the crab meat dressing around the shrimp, holding end of exposed tail.

Dip stuffed shrimp into milk-egg batter and then into flour, back into batter and then into seasoned bread crumbs. Deep fry in remaining oil until golden brown—about 5 minutes.

# MORAN'S LA LOUISIANE

### CREOLE STUFFED EGGPLANT

Diamond Jim Moran made this place famous with an occasional diamond in your meatball. His two sons, Jimmy and Tony, have carried on the tradition with diamond food and diamond fun for New Orleans.

## CREOLE STUFFED EGGPLANT

| | |
|---|---|
| 2 medium eggplants | Salt and pepper to taste |
| 2 cups water | Pinch of thyme |
| ½ cup cooking oil | ¼ cup chopped parsley |
| 1 bunch green onions, chopped | ¼ lb. crab meat, picked |
| ¼ lb. uncooked shrimp, chopped | 1 cup unseasoned bread crumbs |
| 1 red pepper, crushed | 2 lemons, halved |

*Serves 4*

Split the 2 eggplants lengthwise and scoop out all of the insides, being careful not to break the skin. Reserve shells.

In a pot large enough to hold the meat of the eggplants, place the meat and 2 cups water. Bring to a boil, place the lid on the pot and allow to boil for 10 minutes. Drain contents thoroughly.

In another frying pan, over medium heat, add just enough cooking oil so you can sauté without sticking. Now add the chopped green onions and chopped shrimp and cook for 5 minutes, stirring constantly to prevent burning.

Meanwhile, preheat oven to 350°.

Add the drained eggplant to the pan and mix well. Simmer together and add the red pepper, salt, pepper and thyme. Stir over medium heat for about 7–8 minutes.

Remove from heat and add parsley and crab meat, folding them into the dressing

Stuff the eggplant shells with this dressing. Sprinkle with bread crumbs.

Place in the preheated oven for 35–40 minutes.

Serve with ½ lemon per serving.

This is a favorite in Cajun country.

# MORAN'S RIVERSIDE

**STUFFED IMPERIAL PORK CHOPS**

The view from Moran's Riverside is one of the most spectacular. Finally, a restaurant and a view from the French Market, looking across the Mississippi River, of which the Baroness Pontalba would have approved.

## STUFFED IMPERIAL PORK CHOPS

4 Tbs. cooking oil
½ lb. ground beef
1 bunch green onions, chopped
Pinch of cayenne
1 12-oz. package
    frozen chopped spinach, thawed

Salt and pepper to taste
4 cuts pork loin, 2 ribs thick
1 large onion, quartered
2 large carrots, quartered
1 quart water

*Serves 4*

Preheat oven to 375°.

Preheat a frying pan and add the cooking oil. Add the beef and cook along with the green onions, adding a pinch of cayenne. As this cooks, add the chopped spinach and season with salt and pepper. *Do not overcook.* About 5–10 minutes should do it.

Cut a slit between 2 ribs of each pork chop, being careful not to cut all the way through. Stuff as much of the dressing into the pockets as possible. Place the stuffed chops in a roasting pan, surrounded by the onions and carrots. Sprinkle a pinch of cayenne and the salt and pepper on top of the chops.

Place chops in the preheated oven. Brown on all sides, then add a quart of water and place lid (or tinfoil) on roaster.

Reduce heat and roast for 1½ hours at 350°. Remove lid and allow to simmer for 15 minutes.

Serve chops on a heated platter with natural juices. Great with candied yams.

# PASCAL MANALE'S

**COMBINATION PAN ROAST**          **SPAGHETTI AND OYSTERS**

This restaurant has played an important part in my culinary adventure in New Orleans. The beautiful Frances Defelice loves to serve Italian specialties, and if you're lucky, she may offer you a glass of her favorite champagne.

## COMBINATION PAN ROAST

1 pint milk
1 pint oyster liquid
1 lb. margarine
1 cup flour
2 bunches green onions, chopped
½ white onion, chopped
1 bunch parsley, chopped

4 dozen small oysters, shucked
1 lb. lump crab meat, picked
2 Tbs. Worcestershire sauce
1 tsp. Tabasco pepper sauce
1 tsp. salt
1 cup bread crumbs

½ tsp sherry

*Serves 8*

Heat milk and oyster liquid in ½-gallon pot.

Melt margarine (reserving 2–3 Tbs.) and gradually add flour until smooth. Add chopped vegetables. Combine with hot milk and oyster liquid.

Poach oysters for about 5 minutes, until edges curl. Mix with crab meat and combine with vegetable sauce. Cook for about 25–30 minutes. Add Worcestershire and Tabasco. Correct with salt.

Fill 8 ramekins with 6 oysters each. Cover with sauce and sprinkle with bread crumbs. Dot with a little margarine and run under the broiler until golden brown—about 5 minutes.

## SPAGHETTI AND OYSTERS

¼ lb. butter
¼ cup flour
1 pint oysters
4 cups oyster water
   (oyster liquid plus water)
½ cup chopped parsley

1 cup chopped green onions
1 Tbs. Worcestershire sauce
1 tsp. Accent
Salt and pepper to taste
1 lb. spaghetti

*Serves 4*

Melt butter slowly. Blend in flour and cook for 5 minutes. Do not brown. Meanwhile, poach the oysters in the oyster water for 5 minutes. Remove oysters, drain and reserve. Bring oyster water to a boil and add to the roux. Stir rapidly over medium heat and blend well. Cook for 10 minutes.

Add parsley, green onions, Worcestershire sauce, Accent and salt and pepper. Cook over low flame for 15 minutes.

Cook spaghetti in boiling water for 9 minutes. Drain spaghetti and divide among 4 plates.

Drop oysters into sauce and dish over spaghetti.

# THE RIB ROOM, ROYAL ORLEANS HOTEL

**RED SNAPPER ANDALOUSE**            **BRAISED VEAL SHANKS**

The Royal Orleans is on the site of the old Saint Louis Hotel. But for the last 20 years the Rib Room has been a popular gourmet rendezvous in the French Quarter.

## RED SNAPPER ANDALOUSE

*Creole Sauce:*
1 medium onion, sliced
3 medium green peppers, sliced
½ cup sliced celery
6 Tbs. butter
1 cup Chablis wine
1½ cups diced peeled tomatoes
1 tsp. chopped garlic

2 tsp. sugar
Pinch of thyme
Pinch of oregano
Pinch of rosemary
1 bay leaf
Salt and pepper to taste

*Fish and accompaniments:*
2 filets of red snapper, 8 oz. each
4 green onions, chopped
1 lemon, sliced
4 sprigs parsley

½ cup rice, boiled
1½ cups Hollandaise Sauce
(chap. 13)

*Serves 2*

*To make sauce:* Sauté the onion, green peppers and celery in butter for 10 minutes. Add white wine and reduce for 2 minutes. Add tomatoes and all remaining ingredients and cook for another 10 minutes.

*To cook and serve fish:* Poach fish with green onions, sliced lemon and parsley sprigs for 8–10 minutes.

Place fish on a serving platter on a bed of rice. Cover with Creole Sauce and top with hollandaise sauce. Finish in a 350° oven for 5–6 minutes.

# BRAISED VEAL SHANKS WITH TARRAGON

4 veal shanks from hindquarter          4 sprigs parsley
Salt and pepper to taste                2 bay leaves
12 Tbs. butter                          2 pinches thyme
1 medium onion, diced                   ½ tsp. chopped tarragon
2 carrots, diced                        2 Tbs. flour
1 cup diced celery                      2 cups Chablis wine
8 cloves garlic                         1½ cups Beef Stock (p. 183)

*Serves 4*

Preheat oven to 400°.

Sprinkle veal shanks with salt and pepper and grease with 8 Tbs. of the butter. Place them in a heavy pot and cook in the oven for 15 minutes until they reach a nice golden color.

Cut temperature to 350° and add vegetables and seasonings. Cook for another 15–20 minutes until vegetables reach a golden color.

In the meanwhile, make a roux by blending the flour and remaining 4 Tbs. butter; reserve.

Add Chablis to veal and vegetables and reduce to half in oven for about ½ hour. Add the beef stock and thicken with the roux.

Cover pot and cook slowly for 25 minutes or until tender. Before serving, strain sauce and pour over shanks.

# SAZERAC, FAIRMONT HOTEL

**FAIRMONT SPINACH SALAD**     **CHOCOLATE MOUSSE**

The Sazerac Restaurant in the Fairmont Hotel, which used to be the old Roosevelt Hotel, is where I like to go to feel I am in old New Orleans and remember my Paris days.

## FAIRMONT SPINACH SALAD

1 package (10 oz.) fresh spinach
5 strips bacon
1 tsp. herb mixture
   (rosemary, tarragon and
   oregano)
2 tsp. olive oil

2 tsp. red wine vinegar
1 tsp. Worcestershire sauce
1 tsp. Dijon mustard
   (Grey Poupon)
2 tsp. sugar
Black pepper to taste

*Serves 2*

Wash and dry spinach. Remove stems. Place in a salad bowl.

Cut bacon into 1" pieces. Crisp bacon in a skillet. Drain grease.

Add herb mixture. Mix well. Add oil, vinegar, Worcestershire sauce, mustard and sugar and mix well. Heat for 5 minutes. Add pepper to taste from a pepper mill.

Pour this hot dressing over salad, cover with pan and let steam for approximately 15 seconds.

Toss salad. Dish out and pour any remaining dressing with bacon over salad.

## CHOCOLATE MOUSSE

3 egg yolks
4 Tbs. milk
¼ cup corn syrup
2 oz. semisweet chocolate
2 oz. unsweetened chocolate

1 oz. Cointreau or Triple Sec
1 pint whipping cream
3 egg whites
½ cup sugar

*Serves 10*

In the top of a double boiler, combine egg yolks, milk and corn syrup. Cook for about 5 minutes, until well blended.

Cut the chocolate into small pieces and add to the egg-milk mixture. Add the Cointreau or Triple Sec and cook until all lumps are dissolved—about 5–10 minutes. Let cool.

Whip the cream until stiff and fold into the chocolate mixture.

Whip the egg whites and sugar until very stiff and fold gently into the chocolate mixture.

Pour into serving glasses and chill for at least 1 hour.

# THE VERSAILLES

**CRAYFISH VERSAILLES**          **GRAND MARNIER MOUSSE**

This elegant but simple restaurant is in the Garden District. Its chef-owner, Gunther Preusse, has managed to do unusual things with local ingredients and to inspire his menu with originality.

## CRAYFISH VERSAILLES

1 stick butter
1 lb. fresh crayfish tails
   (or frozen)
1 Tbs. French shallots
½ cup minced green onion
½ lb. fresh mushrooms, chopped
1 tsp. Grey Poupon mustard
1 cup Chablis wine

¼ cup Half n' Half
Salt and pepper to taste
Pinch of dillweed, fresh or dry
1 Tbs. *Beurre Manié* (chap. 13)
½ cup Parmesan cheese
Paprika
Rock salt, if available
Lemon wedges

*Serves 6*

Melt butter and sauté crayfish tails until reddish in color—about 5–10 minutes.

Add shallots, green onion, mushrooms and mustard. Blend well. Add Chablis wine and cook for 5 minutes. Add Half n' Half and continue to blend and cook for another 5 minutes. Season with salt, pepper and dill. Gradually add the *beurre manié* until sauce thickens somewhat.

Place in any natural seafood shells (such as oyster or scallop), sprinkle with Parmesan cheese and bake in a moderate oven (350°) until cheese is brown—about 5–10 minutes.

Sprinkle with a little paprika for garnish and color. Serve on a bed of rock salt (if available) and garnish with lemon wedges.

## GRAND MARNIER MOUSSE

6 egg yolks
4 Tbs. sugar
1 cup Chablis wine
½ cup Grand Marnier liqueur
Peelings of 1 lemon, grated
Peelings of 2 oranges
   (but omit white pulp), grated
Juice of 1 lemon, strained

Juice of 2 oranges, strained
1 tsp. Knox gelatine
1 pint cream, stiffly whipped
6 orange shells, hollowed out,
   with caps reserved
Extra whipped cream for garnish
6 Maraschino cherries

*Serves 6*

Place egg yolks, sugar, Chablis, Grand Marnier and gratings in a bowl. Blend well and add lemon and orange juice.

Whip over low heat until eggs and liquid are foamy and stick to side of pan. Add the gelatine and allow to cool in refrigerator for about 10–15 minutes.

After mixture has cooled, add the stiffly whipped cream. Blend very well and chill overnight.

Place mixture in hollowed-out orange shells; top each with more whipped cream, a Maraschino cherry and the orange cap.

Serve on a bed of crushed ice.

# THE VIEUX CARRÉ

**VIEUX CARRÉ BOUILLABAISSE          VIEUX CARRÉ ARTICHOKE BISQUE**
**VIEUX CARRÉ ALMOND TORTE**

The Vieux Carré Restaurant is a tradition in New Orleans. It is linked to France through several families.

## VIEUX CARRÉ BOUILLABAISSE

1 stick margarine
2 large onions, chopped
6 green onions, chopped
2 cloves garlic, minced
2 green peppers,
   cleaned and chopped
3 bay leaves
Pinch of saffron

Salt and pepper to taste
1 No. 2 can tomatoes
2 quarts Fish Stock (p. 184)
1 lb. medium shrimp, shelled
1 medium trout, cut up
1 medium redfish, cut up
1 pint fresh oysters

*Yields 4 quarts*

Melt margarine in a saucepan. Add onions, green onions, garlic and green pepper and cook until tender—about 10–15 minutes.

Add bay leaves, saffron and salt and pepper to taste.

Add tomatoes and fish stock. Cook for about 1 hour.

Add shrimp, cut-up pieces of fish and oysters. Cook until fish pieces are tender but not falling apart—about 10 minutes.

Serve with large croutons of French bread.

## VIEUX CARRÉ ARTICHOKE BISQUE

| | |
|---|---|
| 1 stick margarine | 1 quart water |
| 2 large onions, | 2 No. 2 cans hearts of artichokes, |
| very finely chopped | chopped |
| ½ stalk celery, | 1 pint dry white wine |
| very finely chopped | Salt and pepper to taste |
| 1 cup flour | |

*Yields 2 quarts*

Melt margarine in a saucepan. Sauté onions and celery until tender—about 5 minutes. Add flour and blend well, but do not allow to burn.

Add water and bring to a boil. Reduce heat and blend well. Add chopped artichoke hearts and white wine. Season with salt and pepper. Cook for about 20 minutes.

## VIEUX CARRÉ ALMOND TORTE

| | |
|---|---|
| 1 box confectioners' sugar | 1 dozen coconut macaroons, |
| 1 lb. butter | very finely chopped |
| 1 cup almonds, | 6 egg yolks |
| very finely chopped | Whipped cream |

*Serves 6–8*

Mix all ingredients in a blender. Roll into balls and flatten into 6 or 8 serving portions; place on a sheet pan lined with greased waxed paper.

Place in freezer and freeze until very hard—2 hours or more.

Serve topped with whipped cream.

# 4
# RECIPES OF FRIENDS

IF EVER THERE was something old, something new, something borrowed and something blue (as in cheese) . . . it's a recipe. Aside from cookbooks, magazines and newspapers, no better source of recipes is to be found than the culinary bosom of a dear friend.

There are many types of friends who divulge recipes. There is the type who gives you a recipe because you've asked for it—a true friend. There is the type who deliberately leaves out an important ingredient—a questionable friend. There is the kind who grudgingly gives it to you, saying you are the only one, and then you find out it's been given to everyone—a fair-weather friend. There is the kind who will never give it to you, but if you're good, he'll will it to you—a smart-aleck friend. Then there is the kind who says it's an old family secret he is not permitted to divulge, but you can come over anytime and the cook will prepare it—a devil of a friend. Whatever the method used, whatever the category the friends fit into . . . always take advantage of a good recipe. They are often hard to come by.

I must say that the friends from whom I obtained the recipes included in this book belong only to the first category mentioned above. Their recipes have a very special meaning for me because I have shared them over and over again in the homes of these good friends, who are now kind enough to give them to me so that I may share them with you, my readers.

The friends' recipes contained here represent only those who live in New Orleans. To all my other friends who love to cook and entertain but live outside New Orleans, I can only say . . . next time.

# APPETIZERS

## AVOCADO DIP

2 ripe avocados
Juice of 1 lemon
1 medium tomato,
   peeled and finely diced
½ green pepper, finely diced
3 fresh green onions, finely diced

1 2-oz. can anchovies in oil,
   mashed or puréed
¼ cup olive oil
Dash of Worcestershire sauce
Dash of cayenne pepper
Salt to taste
Dash of chili powder

*Serves 4*

Peel the avocados. Place on a cutting board and squeeze lemon juice over them. Mash with a fork and then place in a bowl. Add the rest of the ingredients one at a time and mix well.
Serve with tacos.

*Recipe courtesy of Chris Owens*

## BAKED OYSTERS

3 dozen oysters, shucked and
   drained of liquid
1 cup bread crumbs
2 Tbs. prepared horseradish
1 Tbs. lemon juice
1 tsp. Worcestershire sauce

2 tsp. light cream
½ cup parsley, finely chopped
1 Tbs. paprika
Salt and pepper to taste
½ lb. butter or margarine

*Serves 6*

Preheat oven to 350°.
Mix together all ingredients except butter.
Melt butter in a baking pan and pour mixed ingredients into it. Bake for 30 minutes.

*Recipe courtesy of Bettie Hanemann*

## CHEESE FRANÇOIS

1 small Camembert or                3 Tbs. white rum
   1 small Brie cheese               2 tsp. sugar
½ cup fresh blueberries

*Serves 6*

   Over a round of Camembert or Brie, pour the blueberries, which have marinated in a mixture of the rum and sugar for 1 hour.
   Serve as an hors d'oeuvre with crackers.

*Recipe courtesy of Frank V. McDonnell*

## COLD MEAT CANAPÉS

1¼ lbs. filet or flank steak,        1 cup chopped parsley
   in 1 piece                     Salt and pepper to taste
½ cup softened butter                1 jigger dry red wine
3 cloves garlic,                     18 Pepperidge Farm party rye
   finely minced or mashed           slices

*Serves 6*

   Broil the meat for 15–20 minutes until pink and allow to get cold. If filet is used, cut medium-thick slices big enough to cover the bread. If flank steak is used, cut on the bias and very thin.
   To the softened butter, add the garlic, parsley, salt, pepper and red wine. Spread each slice of bread quite thickly with this mixture.
   Place slices of meat on each piece of bread. Cover with foil or plastic wrap and allow to chill in refrigerator until butter is hard.
   Allow 3 per person for a cocktail party. This is a good hearty canapé with any drink—guaranteed to keep guests sober.

*Recipe courtesy of Kearny Livaudais*

# FRIED MUSHROOMS À LA CAVIAR

*Fried mushrooms:*
    1 cup plain flour
    2 tsp. baking powder
    1 tsp. salt
    2 eggs
    ¾ cup milk

30 mushrooms, caps only
    (medium size if fresh,
    large if canned)
½–1 cup cooking oil

*Filling or dip:*
    6 oz. caviar
    1 pint sour cream

*Garnish:*
    3 lemons, sliced
    10 slices Melba Toast (chap. 13)

*Serves 6*

Sift flour, baking powder and salt. Add eggs to flour mixture and blend well. Add milk slowly, beating until batter is thin and creamy. If it seems too thick, add a little more milk.

Wash and wipe fresh mushrooms or drain canned mushrooms. Dip mushroom caps in batter. Deep fry a few at a time in the oil. When golden brown, place on paper towels to drain. Serve on a platter with caviar, sour cream, sliced lemons and melba toast.*

*Recipe courtesy of Dorothy Williams*

* You may stuff the mushroom caps with sour cream and top with caviar or mix sour cream and caviar together and serve as a dip.

## OYSTERS À LA GOVERNOR JAMES A. NOE

6 oysters and their liquid
1 cup dry white wine
2 Tbs. butter
¼ cup finely chopped green
    onions, tops and bottoms
1 Tbs. finely chopped parsley
Salt and pepper to taste

1 tsp. Tabasco pepper sauce
2 Tbs. flour
6 oyster shells
6 fried slices good country sausage
    (definitely not breakfast
    sausage)

*Serves 2*

Poach oysters in their own liquid for 2–3 minutes, until they are plump. Remove oysters and reserve. Combine oyster liquid with as much dry white wine as you need to make 1¼ cups liquid; keep warm.

In a saucepan, melt butter and sauté green onions and parsley for 5 minutes. Add salt, pepper and Tabasco and then stir in flour, blending to make a light roux. Add the oyster-wine liquid a little at a time and cook, stirring constantly, until the sauce is thick and smooth.

Place an oyster in each shell. Top generously with the sauce. Place a slice of the lightly fried sausage on each oyster and heat in oven.

These may be made in advance and simply heated when ready to serve.

*Recipe courtesy of the late Governor James A. Noe*

## OYSTERS DOROTHY

¼ cup butter
½ cup flour
6 green onions (white parts plus
    1" of the green), chopped
½ cup chopped parsley
Salt and pepper to taste

½ tsp. Tabasco pepper sauce
2 cups oyster water
    (oyster liquid plus water)
3 dozen medium oysters, shucked
½ cup bread crumbs

*Serves 6*

Make a roux by melting butter in a skillet and, when butter is melted, slowly stirring in flour until well blended.

When roux is nicely browned, add green onions and stir for 3 minutes. Add 3 Tbs. of the parsley, salt, pepper and Tabasco and continue stirring for 2 more minutes. Add oyster water slowly and continue stirring. When well blended, let sauce cook until thick—about 5 minutes.

Add oysters and stir. Sauce will become thin when oysters are added. Let oysters cook for 5 minutes.

Remove oysters from sauce and put in individual ramekins or a single Pyrex dish. Let sauce continue to cook for another 5 minutes or until it is thick again.

When sauce is thick and creamy, pour it over the oysters. Sprinkle with bread crumbs and chopped parsley.

Bake in a 350° oven for 20–30 minutes.

Garnish with the remaining chopped parsley. Pass Melba Toast (chap. 13).

*Recipe courtesy of Dorothy Williams*

# OYSTERS OLIVER

| | |
|---|---|
| 1 Tbs. green onions | Salt and pepper to taste |
| 1 small clove garlic, minced | 1 wineglass dry sherry |
| 1 8-oz. can mushrooms, drained | 1 Tbs. Worcestershire sauce |
| 2 dozen large oysters, shucked | 6 slices buttered French bread, |
| ½ cup flour | toasted |
| 1 stick butter | 2 Tbs. chopped parsley |

*Serves 4*

Chop together the green onions, garlic and mushrooms. Dry the oysters and dredge each in flour.

In a heavy frying pan, heat ½ stick butter until bubbly. Quickly brown oysters in the butter until edges curl. Remove from heat and reserve.

In another pan, place the green onions, garlic and mushrooms. Add the remaining ½ stick butter and cook until melted. Correct with salt and pepper, sherry and Worcestershire sauce. Stir until blended and cook for 10 minutes.

Place oysters on buttered toast, pour sauce over them and garnish with chopped parsley.

*Recipe courtesy of Oliver Evans*

# SOUPS

## CREAM OF BROCCOLI SOUP

1 quart Chicken Stock (p. 183)
1 cup dry white wine
1 bunch fresh broccoli, tops and
   tender, peeled stems only (or 2
   packages frozen broccoli,
   thawed and drained)
1 Tbs. lemon juice

½ tsp. salt
½ tsp. white pepper
1 Tbs. Worcestershire sauce
¼ tsp. Tabasco pepper sauce
4 Tbs. butter
1 cup light cream

*Serves 8*

Combine all ingredients except butter and cream in a soup pot. Bring to a boil; then lower the heat and simmer for about 1 hour or until broccoli falls apart. Allow to cool and purée in a blender.

When ready to serve, add the butter and cream and heat just to the boiling point or until butter has melted.

Serve with thin slices of toasted French bread.

*Recipe courtesy of Dr. John Buddingh*

## FRENCH ONION SOUP WITH CHEESE

4 large yellow onions,
   thinly sliced
4 Tbs. butter
1 Tbs. all-purpose flour
5 cups Beef Stock (p. 183),
   heated

Salt and pepper to taste
8 thick, round French bread
   slices, toasted
½ lb. coarsely grated Gruyère
   cheese or domestic Swiss

*Serves 8*

Separate the onion rings. Melt the butter in a heavy dutch oven or a saucepan. Sauté the onions in the butter over very low heat, stirring frequently, until they are limp—about 20 minutes.

Over the cooked onion rings sprinkle the flour; mix well and add the hot beef stock. Bring to a boil; then reduce heat and simmer for about 45 minutes. Taste for salt and pepper.

Place individual servings of soup in ovenproof bowls, top each with a round of toasted French bread and heap with grated cheese. Place bowls under the broiler until cheese has melted and is golden brown—about 10 minutes.

Alternatively, the entire quantity of soup may be placed in a large ovenproof tureen, topped with the French rounds and cheese, and then placed under the broiler and served family style.

*Recipe courtesy of Larry Jennings*

## OYSTER SOUP

| | |
|---|---|
| 1 bunch green onions, finely chopped | 1 bay leaf |
| 1 Tbs. flour | ½ tsp. ground thyme |
| 1 stick butter | 1 Tbs. Worcestershire sauce |
| 1 cup oyster water (oyster liquid plus water) | ¼ tsp. Tabasco pepper sauce |
| ½ cup chopped parsley | Salt and pepper to taste |
| | 4 dozen fresh oysters, shucked |
| | 1 quart milk |

*Serves 6–7*

Sauté green onions and flour in butter, add oyster water and cook for 10 minutes, until smooth.

Add parsley, bay leaf, thyme, Worcestershire sauce and Tabasco; correct for salt and pepper. Simmer slowly for another 10 minutes.

Just before serving, add oysters and let curl. Add milk. Do not cover after milk is added or it may curdle. Cook for 5–10 minutes.

*Recipe courtesy of Mrs. William B. Burkenroad, Jr.*

## POTAGE AU FENOUIL GLACÉ

1½ lbs. fennel bulbs, trimmed        Pinch each of thyme and savory
5 Tbs. olive oil                     1 bay leaf
1½ cups sliced yellow onions         6 Tbs. tapioca
3½ Tbs. tomato paste                 Salt and pepper to taste
9 cups Beef Stock or                 1 cup heavy cream
  Chicken Stock (p. 183)             A few sprigs fresh dill, chopped

*Serves 6*

Cut bulbs in quarters and blanch them for 5 minutes in boiling salted water. Rinse in cold water and drain. Slice.

Heat the oil in a heavy pot and sauté the onions. When they are limp, after about 10 minutes, add fennel. Sauté until lightly browned. Add tomato paste and simmer slowly, stirring, for 20 minutes. Purée until lightly browned. Add tomato paste and simmer slowly, stirring, for 20 minutes. Purée in the blender and return to the saucepan.

Add stock, thyme, savory and bay leaf. Stir and simmer until reduced by a cup—about 20 minutes.

Remove bay leaf and add tapioca, gradually stirring until thickened. Taste and adjust for seasonings.

Cool and then chill thoroughly.

Before serving, add a cup of heavy cream, stir well and top each serving with a sprinkling of the chopped dillweed.

*Recipe courtesy of Paul Fitzwater*

## POTAGE LAFAYETTE

8 large, very ripe tomatoes,         ½ tsp. Tabasco pepper sauce
  peeled and quartered               1 Tbs. sugar
½ cup chopped onion                  1 tsp. salt
½ cup chopped celery                 ¼ tsp. white pepper
¼ cup chopped parsley                1 quart Chicken Stock (p. 183)
1 10-oz. package frozen green peas   2 cups light cream
2 large pimientos, chopped           4 Tbs. butter
1 cup uncooked long grain rice       Small croutons (optional)

*Serves 8*

Combine all ingredients except stock, cream, butter and croutons. Place in a soup kettle and cover with the chicken stock. Bring to a boil. Reduce heat and simmer for a good hour. Allow to cool.

Purée in a blender.

When ready to serve, add the cream and butter and heat to the boiling point or until the butter is melted. Serve immediately, with small croutons if desired.

*Recipe courtesy of Mrs. William (Monita) Syll*

# ENTRÉES AND ACCOMPANIMENTS

## BARBARA'S CHILI

| | |
|---|---|
| 2 Tbs. Wesson oil | 1 Tbs. cumin |
| 2 large onions, chopped | 1 tsp. crushed red pepper |
| 4 cloves garlic (or more), chopped | 1 tsp. tomato paste |
| 4 lbs. coarsely ground chuck or diced flank steak | 3–4 Tbs. brown sugar |
| 2 medium cans tomatoes | Salt and pepper to taste |
| 6 Tbs. chili powder | About 1 cup Beef Stock (p. 183) and/or tomato juice, red wine, champagne or whatever wine you have on hand |
| 1 Tbs. oregano (or to taste) | |

*Serves 10–12*

Heat oil in a heavy pot. Sauté onions and garlic until limp—about 5 minutes. Add beef a little at a time and sauté until browned—about 10 minutes.

Add all other ingredients except stock or wines.

Cook over medium heat for at least ½ hour. Then reduce heat to low and simmer for 1–2 hours, adding liquid according to thickness of chili desired.

When finished, cool, refrigerate and skim off any excess fat before reheating. It is best the second day.

When reheating, add stock or wine to thin out if necessary.

*Recipe courtesy of Mrs. Barbara Ingram*

AUTHOR'S NOTE: Remember, if you use champagne, no matter how dry, it tends to give the chili a sweetness.

# BEEF AND ASPARAGUS

2 Tbs. olive oil
1½ lbs. New York
    strip sirloin steak
1 lb. fresh asparagus, raw
1 clove garlic, minced

1 Tbs. soy sauce
2 Tbs. oyster sauce (if obtainable)
    or 2 more Tbs. soy
Salt and pepper to taste

*Serves 4*

Heat oil in a large, heavy skillet that has a cover.

Cut steak across the grain in very thin ¼" strips. Cut asparagus diagonally into pieces about 2" long.

Add garlic to pan and fry for a couple of minutes. Add meat and stir constantly for about 5 minutes.

Stir in soy and oyster sauces. Add the cut-up asparagus and stir. Cover and cook for 12 minutes.

Remove cover, correct for salt and pepper and serve.

*Recipe courtesy of Keith Cesare Mora*

# BEEF STROGANOFF

1 Tbs. salt
1 tsp. freshly ground black pepper
2 lbs. filet mignon,
    cut into finger strips
2½ sticks butter
1 cup grated onion
½ lb. fresh mushrooms,
    thinly sliced

2 Tbs. flour
1 cup Beef Stock (p. 183),
    heated
½ pint sour cream
½ cup Italian tomato paste
2 Tbs. large capers

*Serves 6*

Salt and pepper the thin strips of filet and allow to stand in a cool place for 1 hour.

In a heavy skillet, melt 1 stick of the butter and quickly sauté the grated onion. Add the strips of filet several at a time, and cook rare or well done to suit your taste. Remove meat and onions to a mixing bowl. In a separate saucepan, sauté the mushrooms in ½ stick butter for 10 minutes and reserve.

In the original pan, melt the remaining stick of butter and make a roux by adding the flour and blending well. Add the hot beef stock. Stir until thick and allow to cool.

Add the sour cream and tomato paste alternately, a little at a time, blending well after each addition.

To this sauce, add the capers, sautéed meat, onions and mushrooms. Heat but do not boil.

Serve immediately with spinach noodles or new potatoes.

If prepared in advance, reheat in a double boiler. Do not ever allow the sauce to boil.

This version of a classic dish freezes very well.

*Recipe courtesy of Roc Johnson*

# BELGIAN CARBONNADES

4 large onions, quartered
6–8 Tbs. butter
Salt and pepper to taste
Pinch of thyme
1½ lbs. heavy beef, preferably
    chuck roast, cut in thick slices

1 can beer
1 Tbs. Dijon mustard
2 slices day-old bread
    from a whole country loaf

*Serves 4*

Slice onions, but not too thin. Heat about 4 Tbs. of the butter in a heavy pot and gently brown the onions for about 5–10 minutes. Season with salt, pepper and thyme. When they are golden brown, remove with a slotted spoon.

In the same pot, brown meat slices a few at a time, turning once and adding a little more salt, pepper and thyme. Add more butter if needed. When all meat is browned, return onions to pot. Pour in just enough beer to come about halfway up the meat.

Cover pot and simmer slowly for about 1½ hours or until meat is tender. Add more beer if needed, but do not cover the meat completely.

About 15 minutes before meat is done, spread a generous layer of mustard on bread slices and place them on top of the stew. Continue cooking until they have been absorbed into the stew.

*Recipe courtesy of Bettie Hanemann*

# CASCADE CHICKEN

1 fryer (3–4 lbs.), cut up           ½ cup flour, seasoned with
¼–½ lb. butter, melted                  2 tsp. salt and ¼ tsp. pepper

*Serves 4*

Rinse chicken pieces in salted water (1 tsp. salt to approximately 2 quarts water) and drain.

Dip chicken pieces in melted butter and roll in seasoned flour.

In a large skillet, brown chicken pieces in melted butter over medium heat. Cook for about 15 minutes, turning occasionally to brown evenly.

When browned, place chicken in a covered casserole or pan. Correct for salt. Complete by baking for approximately 45 minutes or until tender at 350°. For crispier chicken, remove cover for the last 10 minutes.

*Recipe of Mrs. Hazel Shelton, courtesy of Richard Shelton*

# CHICKEN LEWIS

2 chickens, quartered                2 4-oz. cans button mushrooms,
2 Tbs. butter                           drained
1 package dry onion soup mix         1 cup dry sherry
                                     Parsley flakes

*Serves 4*

Arrange chicken quarters in a buttered baking dish. Sprinkle onion soup mix on chicken; add mushrooms and sherry.

Cover tightly with aluminum foil and bake in a 350° oven for 1 hour.

Remove cover and cook for 1 more hour, turning chicken frequently and basting until done. Sprinkle with parsley flakes.

If a crispier chicken is desired, run chicken in the sauce under the broiler for 10 minutes.

*Recipe courtesy of Max P. Zander*

# CHICKEN SIR MALCOLM

2 fryers, quartered (or the
   equivalent in thighs,
   legs and breasts)
Salt and pepper to taste
4 Tbs. tarragon leaves
3 sticks butter
32 very small whole onions, peeled

1 lb. fresh mushrooms, sliced
1 Bouquet Garni (chap. 13)
2 cups Sir Malcolm Scotch or a
   good medium-light Scotch
2 cups Chicken Stock (p. 183)
½ cup flour

*Serves 8*

Sprinkle chicken pieces with salt, pepper and tarragon leaves.

In a heavy skillet, melt 2 sticks of the butter and lightly sauté the chicken pieces. In 10–15 minutes, when they are delicately browned, remove to a dutch oven.

In the same skillet, lightly brown the onions and sauté the mushrooms for about 10 minutes. Remove the onions and mushrooms and reserve.

Add the bouquet garni to the dutch oven and pour 1½ cups of the Scotch and all the chicken stock over the chicken.

Cover, place in a moderate oven (350°) and baste at 20-minute intervals. Cook for 1 hour or until chicken is tender but not falling apart.

The onions should be added during the final 20 minutes and the mushrooms during the final 10 minutes of cooking time.

In another saucepan, melt the remaining stick of butter and make a roux by stirring in the flour. When the roux is well blended, gradually add the cooking juices from the chicken and stir over moderate heat until sauce is thick.

Remove the bouquet garni and add the sauce to the chicken pieces, mushrooms and onions. Coat well. Add the remaining Scotch immediately before serving.

*Recipe courtesy of Malcolm Woldenberg*

# COQ AU VIN

6 slices bacon
6 Tbs. olive oil, if necessary
1 rooster, cut into serving pieces*
2 cups flour, seasoned
  with salt and pepper
¼ cup brandy
18 very small onions

1 clove garlic, chopped
1 Bouquet Garni (chap. 13)
1 cup Burgundy wine
1 cup Chicken Stock (p. 183)
12 mushroom caps
1–2 Tbs. *Beurre Manié*
  (chap. 13), if necessary

*Serves 6*

Fry bacon in a skillet. If there is not enough fat to brown the meat in, add some olive oil.

Dredge rooster in the seasoned flour and brown lightly in the fat for about 10 minutes. Transfer bacon and rooster to a dutch oven.

Distribute brandy over the rooster pieces and ignite, stirring until flame dies out.

In the remaining fat, sauté the onions and garlic and add to the dutch oven.

Add the bouquet garni and cover with the red wine and chicken stock.

Cover and cook until meat is tender but not falling apart—about 2–3 hours. During the last 10 minutes of cooking time, add mushroom caps.

Correct seasonings, remove bouquet garni and if sauce is not thick enough, correct by blending in 1–2 Tbs. *beurre manié*.

*Recipe courtesy of Vernon Louviere*

* If rooster is not available, you may substitute 2 frying chickens and reduce cooking time to 1–1½ hours.

# FRENCH BOURBON CHICKEN

2 jiggers 100-proof bourbon
1–2 broilers, whole
4 Tbs. olive oil
2 Tbs. paprika
Salt and pepper to taste
  (but more pepper than usual)

1 cup coarsely chopped
  celery leaves
1 onion, coarsely chopped
1 or 2 bay leaves

*Serves 4*

Pour the bourbon into a plastic bag. Place the whole chickens in the bag with the bourbon. Seal. Refrigerate overnight, turning once or twice if possible, to coat evenly with the bourbon.

Preheat oven to 350°.

Rub the marinated chicken with olive oil, paprika, salt and more pepper than usual. The chicken should be well coated and red in color.

Stuff chickens with the celery leaves, onion and bay leaf. Place upside down in the pan and set in the oven. (They remain upside down throughout the cooking process.)

Turn oven up to 500° and cook chickens until they begin to hiss and crackle. Let them do this for 10 minutes or until lightly browned. Turn off the oven, and *do not open the door* for ½ hour. After that, you may check the chickens, but they should remain in the oven for another 2 hours before serving.

*Recipe courtesy of Robert Browne*

## FRESH PARSLEY RELISH

2 cups finely chopped parsley,
   including juice
1 2-oz. can anchovies, minced

3 Tbs. olive oil
1 Tbs. wine vinegar
1 tsp. garlic powder

*Yields 3½ cups*

Combine all ingredients. Refrigerate for at least 4 hours. Excellent with cold meats or fish.

*Recipe of Mrs. Marie Mora, courtesy of Keith Cesare Mora*

## HOT FRUIT

1 large can sliced peaches
1 large can sliced apricots
1 large can sliced pineapple
1 jar Kadota figs
4 bananas, sliced and
   sprinkled with lemon juice

1 package macaroon cookies,
   broken up but not crumbled
1 cup brown sugar
1 large package
   slivered or sliced almonds
1 stick margarine

*Serves 8*

Drain canned fruits thoroughly.

In a 2-quart casserole put a layer of the mixed fruits and top with a layer of macaroons. Sprinkle with brown sugar and almonds. Dot with the margarine.

Repeat until everything is used.

Bake in a 350° oven for 20 minutes or until it bubbles. Serve hot with any meat dish.

*Recipe courtesy of Gay Noe McLendon*

# KELLEY'S POLYNESIAN LAMB

*Polynesian Sauce:* *
    1 pint Kikkoman soy sauce
      (do not substitute)
    Juice of 6 lemons
    ½ cup pineapple juice
    1 large clove garlic, crushed

    1 piece fresh ginger root about
      the size of your palm, cut into
      finger-size pieces and bruised
      with the flat side of a cleaver
    1 Tbs. dry hot Chinese mustard
    1 tsp. Tabasco pepper sauce

*Lamb:*
    1 leg of lamb (5–6 lbs.), boned

*Serves 6*

*To make the sauce:* Pour all ingredients in a mason jar and shake well, allowing the mixture to marinate for 24 hours before using.

Strain the sauce to remove ginger root, lemon and garlic pulp before using with the lamb.

*To prepare, cook and serve lamb:* Have butcher bone a leg of spring lamb so the meat can be laid flat—about the size and shape of a piece of flank steak you would use for London broil.

Marinate the lamb in the Polynesian Sauce for about 2 hours; then drain and broil over coals or on an electric grill as you would do with beefsteak. Slice and serve the same as London broil—i.e., slice diagonally in medium strips from the large end of the piece. Serve with Kelley's Rice Liban (p. 129).

*Recipe courtesy of Kelley Weiss*

* This sauce will keep in the refrigerator for up to 6 weeks and may be used over and over to marinate different kinds of meats. Excellent with beef and pork. Sauce should be strained with cheesecloth after each use to remove any particles of meat and fat.

## KELLEY'S RICE LIBAN

1 Tbs. olive oil
1 cup long grain rice
  (I use Mahatma)
4 green onions, tops and
  bottoms, finely chopped

½ tsp. dried dillweed
Salt and pepper to taste
2 cups Chicken Stock (p. 183),
  heated
2 Tbs. toasted pine nuts

*Serves 6*

You will need a saucepan with a tight-fitting lid.

Heat the olive oil in the saucepan over medium heat. Add the rice, stirring constantly and turning in the oil until the kernels are golden brown—about 10 minutes.

Stir in the onions, dillweed and salt and pepper. Pour in the chicken stock and bring to a vigorous boil.

Cover the pot tightly and reduce heat to simmer. Let steam, covered, until liquid has disappeared—about 15–18 minutes.

Stir only once while steaming; do not uncover more than absolutely necessary.

When rice is *al dente*, add pine nuts, stir thoroughly and serve immediately.

*Recipe courtesy of Kelley Weiss*

## LAMB CHOPS PÉRIGOURDINE

*Lamb chops:*
    4 loin chops, each 2″ thick
    2 lamb kidneys, halved
    4–8 strips bacon, raw

    Coarse pepper
    ½ stick butter

*Sauce:*
    4 Tbs. French shallots, chopped
    2 Tbs. butter
    2 cups Beef Stock (p. 183)

    1 small truffle, finely chopped
    1 Tbs. flour
    1–2 Tbs. good Madeira

*Croutons:*
    4 slices white bread
    ½ stick butter
    4 oz. pâté de foie gras

*Serves 4*

*To prepare chops for cooking:* Have your butcher cut the chops for you. Trim them slightly if necessary. Insert half a lamb kidney between the tail end and body of each chop and secure with a toothpick. Tie around with strips of bacon. Rub with coarse pepper and set to one side.

*To begin sauce:* Sauté the shallots in the butter until golden. Remove shallots and in the same pan reduce the beef stock to 1 cup. Return the shallots, add the truffle and simmer for 20 minutes. Reserve. (Save the flour and Madeira until after you have cooked the chops.)

*To make croutons:* Using the top of a large jar, cut 4 rounds out of the bread slices. Sauté these gently in butter until lightly crisp and brown. Spread each with pâté de foie gras and set to one side.

*To cook chops:* Make sure chops and kidneys are at room temperature before cooking. Place the chops side by side in a heavy, hot skillet and sauté on both sides in butter until brown but still pink inside—about 15–20 minutes in total. Do not overcook.

*To finish sauce:* Remove the chops from the skillet, add a scant Tbs. flour and sauté for 2 minutes. Add the reserved sauce, and stir until smooth and cooked—about 10 minutes. Remove from heat and immediately add the Madeira.

*To assemble:* On heated plates, place the warm croutons with a chop on each and spoon the sauce over.

*Recipe courtesy of Robert Browne*

AUTHOR'S NOTE: This is an expensive dish, and rich—one chop per person is sufficient—and should be accompanied by carefully chosen vegetable garnishes such as Pernod Creamed Spinach (p. 24) or Risotto Araujo (p. 138).

## LEG OF LAMB BARBECUE

1 leg of lamb (6 lbs.)
1 cup ketchup
½ cup Worcestershire sauce
1½ cups water

½ tsp. salt
Dash of Tabasco pepper sauce
1 tsp. chili powder

*Serves 6–8*

Roast the leg of lamb in a 325° oven for about 2 hours or until tender and done to your liking.

Combine the remaining ingredients and blend well to make a barbecue sauce.

During the last hour of baking, baste the lamb with the barbecue sauce.

*Recipe courtesy of Max P. Zander*

# PO BOY BENEDICT

6 round slices Po Boy or other
  French bread, cut 1" thick
1 stick butter
6 poached eggs
6 thick slices tomato, grilled

6 slices barbecued pork
1 cup Hollandaise Sauce
  (chap. 13)
2 Tbs. good barbecue sauce
6 slices black olive

*Serves 6*

Fry bread in butter until golden brown. Reserve and keep warm.

Have poached eggs ready, as well as slices of grilled tomato and hot barbecued pork.

Lay grilled tomato on top of fried bread. Top with a piece of pork and then a poached egg.

Carefully spoon the hollandaise sauce, which has been blended with the barbeque sauce, over each serving. Top with a slice of black olive and serve immediately.

*Recipe courtesy of David Tardo*

# POULET À LA VENITIENNE

6 Tbs. butter
3 Tbs. olive oil
2 carrots, finely chopped
2 stalks celery, finely chopped
1 large onion, sliced
2 3-lb. fryers,
  cut into serving pieces
1 cup dry white wine
1 large can peeled Italian tomatoes

Salt and white pepper to taste
4 cloves
¼ tsp. ground cinnamon
1 lb. fresh button mushrooms
  (or 2 cans)
6 slices toasted bread,
  crusts removed
Chopped parsley

*Serves 6*

Heat butter and oil in a large casserole and sauté the carrot, celery and onion. Add the chicken pieces and brown lightly for about 10 minutes.

Add wine and tomatoes. Season to taste with salt and pepper and flavor with cloves and cinnamon.

Cover and cook gently for 45 minutes or until chicken pieces are tender. Add mushrooms for the last 20 minutes.

Serve on toast squares and sprinkle with chopped parsley.

*Recipe courtesy of Paul Fitzwater*

## SLOVAK CHICKEN PAPRIKASH

2 young chickens, quartered        1 onion, chopped
Salt and pepper to taste           1 cup Chicken Stock (p. 183)
2 Tbs. Hungarian sweet paprika     1 Tbs. flour
8 Tbs. butter                      1 cup sour cream

*Serves 8*

Sprinkle chicken quarters with salt and pepper. Dust them with the Hungarian paprika.

In a heavy pot, brown the chicken quarters lightly in 6 Tbs. of the butter for about 5–10 minutes.

In the remaining 2 Tbs. butter, cook the onion until tender—about 5 minutes. Add to the chicken quarters in the pot. Add a little of the chicken stock and cover.

Stew chicken in a 350° oven, covered, for about 1 hour or until tender, basting from time to time with a little more stock if needed.

About 10 minutes before serving time, combine the flour and sour cream and add to juices in the pot.

Finish cooking gently on top of the stove, stirring from time to time.

*Recipe courtesy of Paul Chase*

## STUFFED LASAGNA

2 Tbs. olive oil                   ½ tsp. basil
1 onion, finely chopped            ½ tsp. black pepper
1 lb. ground meat                  1 lb. package lasagna
¼ cup tomato juice                 1 can (1 lb.) peas, drained
1 can (1 lb.) peeled tomatoes      4 hard-boiled eggs, sliced
1 can (6 oz.) tomato paste         8 oz. mozzarella cheese, sliced
1 tsp. salt                        ¼ cup Parmesan cheese
2 bay leaves

*Serves 4*

Heat oil in a large, heavy skillet. Add onion and cook over medium heat until browned—about 5 minutes. Add meat and cook for 5 more minutes, stirring with a fork to break up meat.

Add next 7 ingredients. Mix well, cover and simmer, stirring occasionally, for about 2 hours.

Preheat oven to 350°.

Cook lasagna according to package instructions and drain well.

Cover the bottom of a large baking pan with a thin layer of the sauce. Add 1/3 of the cooked lasagna, a layer of peas and a layer of egg slices topped with mozzarella cheese. Sprinkle with Parmesan cheese. Repeat layers and end with a layer of sauce. Sprinkle with Parmesan.

Bake for 30 minutes. When ready to serve, cut into squares.

*Recipe courtesy of Mrs. Jennie Ferrara*

# VEAL CHOPS PAPRIKA

1–1½ sticks butter,
   depending on size of chops
1–2 Tbs. paprika
4 thick veal chops

Juice of 1 lemon
2 Tbs. capers with liquid
Salt to taste
½ cup chopped parsley

*Serves 4*

In a heavy skillet, melt butter until foamy. Add paprika and stir well.

Add veal chops and cook until tender—about 10 minutes on each side, depending on thickness. Turn once or twice so that the chops are well coated.

When chops are done, remove to a heated platter.

To the butter add the lemon juice, capers with liquid and salt. Combine well.

Pour this sauce over the veal chops and serve garnished with chopped parsley.

*Recipe courtesy of Mrs. Lena Champenois*

## WALTER MCILHENNY'S FROGS' LEGS CREOLE

*Frogs' legs:*

1 dozen frogs' legs            ½ tsp. Tabasco pepper sauce
Pinch of salt                  ½ tsp. salt
Juice of 1 lemon               3 whole eggs, beaten
1 cup cooking oil              1 cup sifted bread crumbs

*Creole Sauce:*

1½ Tbs. butter                 1 Tbs. chopped parsley
1 Tbs. sifted flour            ½ onion, grated
1 cup fresh milk or cream      2 whole eggs, beaten
½ tsp. salt

*Serves 4*

*To cook frogs' legs:* Take 6 frogs, the more delicate the better. Cut off the hind legs and skin. Scald the legs for about 4 minutes in boiling water to cover, adding salt and lemon juice to the water. Remove and dry with a clean towel.

Heat the cooking oil. Rub the frogs' legs well with Tabasco and salt. Dip in beaten eggs, then bread crumbs, and fry in hot oil to a nice golden brown—about 10–15 minutes.

*To prepare Creole Sauce:* Melt the butter in a saucepan over the fire. Add the flour and stir to make a smooth roux. Add the milk and salt and stir constantly, blending all the time. Add the parsley and onion.

*To finish:* Warm the frogs' legs in the sauce, and when it begins to simmer, briskly stir in the eggs. Cook for another 3–4 minutes. Be careful not to let the sauce boil after the eggs have been added, or it will curdle.

Serve immediately.

*Recipe courtesy of Walter McIlhenny*

# VEGETABLES AND SALADS

## BERTHA'S BAKED OKRA

2 Tbs. bacon grease
1 lb. fresh okra, sliced
1 large onion, chopped

1 green pepper, chopped
Salt and pepper to taste
4 strips bacon

*Serves 4*

Heat bacon grease in a heavy skillet; add sliced okra, chopped onion and green pepper. Stir constantly for 5 minutes. Season with salt and pepper and transfer mixture to a Pyrex pie dish.

Bake in a moderate oven for 15 minutes. Put bacon slices on top of the okra mixture and bake for another 15–20 minutes.

*Recipe courtesy of Patricia O'Brien*

## BROCCOLI SOUFFLÉ

2 boxes frozen chopped broccoli
1½ cups milk, heated
1 stick butter
2 Tbs. flour

½ tsp. Tabasco pepper sauce
Salt to taste
6 egg yolks
7 egg whites

*Serves 10*

Boil broccoli in salted water until tender. When cold, place in a colander to drain. Mash and then place a little at a time in a blender. If too stiff, add a little of the milk. Blend until smooth and reserve.

Melt butter, and when it bubbles, add the flour and blend. Add hot milk slowly and cook until mixture coats spoon—about 10 minutes. Add the Tabasco and salt.

Remove from fire and add egg yolks one at a time. When cool, add broccoli purée and set to one side.

When ready to cook, beat egg whites until very stiff and add to broccoli mixture, folding in lightly.

Butter a 1-quart soufflé dish and fill with mixture. Set in a pan of hot but not boiling water.

Put on shelf 2 notches from bottom in a 350° oven. After 20 minutes, reduce heat to 300°.

Bake the soufflé for 1 hour or until a silver knife comes out clean when inserted into the middle of the soufflé.

*Recipe courtesy of Mrs. William B. Burkenroad, Jr.*

# CHOW CHOW

*Vegetable mixture:*

| | |
|---|---|
| 1 gallon cabbage (3 heads) | ½ gallon onions (5 lbs.) |
| ½ gallon green tomatoes (15) | ⅔ box salt |
| ½ gallon cucumbers (8–9), peeled | 3 pints vinegar |
| | 3 pints water |

*Other ingredients:*

| | |
|---|---|
| 8 pints vinegar | 1 can dry mustard (Coleman's) |
| 6 pods red pepper | 2 Tbs. turmeric |
| 1 Tbs. cloves | 2 Tbs. celery seed |
| 1½ cups sugar | 1 pint olive oil |
| ¾ cup flour | |

*Yields 3 gallons*

*To prepare the vegetable mixture:* Chop the vegetables, combine with the salt, and scald with the 3 pints vinegar and 3 pints water. Let drain overnight.

*To complete the relish:* Boil 6 pints of the vinegar with the red pepper pods and cloves. Sift together the sugar, flour, mustard, turmeric and celery seed; gradually mix in the olive oil and the remaining 2 pints vinegar. Pour this mixture into the boiling seasoned vinegar and cook together until thick—about 5–10 minutes.

Add the drained vegetables, stirring constantly for 5–10 minutes. Place in jars and stir. Allow to cool, seal jars carefully and store until ready to use.

*Recipe of Mrs. Edward Seghers Morrison, courtesy of Mrs. Hale (Lindy) Boggs*

## GERMAN RED CABBAGE

3 or 4 slices lean thick-sliced
   bacon
1 medium onion, chopped
1 head red cabbage, shredded

Salt and pepper to taste
Water, if necessary
½ cup dark brown sugar
¼ cup white vinegar

*Serves 6*

Render bacon, leaving some fat in the pan. Remove bacon and drain. Brown chopped onion in remaining bacon fat.

Add the shredded red cabbage, salt and pepper, and return drained bacon. Add a little water if necessary, but you may not need to because the washed cabbage may have enough. Continue to cook.

Check after 30 minutes and add more water if necessary.

When cabbage is tender, after about another 30 minutes, drain off all liquid. Mix brown sugar with the white vinegar and blend well with the cabbage. Allow to stand for about 30 minutes before reheating and serving.

The flavor improves in proportion to the time the completed recipe is allowed to stand before it is served.

*Recipe courtesy of Mr. William Bohne*

## LOU MARY'S SMOTHERED OKRA

2 Tbs. Mazola oil
1 lb. okra, chopped

1 large onion, finely chopped
Salt to taste

*Serves 4*

Mix all ingredients together in a heavy skillet. (Do not preheat cooking oil.) Smother over low fire for 45–60 minutes. Serve hot.

*Recipe courtesy of Patricia O'Brien*

# RISOTTO ARAUJO

4 cups hot cooked rice
1 stick butter, softened
½ lb. prosciutto ham, diced
1 10-oz. package frozen peas,
    thawed and lightly cooked

4 large pimientos, diced
½ cup chopped green onions
¼ cup grated Parmesan cheese
Freshly ground black pepper
    to taste

*Serves 8*

In a large bowl, combine the hot cooked rice with the softened butter. Add ham, peas, pimientos and green onions. Toss well; then add the Parmesan cheese and a little freshly ground black pepper.

Serve.

If this is prepared in advance, it may be reheated in a 350° oven for 20 minutes before serving.

You will find it indestructible.

*Recipe courtesy of August Araujo*

# SALADE D'OKRA

2 lbs. fresh okra
    (or 3 packages frozen)
1 tsp. salt
3 Tbs. olive oil
1 onion, chopped
1 green pepper, chopped

2 tomatoes, peeled, seeded and
    chopped
1 cup C.B.'s Vinaigrette Sauce
    (chap. 13)
Dash of Tabasco pepper sauce
¼ tsp. each chopped basil,
    parsley and green onion

*Serves 6*

Wash fresh okra thoroughly and cut in 1" pieces. Cook in salted water until just tender—about 15 minutes. (If frozen okra is used, buy the whole okra and follow cooking instructions on package.) Drain.

Heat olive oil in a heavy skillet. Sauté onion and green pepper in this until tender—about 10 minutes. Add tomatoes. Cook for 10 more minutes, stirring constantly.

Toss okra in the vinaigrette sauce, adding Tabasco, and then fold in the cooked vegetables. Refrigerate.

Before serving, sprinkle with the chopped basil, parsley and green onions.

*Recipe courtesy of Paul Fitzwater*

# DESSERTS

## CATHERINE TARDO'S DEVIL

*Cake:*

2½ cups flour, sifted
2 cups sugar
6 Tbs. cocoa
2 tsp. baking soda
½ tsp. salt

2 whole eggs
⅔ cup oil
2 cups buttermilk
1 tsp. vanilla extract

*Icing:*

½ cup milk
2 cups sugar
3 Tbs. cocoa
½ tsp. salt

1 stick unsalted butter
½ tsp. vanilla extract
½ cup chopped pecans

*Serves 8–10*

*To make cake:* Preheat oven to 350°.

Add all ingredients in the order given above. Mix quickly and pour into a baking pan lined with buttered waxed paper. Do not overbeat cake. Place in the oven and bake for 35–40 minutes or until a silver knife comes out clean.

*To make icing:* In a saucepan combine milk, sugar, cocoa, salt and butter. Bring to a boil, stirring occasionally.

When it comes to a boil, remove from heat and add vanilla. Beat with an electric beater for 5–7 minutes or until icing loses its glossy look. Add nuts.

If icing gets too hard, it can be softened by adding a little more butter.

Ice the cake while it is still warm, as the warmth helps spread the icing. It is not recommended to remove this cake from the pan. It is not a layer cake.

*Recipe courtesy of Catherine Tardo*

# CHOCOLATE MAYONNAISE CAKE

*Cake batter:*

1½ cups granulated sugar          1 cup mayonnaise
2 tsp. baking soda                1 cup warm water
2 cups all-purpose flour          1 tsp. vanilla
3–4 heaping Tbs. cocoa

*Icing:*

½ lb. unsalted butter             2 Tbs. cocoa
¾ lb. powdered sugar              3–4 Tbs. strong coffee

*Serves 8*

*To make cake:* Preheat oven to 350°.

Sift sugar, baking soda, flour and cocoa in a large mixing bowl. Add mayonnaise, water and vanilla; with an electric beater, mix to a smooth consistency.

Place equal amounts of the cake batter in 2 round 8″ cake pans which have been coated with butter or shortening and lightly floured. Bake for 40 minutes or until a silver knife comes out dry when inserted in the middle.

*To make icing and assemble:* Cream the butter and gradually add the sugar. (If the icing is too dry as you blend in the sugar, simply add a little more butter.) When thoroughly blended, add the cocoa and then the warm coffee, a little at a time.

When completely smooth, frost the top and sides of the cake and refrigerate until ready to serve.

*Recipe courtesy of Dr. R. Jack Cassingham*

AUTHOR'S NOTE: Don't let the mayonnaise frighten you. It will give the cake a light and moist consistency and help it to rise. This is, without a doubt, one of the best chocolate cakes.

## GAY NOE'S STRAWBERRY CAKE

*Cake:*

1 box strawberry Jell-O powder
1 box white cake mix
1 cup Wesson oil
½ cup milk

½ package frozen strawberries, thawed
½ can coconut
¾ cup chopped pecans
4 eggs

*Icing:*

1 stick margarine
1 box powdered sugar
¾ cup chopped pecans

½ cup coconut
½ package frozen strawberries, thawed

*Serves 6–8*

*To make cake:* Mix the Jell-O powder with the cake mix until well-blended. Add the Wesson oil, milk, thawed strawberries, coconut, pecans and eggs. Mix well, using a rotary beater.

Divide the mixture into 3 greased 9" cake pans and bake in a moderate oven (350°) for 25 minutes. Allow to cool.

*To make icing:* Cream all the ingredients together.

*To assemble:* Ice each layer of the cake and stack them one on top of the other. Cover the sides with the remaining icing and serve.

*Recipe courtesy of Gay Noe McLendon*

## LA DOLCE VITA

*Meringue layers:*

4 egg whites
Pinch of salt

¼ tsp. cream of tartar
1 cup sugar

*Filling:*

6 oz. semisweet chocolate pieces
3 Tbs. water
3 cups heavy cream

1/3 cup sugar
1 pint fresh strawberries

*Serves 6–8*

*To make meringue layers:* Preheat oven to a very low temperature (250°).

Beat the egg whites until stiff. Add the salt and cream of tartar and continue beating until very stiff.

Gradually beat in the sugar and continue to beat until the meringue is stiff and glossy.

Line baking sheets with waxed paper and trace 3 circles 8″ each in diameter. Spread meringue evenly (about ¼″ thick) and bake in very slow oven for 20–25 minutes or until meringue is pale gold but still pliable.

Remove from oven and carefully peel waxed paper from bottom. Put on cake racks to dry.

*To make filling:* Melt the semisweet chocolate pieces with 3 Tbs. water over hot water.

Whip the heavy cream until stiff. Gradually add the sugar and continue to beat until stiff.

Slice the fresh strawberries.

*To assemble:* Spread a meringue layer with a thin coating of melted chocolate. Spread a layer of whipped cream on top (about ¾″) and top with sliced strawberries.

Continue with second layer and the same with the third. Frost sides smoothly with remaining whipped cream and decorate top of cake in an informal manner, using remaining chocolate forced through a small pastry tube.

*Recipe courtesy of Roc Johnson*

## MEXICAN MOUSSE

8 oz. Ibarra Mexican chocolate  
6 eggs, separated  
1 oz. very strong coffee  
1 oz. Coffee Amaretto

½ pint heavy cream, whipped and sweetened with 2 Tbs. sugar

*Serves 6*

Melt chocolate in top of a double boiler. Work quickly and keep stirring, as this chocolate is very sticky.

Remove from heat. Cool slightly and add the egg yolks one at a time, stirring constantly. Add coffee while stirring and then the Coffee Amaretto.

Stiffly beat the egg whites and fold the chocolate mixture into them carefully until there are no spots of egg whites.

Put into 6 stem glasses. Refrigerate for at least 4 hours. Serve with a large spoonful of sweetened whipped cream.

*Recipe courtesy of Keith Cesare Mora*

# MYERS'S JAMAICAN CARROT CAKE

| | |
|---|---|
| 2 bags large carrots | 2 tsp. baking soda |
| 1½ cups Wesson oil | 1 tsp. salt |
| 2 cups sugar | 1 tsp. cinnamon |
| 5 eggs | 2 tsp. vanilla |
| 2 cups flour | 1 cup Myers's Jamaican rum |

*Yields a 2-lb. loaf*

Peel and grate carrots. This should yield 4 cups. If it does not, add a few more carrots. Reserve.

Mix the oil and sugar with an electric beater on low speed. Blend the mixture well for almost an hour.

Add the eggs one at a time until well blended.

Sift flour, baking soda and salt together. Add cinnamon and vanilla. Add this to the first mixture. Blend well again and then add the Myers's Jamaican rum.

Finally add the grated carrots and blend by hand, but do not beat, as this will produce water from the carrots.

Lightly grease and flour 2 loaf pans, 9" x 5" x 2½", and divide cake mixture into them. 2 9" layer pans (round)

Bake in a 350° oven for 1½-2 hours. Cake will rise and then fall. Cool and unmold. rotate ½ way 30 min (check)

Serve with ice cream or whipped cream. Cake may be served warm or cold.

*Recipe courtesy of Carmen Hanson*

*AUTHOR'S NOTE:* This is the most moist carrot cake I have ever tasted.

# PAUL'S SLOVAK CAKE

| | |
|---|---|
| ½ lb. butter | ½ lb. ground walnuts |
| 1 cup granulated sugar | 1 tsp. vanilla |
| 3 eggs | 1 lb. (2 jars) prune jelly or *lekvar* |
| 3 cups flour | Powdered sugar |
| 3 tsp. baking powder | |

*Serves 6*

Cream the butter with the granulated sugar. Add the eggs one at a time. Add the flour and the baking powder. Add the walnuts and the vanilla. Blend together with a wooden spoon until the batter is smooth.

Grease a rectangular pan and line it with waxed paper; grease the waxed paper lightly.

Put half the batter on the bottom of the pan. Spread the prune jelly on top of the batter. Add the remaining batter in a crisscross pattern of strips on top of the prune jelly.

Bake at 350° for 35–40 minutes, until lightly browned.

Sprinkle with powdered sugar when cake is cooled.

*Recipe of Mrs. Charles Rector, courtesy of Paul Chase*


# SUPERBE À L'ORANGE

*Cake:*

3 oranges                          ²/₃ cup flour
2 eggs                             ¼ cup butter, melted
½ cup sugar                        2 tsp. baking powder

*Syrup:*

½ cup sugar
Juice of the 3 oranges

*Serves 4*

*To make cake:* Preheat oven to 400°.

Squeeze the oranges and save the juice for the syrup. Grate the rinds and reserve. Beat the eggs slightly and add the sugar, flour, melted butter and baking powder. Blend until smooth, add the grated rinds and mix well.

Pour into a buttered 10″ Pyrex pie dish. Bake in the oven for 15 minutes. Cool slightly and then unmold.

*To make syrup:* Combine the sugar and orange juice. Boil for 2–3 minutes and pour over the warm cake.

Serve immediately.

*Recipe courtesy of Denise Schweitzer Lagesse*

AUTHOR'S NOTE: I have had this many times in New Orleans and remember making it once myself. If you like, you may substitute a little Cointreau or Triple Sec for some of the orange juice.

# TOAST VILAC
## A French Toast with Bananas

4 eggs
½ cup milk
¼ tsp. salt
¼ tsp. vanilla
6 thick slices white bread

½ cup cooking oil
1 banana, sliced into rounds
¼ tsp. each cinnamon, nutmeg
  and sugar
Powdered sugar (optional)

*Serves 3*

Beat eggs with milk, salt and vanilla. Soak bread in this mixture for a few minutes.

Heat oil in a heavy skillet and fry bread on one side. Arrange sliced bananas, which have been dusted with a mixture of cinnamon, nutmeg and sugar, on top of bread. Then turn bread over and fry other side.

When done, flip bread over so that fried sliced bananas are back on top. Total cooking time is about 10 minutes.

Serve while hot and dust with powdered sugar if you like.

*Recipe courtesy of Frank V. McDonnell*

# 5
# THE
# INTERNATIONAL
# INFLUENCE

I WOULD BE considered prejudiced if I said that New Orleans is the gourmet capital of America. I'll compromise and say that it is certainly one of them and that its reputation as a gourmet city extends beyond this country.

The myth that New Orleans, and especially the French Quarter, is only Cajun and Creole is finally coming to an end. Now we even have what one would call an authentic French restaurant. With all love and respect to those French and Spanish ancestors who gave the city so much of its culture and created the Cajun and Creole cuisine, New Orleans has become a culinary melting pot. It has given and taken from the very best.

Although I have tasted the international recipes included in this chapter in other parts of the world, it has always been a great source of pleasure to me to prepare them in my own home in New Orleans and find an appreciative audience.

Vive Red Beans and Rice . . . but bring on the Spaghetti Carbonara.

# ARABIC

## EGYPTIAN OMELET

| | |
|---|---|
| 2 eggplants, peeled and cubed | 8 eggs, lightly beaten |
| 2 Tbs. butter | Salt and freshly ground pepper |
| 1 medium onion, finely chopped |   to taste |
| 1 clove garlic, chopped | |

*Serves 4*

Put eggplant cubes in a colander. Sprinkle with salt and set aside for 1 hour. Then rinse the eggplant cubes and dry them on paper toweling until ready to use.

In a large frying pan, melt the butter. Add the onion and garlic and fry, stirring, until the onion is soft—about 5 minutes. Add the eggplant cubes and cook until they are tender—about 20 minutes.

Pour in the beaten eggs, season with salt and pepper and mix. Reduce heat to low, cover and cook the omelet for 10–15 minutes or until the bottom is set and the omelet nearly cooked through.

Preheat the broiler. Place the frying pan beneath the heat and broil until the eggs are cooked through and the top is lightly browned—about 5 minutes.

## LAMB AND OKRA STEW

| | |
|---|---|
| 2 cups okra, fresh | 1½ lbs. boned lean lamb, |
|   or frozen (thawed) |   cut into 1″ cubes |
| ¼ cup butter | 3 medium, ripe tomatoes, sliced |
| 2 onions, finely chopped | 2 Tbs. tomato purée mixed with |
| 7 large garlic cloves, chopped |   4 Tbs. water |
|   (use less if you prefer) | Salt and freshly ground black |
| |   pepper to taste |

*Serves 4*

Wash the okra and cut off the stems. Be careful not to cut them too close to the pod, or they will get slimy.

Melt the butter in a large saucepan. Add the onions and garlic and fry, stirring, until the onions are soft but not brown—about 10 minutes. Add the lamb pieces and brown them all over.

Add the okra to the pan and fry, stirring, for 3–5 minutes. Add the tomatoes, tomato purée, salt and black pepper to taste.

Add enough water to cover the meat and vegetables. Bring to a boil. Reduce heat, cover the pan and simmer for 1½ hours or until the meat is tender and the sauce is rich.

# BRITISH

## AUSTRALIAN CARPETBAG STEAK

| | |
|---|---|
| 4 thick tenderloin or filet steaks | 8 very fresh large oysters, shucked |
| Salt and freshly ground black pepper | 4–8 Tbs. melted butter |
| | ½ cup chopped parsley |

*Serves 4*

With a sharp knife, carefully make a slit in the side of each steak to make a pocket. Rub a little salt and pepper inside the pockets.

Insert 2 oysters into each steak and sew up the pockets with some thread or secure with toothpicks or skewers.

Preheat the broiler. Brush each steak liberally with melted butter and sprinkle with black pepper. Broil the steaks 4–8 minutes on each side or until they are done the way you like them. Brush the steaks with more butter when they are turned.

To serve, put the steaks on a heated platter, sprinkle with parsley and pour the juices from the broiler pan over them.

## ENGLISH ROAST BEEF AND YORKSHIRE PUDDING

| | |
|---|---|
| 1 4–6-lb. rib roast | 1 egg |
| 1 cup all-purpose flour | 1¼ cups milk (or a mixture of |
| Pinch of salt | equal parts milk and water) |

*Serves 6*

Run a long skewer through the meat and balance the skewer on the edges of the pan so the meat is suspended. Roast in a 425° oven, allowing 15 minutes to the pound for rare beef.

Mix the flour and salt together. Make a well in the middle and put in the egg and a little milk.

Working from the center, stir the ingredients into a batter, gradually adding the rest of the milk or milk-water.

About 35–40 minutes before the end of the roasting time, pour the batter into the roasting pan. It will rise up at the sides, and the center will be soft. When it is a golden brown, cut into square pieces and serve around the carved roast.

# CHINESE

## ONION PANCAKES

3 cups all-purpose flour  
1½ cups hot water  
4 Tbs. lard  

4 Tbs. green onions, chopped  
½ tsp. salt  
3 Tbs. sesame oil  

*Serves 6*

Sift flour into a mixing bowl and gradually stir in the water. Blend the dough for a few minutes until it is smooth; then cover the bowl with a cloth and set aside for 30 minutes.

Shape the dough into a long roll about 2" in diameter and cut into 1¼" pieces. You should have 12 pieces. Make an indentation with your thumb in the center of each piece and fill with 1 tsp. lard, 1 tsp. chopped green onion and a little of the salt. Fold and pinch the sides up and over the filling ingredients. Now flatten into cakes about 3" in diameter.

Heat the sesame oil in a large, heavy frying pan over moderate heat. Reduce the heat to low and place the pancakes in the pan a few at a time. Cook, turning the pancakes over every 30 seconds, for 4 minutes.

Drain and serve hot.

## PORK AND WATERCRESS SOUP

3 oz. lean pork,  
   cut into thin strips  
½ tsp. salt  
2 Tbs. cornstarch  

2 pints Chicken Stock (p. 183)  
1 bunch fresh watercress  
Freshly ground black pepper  

*Serves 4*

Rub the pork slices with the salt and cornstarch. In a large saucepan, bring the stock to a boil. Add the pork slices. Reduce the heat and simmer, uncovered, for 10–15 minutes.

Add the watercress and pepper to taste. Simmer for 3 more minutes. Pour the soup into a tureen and serve immediately.

# DUTCH

## HOTCHPOTCH WITH SOUP MEAT

| | |
|---|---|
| 1 lb. fat brisket of beef | 3 lbs. potatoes |
| 3/4 lb. lean brisket of beef | 1/2 lb. yellow onions, cut up |
| 3 lbs. old carrots | Salt and black pepper to taste |

*Serves 4–6*

Wash the meat and put it in warm salted water to barely cover. Bring to a boil and simmer for 2 hours.

Peel the carrots and potatoes and cut them up. After meat has cooked for over 1 hour, add the carrots and potatoes. After another 15 minutes add the onions. Simmer for another 1/2 hour, until the vegetables are very tender.

Add more water during the cooking process, if necessary. When the dish is ready, the water should have completely evaporated.

Remove the meat from the saucepan, put on a hot dish and slice. Mash all the vegetables together, season with salt and pepper and arrange them around the dish.

This is a pretty basic dish, and one which reminds the people of Holland of the famous Battle of Leyden, when there was nothing to eat. I came up with a more sophisticated version when some Dutch friends of mine were visiting in New Orleans. They thought it was a delicious variation.

VARIATION: Cook the meat in a good rich Beef Stock (p. 183). Cook the vegetables separately in stock. Drain, mash them together and serve surrounding the meat, as above.

The original version always uses old carrots but you may use smaller, more tender carrots, if you prefer.

# FRENCH

## BOEUF ST.-LOUIS-EN-L'ÎLE

6 steaks or a mixture of steak
    meat (e.g., T-bone,
    porterhouse or filet)*
2 cups all-purpose flour,
    seasoned with salt and pepper
1 cup olive oil

1 clove garlic, minced
1 cup diced carrots
½ cup minced onions
1 cup sliced leeks, if available
2 cups dry white wine
1 small can tomato sauce

*Serves 6*

Preheat oven to 350°.

Dredge steaks in the seasoned flour. Heat olive oil over a high flame and lightly brown the meat for about 5–10 minutes.

Remove to a dutch oven and sprinkle with a little more flour. Add the garlic, carrots, onions and leeks.

Mix the white wine with the tomato sauce and pour the combination over the steaks. Cover and place in the oven for about 30 minutes.

Do not strain. Spoon sauce over steak pieces in individual servings.

Buttered noodles or new potatoes are excellent with this dish.

* I created this dish one night when friends dropped in on the spur of the moment. All I had in my refrigerator was half a T-bone, a small porterhouse and several filets. So—the idea is, use whatever you like or whatever you've got.

## FRENCH SHEPHERD'S PIE

3 onions, chopped
½ cup butter
1 lb. cold boiled beef
    or cold roast beef
4 oz. fat salt pork
    or unsmoked bacon
2 Tbs. chopped parsley
Salt and pepper to taste

½ cup milk
½ cup bread crumbs
1 egg, beaten
3 potatoes, peeled
    and boiled for 20 minutes
1 Tbs. grated Gruyère cheese
1 Tbs. grated Parmesan cheese

*Serves 4–6*

Cook onion gently in half the butter for 15–20 minutes.

Grind the beef with the uncooked salt pork or bacon. Add the parsley and season with salt and pepper. Add enough of the milk to the bread crumbs to make a thick paste and mix this well with the ground meat.

Add the mixture to the softened onions and cook for about 5 minutes. Remove from heat, cool slightly and add the beaten egg.

Grease a round 9″ shallow pan with a little butter. Spread the meat mixture over this.

Mash the hot boiled potatoes with the remaining butter and milk until they are creamy. Spread the mashed potatoes over the meat mixture. Sprinkle with the cheeses.

Bake in a moderate oven (350°) for 30–40 minutes.

## FRENCH-STYLE GREEN BEANS

1 lb. fresh green beans
4 Tbs. butter
1 clove garlic, minced

1 tsp. salt
½ tsp. freshly ground black
    pepper

*Serves 4*

Break off ends and cut beans into long, thin strips. On many vegetable peelers there is a gadget for this purpose. Simply push the bean through the slot, and it is "Frenched."

In a covered pot, cook the beans in 2 cups of cold water for 20–30 minutes or until tender and crisp. Do not overcook.

Drain the beans well and reserve. Melt the butter and add the garlic, salt and pepper. Toss beans in this mixture until well coated.

This recipe may be prepared in advance and heated when ready to serve.

# GARLIC MAYONNAISE

| | |
|---|---|
| 4–8 garlic cloves | 2 cups olive oil |
| ¼ tsp. salt | ½ tsp. white pepper |
| 2 large egg yolks | Juice of 1 lemon |

*Yields 2 cups*

Crush the garlic with a little salt in a wooden bowl. Beat in the egg yolks, and then the olive oil drop by drop, just as for making regular mayonnaise. When the sauce becomes really thick, beat faster. Season with the pepper and lemon juice.

This recipe is definitely for garlic lovers only. In France it is usually served with salt codfish and is called *aioli*. It is also good with cold meats.

Many a friendship has been broken over garlic mayonnaise, but the French won't give it up.

# PORK WITH PRUNES

| | |
|---|---|
| 8 pork chops, boned | ½ bottle dry white wine |
| 1 cup flour, seasoned with | 1 Tbs. red currant jelly |
|     salt and pepper | 2 cups heavy cream |
| ½ cup butter | Salt and black pepper to taste |
| 2¼ cups pitted prunes | Juice of 1 lemon |

*Serves 8*

Dredge pork chops in seasoned flour. Melt butter and fry chops until they are golden brown—about 8–10 minutes on each side. Reduce heat, cover the pan and cook gently for about 20 minutes or until the chops are well cooked but tender.

Simmer the prunes in the white wine until they are soft. Remove prunes and reserve cooking liquid.

Arrange the chops and prunes on a hot platter. Keep hot while preparing the sauce.

Pour the prune liquid into the frying pan and boil it down to approximately half—about 20 minutes—scraping the bottom of the pan with a wooden spoon. Add the red currant jelly.

When the jelly has dissolved, stir in the cream. Boil hard until the sauce is thick, smooth and light-colored. Season with salt and pepper to taste and lastly add the lemon juice.

Pour the sauce over the pork and prunes and serve very hot with small parsley potatoes.

# QUICHE LORRAINE

*Crust:*

3 cups all-purpose flour
5 egg yolks
1 Tbs. olive oil

3/4 cup softened butter
1/2 tsp. salt
1/4–1/2 cup cold water

*Filling:*

12 thick slices Canadian bacon
12 thick slices Gruyère or
    domestic Swiss cheese

*Custard:*

3 whole eggs
1 Tbs. flour
Generous grating of nutmeg
1/2 tsp. salt

1/4 tsp. Tabasco pepper sauce
2 cups light cream
1 1/2 Tbs. melted butter

*Serves 8*

*To make crust:* Place flour in a mixing bowl and make a well. Place egg yolks, olive oil, butter and salt in the well and mix thoroughly, bringing in the flour from the sides of the bowl.

Add enough cold water to moisten and make a good dough, ready to knead out. If time permits, form the pastry into a ball, place in a towel and refrigerate for an hour or so. Return to room temperature before using.

Roll the dough out and line a standard quiche pan or 9″ pie plate with it. Prebake the pie shell for about 10 minutes in a moderate oven (350°). Allow to cool.

*To prepare filling:* Partially cook the Canadian bacon for 5–10 minutes, drain and cut into thin julienne strips. Cut the cheese into thin julienne strips.

*To prepare custard:* Beat the eggs. Add the flour, nutmeg, salt and Tabasco. Add the light cream and beat again. Stir in the melted butter.

*To assemble and serve:* Fill the prebaked pie shell with overlapping strips of the Canadian bacon and cheese. Strain the custard mixture over this through a cheesecloth.

Bake in a moderate oven (350°) for 45–60 minutes or until a silver knife comes out clean when inserted into the custard.

I like to cook my quiche in advance and then refrigerate it. It slices much better this way. When ready to serve, simply heat on a cookie sheet for 15 minutes in a 300° oven.

Serve quiche warm, not piping hot. It may also be cut up into bite-size pieces and used as an hors d'oeuvre.

# RATATOUILLE

4 unpeeled zucchini, sliced
2 unpeeled eggplants, sliced
1 tsp. salt
3 sweet peppers
   (1 red, 1 yellow and 1 green)
4–5 Tbs. olive oil
2–3 white onions, sliced
3 cloves garlic, chopped

6 tomatoes, parboiled,
   peeled and chopped
Freshly ground black pepper
1 Tbs. sugar
½ cup white wine
8 black olives, pitted and sliced
½ cup chopped parsley

*Serves 6*

Sprinkle zucchini and eggplant slices with salt and allow to sit for 1 hour. Dry them with paper toweling. Clean the peppers and cut them into strips. Mix with zucchini and eggplant and reserve.

Heat the olive oil in a deep saucepan. Add the onions and garlic and cook until the onions are soft—about 10 minutes.

In a dutch oven, arrange alternate layers of the onions, the zucchini-eggplant-peppers mixture and the tomatoes. Season with black pepper and a little more salt as you make the layers. Pour the sugar mixed with the white wine over all.

Cook for about 1 hour, uncovered, over very low heat, until the vegetable stew is thick. Stir from time to time. Correct seasonings, add the black olives and sprinkle with parsley for garnish.

Serve hot or cold as a first course or as a vegetable with meat or fish.

# STRAWBERRY TART

*Crust:*

12 Tbs. flour
8 Tbs. sugar
¹/₃ lb. unsalted butter

2 egg yolks
8 Tbs. ground blanched almonds

*Filling:*

1 pint fresh strawberries
2 Tbs. sugar
Juice of ½ lemon

*Meringue:*

2 egg whites
1 Tbs. sugar

*Serves 6*

*To make crust:* Make a short pastry with the flour, sugar and butter, which has been cut up into small pieces. Add the egg yolks and almonds. Blend well.

Roll out, a little on the thick side, to the shape of a 9″ tart pan. Prebake for 35 minutes in a 350° oven.

*To make filling:* Wash and clean the strawberries, drain well and cut them in half lengthwise. Sprinkle with sugar and lemon juice. Arrange in tart pan.

*To make meringue and serve:* Beat the egg whites with 1 Tbs. sugar until stiff. Spread over the strawberries and return to a 350° oven. Bake until the meringue is slightly browned—about 10–15 minutes.


## TRIPE ST. LOUIS

3 lbs. fresh tripe
2 calves' feet or pigs' feet
2 medium onions, sliced
2 large carrots, sliced
2 stalks celery, sliced
2 leeks, sliced
2 sprigs parsley
½ lb. chopped kidney suet
1 tsp. dried thyme (or 2 Tbs.
  chopped fresh thyme)
1 bay leaf
2 cloves garlic

6 peppercorns
3 whole cloves
Blade of fresh mace or
  pinch of dried
1 tsp. salt
½ tsp. black pepper
¼ cup Calvados
½ cup hard cider
1½–2 cups Beef Stock (p. 183)
2 cups flour
Cold water

*Serves 8*

Wash the tripe well and cut into 2″ squares. Set aside. Wash and split the calves' feet. Set aside.

In a 3-quart casserole, put the vegetables, tripe, calves' feet, suet and seasonings, in that order. Pour in the Calvados and then the cider and enough of the beef stock to barely cover all the ingredients.

Cover the casserole and seal it with a roll of dough made by mixing the flour with enough cold water to make a stiff paste. Bring the liquid to a boil.

Place the casserole in slow oven (250°–300°) and cook anywhere from 8–10 hours (or even overnight in a lower oven). Never open the casserole or disturb the tripe while it cooks.

When finished, open and transfer the tripe to another casserole, reserving the stock and discarding the dough. Remove the calves' feet and pick over for the meat, discarding the bones. Add meat pickings to the tripe. Skim off the fat from the stock and strain it over the tripe. Heat.

Serve hot with parsley potatoes.

# VEAL MARENGO

3 lbs. lean veal stew meat,
   cut into 1½" squares
2 cups all-purpose flour,
   seasoned with salt and pepper
1 cup olive oil
1 stick butter
2 cloves garlic, chopped
1 Bouquet Garni (chap. 13)
8 very ripe tomatoes,
   peeled and quartered

2 cups dry white wine
36 small white onions, peeled
1 small can tomato sauce
1 lb. mushrooms, stems removed
½ Tbs. salt
¼ tsp. white pepper
¼ tsp. Tabasco pepper sauce
2 Tbs. *Beurre Manié* (chap. 13),
   if necessary

*Serves 6*

Dredge veal pieces in seasoned flour. Heat olive oil and butter in a heavy skillet and brown veal pieces lightly for about 5 minutes. Add chopped garlic. Drain excess fat and transfer to a heavy dutch oven.

Add the bouquet garni and crush the tomato wedges over the meat. Add the white wine and bring to a boil, reduce heat and simmer for 30 minutes.

Add the peeled onions, return cover and continue to cook until meat and onions are tender but not falling apart—about another 20–25 minutes.

Add tomato sauce and mushroom caps and correct seasoning with salt, pepper and Tabasco. Cook for an additional 10 minutes.

Remove bouquet garni. If sauce is too thin, add the *beurre manié* and work into the sauce. Serve.

## WALNUT OIL SALAD

1 large head lettuce,           ½ tsp. sugar
  such as romaine         1 tsp. chopped parsley
1 Tbs. white wine vinegar       ½ tsp. chopped tarragon
8 Tbs. walnut oil               ½ tsp. chopped chervil
1 small garlic clove, crushed   4 thick slices French bread,
Salt and freshly ground black     with crusts
  pepper to taste          2 cloves garlic, cut in half

*Serves 4–6*

Pull the lettuce apart, wash it and drain well. Keep in toweling.

In a salad bowl mix vinegar, 4 Tbs. of the walnut oil and all other ingredients except bread and garlic halves.

Just before serving, rub the bread all over with the garlic. Cut the bread into small cubes. Heat the remaining walnut oil in a frying pan and fry the bread until golden brown—about 5–8 minutes.

Break the lettuce leaves into the salad dressing. Meanwhile, drain the bread pieces on paper toweling.

Toss the salad at the very last minute. After the last turning, toss in the fried bread cubes (called *chapons*) and toss once again. Serve immediately.

This is a nostalgic salad: Alice B. Toklas taught me to make it originally with hazelnut oil, but a nut is a nut is a nut!

Walnut oil is now available in gourmet shops. It's delicious . . . but it ain't cheap.

# GERMAN

## BAVARIAN LIVER DUMPLINGS

6 stale crusty rolls, thinly sliced
½ tsp. salt
1¼ cups lukewarm milk
½ lb. beef liver
⅛ lb. beef suet

1 small onion, coarsely chopped
2 eggs, lightly beaten
1 tsp. marjoram
1½–2 quarts Beef Stock (p. 183)

*Serves 4*

Put the sliced rolls in a large bowl. Sprinkle with salt and pour in the lukewarm milk. Leave them to soak until ready to use.

Trim the liver and put it through a meat grinder together with the suet and onion. Add the soaked bread, eggs and marjoram, and mix with a wooden spoon until well blended. The mixture will be very soft.

Bring the stock to a boil in a large kettle. Reduce heat to low and simmer. Divide the dumpling mixture into 8 portions. With wet hands, shape a portion at a time into a ball and drop into the stock. Simmer gently for 15–20 minutes or until the dumplings are cooked.

Serve 2 dumplings per person in soup plates together with some of the stock. This may also be served as an accompaniment to Boiled Beef (below).

## BOILED BEEF

1 lb. beef bones
2½ quarts water
1 Tbs. salt
2–2½ lbs. top round of beef,
    tied with a string
1 large leek, halved

2 celery stalks, sliced
1 large carrot, halved
1 onion, sliced
4 sprigs parsley
6 black peppercorns

*Serves 6–8*

In a large saucepan, cover the beef bones with 2½ quarts salted water. Bring to a boil slowly, skimming off the scum as it rises to the surface.

Add the beef and the remaining ingredients. Slowly bring to a boil again.

Lower the heat so that the liquid barely simmers. Partly cover the pot and cook for 2½–3 hours or until the beef is very tender.

To serve, cut the beef into thick slices and arrange them on a warm platter. Serve with boiled potatoes or Bavarian Liver Dumplings (above).

## WIENER SCHNITZEL À LA HOLSTEIN

6 individual veal rounds, pounded
2 whole eggs, beaten with
   1 Tbs. water
1½ cups flour, seasoned with
   salt and pepper
2 cups bread crumbs
1½ cups cooking oil
   (or 1½ sticks butter)

12 anchovies
6 hard-boiled eggs, quartered
12 thin lemon slices
½ cup capers
Paprika
Finely chopped parsley

*Serves 6*

Pound the veal rounds between 2 pieces of waxed paper until very thin. If they are large, cut them in half, allowing 2 per person.

Dip each round in egg wash, then in seasoned flour and lastly in bread crumbs. Lay flat on a platter, and be certain that schnitzels are well coated with bread crumbs. Refrigerate for several hours until ready to use.

When ready to cook, heat the oil or butter. Depending on the size of the skillet, sauté a few at a time until they are golden brown on each side—about 10 minutes in all.

Drain on paper toweling and garnish each schnitzel with anchovies, hard-boiled egg, lemon slices and capers. Dust egg with paprika and parsley.

# GREEK

## LEMON SOUP

1 quart Chicken Stock (p. 183)
¼ cup raw rice
2 egg yolks

Juice of 1½ lemons
Fried Croutons (chap. 13)

*Serves 4*

Heat the stock, add the rice and simmer for about 10 minutes or until the rice is cooked.

Before serving, blend in the egg yolks, which have been diluted with a little of the hot stock.

Add the lemon juice, stir for a few minutes and serve immediately with croutons.

# PILAF

2 Tbs. butter
1 cup raw rice
1 quart Beef Stock (p. 183) or
    mutton stock

2 medium tomatoes, sliced
Salt and black pepper to taste

*Serves 4–6*

In a heavy saucepan, melt butter and fry rice for about 8 minutes. Add the hot beef stock gradually and simmer the rice for 20–25 minutes.

Add the sliced tomatoes and salt and pepper. Continue to cook for another 10 minutes. When properly done, the rice should be just moist, with each grain separate.

# HUNGARIAN

## HUNGARIAN PANCAKES WITH WALNUT FILLING

*Batter:* *
    2 cups flour
    2 eggs
    Pinch of salt

1 tsp. cognac
1 tsp. olive oil
2 cups milk

*Filling:*
    1 cup milk
    1 cup sugar

1½ cups ground walnuts
3 Tbs. powdered sugar

*Serves 4–5*

*To make pancakes:* Put flour in a mixing bowl and break in eggs. Add salt, cognac and olive oil. With a wooden spoon or an electric beater mix ingredients well.

Beating all the time, very slowly dilute with the milk until the mixture is smooth and has the consistency of light cream. Allow to stand for 1 hour before using.

Heat a small pancake pan or griddle and lightly brush with cooking oil. Spoon out batter and cook pancakes one at a time for 2–3 minutes on each side, until golden.

These may be made in advance and simply reheated when ready to serve.

*To make filling and assemble:* Put milk, sugar and walnuts in a saucepan.

Carefully bring this to a boil; reduce heat and allow to cook, uncovered, until mixture is thick—about 15 minutes.

Fill each pancake with this mixture and roll. Dust with powdered sugar and reheat for 5 minutes in a 350° oven.

*Yields 8–10 pancakes.

## PORK GULYÁS

1 lb. pork shoulder
1 lb. ribs of pork
1 lb. lean pork loin
2 Tbs. ham fat or cooking oil
2 large red onions, chopped
2 cloves garlic, crushed
1 tsp. caraway seeds

½ Tbs. Hungarian sweet paprika
Salt and black pepper to taste
1 cup dry white wine
2 lbs. sauerkraut
2 Tbs. flour
1 pint sour cream

*Serves 6–8*

Cut meat in 2″ pieces. (Saw the pork ribs or have your butcher do it.)

Melt fat in a dutch oven and cook onions until yellow and soft—about 5–10 minutes. Add meat, garlic, caraway seeds, paprika, salt and pepper. Cover with white wine and simmer for 1 hour.

Add the sauerkraut and a little more white wine if needed and cook for another ½ hour or until meat is tender, stirring occasionally.

Blend flour and sour cream, add to the *gulyás* and simmer for 5 more minutes. Never allow it to boil.

Serve with buttered noodles.

## POT ROAST ESTERHAZY

2 lbs. flank steak or top round or
  stewing beef
1 cup flour, seasoned with
  salt and pepper
3 Tbs. bacon fat or cooking oil
1 small red onion, chopped

2 tsp. Hungarian sweet paprika
Salt and pepper to taste
1 carrot, diced
2 sprigs parsley
2 cups Beef Stock (p. 183)
4 Tbs. sour cream

*Serves 4–6*

Cut beef into thin slices and pound well with a meat hammer. Dredge in flour. Melt the fat in a saucepan and fry the meat over brisk heat for about 5 minutes on each side.

Remove meat and in the same fat fry the onion until golden—about 5 minutes. Sprinkle with paprika, replace meat and add salt, pepper, carrot and parsley. Add 1 cup of the beef stock and cover. Cook very slowly, moistening occasionally with the remaining stock if necessary.

When meat is tender—about 1 hour—remove to a heated platter. Strain gravy and blend in the sour cream. Pour this back over the meat slices.

# IRISH

## IRISH SODA BREAD

1 lb. flour  
½ tsp. salt  

½ tsp. baking soda  
½ pint buttermilk or sour milk  

*Serves 6*

Sift flour, salt and baking soda into a bowl. Mix to a loose dough with the milk.

Turn out onto a floured board and knead lightly until the underside is smooth. Turn the smooth side up. Place in a preheated, greased 8″ cast-iron pot.

Make a cross on top with a knife. Cover with a lid. Bake in a hot oven (400°) for about 40 minutes.

# IRISH STEW

| | |
|---|---|
| 2 lbs. mutton or lamb chops | Salt and white pepper to taste |
| 2 lbs. white potatoes | 1 pint water |
| 5 medium onions | 1 tsp. chopped parsley |

*Serves 4–6*

Cut the meat into small pieces, removing the skin and fat. Do not remove all fat, because the potatoes will absorb a certain amount.

Put the meat in the bottom of a heavy pot. Cube the potatoes and the onions and add half of them to the pot. Season with salt and pepper. Add water, bring to a boil and skim. Simmer for 1 hour.

Arrange the remainder of the potatoes and onions on top and cover. Simmer for ½ hour or until meat is tender.

When thoroughly cooked, place meat pieces on a heated platter, arrange vegetables around them and pour some of the sauce over all, reserving the rest for a sauceboat.

Garnish with chopped parsley.

# MARY'S TAVERN OYSTER STEW

| | |
|---|---|
| 4 dozen oysters and their juices | 1 pint milk |
| 4 Tbs. butter | ½ cup coarse white-bread crumbs |
| Salt and white pepper to taste | ½ tsp. Tabasco pepper sauce |
| ½ tsp. paprika | Juice of 1 lemon |
| 1 bay leaf | ¼ cup chopped parsley |

*Serves 6*

Shuck oysters and reserve the juices. Put butter in a saucepan and melt. When it begins to sizzle, add the oysters and cook for 3 minutes. Season with salt, pepper, paprika and bay leaf. Mix well.

Add the milk and the oyster juices. Cook for a few more minutes, just to the boiling point.

Thicken with the bread crumbs. Remove the bay leaf and correct seasonings with salt, pepper and Tabasco. Lastly, add the lemon juice and the chopped parsley.

Serve with crisp bread.

# ITALIAN

## BOLOGNESE MEAT SAUCE

¼ cup butter
⅓ cup diced bacon or salt pork
1 onion, finely chopped
1 carrot, diced
½ cup chopped celery
½ lb. ground lean pork
¼ lb. ground lean beef
¼ lb. ground smoked ham

2 Tbs. dried mushrooms,
    soaked in water for 1 hour
1 Tbs. tomato purée
½ tsp. dried oregano
⅔ cup Beef Stock (p. 183)
⅔ cup dry red wine
4 Tbs. hot cream or milk
Salt and freshly ground black
    pepper to taste

*Serves 4*

Melt butter in a large, heavy pan; add the diced bacon and cook until it is transparent—about 5–10 minutes. Add the onion, carrot and celery and cook over moderate heat, stirring, for about 5 minutes.

Add the ground meats one at a time. Increase heat and sauté, stirring, until the meats are lightly browned.

Drain the mushrooms and chop. Add the mushrooms, tomato purée, oregano, stock and wine and bring to a boil.

Lower the heat, cover the pot and simmer gently for 40 minutes. Stir occasionally.

Finally, add the hot cream or milk. Correct for salt and pepper. Bring sauce to a boil once again and cook for another 5 minutes, stirring until the cream has blended with all the other ingredients.

Serve with your favorite pasta.

## MOZZARELLA SANDWICHES

8 large slices white bread
4 thick slices mozzarella cheese
2 eggs
2 Tbs. milk

Pinch of salt
½ cup flour
²/₃ cup olive oil

*Serves 4*

Trim the crust from the bread slices and make sandwiches with the mozzarella cheese. Dip edges of the bread in cold water for a second and press them together to seal the cheese.

Beat the eggs with milk and a pinch of salt. Dust the sandwiches very lightly with the flour. Soak them thoroughly in the egg mixture and fry them in hot oil a few at a time until golden—about 5 minutes on each side.

Drain sandwiches on paper toweling and serve immediately.

## SPAGHETTI CARBONARA

1 lb. spaghetti
²/₃ cup diced bacon
1 Tbs. olive oil
4 eggs
2 Tbs. light cream

Salt and freshly ground black
    pepper
³/₄ cup freshly grated Parmesan
    cheese

*Serves 4*

Boil the spaghetti in a large pan of salted water until it is cooked through but still firm to the bite—about 10–12 minutes.

Fry the bacon gently in the oil until done and reserve.

In a large tureen, beat the eggs with the cream. Add salt and pepper to taste and the grated cheese.

Drain the cooked spaghetti thoroughly and immediately toss it with the egg-cheese mixture. The heat of the pasta will cook the sauce.

Add the drained, hot bacon bits. Toss again and serve immediately with more cheese on the side.

# STUFFED PEACHES

6 large peaches, not too ripe
½ cup sweet almonds or pecans
3 bitter almonds
¼ cup sugar
4 small ladyfingers or the
   equivalent in sponge cake

1 strip candied lemon or
   orange peel
½ cup sweet white wine
Fresh mint leaves

*Serves 6*

Blanch the peaches long enough to remove the skins easily—about 10 minutes in boiling water. Peel. Cool, cut in half and remove stones. Also remove some of the peach pulp and reserve. This will allow more room for the stuffing.

Pound the nutmeats in a mortar with half the sugar and then place in a bowl. Finely chop the cake and candied fruit and add, along with the peach pulp. Blend well.

Fill the peach halves with this mixture; then put the halves together so they look whole again.

Place in a buttered baking dish, pour the wine over them, sprinkle generously with the remaining sugar and cook in a moderate oven (350°) for about 10 minutes. The sugar should form a crust over the peaches.

Serve hot or cold and garnish with fresh mint leaves.

# VEAL MARCELLO

8 small veal scallops
4 large, or 8 small, very thin
   slices smoked ham or prosciutto
Salt and white pepper to taste
8 fresh sage leaves

6 Tbs. butter
4 Tbs. dry white wine
   or dry Marsala
Chopped parsley
Lemon wedges

*Serves 4*

Pound the veal until each piece is very thin. Trim the slices of ham to about the same size as the veal.

Sprinkle each piece of veal with very little salt and white pepper. Lay a sage leaf on it and cover with the slice of ham. The little sandwiches may be secured with a toothpick. Do not roll up.

Heat 3 Tbs. of the butter in a frying pan until foaming. Sauté the sandwiches briskly for 6–8 minutes on each side or until they are cooked through and golden. Transfer them to a heated platter and keep warm.

Add the dry white wine or dry Marsala to the butter and juices remaining in the pan and bring to a boil, scraping the bottom of the pan. Stir in the remaining butter and spoon the hot sauce over the veal.

Garnish with chopped parsley and lemon wedges.

# JAPANESE

## CHICKEN SUKIYAKI

1 Tbs. butter or chicken fat
1 bunch green onions,
   cut in 1″ pieces
1 Tbs. soy sauce
2 Tbs. sugar
1 cup raw white meat
   from breast of chicken,
   cut in julienne strips
2 cups sliced celery

1 cup thinly sliced water
   chestnuts
1 cup thinly sliced bamboo shoots
1 cup sliced mushrooms
¼ lb. young, fresh spinach
   leaves, well washed
2 squares bean curd (optional)
½ cup chicken broth, sherry or
   rice wine

*Serves 4*

In a heavy pan melt butter or fat and cook green onions over high heat for about 5 minutes. Sprinkle with soy sauce and sugar. Toss.

Add all remaining ingredients except broth or wine. Toss again.

Reduce heat to moderate. Cook for 4–5 minutes, adding wine or broth as needed to prevent mixture from becoming too dry. There should be very little liquid in the pan.

Serve hot with fluffy white rice.

# FISH AND VEGETABLE TEMPURA

*Batter:*
> 1 cup ice water
> 1½ cups all-purpose flour
> 1 large egg

*Fish and vegetables:*
> 1½ lbs. fresh fish, shellfish or
> vegetables, or a combination
> 2 cups vegetable oil

*Serves 6*

*To make batter:* Gradually stir the ice water into the flour. Blend well. Add the egg, blend again and reserve.

*To cook fish and vegetables:* Cut the fish, shellfish and/or vegetables into small pieces.

In a large saucepan, heat the vegetable oil. Test to see if it's ready by dropping in a bit of the batter. If it sinks and then rises rapidly to the surface, the temperature is right.

Dip the fish and vegetable pieces into the batter and fry for 3–5 minutes.

Maintain the same temperature throughout the cooking of the tempura, removing any extra pieces of batter.

# SASHIMI

> 1 lb. fresh, ice-cold, paper-thin
> slices of redfish or raw tuna
> (fish must be firm)
> 2 daikon radishes, shredded

> ½ cup Japanese soy sauce
> Pinch of English mustard
> Gratings of fresh ginger

*Serves 4*

Arrange paper-thin slices of fish on a bed of daikon radish.

Thoroughly mix the soy sauce, mustard and gratings of ginger in a separate bowl.

With a fork or chopsticks, dip small pieces of the fish into the sauce and eat with daikon radish.

I find this better than an olive to accompany a martini.

## VINEGARED SEAFOOD

*Dressing:*
    6 Tbs. su (rice vinegar)
    2 Tbs. sugar

    1–2 tsp. shoyu
      (Japanese soy sauce)
    Salt to taste

*Seafood salad:*
    ½ lb. scallops
    ½ daikon (Japanese radish),
      finely grated
    1 large carrot, finely grated
    ½ cucumber,
      cut in julienne strips

    ½ lb. green beans,
      cut in 2″ lengths and
      blanched for 10 minutes
    1–1½ lbs. spinach or broccoli,
      blanched and well drained
    ½ lb. cooked shrimp (p. 247),
      cut into pieces
    Dried bonito flakes

*Serves 4*

*To make the dresing:* Combine the su, sugar, shoyu and a little salt in a small bowl. Mix well.

*To cook and serve:* Cook scallops in salted water for 10–15 minutes. Drain, shred and combine with vegetables and shrimp, dividing the mixture into 4 bowls.

Pour a little of the dressing over each bowl. A few dried bonito flakes may be sprinkled over each bowl to add texture and a subtle flavor.

# JEWISH

## CARP IN THE JEWISH STYLE

    1 large or 2 small carp (4–5 lbs.),
      cleaned and washed
    1¼ cups olive oil
    2 large onions, chopped
    4 green onions, chopped
    2 Tbs. flour
    1 Tbs. sugar (more if needed)

    7½–8 cups water
      or Fish Stock (p. 184)
    1 Tbs. vinegar
    1 Bouquet Garni (chap. 13)
    ½ cup raisins
    1 cup halved blanched almonds
    Salt and freshly ground black
      pepper to taste

*Serves 6–8*

If the fish is large, cut it into thick slices. If small, leave whole. Place the fish on the perforated tray of a fish kettle or steamer.

Heat the oil in a saucepan. Add the onions and green onions and fry lightly, stirring until they begin to turn golden—about 10–15 minutes. Stir in the flour, sugar and 7½ cups of the water or stock. Add the vinegar, bouquet garni, raisins, almonds, salt and pepper. Bring the mixture to a boil and pour it over the fish. If the sauce does not cover the fish, add more water or stock.

Cover the steamer and simmer the fish until it is cooked—about ½ hour. Transfer the fish carefully to a deep dish.

Increase the heat and boil the sauce down until it has a good strong flavor. Correct the seasonings for salt and pepper and more sugar if needed.

Pour the sauce over the carp and set aside to cool.

Serve the fish chilled.

## GEFILTE FISH

| | |
|---|---|
| 3 lbs. fish (pike and whitefish or pike and carp) | 1 tsp. black pepper |
| | Pinch of sugar |
| 1 stalk celery | 2 Tbs. matzoh meal |
| 1 carrot | 1 egg |
| 2 onions | 2 quarts Fish Stock (p. 184) |
| 1 tsp. salt | 2 Tbs. gelatine |

*Serves 6*

Clean and wash fish thoroughly. Filet the fish, reserve the filets and put the bones and heads in a heavy kettle.

Dice celery, carrot and 1 onion and add to the kettle.

Cover to about 2" above contents with cold water. Season with salt, pepper and sugar. Bring to a boil. Cook for 1 hour.

Meanwhile, grind the filets. Chop the remaining onion and blend with filets in a wooden bowl, adding the matzoh meal and the egg. Beat until the mixture is stiff.

With fingers dipped in cold water, form mixture into little oval cakes. Drop each gently into rapidly boiling fish stock.

Reduce heat and cook them gently for 1½–2 hours, shaking the pot occasionally to keep the fish cakes separate. Allow them to cool before removing from the pot.

Chill thoroughly. You may combine 2 cups of the stock, strained, with the gelatine and allow to set in refrigerator. Cut up for garnish surrounding the fish.

## NOODLE AND CHEESE PUDDING

1 lb. thin noodles
4 eggs, separated
1 cup sugar
1 small can evaporated milk

1 lb. cream cheese
1 pint sour cream
½ lb. butter or margarine, melted
1 tsp. vanilla

*Serves 6*

Cook noodles according to directions on package. Drain well.

Beat egg yolks with sugar until thick and lemon-colored—about 5 minutes. Add milk, cream cheese, sour cream, melted butter and vanilla to egg yolks and beat until thoroughly mixed.

Beat egg whites until stiff. Add egg-yolk mixture to cooked noodles. Fold in beaten egg whites. Mix thoroughly.

Grease and lightly flour a deep pan. Bake for 1 hour at 350° until lightly browned on top.

This dish may be made in advance and simply reheated.

# RUSSIAN

## BLINI
### Russian Pancakes

1 envelope granulated yeast
1½ pints milk
³/₄ lb. buckwheat flour

3 eggs, separated
Pinch of salt
½ cup cooking oil

*Serves 4–6*

Dissolve the yeast in ½ pint of the warm milk and make a dough with a little of the flour. Let stand in a warm place for 2 hours.

Now add the rest of the flour, the egg yolks, salt and remaining warm milk. Mix thoroughly but do not overmix or the batter will get too thick.

Lastly, add the egg whites, beaten to a stiff froth; let stand for another ½ hour.

Lightly oil a very small skillet* and heat, being careful not to let it get too hot. Pour in batter until surface of the pan is thinly covered. Cook about 3 minutes on one side, then slip over and cook about 3 minutes again or until golden. Keep hot in a warm oven until ready to serve.

These are very often served with caviar and sour cream. They are best served with any kind of savory.

*Some gourmet shops now carry special blini pans.

# VEAL WITH CAVIAR SAUCE

*Stewed veal:*

| | |
|---|---|
| 2 lbs. filet of veal, larded | Rind of 1 lemon |
| 1 cup Veal Stock (p. 185) | A few whole cloves |
| 1 cup dry white wine | Salt and black pepper to taste |
| 1 bay leaf | |

*Caviar sauce:*

| | |
|---|---|
| 1 cup stewing liquid from veal, skimmed and strained | Juice of 1 lemon |
| 4–5 Tbs. fresh caviar | 4 Tbs. unsalted butter, in a lump |

*Serves 4–6*

Stew the veal in a mixture of the remaining veal ingredients for 1 hour, until tender.

To make the sauce, put the stewing liquid in a saucepan and add the caviar and a little of the lemon juice. Stir well and simmer for a few minutes. Finally, add the lump of butter just before serving, and the rest of the lemon juice, if needed for taste.

Slice the veal, cover with the sauce and serve.

# SCANDINAVIAN

## FISH MOUSSE

2½ lbs. fresh haddock,*
   skinned and boned
1¼ cups butter
4 eggs, separated
½ cup cream

½ cup flour
½ Tbs. salt
½ tsp. white pepper
Pinch of sugar
Bread crumbs

*Serves 4–6*

Dry fish and grind with butter in a food grinder at least 3 times. Then pound in a mortar until you have a smooth and creamy paste.

Mix the egg yolks in a bowl with half the cream, adding the flour, salt, pepper and the sugar. Alternately mix in the fish and the rest of the cream and work very well. This will take some time—about ½ hour or so.

Finally add the stiffly beaten egg whites and pour mixture into a buttered 1½-quart soufflé dish or pie dish. Top with bread crumbs.

Place dish in a pan of hot water and steam the mousse for 1 hour in a moderate oven (350°). Serve it with either Lobster Sauce (below) or Mushroom Sauce (p. 177).

*In New Orleans, redfish or trout may be substituted for the haddock.

## LOBSTER SAUCE

2 Tbs. butter
2 Tbs. flour
1 cup Fish Stock (p. 184)

Salt and white pepper to taste
1 cup finely grated cooked lobster
   meat (p. 247)
1 egg yolk

*Yields 1–1½ cups*

In a small saucepan melt butter and then stir in flour, being careful not to brown. Add fish stock, stirring constantly. Season with salt and pepper.

When sauce thickens, add the grated lobster meat and finally the egg yolk, which has been previously beaten with a little of the hot sauce.

If sauce is too thick, add a little more fish stock.

# MUSHROOM SAUCE

1 cup finely chopped mushrooms          2 Tbs. flour
1 cup water                             Salt and white pepper to taste
2 Tbs. butter                           1 egg yolk

*Yields 1–1½ cups*

Boil mushrooms in 1 cup water for about 5–10 minutes. Drain and reserve mushroom water. Chop mushrooms.

In a saucepan, melt butter and add flour. Add the mushroom water, stirring constantly. Season with salt and pepper.

When sauce thickens, add chopped mushrooms and the egg yolk, which has been previously beaten with a little of the mushroom water.

If sauce is too thick, add a little hot water.

# SOUR PICKLED HERRING

3 large herring,                        1 tsp. peppercorns
  skinned and boned                     2–3 bay leaves, crumbled
1 cup water mixed with                  Sprig of dill, chopped
  1 cup milk                            1 pint vinegar mixed with
3 white onions, thinly sliced             ¾ Tbs. sugar

*Serves 6*

Soak the herring filets in the water-milk mixture for 6 hours.

Dry thoroughly and cut in slices crosswise, working from the tail end. Put alternate layers of herring and thinly sliced onions in a glass jar. Sprinkle peppercorns, bay leaves and dill in between layers.

Cover with the cold vinegar-sugar mixture.

Seal and refrigerate. The herring is ready to eat in 24 hours.

# SOUTH AMERICAN

## CHILEAN SAUCE

½ cup plus 1 Tbs. olive oil
2 cups Beef Stock (p. 183)
1 medium onion, finely chopped
2 medium tomatoes, blanched,
  peeled and chopped

Juice of 2 lemons
Salt and freshly ground black
  pepper to taste
½ tsp. Tabasco pepper sauce

*Yields 2 cups*

In a saucepan, combine the 1 Tbs. of oil, stock and onion and simmer until the onion is tender—about 10 minutes. Push through a strainer and set to one side.

Purée the tomatoes in an electric blender or a food mill. In the original saucepan cook the tomato purée until it is thick—about 25 minutes. Now mix in the onion-stock mixture, lemon juice, salt, pepper and Tabasco.

Gradually beat in the ½ cup olive oil. The sauce should be thick. Beat in more oil if necessary.

Serve with omelets, steaks or fish.

## FEIJOADA
### Brazilian Black Beans

4 cups black beans
1 lb. beef jerky or dried beef
3 Tbs. lard or bacon grease
3 medium onions, chopped
3 cloves garlic, chopped
1 lb. Portuguese linguica sausage
  or Polish sausage
1 lb. blood sausage or chorizo
½ lb. salt pork or lean bacon or
  pickled pork
1 lb. fresh pork sausages
1 lb. chuck beef,
  cut into 1″ cubes
1–2 pigs' feet (optional)

1–2 pigs' ears (optional)
1 lb. pork tenderloin,
  cut into 1″ cubes
1 bay leaf
1 hot red chili pepper,
  seeded and chopped
  (or ¼ tsp. Tabasco pepper
  sauce)
Salt to taste
2 lbs. kale or collard greens
¼ lb. raw bacon, diced
4–5 cups rice, boiled
4–6 oranges, peeled and sliced
2 cups cassava (manioc) meal

*Serves 8–10*

Cover beans with water and soak overnight. Soak beef jerky in water overnight.

Place beans in a large kettle with the same soaking water and simmer for 2 hours.

Melt the lard or bacon grease and fry the onions and garlic until tender but not browned—about 10 minutes. Add this to the beans.

Simmer the linguica, blood sausage and salt pork in water to cover for 15 minutes. Add pork sausages and simmer for another 15 minutes. Drain and set to one side.

Drain beef jerky, combine with all the above meats and add to the bean mixture.

Next add the cubed beef, the pigs' feet and ears and the pork tenderloin.

Add bay leaf and chili pepper or Tabasco. Simmer 1 hour longer or until meat and beans are tender. Taste for salt.

Meanwhile, wash kale thoroughly and dry. Remove and discard stems, shred leaves and combine with diced bacon. Sauté kale for about 15 minutes or until tender. Taste for salt.

Arrange beans and meats on a large platter and top with kale. Then sprinkle with the cassava meal, which has been browned in a large frying pan over low heat. In areas where this is not available, omit from recipe.

Surround with boiled rice and garnish with sliced oranges.

# SPANISH

## DULCE DE LECHE

1 quart milk
1 cup sugar

1 tsp. vanilla extract
¼ tsp. baking soda

*Yields 1 quart*

Combine all ingredients in a heavy saucepan and bring to just under the boiling point.

Cook over very low heat, stirring occasionally, until the mixture begins to thicken; then stir constantly until the mixture is thick—about 15–20 minutes.

Good with pound cake.

# PAELLA VALENCIANA

½ cup butter
2 young chickens (legs, thighs
    and breasts cut in half)
½ lb. lean loin of pork, cubed
1 clove garlic, crushed
2 cups raw long grain rice
½–1 tsp. saffron
4–5 cups hot Chicken Stock
    (p. 183)
12 chunks lobster meat,
    cooked (p. 247) or uncooked

1 dozen shelled shrimp, uncooked
1 raw redfish steak,
    cut into pieces
1 chorizo (sausage),
    sliced and quartered
½ cup diced pimientos
1 dozen fresh clams
    in their shells*
Extra strips of pimiento
    for garnish

*Serves 6*

Melt butter in a heavy skillet. Sauté the chicken pieces, pork cubes and garlic for about 15 minutes, until golden brown. Remove and set to one side.

In the juices remaining in the pan, sauté the raw rice until it is golden. Add saffron and 4 cups of the hot chicken stock and cook over a very low fire until all the liquid is absorbed—about 25 minutes. The rice will be only partially cooked.

Butter the bottom and sides of a paella pan or a deep casserole. Put half the pieces of chicken and pork in the casserole and cover with half the cut-up pieces of lobster meat, shrimp, redfish, chorizo and diced pimientos.

Add almost all of the rice and top with the remaining pieces of chicken and pork. Add the other ingredients to cover the chicken exactly as before. Add the rest of the rice and bake the paella, covered, in a moderate oven (350°) for 45 minutes, adding a little of the remaining chicken stock from time to time, if needed.

The last 15 minutes, arrange clams in their shells on top of the paella, and they will pop open and cook.

Garnish with strips of pimiento and serve from the paella pan with garlic bread and a tossed green salad.

*If you can't obtain clams, you may substitute oysters.

PART TWO
# BLAKE'S BASICS

# 6
# SOUPS

THE FAMILY soup kettle or pot, so important all over the world, is no less respected, loved and needed in New Orleans. From red bean soup to the many, many gumbos, New Orleans has become famous for its own soups and potages. It has also incorporated those from other places.

Because so many of us today depend on canned, frozen and dried soup mixtures, we have not been able to enjoy the wonderful romance of preparing a soup from scratch. I defy any of these modern concoctions to rival the first homemade soups that came steaming from a peasant's kitchen. With all due respect to convenience, let us not forget the noble soup, its method of preparation and its infinite potential for variations on a theme.

To my mind, all soups, great and modest, depend upon the stock from which they are made. Beef, chicken, veal or fish stocks are the ABCs of many a soup, including the ones found in this collection.

These soups have been selected with an eye to variety, ease of preparation and, in some cases, economy. Any number of them can serve as a first course or a main course for lunch or dinner. And don't overlook a bowl or a cup of good soup for breakfast.

Prince Curnonsky, that prince of gastronomes, is said to have insisted on tasting a cup of clear chicken consommé in a restaurant before ordering a meal. If that passed the test, then he proceeded. While his cup of soup may not be yours, I'm sure you'll find many in this chapter to suit your taste.

# STOCKS

## BEEF STOCK

½ bunch celery tops
½ bunch parsley
3 carrots
1 bay leaf
2 large onions,
    studded with 3 cloves each
½ cup Kitchen Bouquet

5 lbs. good beef bones,
    marrowbones included
3 lbs. lean brisket of beef or
    chuck or short ribs
1 Tbs. salt
1 tsp. black pepper
Water to cover

*Yields 5–6 quarts*

Tie celery tops, parsley, carrots and bay leaf with a string. Place all ingredients in a large stockpot (8–10 quarts) and cover with water.

Bring to a boil and then skim off all impurities. Reduce heat and simmer for 5–6 hours, adding more water if necessary.

When finished, strain, taste for salt and pepper and allow to cool.

Refrigerate overnight and skim off all the fat the next day. Heat gently and strain once again through a sieve or cheesecloth. Cool and store in plastic jars.

This freezes very well and is essential to any beef-base soups or brown sauces. The beef itself may be used for your favorite recipe.

## CHICKEN STOCK

½ bunch celery tops
½ bunch parsley
2 large carrots
1 bay leaf
2 large onions,
    studded with 3 cloves each

6 chicken bouillon cubes
5 lbs. chicken,
    backs and wings only
1 Tbs. salt
1 tsp. white pepper
Water to cover

*Yields 5–6 quarts*

Tie celery, parsley, carrots and bay leaf with a string. Place all ingredients in a good stockpot (6–8 quarts). Cover with water and bring to a boil. Skim off impurities, reduce heat and simmer for 2–3 hours, adding more water when necessary.

When finished, taste for salt and pepper again. Strain, allow to cool and keep refrigerated overnight. Next day, skim off all the fat. Heat again and strain through a fine sieve or cheesecloth. Allow to cool.

This stock will freeze and is essential to any chicken-base soups or white sauces which require a chicken stock. Also great for cooking certain vegetables such as carrots, broccoli, potatoes and even rice.

## FISH STOCK

2 lbs. bones and heads from any
    fresh fish (you may mix any
    fish)
2 quarts water
1 lemon, sectioned
1 bay leaf

2–3 sprigs parsley
1 medium onion, chopped
1 medium carrot, peeled and
    sliced
½ tsp. chervil
Salt and pepper to taste

*Yields 2 quarts*

Place bones and heads in a heavy soup kettle. Cover with about 2 quarts of water and add all other ingredients. Bring to a boil slowly, skimming constantly. Reduce heat to moderate and cook for about 1 hour. Strain once or twice.

Leftover stock may be frozen and saved, but I don't recommend keeping the stock frozen for a long period of time.

*NOTE:* For stock made from shellfish, which I call "swamp water," simply use the shells and heads of shrimp or other shellfish and follow the same amounts and directions as above.

## FISH VELOUTÉ BASE FOR SHELLFISH BISQUES

Bones and trimmings of 6 white-
    fleshed fish
2 quarts water
1 cup dry white wine
1 carrot, sliced
1 onion, sliced
1 bay leaf

Pinch of thyme
2 sprigs parsley
8 peppercorns
Salt to taste
¾ cup flour*
¼ cup butter

*Yields 2 good quarts*

In a heavy saucepan, place all the fish trimmings and cover with the water. Add the wine and all other ingredients except flour and butter. Bring the mixture to a boil and simmer for 30 minutes, skimming as necessary.

In another saucepan, melt the butter and stir in the flour. Cook this roux, stirring constantly until the mixture begins to turn golden. Now strain the fish stock into the roux, stirring until the *velouté* is thick and smooth. Cook it for 20 minutes longer, stirring occasionally and skimming as necessary. Strain the *velouté* through a fine sieve or cheesecloth.

Keep refrigerated or freeze.

\* Rice flour is used traditionally.

## VEAL STOCK

| | |
|---|---|
| 6 lbs. shoulder of veal | 2 medium onions |
| 1/3 cup shortening | 1 large Bouquet Garni (chap. 13) |
| 5 lbs. veal knuckles | 7 quarts Chicken Stock (p. 183) |
| 2 lbs. veal bones | 1 Tbs. salt (or salt to taste) |
| 2 large carrots | White pepper to taste |

*Yields about 3 quarts*

Tie up meat with a string and coat it with shortening. Brown on all sides on top of the stove.

Crush the knuckles and bones, peel and slice carrots and onions, and put all in the bottom of a 10-quart saucepan along with the bouquet garni. Top with browned meat. Cover and let stand 15 minutes.

Add 2 quarts of the chicken stock and the salt and pepper. Simmer 1 hour, having the pot partially covered with lid. Add remaining stock. Bring to the boiling point; skim off scum from surface. Reduce heat and simmer 5 hours.

Remove meat and bones from the stock, strain through a fine sieve or cheesecloth and skim off fat. Or store overnight in refrigerater and remove fat the next day.

This freezes well. Use for making thin veal gravy or brown sauces, for braising vegetables and red meats, for making consommés or anything that calls for veal stock.

# BEEF SOUPS

## GOULASH SOUP

2 lbs. shin beef
6 medium potatoes
4 Tbs. ham fat
2 medium red onions, chopped

4–5 heaping Tbs. Hungarian
    sweet paprika
Salt and pepper to taste
1–2 cups hot water

*Serves 8–10*

Cut beef into small cubes. Peel and cut the potatoes as for thick french fries. Melt and render the ham fat.

In a heavy pot, fry the onions in ham fat until golden in color. Blend in paprika and add the meat immediately. Fry the meat slightly, stirring constantly so that the pieces are well coated with the paprika.

Add salt and pepper. Reduce heat. Add a cup of the water and cover the pot with a lid. Cook, adding a little of the rest of the water from time to time.

When the meat just begins to feel fork tender and there is enough liquid to cover, add the potatoes and continue cooking, covered, until the potatoes are tender but not falling apart.

NOTE: This can be prepared the night before and simply reheated. It gets better the longer you keep it, as much as a week. The potatoes are the thickening agents.

## OXTAIL SOUP

2½ lbs. oxtail
½ lb. beef suet
1 cup sliced onions
2 cups sliced carrots
2 Tbs. flour
2 quarts plus 1 cup Beef Stock
    (p. 183)
1 cup sliced white part of leeks or
    scallions

½ tsp. dried basil
½ tsp. dried marjoram
½ tsp. dried rosemary
½ tsp. sage
Salt and pepper to taste
8 Tbs. port

*Serves 8*

Cut oxtail meat into 2″ pieces. Brown these pieces in the beef suet along with the onions and carrots. Sprinkle all this with flour. Stir and cook until flour has browned.

Add the 2 quarts beef stock and leeks or scallions. Cover and simmer for 2 hours. Strain the soup through a fine sieve. (It should be full-bodied and gelatinous.)

Steep all the herbs together in the 1 cup beef stock in a pot for 10 minutes. Then strain through a fine sieve into the soup. Season for salt and pepper.

Divide the oxtail meat and place on the bottom of each serving dish. Pour the hot soup over the meat and at the last minute splash 1 Tbs. of port into each serving dish.

## PETITE MARMITE

| | |
|---|---|
| 2 lbs. chicken backs and necks | 1 cup thinly sliced carrots |
| 1 lb. brisket of beef | 1 cup diced turnips |
| 1 lb. beef ribs | ¼ cup diced celery |
| 1 stalk celery | 1 cup shredded cabbage |
| 1 large onion, whole | Salt and pepper to taste |
| 2 quarts Beef Stock (p. 183) | |

*Serves 6*

Lightly brown the chicken pieces in a moderate oven (375°). Drain off the fat and discard. Put chicken pieces in a 4-quart saucepan. Add brisket, ribs, celery, onion and beef stock. Cover. Slowly bring to a boil. Reduce heat and simmer 1½ hours, skimming as necessary.

Remove from fire and discard onion and celery. Pick meat from chicken bones and beef ribs and cut beef brisket into ½" squares. Set to one side.

Skim broth; bring to the boiling point. Add carrots, turnips, diced celery. Cover and cook 15 minutes longer or until vegetables are tender. Add cabbage and meat. Cover and cook 5 minutes or until cabbage is tender but still crisp. Taste for salt and pepper.

Serve from an earthenware casserole accompanied by croutons of French bread.

# CHICKEN SOUPS

## COCKALEEKIE

18 dried prunes
2 cups Chicken Stock (p. 183)
4 cups sliced white parts of leeks
4½ cups boiling water
1½ tsp. salt

4 peppercorns
2 cups cooked white chicken
  meat, cut in julienne
2 Tbs. butter or chicken fat

*Serves 6*

Soak the dried prunes in the chicken stock for 1 hour and then cook for 15–20 minutes or until tender. Drain prunes and reserve chicken stock.

Cook the leeks for 5 minutes, or until they are soft, in 2 cups of the boiling water with the salt. Drain and reserve leeks.

Combine the reserved chicken stock and the remaining 2½ cups boiling water. Add peppercorns. Cover and bring to a boil.

Reduce heat; add chicken juliennes that have been sautéed in the butter or chicken fat. Add leeks. Adjust seasonings.

Serve hot with 3 prunes added to each serving.

## COLD SENEGALESE

3½ cups Chicken Stock (p. 183)
1 cup finely chopped chicken
  meat, cooked
½ tsp. good curry powder

4 egg yolks
2 cups heavy cream
Salt and pepper
Shredded chicken

*Serves 4–6*

In a heavy saucepan, bring the chicken stock to a boil and add the chopped chicken pieces. Stir in the curry powder, using more to taste.

Beat the egg yolks, stir in a little of the hot chicken stock and blend well with the cream. Gradually add this to the chicken stock, stirring constantly over low heat until the soup just begins to thicken. Be careful not to allow the eggs to curdle.

Taste for salt, pepper and extra curry if you wish. Cool and refrigerate. Serve cold with shredded chicken for garnish.

# WAR OF 1812 SOUP

1 tsp. finely chopped onion
1 Tbs. butter
½ cup chopped mushrooms
1 cup diced celery
4 cups Chicken Stock (p. 183)
1 Tbs. quick tapioca
½ cup diced chicken, cooked

½ cup diced ham, cooked
Sage, nutmeg and onion salt
  to taste
½ tsp. Tabasco pepper sauce
2 hard-boiled eggs, chopped
2 cups cream
Chopped parsley

*Serves 8*

Sauté onion in butter until tender. Add mushrooms and celery; cook for 10 minutes. Stir in chicken stock, tapioca, chicken, ham and seasonings to taste. Cook for 20 minutes. Add chopped eggs and cream.

Serve in large bowls garnished with chopped parsley.

# FISH AND SHELLFISH SOUPS

## BRITTANY BOUILLABAISSE

1 stick butter
1 large white onion, chopped
1 large white potato, cubed
1 large carrot, cubed
5 cups heated Fish Stock (p. 184)
¼ cup parsley, chopped

¼ cup fresh mint, finely chopped
Salt and white pepper to taste
2 lbs. fresh filets—such as a
  combination of flounder,
  pompano, salmon, halibut—
  cubed

*Serves 6*

In a large saucepan, melt butter. Add onion, potato and carrot and cook until tender but not falling apart. Add the hot fish stock with the parsley and mint and continue cooking for about 10 minutes. Taste for salt and pepper.

Reduce the heat to a simmer and add the cubed fish a little at a time. Cook just long enough so that the fish cubes are done but not falling apart—approximately 10 minutes.

Serve immediately with hot bread.

## CRAB MEAT BISQUE

1 lb. fresh crab meat,
   picked and cleaned
2 Tbs. boiled rice
5 cups Chicken Stock (p. 183)
2 egg yolks

2 Tbs. Calvados, applejack or
   brandy
Salt and white pepper to taste
6 cooked shrimp (p. 247)
2 Tbs. butter
4 Tbs. flour

*Serves 4–6*

Pound crab meat with a mortar and pestle or put through a blender until very fine. To ease the chopping or pounding, add the boiled rice and a small amount of the chicken stock.

Place the crab meat mixture in a heavy saucepan and add the rest of the chicken stock. Bring to a boil, remove from heat and stir in the 2 egg yolks beaten with the 2 Tbs. of liquor.

Return to the fire and heat without boiling. Season with salt and white pepper.

Make a shrimp butter by pounding the shrimp until they are a paste and blending them with 2 Tbs. butter. Knead shrimp butter with 4 Tbs. flour and add to bisque to thicken.

Serve hot with any of these garnishes: a large crouton, a hot lump of crab meat or some chopped boiled peanuts (raw peanuts that have been boiled in their shells).

## CREOLE SHRIMP BISQUE

½ carrot, finely chopped
½ onion, finely chopped
2 sprigs parsley, finely chopped
Pinch of thyme
½ bay leaf
4 Tbs. butter

1 cup white wine
24 large shrimp, in their shells
2 quarts Fish *Velouté* Base (p. 184)
3 Tbs. cream
2 Tbs. brandy, sherry or Madeira
Tabasco pepper sauce

*Serves 4–6*

Make a mirepoix by stewing the carrot, onion, parsley, thyme and bay leaf in 2 Tbs. of the butter. Add the white wine, bring mixture to a boil and reduce heat.

In this mixture poach the shrimp for 8 minutes. Shell the shrimp and devein. Dice half the shrimp and reserve for garnish.

Crush the shells and the remaining shrimp in a mortar, or with a food chopper or blender. Combine this purée with the 2 quarts of *velouté* base and the liquid in which the shrimp were poached. Bring mixture to a boil and simmer for 20 minutes.

Strain the soup through a fine sieve and if it seems a bit too thick, add a little white wine. Strain it again through several thicknesses of cheesecloth.

At serving time, bring the bisque to the boiling point and finish with the remaining 2 Tbs. butter, the cream and the liquor. Garnish with the reserved shrimp and a few dashes of Tabasco pepper sauce.

## FISH BROTH

1½ lbs. pike or whiting
½ cup shredded white parts of
    leek
1 cup finely chopped mushroom
    stems

¼ cup finely chopped parsley
2 egg whites
2 cups dry white wine
1 quart Fish Stock (p. 184)
Salt and white pepper to taste

*Serves 6–8*

In a 4-quart saucepan, thoroughly mix the first 6 ingredients. Add the fish stock and simmer for 30 minutes. Cool and strain through 2 thicknesses of cheesecloth or through a very fine sieve.

Serve hot, seasoned to taste with salt and pepper. Accompany with thick slices of toasted French bread sprinkled with grated Parmesan cheese.

## LOBSTER SOUP

3 cups Fish *Velouté* Base (p. 184)
2 cups Béchamel Sauce
    (chap. 13)
½ cup fresh tomatoes,
    peeled, seeded and crushed
1 Tbs. tomato paste

1–1½ lb. lobster, enough to
    make ⅓ cup cooked lobster
    meat (p. 247) and coral, and
    extra for garnish
⅓ cup softened butter
Salt and white pepper to taste

*Serves 6*

Combine *velouté* base, béchamel, tomatoes and tomato paste in a 2-quart saucepan. Heat.

Pound and mash the lobster meat with the red coral and blend with the butter. Add this to the soup, mixing well. Season with salt and white pepper.

Serve hot, garnished with chunks of cooked lobster meat.

## NEPTUNE CHOWDER

6 Tbs. butter
3 oz. salt pork, finely diced
1 onion, finely chopped
1 clove garlic, minced
2 large potatoes, diced

½ lb. codfish, diced
3 oz. prawns
2–3 cups milk
Salt and pepper to taste
Chopped parsley

*Serves 4*

In a heavy saucepan, melt the butter and sauté the pork and onions until soft. Add the garlic. Add the potatoes, codfish and prawns. Cover with the milk. Bring to a boil and simmer gently for 30 minutes. Season for salt and pepper.

Sprinkle with chopped parsley and serve immediately with plain crackers.

## OYSTERS POINT LA HÂCHE

1 pint oysters
3 Tbs. butter
½ tsp. Worcestershire sauce
½ tsp. celery salt

½ cup liquor from oysters
½ cup clam juice
2 cups milk
Dash of paprika

*Serves 2*

Drain oysters, reserving the liquor.

Heat together 1½ Tbs. of the butter, the Worcestershire sauce and celery salt; bring to a boil. Add oysters and mixed oyster and clam liquors; heat until edges of oysters curl. Pour in milk and heat just to boiling.

When serving, add ¾ Tbs. butter and a dash of paprika to each bowl.

## POTAGE BELLE HÉLÈNE

60 raw medium shrimp with
   heads
⅔ stick butter
1 large onion, chopped
½ cup chopped parsley
6 Tbs. flour
1 can tomato sauce
1 Tbs. sugar

½ tsp. Tabasco pepper sauce
Salt and pepper to taste
12 ripe Creole tomatoes,
   peeled and cut into wedges
1 pint dry white wine
½ pint heavy cream
8 round pieces fried French bread

*Serves 8*

In a heavy soup pot, cook unseasoned shrimp until tender, using enough water to barely cover. Drain shrimp and reserve liquid.

Remove heads from the shrimp and return the heads to the liquid. Bring to a boil and simmer for ½ hour or so until a good shrimp stock is reached. Reserve at least 1 quart of this liquid for the soup; the rest can be frozen. I call this "swamp water."

Peel and devein the shrimp. In a heavy soup pot, melt butter and sauté the onions and parsley. Add about 30 shrimp and sauté for 10 more minutes. Add flour and stir well.

Add the can of tomato sauce, the sugar and Tabasco pepper sauce; salt and pepper to taste and squeeze all the fresh tomato wedges over this mixture.

Add a quart or a bit more of the shrimp stock and the white wine. Bring to a boil, reduce heat and simmer for 1 hour. Taste for salt and pepper.

Allow to cool; purée in a blender. Add cream and gently reheat until ready to serve hot.

Chop the remaining shrimp for garnish. Pile a spoonful of the hot chopped shrimp on a slice of fried French bread and top each bowl of soup with this garnish. Any leftover shrimp may be added to the potage while heating.

## POTAGE PONT BREAUX

| | |
|---|---|
| 7 cups Fish *Velouté* Base (p. 184) | ½ cup cooked peas |
| 2 egg yolks | ½ cup cooked carrots, diced |
| ½ cup heavy cream | 1¹/₃ cups cooked rice |
| Salt and pepper to taste | Chopped crayfish tails (p. 247) |

*Serves 8*

Heat *velouté* base just to the boiling point. Mix egg yolks with cream and salt and pepper to taste. Add this to the *velouté* and mix well.

Stir in the cooked vegetables and rice, blend well and heat for a few more minutes.

Serve garnished with chopped crayfish tails.

# FRUIT, NUT AND CHEESE SOUPS

## APPLE AND RAISIN SOUP

1½ lbs. sour apples
2 thick slices stale white bread
1 quart red wine
1 stick cinnamon (about 2″)
3 whole cloves, heads removed
2 lemon slices, seeded
Salt to taste

2 Tbs. butter
½ cup seedless raisins
3 Tbs. sugar
1 egg yolk
1 Tbs. brandy
Extra raisins, for garnish

*Serves 4–6*

Wipe the sour apples with a damp cloth and quarter them without peeling. Put them in a heavy saucepan; add the white bread, wine, cinnamon, cloves, lemon slices and very little salt. Cook very slowly until the apples are tender—about 30 minutes.

Discard the spices and run the mixture through a fine sieve or a blender.

Add the butter, the ½ cup of raisins and the sugar. In the saucepan, heat slowly to the boiling point and simmer gently for 4–5 minutes or just until the raisins are plump.

Beat the egg yolk and the brandy together and very slowly pour into the soup, stirring constantly. Bring to the boiling point and serve at once, garnished with more raisins.

## CHEDDAR SOUP

2 Tbs. butter
2 Tbs. flour
3 cups hot milk
1 clove garlic
1 cup dry white wine
1 cup grated Cheddar cheese
Salt and pepper to taste

Pinch of nutmeg
Pinch of cayenne
2 egg yolks
2 Tbs. heavy cream
Extra grated Cheddar cheese
Paprika

*Serves 4*

In a heavy saucepan, melt butter and add flour. Gradually stir in the hot milk with the clove of garlic and cook mixture for 20 minutes, stirring constantly in order not to burn. You may transfer this to the top of a double boiler if you prefer.

Discard the garlic; stir in the white wine, cheese, salt and pepper to taste and the nutmeg and cayenne. Cook gently, stirring constantly until cheese is melted.

Beat the 2 egg yolks lightly with the heavy cream; stir gradually into the soup and cook, stirring for about 3 minutes longer.

Pour into individual serving bowls and garnish with a little grated cheddar cheese and paprika.


## CHESTNUT SOUP

| | |
|---|---|
| 1¾ quarts chestnuts in shells | Dash of baking soda |
| 1 Bouquet Garni (chap. 13) | ⅓ cup dry sherry |
| 1 quart Chicken Stock (p. 183) | 2 egg whites for meringue |
| 1 cup heavy cream | Dash of salt |
| ¼ tsp. dry mustard | |

*Serves 8*

Make a slit in each chestnut; spread in a shallow greased pan. Bake at 450° for 15 minutes; cool.

Shell and skin chestnuts. Chop enough for 3 Tbs. and reserve. Place the rest in a deep saucepan with a bouquet garni. Add enough water to cover. Bring to a boil. Cover and reduce heat; simmer for 20–25 minutes or until tender. Drain.

Purée the boiled chestnuts and put into a deep saucepan. Add chicken stock. Bring to a boil; add heavy cream, mustard and baking soda. Cook for another 5 minutes, being careful not to boil; remove from heat. Stir in sherry and keep warm.

While the soup is cooking, beat egg whites until stiff but not dry. Gradually add salt and beat until very stiff. Fold in the reserved chopped chestnuts. Drop by the spoonful on greased brown paper on a baking sheet and place under broiler until lightly browned—about 5 minutes.

Spoon soup into soup cups; top each with a meringue and serve hot.

## SWEET CHERRY SOUP

1½ lbs. dark sweet cherries,            2 cups hot water
   pitted                             3 cups Veal Stock (p. 185)
2 Tbs. sugar                            Unsweetened whipped cream

*Serves 6*

Put the cherries in a saucepan with the sugar and hot water. Simmer for 10 minutes.

Reserve 24 cherries for garnish and put the rest through a fine sieve or a blender.

Mix the cherry pulp and cooking liquid together into a thin purée; stir in the veal stock and heat again to boiling in the saucepan.

Cut the garnishing cherries into quarters and place them in the bottom of 6 bouillon cups. Pour the hot soup over them and top with a little unsweetened whipped cream.

# VEGETABLE SOUPS

## BARLEY AND MUSHROOM SOUP

4 Tbs. butter                           Salt and white pepper to taste
5 Tbs. flour                            2 egg yolks
5 cups Chicken Stock (p. 183)           ¾ cup milk
2 oz. dried mushrooms,                  ¼ cup heavy cream
   soaked and sliced                Dry sherry (optional)
½ cup barley                            Blanched toasted almonds

*Serves 4–6*

In a 2-quart saucepan, melt butter and then blend in flour and cook until mixture is golden. Add chicken stock and cook until mixture thickens slightly.

Add sliced dried mushrooms, which have been previously soaked in hot water for 1 hour. Add barley.

Cook until barley is tender—about 30 minutes. Season with salt and pepper.

Blend egg yolks with milk and gradually add to the soup mixture. Continue cooking until well blended. Finally add cream and taste again for seasonings. A little dry sherry may be added at the last moment.

Garnish with blanched toasted almonds.

# BAYOU CARROT SOUP WITH RICE

½ cup diced onion
2 strips bacon, diced
4 cups sliced carrots
1½ quarts Chicken Stock
  (p. 183)
¼ cup uncooked rice

Salt and ground black pepper
  to taste
2 Tbs. butter
½ cup heavy cream
6 Tbs. cooked rice

*Serves 6*

Lightly fry onion with diced bacon until onion is soft. Add carrots, chicken stock and raw rice. Cover and cook for 20 minutes.

Put through a sieve. Return to saucepan, bring to the boiling point and add salt, pepper, butter and cream.

Serve hot and sprinkle 1 Tbs. cooked rice over each serving.


# BOTVINIA

1 cup sorrel (sour grass) or chard,
  chopped
3 cups spinach, finely chopped
3 cups young and tender beet
  tops, finely chopped
¼ tsp. salt
5 cups light beer or
  dry white wine

½ tsp. sugar
Fresh ground black pepper
  to taste
1½ cups raw cucumber, peeled
  and diced
Chopped parsley

*Serves 6*

Wash vegetables. In a covered saucepan, cook sorrel or chard, spinach and beet tops with the salt and with only the water that clings to the leaves after washing. Cook until the vegetables are wilted and soft—about 15–20 minutes.

Put through a sieve, pushing through as much of the vegetables as possible. Add the beer or wine and season with sugar and pepper. Correct for salt. Chill.

Divide the diced cucumber into each bowl and pour the chilled soup over this.

If desired, place 2 ice cubes in each serving. Sprinkle with chopped parsley.

This dish is usually accompanied by cubes of smoked salmon or sturgeon served in a separate dish with a little grated horseradish mixed with vinegar, and some good black bread.

## COLD SUMMER SQUASH SOUP

1 medium Spanish onion,          ½ cup Chicken Stock (p. 183)
   thinly sliced                      Salt and white pepper to taste
1 Tbs. butter                            1 cup milk
6 medium yellow squash, sliced   Chopped chives

*Serves 4–6*

In a heavy saucepan sauté onion in butter until limp but not brown. Add the squash. Add the chicken stock and cover; cook until tender—about 15 minutes. Season with salt and pepper to taste. Cool, then purée the mixture in a blender.

Serve cold with milk added for taste and consistency. Garnish with chopped chives.

## CREAM OF CAULIFLOWER CREOLE

1 small cauliflower              ⅔ cup tomato purée
2 Tbs. butter                    1 Tbs. sugar
2 Tbs. flour                     2 egg yolks
1½ quarts Chicken Stock          ½ pint heavy cream
   (p. 183)                      Chopped shrimp

*Serves 4–6*

Clean cauliflower and blanch in hot water. Allow to cool and cut up into pieces.

In a saucepan, melt butter and add flour to make a roux. When mixture is smooth and very light in color, add chicken stock and bring to a boil. Reduce heat and add cauliflower pieces along with the tomato purée and the sugar.

Cook for about 40 minutes or until cauliflower is falling apart. Cool and purée through a sieve or in a blender. Correct for seasonings.

Combine egg yolks and cream and add gradually to the hot but not boiling soup mixture.

Serve hot garnished with a few chopped shrimp.

## CREAM OF FRESH CORN SOUP

6–8 ears fresh corn, enough to
  make 2½ cups finely cut raw
  kernels
1 cup boiling water
2 Tbs. finely chopped onion
3 Tbs. butter
3 Tbs. flour

1½ cups Veal Stock (p. 185) or
  Chicken Stock (p. 183)
1½ cups milk
Salt and white pepper to taste
½ cup heavy cream
Chopped pimientos
Cayenne pepper

*Serves 6*

Run a sharp knife down the center of each row of corn kernels, splitting them in half. Cut off the tips of the kernels and discard. Then cut the remainder of the kernels from the cob and reserve. Scrape the cob well, getting out all the milk.

Cook the kernels in boiling water for 5–6 minutes. Set aside.

Sauté onion in butter until transparent. Remove from heat and blend in flour. Stir and cook for 1 minute.

Add corn, stock and milk. Cook for 5 minutes longer, stirring frequently. Add salt and pepper. Finally add cream and heat, being careful not to boil.

Serve hot, garnished with chopped pimientos that have been heated in their own liquid with a little cayenne pepper.

## CREAM OF MUSHROOM SOUP

2 Tbs. butter
3 Tbs. flour
Pinch of dry mustard
1 tsp. salt
Pinch of cayenne
Pinch of baking soda

1 quart hot Chicken Stock
  (p. 183)
¾ lb. fresh mushrooms,
  cleaned and chopped
1/3 cup dry sherry
½ cup scalded cream
Unsweetened whipped cream

*Serves 6*

Melt butter in a heavy saucepan. Blend in flour and add dry mustard, salt, cayenne and baking soda. Gradually stir in the hot chicken stock and then add the chopped mushrooms.

Cook very gently, covered, for about 35 minutes. Strain through a fine sieve and correct seasonings.

Stir in the sherry and the scalded cream. Heat gently but do not boil. Serve hot. Garnish with a little of the unsweetened whipped cream and a sprinkle of paprika for color.

## CREAM OF SPINACH SOUP

1 pound fresh spinach
3 Tbs. butter
2 Tbs. finely chopped onion
3 Tbs. flour
1½ cups milk
Salt and white pepper to taste

Ground nutmeg
2 egg yolks, lightly beaten
¾ cup heavy cream
2 hard-boiled egg yolks, sieved
  (optional)

*Serves 4–6*

Wash spinach thoroughly. Place in a saucepan without adding any extra water. Cover and cook over low heat for 10 minutes, stirring once. Remove from heat, drain and reserve liquid. Force spinach through a sieve.

Melt butter in a deep saucepan; add onion and cook until tender. Blend in flour. Gradually add milk and cook, stirring constantly, until mixture thickens and comes to a boil.

Add strained spinach and liquid. Season to taste with salt, pepper and nutmeg. Simmer until spinach is heated through.

Beat egg yolks with cream. Add this to the spinach soup, stirring rapidly until slightly thickened.

Serve hot but be careful not to boil.

Sieved egg yolks may be used for garnish.

## CREAM OF VEGETABLE SOUP

4 Tbs. butter
2 Tbs. flour
5 cups Veal Stock (p. 185)
4 medium tomatoes, peeled,
  seeded and chopped (or 2 cups
  canned tomatoes)
1½ cups diced potatoes
1 cup diced turnip

1½ cups diced carrots
1 cup green beans,
  cut in ½" pieces
Salt and ground black pepper
  to taste
½ tsp. sugar
Chopped parsley

*Serves 6*

Melt 2 Tbs. of the butter in a 2½-quart saucepan. Remove from fire and blend in the flour. Stir and cook for 1–2 minutes.

Remove from heat, add stock and mix well, bringing to a boil. Add tomatoes and potatoes. Cook slowly for 30 minutes.

Cook turnips in a separate saucepan in enough salted water to cover for 45 minutes. Cook carrots and beans together in water until they are tender for 20–25 minutes.

Purée the soup mixture. Season with salt, pepper and sugar. Bring to a boil, stirring in the remaining 2 Tbs. butter.

Drain the turnips, carrots and green beans and add to the soup. Heat gently without boiling.

Serve hot, garnished with chopped parsley.

## CREOLE DRIED BEAN SOUP

| | |
|---|---|
| 2 cups dried lima beans | 4 whole cloves |
| 7 cups boiling water | 6 whole peppercorns |
| 1 Tbs. Creole seasonings | 2 tsp. salt (or to taste) |
| 1 ham bone, with meat on it | 1 cup milk |
| 1 carrot, quartered | 3 Tbs. butter |
| 1 large onion, sliced | ½ tsp. ground black pepper |
| 3 sprigs parsley | ¼ cup heavy cream |

*Serves 8*

Wash beans; place in kettle and add 4 cups boiling water. Boil for 2 minutes. Remove from heat and soak for 1 hour.

Add remaining boiling water and the Creole seasonings, ham bone, carrot, onion, parsley, cloves, peppercorns and salt. Cover and cook slowly for 2 hours or until the beans are very soft.

Remove ham bone. Purée the soup a little at a time, adding the milk and butter in so doing.

Heat and lastly stir in the black pepper and heavy cream just before serving.

## CREOLE TOMATO AND RICE SOUP

2 slices bacon,
   cut into small pieces
1 cup diced carrots
½ cup chopped onion
4 Tbs. flour
5 cups Veal Stock (p. 185)
8 medium Creole tomatoes,
   quartered
1 tsp. sugar

1 Tbs. Creole seasonings
2 sprigs parsley
Salt and ground black pepper
   to taste
¼ cup heavy cream
½ tsp. Tabasco pepper sauce
8 Tbs. cooked rice
Fried Crouton cubes (chap. 13)

*Serves 8*

Cook bacon with carrots and onion until bacon is browned. Remove from heat and blend in the flour. Stir and cook for about 2 minutes.

Add stock, tomatoes, sugar, Creole seasonings and parsley. Cover and cook for 30 minutes over low heat.

Strain through a sieve or purée in a blender. Season for salt and pepper. Return to saucepan and bring to the boiling point. Add the cream and the Tabasco.

Put 1 Tbs. cooked rice into each bowl and fill with the hot soup. Garnish with fried crouton cubes.

## FRENCH QUARTER JELLIED AVOCADO SOUP

2–3 ripe avocados, enough to
   make 2 cups avocado purée
2 cups sour cream
2 cups jellied chicken consommé
1 tsp. Creole seasonings

¼ tsp. Creole mustard
1 tsp. lemon juice
Salt and pepper to taste
Diced avocado

*Serves 6*

In a blender, purée enough very ripe avocados to make 2 cups. Combine this with the sour cream and the jellied chicken consommé. Beat the mixture with a fork; add seasonings, mustard, lemon juice and salt and pepper to taste.

Divide into 6 crystal bowls and refrigerate.

Serve very cold, garnished with diced avocado.

# GARBURE SOUP

2 medium carrots
2 medium turnips
3 medium potatoes
4 Tbs. butter
1 cup hot Beef Stock (p. 183)
2 cups shredded cabbage
1 cup cooked dried beans

2 cups diced fresh tomatoes
Salt and pepper to taste
1 egg
1 cup grated Parmesan or
    Cheddar cheese
6 slices French bread

*Serves 6*

Peel carrots, turnips and potatoes and slice thin. Place in a saucepan with 2 Tbs. of the butter. Heat and toss for 3 minutes. Add hot beef stock. Cover and cook until vegetables are tender, adding cabbage 5 minutes before the other vegetables are done.

Heat beans with tomatoes and put them through a sieve along with the other vegetables, pushing as much of the vegetables through as possible. Thin to the desired consistency with stock. Adjust seasonings. Add remaining butter, and heat.

Beat egg, mix with cheese and spread over slices of French bread. Toast in a very hot oven or broiler.

Place a slice of bread in each soup plate, pour hot soup over this and serve immediately.

# GAZPACHO
## A Cold Spanish Soup

2 cloves garlic, minced
1 Tbs. salt
½ tsp. Tabasco pepper sauce
2 cups cucumbers, peeled, seeded
    and diced
3 cups firm tomatoes, peeled,
    seeded and diced
½ cup celery, diced
1 cup white onions, diced

½ cup parsley, minced
2 large bell peppers, diced
½ cup olive oil
1 large can V-8 juice
    (46 fluid oz.)
2 cups cold water, preferably iced
8 large croutons from a loaf of
    French bread

*Serves 8*

Rub the bottom of a glass bowl with the garlic. Add salt and Tabasco and then all the vegetables. Toss well. Add the olive oil and the V-8 juice and mix well. Add the iced water. Refrigerate.

When ready to serve, place a crouton in each serving bowl and ladle the gazpacho over the croutons.

## GREEK-STYLE GARBANZO SOUP

½ cup olive oil
2 medium onions, cut fine
2 stalks celery,
  cut into small pieces
1 clove garlic, minced
1 or 2 carrots, sliced
1 large potato, peeled and diced
1 sprig parsley, chopped fine

1 small green pepper,
  cut in julienne
2 Tbs. tomato paste
1 8-oz. can tomato sauce
Salt and pepper to taste
2 No. 2 cans garbanzo beans
5 cups Beef Stock (p. 183)
Juice of 1 lemon

*Serves 8–10*

In a heavy skillet, heat the olive oil and cook the onions, celery and garlic for about 5 minutes. Add the remaining cut-up vegetables, tomato paste and sauce. Stir in salt and pepper to taste and boil gently for about 30 minutes.

Add the 2 cans of well-drained beans and 5 cups of beef stock. Bring to a boil and simmer for 10 minutes.

Add the lemon juice and stir well just before serving.


## GUMBO Z'HERBES

1 bunch spinach
1 bunch mustard greens
½ green cabbage, shredded
1 bunch beet tops
1 bunch watercress
1 bunch radish tops
½ bunch parsley
1 large onion, chopped
1 bunch green onions, tops only

1 ham bone or
  1 or 2 veal shanks, cut up*
1 thick strip bacon, diced
1 Tbs. lard
3 Tbs. flour
Salt and white pepper to taste
Dash of Tabasco pepper sauce
1 or 2 sprigs thyme
1 bay leaf
2 Tbs. butter

*Serves 6*

Wash all the greens in several changes of water to be sure they are absolutely clean. Chop all greens, along with onion and green onions. Place them in water to barely cover. Bring to a boil and cook until tender—about 10–15 minutes. Drain and save the water.

Add ham bone or veal shanks to the water and cook until falling apart—about 1 hour. Remove ham bone or veal shanks and reserve water.

Fry the diced bacon in the lard. Add any bits of meat picked from the ham bone or veal shanks. Add to this all the greens and onions (you may purée them if you wish) and fry. Stir constantly, lest the greens burn. When they are well fried, add 1 Tbs. of the flour and stir some more. Now add salt, pepper, a dash of Tabasco, the thyme and the bay leaf.

Add all this to the reserved waters and simmer for 1 hour. When done, remove the bay leaf and sprigs of thyme.

Make a *beurre manié* by kneading the remaining 2 Tbs. flour with 2 Tbs. butter. Just before serving, blend this gradually into the liquid until the gumbo is smooth.

Serve hot with white rice.

*Peeled shrimp, shucked oysters or picked crab meat may be used instead of the ham bone or veal shanks. Use the same process. This is an old Lenten recipe.

## HEARTY BEAN SOUP

| | |
|---|---|
| 1 cup navy beans | 1½ Tbs. cooking oil |
| 2 quarts Veal Stock (p. 185) | 2 Tbs. flour |
| 3 slices bacon, diced | 1 tsp. chopped parsley |
| Salt and pepper to taste | 4 frankfurters, sliced |
| 2 bay leaves | Red wine vinegar to taste |

*Serves 4–6*

Soak beans overnight. Drain and set to boil in the veal stock, combined with the bacon, salt, pepper and bay leaves.

Simmer and cook until beans are very tender—about 1½–2 hours. Drain and reserve liquid. Force beans through a sieve or use a blender to make a purée.

Heat cooking oil and gradually add flour, making a smooth roux. Add parsley, and when mixture is golden add the reserved liquid. Combine this with the puréed navy beans.

Add the sliced frankfurters and correct for seasonings. As the soup is being heated, add the few drops of wine vinegar to taste.

## ICED CUCUMBER SOUP

3–4 large cucumbers            2–3 cloves garlic, crushed
Salt to taste                  4 oz. coarsely chopped walnuts
4 cups yogurt                  2–3 Tbs. olive oil
4 cups water                   Slices of unpeeled cucumber

*Serves 4–6*

Peel cucumbers and chop them finely. Sprinkle with salt and place in a covered bowl. Refrigerate for about 1 hour.

Dilute yogurt with water. Add garlic and walnuts. Blend thoroughly with olive oil. Drain cucumbers and combine ingredients. Chill very well before serving.

Garnish with thin slices of unpeeled cucumber.

## LEEK AND POTATO SOUP

9–10 Tbs. butter                        1 small ham bone
3 leeks, white parts only, sliced       1 cup cream
1 white onion, sliced                   Salt and white pepper to taste
5 cups hot Chicken Stock (p. 183)       Pinch of ground mace
4 medium potatoes, cubed                $1/3$ cup heavy cream

*Serves 6*

In a heavy saucepan, melt 6 Tbs. of the butter and cook the sliced leeks and onion until soft—about 15 minutes. Add the hot stock. Add the cubed potatoes along with the ham bone. Cover, bring to the boiling point, reduce heat and cook slowly for almost 1 hour.

Remove ham bone and add cream and salt and pepper. Bring to the boiling point. Just before serving, stir in the remaining butter.

Correct for seasonings. Add the ground mace and lastly the $1/3$ cup heavy cream.

Serve hot.

# PEA SOUP WITH CREAM

1½ cups (1½ lbs.) shelled green
   peas
½ tsp. salt
Boiling water
4 Tbs. all-purpose flour or
   rice flour
3½ cups Chicken Stock (p. 183)

3¼ cups milk
Salt to taste
Ground black pepper to taste
2 Tbs. butter or bacon drippings
½ cup heavy cream
2 strips crisp bacon

*Serves 6*

Cook peas with salt in boiling water for about 5 minutes or until they become soft. Drain off water and reserve ⅓ of the peas for garnish.

Put remaining peas through sieve or blender. Mix flour with ½ cup of the stock until mixture is smooth and then add the remaining stock along with the milk. Stir and cook for about 5 minutes. Stir in pea purée, salt, pepper, and bacon drippings or butter. Bring to a boil. Just before serving, remove from heat and stir in cream.

Place 1 Tbs. reserved cooked peas in each bowl and fill with soup. Garnish with crumbled crisp bacon.

# PISTOU SOUP

1 cup diced onion
1 leek or 3 scallions,
   white part only, sliced
2 Tbs. butter
1 cup green beans,
   cut into ½" pieces
1 cup diced potatoes
1½ cups diced tomatoes
   (or 1 cup canned)
6 cups Beef Stock (p. 183)
½ cup vermicelli,
   broken into 1" pieces

Salt and ground black pepper
   to taste
2 cloves garlic
2 tsp. chopped fresh thyme
   (or ¼ tsp. dried)
2 tsp. chopped fresh sage
   (or ¼ tsp. dried)
2 egg yolks
¼ cup olive oil or salad oil
2 Tbs. tomato purée
½ cup grated Cheddar or
   Gruyère cheese

*Serves 6–8*

Cook onions and leeks in butter until transparent. Add vegetables and stock.

Cover and bring to a boil. Reduce heat; cook 30 minutes or until vegetables are soft.

Add vermicelli after 15 minutes. Season with salt and pepper.

Pound garlic with herbs. Add egg yolks. Gradually beat in oil as in making mayonnaise. Add tomato purée, beating constantly.

Put this mixture in a soup tureen and stir the soup in gradually to prevent cooking the egg yolks. Sprinkle with grated cheese.

Serve as a main-dish soup.

## POTAGE BARONESS PONTALBA

4 Tbs. butter
2 small onions, finely chopped
6 Creole tomatoes,
    peeled, seeded and chopped
1 Tbs. tomato paste
1 bay leaf
1 tsp. Creole seasonings

1 garlic clove, crushed
6 peppercorns
6 cups Chicken Stock (p. 183)
¼ cup cooked rice
Pinch of sugar
2 Tbs. chopped parsley

*Serves 6*

In a heavy saucepan, melt butter and sauté the onions until they become transparent. Add the tomatoes and cook briskly for 3–4 minutes. Add the tomato paste, bay leaf, Creole seasonings, garlic and peppercorns. Cover and cook gently, stirring occasionally, for 10 minutes.

Press this mixture through a fine sieve so that the peppercorns are removed, and add the purée to the chicken stock. Bring the soup to a boil, add the cooked rice and simmer for another 15 minutes. Correct seasonings.

Just before serving add a pinch of sugar and the chopped parsley.

## POTAGE RUE DAUPHINE

4 large fresh beets,
    peeled and quartered
1 quart hot Chicken Stock
    (p. 183)
1½ envelopes Knox gelatine
⅓ cup dry sherry

1 Tbs. strained lemon juice
Pepper to taste
4 Tbs. red caviar
½ pint whipped sour cream
Gratings of fresh nutmeg

*Serves 4*

Boil the beets in water to cover to make 1 cup good concentrated beet juice. Add this to the hot chicken stock. Heat to the boiling point. Stir in the gelatine, which has been dissolved in the sherry and lemon juice. Taste for pepper and cool. Do not add salt.

In the bottom of your serving cups, put 1 Tbs. red caviar for each dish. Very gently pour enough of the bouillon mixture until each dish is filled. Chill in refrigerator until very firm.

When set and ready to serve, scoop out 1 Tbs. jellied bouillon from the center of each dish and fill the hole with whipped sour cream that has been forced through a pastry bag with a rose or star tube.

Sprinkle the cream with a grating of nutmeg and surround with the rest of the finely diced jellied bouillon.

## ROMAINE SOUP

| | |
|---|---|
| 2 Tbs. butter | Salt and white pepper to taste |
| 1 small onion, minced | 4 egg yolks |
| 1 quart Chicken Stock (p. 183) | 1 cup heavy cream |
| 2 large heads romaine lettuce, | |
|    outside leaves only, chopped | |

*Serves 4–6*

In a large saucepan, melt butter, add the onion and cook until tender. Add chicken stock and bring to a boil. Add the chopped romaine lettuce leaves, and simmer for 10 minutes or until the lettuce leaves have wilted. Season with salt and pepper.

Beat together the egg yolks and the cream. Stir this into the soup mixture and cook over very low heat until soup mixture thickens slightly. Do not allow to boil.

Correct for seasonings and serve hot with crisp French bread.

## UKRAINIAN BEET SOUP

1½ lbs. lean beef
1 lb. lean fresh pork
½ lb. smoked pork
10 cups cold water
1 bay leaf
8 peppercorns
1 clove garlic
A few sprigs of parsley
1 carrot
1 stalk celery
2 leeks
9 raw beets, whole and unpeeled
¼ cup cold water

1 cup shredded cabbage
2 onions, quartered
3 potatoes, peeled and quartered
6 tomatoes,
  peeled, seeded and quartered
1½ tsp. tomato purée
1 Tbs. vinegar
1 tsp. sugar
½ cup cooked navy beans
4 frankfurters, thickly sliced
1 Tbs. *Beurre Manié* (chap. 13)
Salt to taste

*Serves 6–8*

In a heavy soup kettle place the beef, fresh pork and smoked pork and cover with the water. Bring water slowly to a boil, skim carefully and add the bay leaf, peppercorns, garlic, parsley, carrot, celery and leeks. Simmer, covered, for 1½ hours.

Meanwhile cook 8 of the beets, unpeeled, in salted water to cover for about 40 minutes, or until tender. Peel and cut each beet into 8 segments. Peel and grate the remaining raw beet and soak it in ¼ cup cold water.

Remove meats from soup and strain soup into another saucepan. Add the cooked beets, the shredded cabbage, the onions, potatoes, tomatoes, tomato purée, vinegar and sugar and return the meats. Bring to a boil and simmer for another 40 minutes. Add the cooked navy beans and the frankfurters and continue to simmer for 20 more minutes.

Thicken the soup with the *beurre manié*, which has been blended with the liquid strained from the raw beet. Correct seasonings.

Cut the meat into thick slices and place in a large soup tureen. Add the raw grated beet to the hot soup mixture and pour over the meat.

# U.S. SENATE SOUP

1 lb. navy beans,
   soaked overnight
1 ham bone,
   with plenty of meat on it
3 quarts cold water
1 cup cooked mashed potatoes

3 onions, chopped
1 small bunch celery, including
   tops, finely chopped
2 cloves garlic, finely chopped
¼ cup finely chopped parsley

*Serves 4–6*

Drain soaked beans and place in a heavy soup kettle. Put in ham bone and cover with 3 quarts cold water. Bring to a boil and simmer for 2 hours.

Stir in the mashed potatoes, onions, celery, garlic and parsley. Simmer soup for 1 hour more or until beans are thoroughly cooked.

Remove ham bone and dice any remaining meat clinging to the bone. Add the meat to the soup mixture, heat thoroughly and serve at once.

# VICHYSSOISE

8 leeks, white parts only
2 medium onions
4 Tbs. butter
10 medium potatoes,
   peeled and quartered

2 quarts Chicken Stock (p. 183)
2 Tbs. salt
White pepper to taste
2 cups Half n' Half
Chopped chives

*Serves 6–8*

Slice the leeks and onions. In a heavy soup pot, melt the butter and sauté the vegetables until they just begin to turn color. Add the potatoes and cover with the chicken stock. Add the 2 Tbs. salt and a little pepper.

Bring to a boil, reduce heat and simmer for about 40 minutes or until potatoes are falling apart. Allow to cool, and gradually purée in a blender, adding the Half n' Half, until mixture is very smooth.

Place smooth mixture in a bowl or large plastic container and refrigerate. When thoroughly cold, taste for seasonings and add a little more cold cream if mixture is too thick.

Serve sprinkled with chopped chives.

## WATERCRESS SOUP

3 leeks or 6 scallions,
  white parts only, sliced
1 small onion, sliced
2 Tbs. butter
3 medium potatoes,
  peeled and thinly sliced
3 cups Chicken Stock (p. 183)
1 cup milk

1 bunch fresh watercress with
  stems removed
½ cup boiling water
Salt and ground black pepper
  to taste
1 cup heavy cream
Watercress leaves

*Serves 6*

Sauté leeks and onion in butter until they turn golden. Add potatoes and stock. Cover and bring to a boil. Reduce heat and simmer for 30 minutes.

Pour soup through a strainer, rubbing as much of the potatoes and onion through as possible, or purée in a blender a little at a time.

Return purée to saucepan, add milk, stir and cook for another 5 minutes.

Cook watercress in ½ cup boiling water in a covered saucepan until cress is limp. Force it through a sieve or purée in a blender.

Add this to the soup and heat. Add salt, pepper and cream, being careful not to boil the cream.

Serve hot or cold, garnished with watercress leaves.

# WHITE BEAN AND NOODLE SOUP

1 1/3 cups dried white beans,
    soaked overnight and drained
½ lb. fresh pork belly, with skin
1 onion, finely chopped
1 carrot, finely chopped
1 celery stalk, finely chopped
1 clove garlic, finely chopped

2 sprigs parsley, finely chopped
Pinch of sage
1 bay leaf
Salt and ground black pepper
    to taste
¼ lb. spaghetti or ribbon noodles
2 Tbs. olive oil

*Serves 4–6*

In a heavy saucepan place the beans along with the pork belly, onion, carrot, celery, garlic, parsley, sage and bay leaf and cover with water. Bring to a boil, reduce heat, cover and simmer gently for 2 hours or until beans are soft.

Purée 1 cup beans in a blender, leaving the rest in the soup. Stir the bean purée back into the soup. Season to taste with salt and freshly ground black pepper and bring to a boil again.

Now add the spaghetti or ribbon noodles and boil for about 12 minutes or until they are cooked but firm to the bite.

Remove the piece of pork belly and cut into thin strips. Just before serving, dribble the olive oil into the soup and add another grinding of fresh black pepper.

Serve the soup warm rather than piping hot, accompanied by the strips of pork belly on another plate.

# 7
# EGGS

JUST AS ONE doubts that Voltaire said, "A meal without wine is like a day without sun," so I question the claim that the great Escoffier had two thousand recipes for the preparation of eggs.

Be that as it may, there are enough egg recipes around to fill several cookbooks. The important thing is that the egg graces any kitchen and any gourmet meal. Leaving the World Poultry Congress and the American Medical Association to debate the pros and cons of eating eggs, the world of gastronomy regards them with respect.

Once you get out of the "eggs for breakfast" syndrome, you will emerge into a completely new world of what to do with the egg. No matter how the price of eggs fluctuates, working with them for a good menu, you will come out within your family budget. Of course, this does not mean that you can indulge in quail eggs, thousand-year-old eggs or any such exotic variations.

These recipes are designed for those eggs that, hopefully, come fresh from the farm to your supermarket. For those who know the glories of country-fresh eggs straight from the farm, these recipes will have a special meaning.

# HINTS

## USES FOR EGGS IN COOKING

*Thickening agent:* for custards, puddings, sauces, soufflés. The yolks or whites of 2 eggs are equal to 1 whole egg in thickening power.

*Binding agent:* to hold ingredients together in mixtures such as meat loaf or croquettes. Also to hold a coating of bread crumbs, flour or cornmeal to the surface of foods for frying.

*Strengthening agent:* for doughs and batters.

*Clarifying agent:* as a magnet to attract and agglomerate particles which cloud broths or stocks.

*Emulsifying agent:* to blend dissimilar liquids into a stable mixture, as melted butter and lemon juice in hollandaise sauce. Heat is not essential in forming an emulsion; for example, eggs emulsify the oil and vinegar in mayonnaise.

*Leavening agent:* for cakes and baked goods. Air beaten into egg whites expands when heated. The whites are thus stretched and coagulate to form a light, porous product, as in sponge cake.

*Glazing agent:* for bread, rolls, cookies or pie crusts. Eggs beaten with a little water and brushed over the surfaces of baked goods will create an attractive, shiny crust.

## HOW TO SCRAMBLE EGGS

Break the desired number of eggs into a bowl. Add milk or light cream in the following proportions:

For creamy scrambled eggs: Add 1 Tbs. milk or light cream for each egg.

For dry scrambled eggs: Add ½ Tbs. milk or light cream for each egg.

Beat the mixture only until yolks and whites are blended. If flecks of the whites are preferred in scrambled eggs, omit milk or cream and beat the eggs very slightly.

Season to taste with salt and ground black pepper.

Pour the mixture into a heated skillet in which a small amount of butter or other fat has been melted. Stir and cook slowly until the eggs are set but still moist.

Scrambled eggs may also be cooked in a little butter in the top of a double boiler over simmering (but not boiling) water.

Allow 1–2 eggs per person.

## HOW TO FRY EGGS

Heat butter, bacon drippings or other fat in a skillet, using only enough to grease the bottom of the pan.

Break eggs into a saucer, one at a time, and then slip them into the pan. Sprinkle with salt and ground black pepper.

Cover pan tightly and cook over very low heat for 2–3 minutes or until the egg whites are firm and the yolks are covered with a film of coagulated white.

## HOW TO FRENCH FRY EGGS

Heat 1 cup cooking oil in a small skillet until very hot. Break 1 egg at a time into a saucer and salt the white lightly.

Holding the pan at a slight angle, slide the egg into the hot oil. Turn it over at once with a wooden spoon to prevent the white from spreading. Gently press the white down with the spoon, and when the bottom side is browned, turn the egg over to brown the other side and to aid the egg in retaining its oval shape. The white must be firm, and the yolk remain soft.

Remove egg from skillet, drain on a paper towel and keep warm while cooking the rest of the eggs. Cook only 1 egg at a time.

If doing this for the first time, you may ruin about a dozen eggs, but keep trying, as it is well worth the effort for a beautiful-looking, delicious egg dish.

## HOW TO SOFT-BOIL EGGS IN THE SHELL

Place eggs in a saucepan with enough water to cover completely. Cover, bring to the boiling point, remove from heat and let stand 3–5 minutes, allowing the longer time for a firmer consistency.

If soft-boiled eggs are to be peeled, let stand for 5–6 minutes beyond initial cooking time and then plunge into cold water.

Serve soft-boiled eggs for breakfast or make them into hot or cold dishes for lunch or supper or for a buffet.

## HOW TO HARD-BOIL EGGS IN THE SHELL

Place eggs in a saucepan with sufficient water to cover completely. Cover, bring to the boiling point, remove from heat and let stand for 20 minutes. Cool eggs immediately in cold water.

Use hard-boiled eggs in hot or cold entrées and main dishes, hors d'oeuvres, sandwiches, salads and garnishes.

*HOW TO POACH EGGS*

Put 2 cups water in a skillet (I prefer an iron skillet) with ½ tsp. salt and 1 Tbs. vinegar. Bring to a rolling boil and reduce heat.

Break eggs into a cup or saucer, one at a time, and gently slide into water. Do not cook more than 2 eggs at a time.

With a spoon, baste the egg with the water, making sure that the whites cover the yolks.

When whites are firm and set remove with a slotted spoon or spatula. Drain. These may be used for hot or cold recipes.

# COLD DISHES

## ASSORTED COLD STUFFED EGGS

| | |
|---|---|
| 12 hard-boiled eggs | 3 Tbs. red caviar |
| ¾ cup softened butter | 8 large shrimp, finely chopped |
| ⅓ cup mayonnaise | 4 Tbs. smooth liver pâté |
| 3 Tbs. tomato purée | 1 cup Aspic (chap. 13) |

*Serves 12*

Cut eggs into crosswise halves and cut a thin slice from each end so they will stand upright, reserving end slices to use later.

Remove yolks, keeping whites intact, and put yolks through a sieve. Mix yolks with butter and mayonnaise. Divide the mixture into 4 equal parts and mix 1 part with tomato purée, another with red caviar, another with the shrimp and the last with the liver pâté. Using a pastry bag fitted with a large, smooth tube, fill the egg-white halves with the various stuffings.

Chill the stuffed eggs. Coat them lightly with the aspic and refrigerate until set, at least 1 hour.

Serve on a buffet table as a garnish for a platter of meat, vegetables, fish, salad or by themselves.

## DUCK LIVER EGGS

2 duck livers, sautéed
4 hard-boiled eggs,
   cut in half lengthwise
Salt and ground black pepper
1 Tbs. chopped parsley
Pinch of dried chervil

Pinch of dried tarragon
Pinch of chopped fresh chives
2 Tbs. Madeira wine
   (or enough to moisten)
1 small truffle, chopped

*Serves 4*

Slice livers thinly, trim slices into 6 medallions slightly smaller in diameter than the eggs used, and set to one side. Remove egg yolks from whites.

Purée the remaining liver trimmings in a blender and mix with 2 of the egg yolks. (Save the other yolks for future use.)

Season to taste with salt, pepper and herbs. Moisten with Madeira.

Fill egg-white halves and decorate each with a liver medallion and some truffle.

## EGGS CASINO

½ cup Jellied Mayonnaise
   (chap. 13)
1 Tbs. tomato purée
12 soft-boiled eggs, cooled in
   their shells
1 hard-boiled egg
¾ cup finely chopped cooked
   chicken, cold
3 Tbs. mayonnaise

Salt and ground black pepper
   to taste
6 Basic Tart Shells (p. 383),
   approximately 3" in diameter,
   baked
12 cooked asparagus tips, cold
12 slices cooked ham, cold
1 truffle, sliced (or 4 black olives,
   sliced)

*Serves 6*

Combine jellied mayonnaise and tomato purée.

Peel the soft-boiled eggs. Coat 6 of them with the jellied mayonnaise. Using the white and yolk of the hard-boiled egg, make a design on each to simulate a daisy. Chill and set.

Mix the chicken with the mayonnaise and season with salt and pepper. Spoon the mixture into the tarts.

Place 2 asparagus tips and a tomato-mayonnaise-coated egg on each tart. Garnish the ends of the asparagus tips with a bit of the jellied mayonnaise. Arrange the tarts in the center of a platter.

Fold the ham slices in quarters and arrange 6 folded slices in a circle at each end of the platter. Decorate the remaining 6 soft-boiled eggs with a bit of truffle or sliced black olive and arrange around the platter.

## EGGS IN ASPIC WITH PARMA HAM

6 firmly soft-boiled eggs
3 cups Aspic (chap. 13)
6 thin slices truffle

Tarragon or parsley leaves
6 thin slices cooked ham
   such as prosciutto

*Serves 6*

Peel eggs and set to one side.

Coat the insides of 6 small oval-shaped molds (or small Old-Fashioned glasses) with aspic and chill them until the aspic begins to jell—about 5–10 minutes. At the same time refrigerate the remaining aspic.

Decorate the aspic in the molds with truffle slices and tarragon or parsley leaves.

Wrap each egg in a slice of ham and place 1 egg in each mold. Finish filling the molds with the remaining aspic. Chill until the aspic is firm—about 2 hours or longer.

There will be some aspic left over; chill this until set and reserve for garnish.

To serve, unmold* eggs onto a cold serving platter. Arrange them in a circle. Chop firm aspic and spoon it around the eggs. Serve for a buffet, lunch or supper.

*To unmold, run a sharp knife around the mold and invert it onto the platter.

## EGGS VERT PRÉ

12 small hard-boiled eggs,
   cut in half lengthwise
1 Tbs. Dijon-style mustard
3 Tbs. softened butter

Salt and white pepper to taste
½ cup chopped watercress
1 Tbs. heavy cream
1 cup Jellied Mayonnaise
   (chap. 13)

*Serves 4*

Separate the egg yolks from the whites. Sieve the yolks into a bowl. Blend in the mustard, softened butter and salt and pepper. Stuff only half the egg whites, reserving the rest for another time.

Fill a pastry bag fitted with a large fluted tip with the yolk mixture and force into the whites, or simply spoon the yolk mixture into the whites. Chill for at least 1 hour.

When properly chilled, set the filled whites on a rack over a tray. Add the chopped watercress and heavy cream to the jellied mayonnaise. Before it begins to set, quickly spoon the watercress mayonnaise over the eggs, covering the yolks completely.

Arrange the eggs on a bed of watercress and parsley. Refrigerate for 1 hour or until ready to serve.

## MIMOSA TARTS

1 cup mixed cooked green peas
  and diced carrots
½ cup finely diced celery
¾ cup finely diced ham,
  preferably smoked
¾ cup flaked cooked lobster meat
  (p. 247)
Salt and ground black pepper

²/₃ cup mayonnaise
16 Basic Tart Shells  (p. 383),
  approximately 3″ in diameter,
  baked*
2 Tbs. butter, softened
4 hard-boiled egg yolks
Chopped parsley

*Serves 8*

Combine cooked vegetables, celery, ham, lobster, salt, pepper and a little more than ¹/₃ cup of the mayonnaise. Chill.

Coat the bottom of the tart shells with the remaining mayonnaise mixed with the butter. Chill.

Shortly before serving, fill the tarts with the vegetable mixture. Put the 4 hard-boiled egg yolks through a sieve and sprinkle evenly over the tarts.

Garnish with chopped parsley and chill for 1 hour or until ready to serve.

*If you prefer, you may substitute 16 halves of hard-boiled eggs, whites only, for the tart shells.

# MOLDED EGG SALAD

2 envelopes Knox gelatine
¾ cup water
3 Tbs. vinegar
1 tsp. Worcestershire sauce
1 tsp. salt
White pepper to taste
¼ tsp. dry mustard
1 cup mayonnaise
1 Tbs. chili powder

1 tsp. green pepper, finely
  minced
1 tsp. green onion, green parts
  only, finely minced
¾ cup chopped celery
$1/3$ cup chopped green pepper
$1/3$ cup chopped pimiento
1 Tbs. chopped green onion
10 hard-boiled eggs, coarsely
  chopped

*Serves 6*

Dissolve gelatine in water in the top of a double boiler. Add vinegar, Worcestershire sauce, salt, pepper and mustard. Cool for about 10 minutes.

Meanwhile, make a chili mayonnaise by mixing the homemade mayonnaise, chili powder, minced green pepper and minced green parts of green onion. Stir into the cooled gelatine mixture.

Add celery, green pepper, pimiento, chopped green onion and the hard-boiled eggs. Correct for seasonings. Pour into a greased ring mold. Refrigerate until well set.

Unmold* and fill the center of the molded salad with any garnish such as wedges of tomatoes, radishes, gherkins or shrimp.

*To unmold, run a sharp knife around the mold. Dip the mold in hot but not boiling water for a few seconds and invert onto a cold platter.

# SCANDINAVIAN EGGS

6 hard-boiled eggs,
  cut in half lengthwise
6 anchovy filets*
Pepper to taste
1 tsp. chopped parsley

Pinch of chopped fresh chives
Pinch of dried tarragon
Pinch of dried chervil
4 pimiento-stuffed green olives,
  sliced

*Serves 6*

Remove the egg-yolk halves from the whites. (Save 8 of them for future use or use some, grated, as garnish.)

Mash the anchovy filets and blend with 4 egg-yolk halves. Finely chop 2 halves of egg white and add. Mix well. Add pepper and herbs to taste. (Do not add any salt.)

Fill 10 egg-white halves with the anchovy mixture and garnish each with a slice of stuffed olive.

*Use Scandinavian anchovy filets packed in brine, available at gourmet shops. Do not use the regular canned variety. You may substitute sprats, boneless and skinless sardines or smoked salmon. If you use sprats, be sure to wash them thoroughly first.

## STUFFED EGGS ARNONVILLE

| | |
|---|---|
| 6 hard-boiled eggs | About ½ cup Jellied Mayonnaise |
| 1 cup cooked shrimp (p. 247), diced | (chap. 13) |
| 1 cup mayonnaise | 1 cup cooked mixed vegetables, cold |
| Salt and white pepper to taste | Lettuce |
| ½ tsp. Tabasco pepper sauce | Paprika |

*Serves 6*

Cut eggs in half lengthwise and remove yolks, leaving the whites intact. Reserve both yolks and whites.

Combine shrimp, ⅓ cup of the mayonnaise, and salt, pepper and Tabasco pepper sauce. Spoon the mixture into the cavities of the egg whites, mounding it over the tops.

Then coat the stuffed eggs thinly with jellied mayonnaise. Chill until mayonnaise is set—about 1 hour.

Combine the vegetables with the remaining ⅔ cup mayonnaise and correct for salt and pepper.

Arrange lettuce on the bottom of a serving dish. Spoon the vegetable mixture into the center and surround it with the stuffed eggs.

Chop the hard-boiled egg yolks and sprinkle them over the eggs. Dust with some paprika.

# SUPERDOME EGGS

6 hard-boiled eggs,                    Salt and pepper to taste
   cut in half lengthwise      ¼ tsp. Tabasco pepper sauce
½ avocado, puréed                      ½ head of lettuce, shredded
2 Tbs. cooked ham, chopped             6 slices smoked tongue or turkey
2 Tbs. mayonnaise                      Chopped parsley

*Serves 3*

Remove yolks from eggs and set whites aside. Mash yolks together with avocado, chopped ham, mayonnaise, salt, pepper and Tabasco.

Lay shredded lettuce on a platter. Stuff egg whites with the mixture. Lay 2 egg whites on each slice of smoked tongue or turkey.

Garnish with chopped parsley and serve.

# HOT DISHES

## BAYOU POACHED EGGS

6 medium Creole tomatoes               6 Tbs. crisp bacon, crumbled
Salt and pepper to taste               6 poached eggs
18 crayfish tails, cooked              Chopped parsley
   (p. 247)*             Tabasco pepper sauce (optional)

*Serves 6*

Cut the tops from the tomatoes. Scoop out enough of the pulp so the shell will hold the crayfish tails and the poached egg.

Sprinkle the tomatoes with salt and pepper. Put the crayfish tails in them and place them in the oven for 8–10 minutes. The tomatoes should be cooked through but not mushy, and the crayfish tails hot.

Transfer the tomatoes to a heated serving platter and sprinkle the hot, crumbled bacon bits over the crayfish tails. Cover each tomato with a freshly poached egg.

Garnish with chopped parsley and a dash of Tabasco, if you wish.

*You may substitute 18 medium shrimp, cooked (p. 247) and cut up, or 1 can Alaska king crab meat.

## BAYOU POM-POM EGG PIE

6 hard-boiled eggs
3–4 Tbs. butter
6 1″ slices firm tomato, peeled
6 shrimp, cooked and shelled
   (p. 247)
Dash of Tabasco pepper sauce
1 clove garlic, crushed

3 Tbs. mixed basil and parsley,
   finely chopped
8–9 Tbs. fine bread crumbs
Salt and pepper to taste
6 whole eggs
1–1½ cups light cream

*Serves 4–6*

Slice the hard-boiled eggs crosswise.

Use some of the butter to grease a pie pan generously. Lay the tomato slices on the bottom.

Pound the shrimp until very fine. Blend with 2 Tbs. butter. Add a dash of Tabasco and chill.

Brush each slice of tomato with the shrimp butter and then sprinkle with the combined garlic, basil and parsley.

Cover with alternate layers of sliced egg and bread crumbs. Season each layer with salt and pepper and dot with the remaining butter.

Beat the whole eggs with the light cream, also seasoned with salt and pepper. Pour over the hard-boiled-egg mixture.

Bake in a moderate oven (350°) for about 35 minutes, or until the custard is firm in the center.

Serve the pie piping hot.

## BERCHERON HARD-BOILED EGGS

10 hard-boiled eggs
3 medium potatoes, boiled
   (15–20 minutes) and peeled
Salt and ground black pepper
   to taste

1¾ cups Béchamel Sauce
   (chap. 13)
Paprika
Chopped parsley

*Serves 6*

Slice eggs and potatoes while they are hot. Sprinkle with salt and pepper.

Arrange them in a serving dish in alternate layers with béchamel sauce, having the potatoes as the bottom layer and the sauce as the top layer.

Sprinkle with paprika and chopped parsley.

# BRITTANY HARD-BOILED EGGS

1 small onion, sliced
¼ cup sliced leeks
1 Tbs. butter
3 Tbs. Chicken Stock (p. 183)
½ cup sliced mushrooms, sautéed

1 cup Béchamel Sauce (chap. 13)
Salt and ground black pepper
  to taste
10 hard-boiled eggs
Paprika

*Serves 6*

Cook onion and leeks in butter until they are soft. Add stock and cook 1 minute. Stir in mushrooms and blend with béchamel sauce. Heat, without boiling. Season with salt and black pepper.

Pour ⅓ of the mixture into a serving dish. Slice eggs, saving one of the yolks, and arrange over the sauce. Cover with remaining sauce. Put the reserved egg yolk through a sieve and sprinkle on top. Dust with paprika.

Serve as a main dish for lunch or late supper.

# CAJUN-STYLE FRIED EGGS

1 clove garlic
2 Tbs. chopped parsley
3 Tbs. cooking oil
8 firm tomatoes
16 *cèpes* or whole mushroom caps

2 Tbs. butter
8 hot fried eggs
Salt and ground black pepper
  to taste
Fried parsley

*Serves 4*

Split garlic and place it in an 8″ skillet along with chopped parsley and oil. Heat for 1–2 minutes.

Cut tomatoes in half, place them in the hot oil cut side down, and cook for 1 minute (do not overcook). Discard garlic.

Sauté *cèpes* or mushroom caps in butter until they are tender.

Arrange tomatoes in a ring on a serving dish and top each with a sautéed *cèpe* or mushroom cap. Place hot fried eggs in the center of the dish and sprinkle with salt and pepper.

Garnish with fried parsley.

## C.B.'S ITALIAN FONDUE

½ lb. fontina cheese, chopped            6–7 Tbs. butter
   (or enough to equal 1½ cups)          4 egg yolks
2 cups milk (or enough                   Dash of white pepper
   to cover cheese for soaking)

*Serves 4–6*

Soak the cheese in enough milk to cover for at least 2 hours.

In a heavy saucepan, melt the butter, and when it begins to color, add the cheese and 2 Tbs. of the milk in which the cheese has soaked. Stir constantly, but never allow to boil.

When the cheese is completely dissolved, remove saucepan from the fire. Mix in gradually the yolks of eggs and season with white pepper. Replace saucepan on fire and continue to stir.

As soon as the mixture has the consistency of thick cream, serve in a bowl accompanied by small pieces of toasted French bread.

## CHEESE SOUFFLÉ

2 Tbs. butter                            4 egg yolks
2 Tbs. flour                             ¾ cup sharp Cheddar or
¾ cup milk, heated                          Parmesan cheese, grated
Salt to taste                            5 egg whites
Dash of cayenne                          Paprika
Dash of nutmeg

*Serves 6*

Melt butter in the top of a double boiler over a direct, medium flame. Stir in the flour and blend well, continuing to stir for 5–10 minutes. Stir in the milk and season with salt, cayenne and nutmeg.

Remove from the fire and beat in 4 egg yolks, one at a time, alternately with the Cheddar or Parmesan cheese. Stir the mixture over hot but not boiling water until the cheese is completely melted.

When all ingredients are well blended, remove the double-boiler top from the hot water and cool slightly.

Fold in 5 stiffly beaten egg whites and pour the batter into a generously buttered soufflé dish (1½-quart size).

Decorate the top of the mixture with *very* thin slices of the Cheddar cheese (or grated Parmesan, if that's what you've used) and dust with paprika.

Bake in a moderate oven (375°) for about 30 minutes or until the top is delicately browned. Serve at once.

## CHEESE-STUFFED EGGS

9 hard-boiled eggs
½ cup Mornay Sauce (chap. 13)
1 Tbs. Béchamel Sauce
  (chap. 13)
½ cup finely chopped mushrooms
6 Tbs. softened butter

Salt and ground black pepper to
  taste
½ cup fine dry bread crumbs
¼ cup grated Cheddar or
  Parmesan cheese

*Serves 6*

Preheat oven to 350°.

Cut eggs into lengthwise halves. Remove yolks and put them through a sieve. Blend with Mornay and béchamel sauces.

Sauté mushrooms in 2 Tbs. of the butter and combine with the yolk mixture. Season with salt and pepper. Stuff into the egg whites. Arrange in a buttered baking dish.

Melt remaining 4 Tbs. butter and mix with bread crumbs and cheese. Sprinkle over the eggs and place them in the oven to brown for 5 minutes.

Serve hot for lunch or supper.

## CREOLE EGG BALLS

4 hard-boiled eggs
1 Tbs. tomato purée
Salt and white pepper to taste
½ tsp. Tabasco pepper sauce

1 stiffly beaten egg white
Flour, sifted and seasoned
  with salt and pepper
4–5 Tbs. butter

*Serves 4*

Chop hard-boiled eggs very fine. Add tomato purée. Season with salt, pepper and Tabasco pepper sauce. Add enough of the stiffly beaten egg white to moisten the eggs.

Form the mixture into small balls and roll them in the flour. Brown them in the melted butter for 2–3 minutes.

Use as a garnish for soup.

## CREOLE TOMATOES AND EGGS

4–5 Tbs. olive oil
1½ lbs. ripe Creole tomatoes,
   peeled, seeded and chopped
1 clove garlic, chopped
1 Tbs. chopped parsley
Salt and pepper to taste

4–6 eggs, lightly beaten with
   1 Tbs. water
¼ cup grated Parmesan cheese
4 Tbs. butter
1 Tbs. chopped fresh mint
½ tsp. marjoram

*Serves 4–6*

In a heavy skillet heat the oil; add the tomatoes, garlic and parsley. Season with salt and pepper and simmer until the tomatoes are reduced to a pulp.

Rub all this through a sieve and add the eggs. Add the grated cheese and mix well.

Heat the butter in another skillet to cook the eggs. When butter is hot, pour in the egg-tomato mixture and cook, stirring, until eggs are set but soft, about 10 minutes.

Remove from fire and put on a hot dish. Sprinkle the eggs with chopped mint and marjoram.

## CRESCENT CITY EGGS

5 Tbs. butter
1 onion, minced
1 green pepper, chopped
1 very small eggplant,
   cut into very small cubes
3 Creole tomatoes, peeled, seeded
   and chopped
1 cup frozen peas, thawed

1 tsp. salt
2 Tbs. Worcestershire sauce
½ tsp. Tabasco pepper sauce
2 cups Béchamel Sauce (chap. 13)
8 hard-boiled eggs, sliced
1 cup plain bread crumbs
1 cup sharp Cheddar cheese,
   grated

*Serves 6*

Melt 4 Tbs. of the butter in a saucepan and sauté the onion, green pepper and eggplant for about 20 minutes. When tender, add the tomatoes and peas and the salt, Worcestershire and Tabasco. Pour the béchamel sauce into this and mix well.

In a buttered 2-quart casserole, place alternate layers of the vegetable sauce and sliced eggs, ending with the sauce.

Top with bread crumbs mixed with the remaining butter and the cheese. Bake at 350° for 15–20 minues.

# EGG CURRY

4 Tbs. vegetable oil
2 medium onions, finely chopped
1″ piece fresh ginger,
   peeled and finely chopped
2 garlic cloves, chopped
1 tsp. turmeric
1 tsp. ground cumin
2 tsp. ground coriander
1 tsp. cayenne pepper
¼ tsp. ground fennel seeds

1 Tbs. finely chopped coriander
   leaves (Chinese parsley)
1 lb. tomatoes, blanched, peeled,
   seeded and chopped
1 tsp. salt
½ tsp. sugar
½ cup thick coconut milk
6 hard-boiled eggs,
   cut in half lengthwise
1 Tbs. lemon juice

*Serves 4*

Heat the oil in a large saucepan. Add the onions, ginger and garlic; fry until golden brown.

Add the tumeric, cumin, coriander, cayenne pepper and fennel seeds. Cook, stirring for 8 minutes, adding a spoonful or so of water if the spices get too dry.

Add the coriander leaves, tomatoes, salt and sugar and bring to a boil. Reduce the heat to low, cover the pan and simmer for 30 minutes.

Stir in the coconut milk and add the eggs. Simmer, covered, for 20 minutes. Stir in the lemon juice. Taste and adjust seasonings.

Serve hot with steamed or boiled rice, chutney and pappadums.

# EGGS PONT BREAUX

6 slices eggplant
1 stick butter
Salt and white pepper to taste
6 slices Creole tomato

6 poached eggs
18 cooked crayfish tails (p. 247)*
1 cup Hollandaise Sauce (chap. 13)
½ tsp. Tabasco pepper sauce

*Serves 6*

Fry the eggplant slices in about ⅔ of the butter, add salt and pepper to taste and keep warm. Lightly grill the tomato slices and keep warm. Poach the eggs, trim and reserve.

On each eggplant slice, lay 1 slice of tomato. Sauté the crayfish in the remaining butter and place some on each slice of tomato. On top of this place a poached egg. Top with the hollandaise sauce, to which has been added the Tabasco.

Top each serving with a few more crayfish and serve immediately.

*You may substitute 18 medium shrimp, cooked (p. 247), or 1 can Alaska king crab meat.

# EGGS SHADOWS ON THE TECHE

12 hard-boiled eggs
3 Tbs. butter
6 Tbs. concentrated tomato purée
1 tsp. salt
½ tsp. Tabasco pepper sauce
12 cooked, peeled shrimp
  (p. 247), finely chopped
2 cups Béchamel Sauce
  (chap. 13)

1 cup Creole tomatoes,
  finely chopped, cooked and
  drained of any excess liquid
  (approximately 2 tomatoes)
1–2 hard-boiled eggs, yolks and
  white separated and chopped
Finely chopped parsley
Paprika

*Serves 6*

Cut the hard-boiled eggs lengthwise. Remove the yolks from the whites.

Mash the yolks with the butter, tomato purée, salt and Tabasco. Add the finely chopped shrimp.

Stuff the egg whites and arrange the halves in a shallow buttered casserole. Put the casserole in a 350° oven until the eggs are heated but not browned—about 15 minutes.

Combine the béchamel sauce with the chopped tomatoes and heat for 5 minutes or until very hot. Coat the eggs with this mixture and garnish with sprinklings of the chopped hard-boiled eggs, chopped parsley and some paprika.

NOTE: *Shadows on the Teche* is a historic house in New Iberia, the heart of the Bayou Teche country in south Louisiana.

# EGGS SUPREME

6 hard-boiled eggs,
  cut in half lengthwise
4 Tbs. purée of foie gras
1 Tbs. finely chopped
  black olives
Pinch of dried chervil
Salt and white pepper to taste

4 Tbs. butter
2 cups Béchamel Sauce
  (chap. 13)
6 Tbs. grated Swiss cheese
Paprika
Parsley

*Serves 6*

Mash egg yolks and blend well with purée of foie gras, black olives and chervil. Season with salt and white pepper.

Stuff the egg whites and press the halves together. Place the stuffed eggs in

6 individual ramekins that have been buttered with some of the butter. Spoon enough béchamel sauce over each egg to cover.

Sprinkle each egg with 1 Tbs. grated Swiss cheese and some paprika. Dot with the remaining butter and set under the broiler until the topping is well browned, about 5 minutes.

Garnish with sprigs of parsley.


## FRENCH FRIED EGG PO BOY

1 8" slice New Orleans Po Boy
   bread (or 1 small French loaf of
   equivalent size)
2 Tbs. melted butter

½ tsp. Creole mustard
3 French fried eggs
¼ cup fried parsley

*Serves 1*

Hollow out the slice of Po Boy or French bread loaf. Melt butter, add Creole mustard and brush inside of bread.

French fry 3 eggs. When cooked, lay them side by side in the bread. Dust with fried parsley and cover loaf.

Place in oven for about 2–3 minutes and serve immediately.

This will be messy to eat but oh-so-New-Orleans good. A different breakfast dish.


## FRIED EGGS HUEY LONG

8 chicken livers
4 Tbs. butter
12 slices firm tomato

Salt and ground black pepper
8 fried eggs
1 cup Madeira Sauce (chap. 13)

*Serves 4*

Sauté chicken livers in butter. Set aside to keep warm.

Sauté tomatoes in remaining butter. Sprinkle both livers and tomatoes with salt and pepper.

Arrange eggs and tomato slices alternately on a serving dish. Garnish each serving with chicken livers. Surround with Madeira sauce.

Serve for lunch or supper.

## FRIED EGGS WITH BLACK BUTTER

8 hot fried eggs                    Salt and ground black pepper
4 Tbs. butter                       1 tsp. vinegar

*Serves 4*

Arrange fried eggs in a serving dish.

Brown the butter in a saucepan. Add a dash each of salt and pepper and pour over the eggs. Pour the vinegar into the saucepan, heat and pour over the eggs.

Serve for breakfast, lunch or supper.

## GYPSY EGGS

2 Tbs. olive oil                    ½ tsp. cumin
2 or 3 cloves garlic                Pinch of nutmeg
10–12 blanched and skinned          Salt and pepper to taste
  almonds, unsalted                 ¼ cup boiling water
2 slices white bread                6 eggs
Pinch of powdered saffron           Chopped parsley

*Serves 6*

Heat some olive oil in a heavy frying pan and lightly fry the garlic, almonds and bread.

In a mortar, pound the saffron, cumin and nutmeg. Add the fried garlic, almonds and bread and pound thoroughly.

When reduced to a paste, add a little of the oil in which the garlic has been fried. Season with salt and pepper and add a little boiling water to thin the sauce.

Pour this mixture into a fireproof dish. Break the eggs carefully into it and put in a 400° oven until the eggs are nicely set—about 5 minutes.

Serve immediately, garnished with chopped parsley.

# HUEVOS RANCHEROS

| | |
|---|---|
| 3 Tbs. olive oil | Salt and pepper to taste |
| 1 large onion, sliced | A pinch of chili powder |
| 1 large green pepper, sliced | Cumin and oregano to taste |
| 1 clove garlic, crushed | ½ tsp. Tabasco pepper sauce |
| 1 Tbs. flour | 6 large eggs, raw |
| 3½ cups tomatoes, peeled, seeded, chopped and cooked in butter 5–10 minutes | 18 small cubes sharp Cheddar cheese or Monterey Jack cheese |
| | 6 black olive halves |

*Serves 6*

In a saucepan, heat the olive oil; add the onion, green pepper and garlic. Cook gently for 3 minutes.

Blend in the flour and the cooked tomatoes. Cook, stirring for a few minutes, and season with salt, pepper, chili, cumin, oregano and Tabasco. Cook for 5 more minutes. Pour the sauce into a shallow baking dish.

Break the eggs into the dish. Around and in between the eggs, put the cheese cubes. Place an olive half on each egg yolk.

Bake the dish in a moderate (350°) oven for about 10–12 minutes or until the eggs are set.

*NOTE:* Also good served with slices of avocado (that have been heated in a little chicken stock and drained) in addition to the other ingredients.


# HUNGARIAN-STYLE STUFFED EGGS

| | |
|---|---|
| 9 hard-boiled eggs | Salt and ground black pepper |
| 4 Tbs. finely chopped red onion | 4 firm medium tomatoes |
| 4 Tbs. butter | Lemon juice to taste |
| 1 tsp. paprika | ½ cup heavy cream |

*Serves 6*

Preheat oven to 350°.

Cut eggs into lengthwise halves. Remove yolks and put them through a sieve.

Cook onions in butter until they are soft and blend half of them with the yolks, reserving the other half.

Add ½ tsp. of the paprika to the yolk mixture and season with salt and pepper to taste. Stuff the egg whites and set aside.

Cut tomatoes into slices ½" thick. Sauté them in the reserved butter-and-onion mixture.

Place tomato slices in the bottom of a baking dish and arrange the stuffed eggs on top. Bake for 5 minutes.

Add lemon juice and the remaining paprika to the cream and pour over the eggs.

This is a good luncheon or supper dish.


# JANSSON'S TEMPTATION

7 medium boiling potatoes,
   peeled and cut into strips
   2" long and ¼" thick
4½ Tbs. butter
2 Tbs. vegetable oil
2–3 large yellow onions,
   thinly sliced (4 cups)

White pepper to taste
16 flat anchovy filets, drained*
8 hard-boiled eggs, sliced
2 Tbs. fine dry bread crumbs
1 cup heavy cream
½ cup milk

*Serves 4–6*

Preheat oven to 400°.

Place the potato strips in cold water to keep them from discoloring.

Heat 2 Tbs. of the butter and the 2 Tbs. oil in a 10"–12" skillet. When the foam subsides, add the onions and cook for 10 minutes, stirring frequently, until they are soft but not browned.

With a pastry brush or paper towel, grease a 1½–2-quart soufflé dish or baking dish with ½ Tbs. of the butter.

Drain the potatoes and pat them dry with paper towels. Arrange a layer of potatoes on the bottom of the dish and sprinkle with white pepper as you alternate layers of onions, anchovies and hard-boiled egg slices, ending with the potatoes.

Scatter bread crumbs over the top layer of potatoes and dot the casserole with the remaining 2 Tbs. butter cut into bits.

In a small saucepan, heat the cream and milk until they barely simmer; then pour over the casserole.

Reduce heat to 350° and bake in the center of the oven for 45 minutes, or until the potatoes are tender when pierced with the tip of a sharp knife and the liquid is nearly absorbed.

In a cold climate excellent for breakfast or for an after-theatre supper.


*Use Scandinavian anchovy filets packed in brine, available at gourmet shops. Do not use the regular canned variety. If the Scandinavian kind is not available, use sprats. Be sure to wash them thoroughly first.

# KING MARDI GRAS EGGS

6 Tbs. butter
1 Tbs. onion, grated
3 Tbs. green pepper, finely
  minced
3 Tbs. fresh mushrooms,
  finely chopped
1 large Creole tomato,
  peeled, seeded and chopped
4 Tbs. flour
2 cups light cream, scalded

Salt and white pepper to taste
½ tsp. Tabasco pepper sauce
7–8 hard-boiled eggs, thickly
  sliced
2 slices pimiento, chopped
3 Tbs. dry sherry
1 cup plain French bread crumbs
  mixed with ¼ cup grated
  Gruyère or Parmesan cheese

*Serves 4–6*

In a heavy saucepan, melt 4 Tbs. of the butter and cook the onion, green pepper and mushrooms, stirring constantly until the vegetables are tender. Add the tomato and cook for 5 more minutes.

Stir in the flour. When it is well blended, add the cream a little at a time, stirring constantly. The sauce should be thick. You may not require the full 2 cups of cream. Season with salt, pepper and Tabasco.

When the sauce is thick and smooth, transfer to the top of a double boiler. Mix in gently but thoroughly the thick slices of hard-boiled egg. Add the pimiento and the sherry.

Finish cooking over hot but not boiling water, until the mixture is thoroughly heated—about 10–15 minutes.

Pour the mixture into a large, shallow casserole or individual casseroles that have been buttered. Sprinkle with the bread-crumb-and-cheese mixture and dot with the remaining butter. Brown quickly under the broiler flame.

# NEW ORLEANS EGGS EN CROÛTE

6 slices French bread
Butter
1½ cups diced, cooked shrimp
  (p. 247), (about 24 shrimp)
2 cups Béchamel Sauce (chap. 13)

6 eggs
Salt and pepper to taste
Chopped parsley
Paprika

*Serves 6*

Partially scoop out the slices of French bread to make shells. Spread inside and out with softened butter. Place the bread shells in individual shallow ramekins.

Combine the shrimp with the hot béchamel sauce. Fill the bread shells with this mixture.

On top of each shell break a fresh egg. Dot the eggs with butter and salt and pepper.

Bake in a moderate (350°) oven for about 12 minutes or until the whites are set. Garnish with chopped parsley and paprika.

## POACHED EGGS MARIE LAVEAU

6 large Creole tomatoes,
  firm and ripe
Salt and ground black pepper
  to taste
24 medium shrimp, cooked
  (p. 247), peeled and deveined
1½ cups Béchamel Sauce
  (chap. 13)

½ cup sliced mushrooms,
  sautéed and drained
6 hot poached eggs
1 Tbs. heavy cream
3 black olives, sliced

*Serves 6*

Cut a slice from the stem end of each tomato. Scoop out the center with a spoon and sprinkle the tomatoes with salt and pepper. Invert on a plate to drain.

Combine 16 whole shrimp with the mushrooms and 1 cup of the béchamel sauce. Adjust seasonings. Spoon into the tomato cups and top each with a poached egg.

Mix together the remaining ½ cup béchamel sauce, the remaining shrimp, finely chopped, and the cream. Spoon this over the eggs and garnish each with a slice of olive.

Serve hot.

## POACHED EGGS METAIRIE

1 cup cooking oil, for frying
8 cold poached eggs
2 raw eggs, beaten with
  1 Tbs. water

1 cup fine dry bread crumbs
¾ cup tomato sauce flavored with
  ½ tsp. Creole seasonings
Chopped parsley

*Serves 4*

Preheat oil to 375°.

Carefully dip 1 poached egg at a time in beaten raw egg and roll in bread crumbs. Let stand for 30 minutes, refrigerated, for crumbs to set.

Fry in preheated cooking oil until browned—about 2–3 minutes. Drain on paper towel.

Serve hot with seasoned tomato sauce. Garnish with chopped parsley.

# POACHED EGGS MORNAY

8 poached eggs
8 slices sandwich-size fried bread
   or buttered toast
Salt and ground black pepper
   to taste

¾ cup Béchamel Sauce (chap. 13)
4 Tbs. grated Gruyère cheese
2 Tbs. fine dry bread crumbs
3 Tbs. melted butter
Watercress

*Serves 4–8*

Preheat oven to 450°.

Place 1 poached egg on each slice of fried bread or toast. Arrange on a baking sheet. Sprinkle with salt and black pepper. Coat with béchamel sauce.

Combine cheese and bread crumbs and sprinkle over the eggs. Drizzle with melted butter. Place in the oven for about 4–5 minutes to melt the cheese, being careful not to overcook eggs.

Garnish with watercress.

# POACHED EGGS VERSAILLES

*Eggs Versailles:*
24 medium shrimp, cooked
   (p. 247)
1 Tbs. butter
¾ cup Béchamel Sauce (chap. 13)
1 lb. filet of sole or flounder
½ cup sliced, sautéed mushrooms
Salt and black pepper to taste

8 slices French bread,
   partially scooped out and
   toasted lightly
8 hot poached eggs
1 truffle, cut in julienne strips
   (or 8 mushroom caps,
   sliced and sautéed in butter)

*Sauce Normande:*
2 Tbs. butter
1 tsp. flour
1 cup cooking liquor from fish or
   shellfish used above

Liquor from mushrooms used
   above
2 egg yolks
½ cup cream

*Serves 4*

Chop 12 of the shrimp and pound together with the butter. Combine with béchamel sauce to make a shrimp sauce.

Dice the remaining shrimp. Poach the fish in simmering water for 8 minutes, drain and flake.

Mix fish and diced shrimp with mushrooms and shrimp sauce. Season to taste with salt and black pepper.

Spoon into French bread shells. Top each with a poached egg.

*To prepare the Sauce Normande:* Melt the butter in a saucepan, add flour and cook until it just starts to turn golden. Add the fish and mushroom liquors and cook for about 10 minutes. Beat the egg yolks slightly with the cream and combine with the sauce. Heat, but do not boil, and strain through a fine sieve.

Coat the poached eggs in the bread shells with the hot sauce Normande. Garnish with truffle or mushroom slices and serve immediately.

# RICH BOY EGGS

| | |
|---|---|
| 2 cups Basic Brown Sauce (chap. 13) | 8 round pieces fried bread |
| ½ cup Madeira or dry sherry | 8 truffle slices |
| 8 hot poached eggs | |

*Serves 4*

Cook brown sauce slowly until reduced to 1 cup. Add wine, mix well and heat.

Spoon this mixture over the hot eggs after placing 1 egg on each piece of fried bread.

Top each egg with a truffle slice and serve.

## SCRAMBLED EGGS BUDAPEST

6 eggs
3 Tbs. lukewarm water
Salt to taste
4 oz. smoked bacon (or
  Hungarian *szalonna,* if
  available)

1 medium red onion, finely
  chopped
1 tsp. Hungarian sweet red
  paprika

*Serves 4*

In a bowl beat eggs with the lukewarm water and season with salt. Cut the bacon or *szalonna* into very small cubes.

In a heavy iron frying pan, fry the bacon over low heat until the fat is all out. Remove the pieces of crisp bacon and keep warm.

In the same frying pan, fry the onion until golden. (If you have too much fat, drain some off.) Immediately pour the eggs over them and scramble until set. Mix in the fried bacon pieces or scatter them on top.

Dust top with paprika before serving.


## SCRAMBLED EGGS WITH CHEESE

8 large eggs
1/3 cup light cream
1/2 cup grated Cheddar
  or Gruyère cheese

Salt and ground black pepper
  to taste
1 Tbs. butter
8 slices Cheddar
  or Gruyère cheese

*Serves 4*

Beat eggs lightly; add cream, grated cheese, salt and pepper. Melt butter in an 8″ skillet. Pour in the egg mixture. Stir and cook over low heat until eggs are set but soft.

Serve over slices of cheese at room temperature.

## SCRAMBLED EGGS WITH CRAYFISH

32 peeled crayfish tails*          ⅓ cup light cream
3 Tbs. butter                      Salt and ground black pepper
8 large eggs                         to taste

*Serves 6*

Cook crayfish in 2 Tbs. of the butter over moderately low heat until they are tender—about 5 minutes.

Beat the eggs lightly and add crayfish tails, cream and salt and pepper.

Melt the remaining 1 Tbs. butter in an 8" skillet. Pour in the eggs. Stir and cook over low heat until eggs are set but soft.

Serve hot.

*You may substitute 32 small shrimp, 1½ cans Alaska king crab, or 4 oz. fresh beluga caviar. (When I'm really broke I use lumpfish, a.k.a. "Texas caviar.")

# SCOTCH EGGS

4 hard-boiled eggs
¼ cup flour, seasoned with
  salt and pepper
1 lb. sausage meat, breakfast type
Pinch of sage, thyme, tarragon,
  Tabasco

2 egg yolks beaten with
  a little milk
1 cup bread crumbs
1 cup cooking oil (more if
  needed)

*Serves 4*

Cool the hard-boiled eggs, peel and roll lightly in seasoned flour.

Season the sausage meat with any one or a combination of the seasonings.

Cover the eggs with the sausage meat. See that they are well sealed in at least ¼" of the meat, or more if you like it thicker. Roll again in flour and then in the egg mixture and finally the bread crumbs.

Refrigerate for at least 1 hour or until ready to use. Then deep fry in cooking oil until golden brown—about 15 minutes.

When ready to serve, slice in half lengthwise and you will have an egg in a neat sausage basket.

May be served hot or cold.

# 8
# FISH & SHELLFISH

I LIKE to think that man came from the sea and will return to it. I know I did—I'm a Pisces.

The fish and shellfish recipes in this chapter reflect authentic French cuisine with an accent of Cajun and Creole.

While salmon, lobsters, clams and scallops are not native to Gulf waters, with deep freezing and air freight, these seafoods are now available in New Orleans, and when I'm home I enjoy varying my seafood menus to include them.

The Lummi Coho salmon, which now can be purchased around the country, comes from an Indian tribe in the Pacific Northwest which has lived by the sea for centuries. My salmon recipes were created for the Lummi Coho salmon.

Naturally, fresh fish and shellfish, when available, always bring these recipes to their fullest perfection. However, in areas where fresh items cannot be found, these recipes may be prepared from their frozen companions.

For any readers who wish to send for local Louisiana shellfish or fish, my contact in New Orleans is: Mr. Johnny Ferrara of Ferrara Bros. Seafood, 729 Gov. Nicholls St., New Orleans, LA 70116; (504) 523–4273. Johnny Ferrara ships everywhere—even overseas.

# HINTS

## *HOW TO COOK SHRIMP*

Shrimp sizes are: small (40–45 per lb.), medium (26–30 per lb.) and large (15–20 per lb.). Your cooking time will depend on the size: 3–5 minutes for the small, 8–10 minutes for the medium and sometimes as much as 12–15 minutes for the very large or jumbo.

I prefer to use beer in cooking my shrimp, or a mixture of beer and water. Cook them unpeeled.

For 2 lbs. of shrimp, put 2 cans of beer and 1 can of water in a large kettle. Add 1 onion, 1 lemon cut in half and 1 carrot. Use crab boil, if available. Bring the liquid to a boil, add the shrimp and cook for the desired time.

Be careful not to overcook or your shrimp will get mushy. When ready remove shrimp, cool and then peel and devein.

Now your shrimp are ready for use in any recipe calling for cooked shrimp. Or you may eat them just as they are with Chris's Cocktail Sauce (chap. 13).

## *HOW TO COOK CRAYFISH*

If you are fortunate enough to get live crayfish or uncooked crayfish tails, you can cook them as you do shrimp (above).

However, most crayfish tails now come already peeled, cooked and frozen—even in New Orleans. Many seafood markets around the country have them shipped in.

When you buy frozen, precooked crayfish tails, you may use them just as they are after thawing. Or they can be further cooked according to the directions in the individual recipes.

## *HOW TO COOK LOBSTER*

When I feel extravagant and send for live lobsters, this is the way I prepare them.

In the bottom of a large steamer, place some clams with a bit of seaweed. Add about 3 cups of water with a little salt and bring to a boil. Then put the live lobsters in the top half, cover tightly and steam them for about 20 minutes, until they are red and tender.

Another method of cooking live lobsters is to throw them into salted boiling water to cover for 20–25 minutes or until they are bright red.

Most of the lobster dishes in this book were created with either Florida rock lobster tails or South African lobster tails.

I have found that 1 large lobster tail will make 1 cup of cooked lobster meat, more or less.

## HOW TO USE CRAB

Fresh crab meat in New Orleans comes in the form of lump, white and claw.

The lump is the very meaty part and is used for special recipes as indicated. The white and claw are what I use for recipes that call for stuffing with crab.

If the crab meat is fresh, pick over and use it immediately. If frozen, be sure to thaw out completely and pick over before using.

# CLAMS

## CLAM BALLS

| | |
|---|---|
| 1 cup bread ends, very finely cut up | 1 Tbs. butter |
| 2 bottles clam juice | 1 Tbs. flour |
| 1 cup chopped clams | 1 cup flour, seasoned with salt and pepper |
| ½ large onion, minced | 2 whole eggs, mixed with a little water |
| ¼ cup celery, minced | |
| ½ Tbs. Worcestershire sauce | 1–1½ cups bread crumbs |
| 1 Tbs. pimiento, minced | 2 cups cooking oil |
| ¼ tsp. Tabasco pepper sauce | Parsley or watercress |

*Serves 6*

Soak the bread ends in 1 bottle of clam juice. Mix chopped clams with the bread ends and combine thoroughly. Add the next 5 seasoning ingredients and combine again.

Melt butter, add 1 Tbs. flour and then add the remaining bottle of clam juice to make a thick clam sauce.

Add the sauce to the chopped clam mixture and work once more so that everything is well blended. Place this mixture in a bowl and allow to refrigerate overnight.

When mixture is ready for use, prepare a bowl for the seasoned flour, another for the egg wash and a third for the bread crumbs.

Roll the clam balls in the palms of your hands to the size of a melon ball. Roll in seasoned flour, then in the egg wash and finally in the bread crumbs.

Refrigerate once more until ready to fry—at least 1 hour. Then deep fry or fry in a skillet for about 5 minutes, until golden brown. Be careful not to overcrowd.

Drain on paper towels and serve on a bed of parsley or watercress.

## CLAMS CASINO

6 cherrystone clams
3 Tbs. butter
½ tsp. anchovy paste
Rock salt

½ cup finely chopped green
  pepper
½ cup finely chopped pimiento
2 strips raw bacon
Watercress

*Serves 1*

Loosen the clams in the bottom of each shell.

Combine the butter with the anchovy paste. Divide this anchovy butter among the shells, placing a bit underneath each clam.

Set the shells firmly on a layer of rock salt in a shallow baking pan.

Combine the green pepper and pimiento and top each clam with a pinch of this mixture. Cover with a piece of raw bacon cut the size of the clam.

Broil 3″ from the flame for 6–8 minutes, turning the bacon once to broil on each side. When the bacon is crisp, serve immediately, garnished with crisp watercress.

## NEW ORLEANS CLAM DIP

1 pint Creole cream cheese*
½ pint sour cream
½ tsp. Tabasco pepper sauce
1 Tbs. Worcestershire sauce

2 tsp. chives
½ tsp. seasoned salt
1 cup clams, finely minced

*Serves 6*

Mix well all ingredients except clams. Add minced clams. Blend well and chill thoroughly before serving as a dip.

*The nearest substitute is creamed cottage cheese.

## STUFFED CLAMS NORMANDY

18 large clams, fresh or canned,
   well cleaned,
   with shells reserved
2 Tbs. butter
3 Tbs. mushrooms, finely
   chopped
2 Tbs. shallots, finely chopped

½ tsp. Tabasco pepper sauce
1½ Tbs. chives, finely minced
1 tsp. chervil
1 tsp. parsley, minced
2 Tbs. bread crumbs
1 tsp. dry sherry
¼ cup dry white wine

*Serves 6*

Chop the clams finely.

Heat butter, sauté the mushrooms and add all other ingredients except bread crumbs and wines. Blend well.

Add bread crumbs and clams. Add sherry and wine to moisten.

Using either the fresh clam shells or imitation shells, fill each with this mixture.

Bake in a moderate oven (325°) for about 10 minutes or until golden brown.


# CRAB


## CRAB MEAT DAN FUSELIER

½ cup olive oil
4 Tbs. butter
1 carrot, diced
3 shallots, minced
1 large tomato,
   peeled, seeded and chopped
½ green pepper, diced
2 whole pimientos, diced

1 clove garlic, minced
½ cup celery, minced
1 Tbs. Creole mustard
1 Tbs. Worcestershire sauce
½ tsp. Tabasco pepper sauce
Salt and pepper to taste
½–1 cup dry white wine
1 lb. lump crab meat, picked over

*Serves 4*

Heat oil and butter in frying pan. Add carrot and cook over low heat until almost tender—about 10 minutes. Add shallots, tomato, green pepper, pimientos, garlic and celery; cook for 15 minutes.

Add mustard, Worcestershire sauce, Tabasco, salt and pepper. Cook for 5 minutes longer. Add white wine and continue to cook until wine has reduced by half—about 10 minutes. If the consistency is too thick, a little more white wine may be added.

Finally gently blend in the lump crab meat and cook until mixture is thoroughly heated.

Serve with fluffy rice or plain pasta.

## CRAB MEAT CHELSEA

| | |
|---|---|
| 24 stalks fresh asparagus | 2 pimientos, chopped |
| 5 Tbs. butter | ¼ cup chopped parsley |
| 1 medium or 2 small | 2 Tbs. flour |
|    white onions, chopped | 1 lb. lump crab meat, picked over |
| ½ green pepper, chopped | Salt and pepper to taste |
| ¼ cup chopped celery | 1 Tbs. Worcestershire sauce |
| 1 medium tomato, | ¼ cup dry sherry |
|    peeled, seeded and chopped | Toast points |

*Serves 4*

Clean and wash asparagus and cook in salted water until just tender—about 15 minutes. Keep warm.

Melt butter in a heavy skillet. Add onion, green pepper and celery and sauté for 10 minutes. Add tomato, pimiento and parsley and cook for 5 minutes longer. Add flour and blend well. Gently toss in the carb meat. Add salt, pepper and Worcestershire sauce and cook until thoroughly heated—about 5 minutes. Lastly, add the sherry.

Lay 6 hot asparagus per person on individual dishes. Cover each serving with the crab meat and serve with toast points.

# CRAB MEAT LOUIS

*Crab meat salad:*

| | |
|---|---|
| 1 medium head lettuce, shredded | 3 hard-boiled eggs, sliced |
| 1½ lbs. lump crab meat, picked over and chilled | 9 ripe olives, sliced |
| 2 pimientos, cut into strips |
| 2 large tomatoes, peeled and cut into wedges | 2 Tbs. capers |
| Finely chopped parsley |

*Louis dressing:*

| | |
|---|---|
| 1½ cups mayonnaise | ½ tsp. fresh tarragon (a little less if dried) |
| ¾ cup chili sauce |
| 1½ tsp. grated onion | ¼ tsp. Tabasco pepper sauce |
| 1½ tsp. horseradish | Salt and white pepper to taste |
| 1 tsp. lemon juice | |

*Serves 6*

Arrange lettuce in individual serving bowls. Mound crab meat on top. Garnish with tomato wedges, egg slices, olive slices and pimiento strips, reserving capers and parsley until ready to serve.

Cover bowls with foil or plastic wrap and chill.

To make the Louis dressing, blend all ingredients and chill.

When ready to serve, spoon the dressing over each bowl of crab meat and garnish with capers and parsley.

# CRAB MEAT POLAUMBO

| | |
|---|---|
| 1 stick butter | ⅔ cup Béchamel Sauce (chap. 13), hot |
| ½ cup onions, minced |
| ½ lb. fresh mushrooms, diced | 1 cup Italian seasoned bread crumbs |
| Salt and white pepper to taste |
| 1 Tbs. Worcestershire sauce | Paprika |
| 1 lb. lump crab meat, picked over | |

*Serves 6*

Over medium heat, melt most of the butter in an iron skillet. (Reserve just enough to dot the ramekins later.) Add onions and cook for 10 minutes. Add mushrooms and cook for about 5 more minutes. Add salt, pepper and Worcestershire sauce.

Now add crab meat and cook until thoroughly blended and heated through—

about 10 minutes. Gradually add enough of the hot béchamel sauce to bind the mixture.

Fill small ramekins with this mixture, top with seasoned bread crumbs and dot with the remaining butter. Sprinkle with paprika and broil in a moderate oven until crumbs are golden brown on top—about 3–5 minutes.

This dish may be made in advance and heated in the oven for 15–20 minutes, omitting the final broiler step.

## DEVILED CRABS

6 Tbs. butter
½ cup shallots, minced
¼ cup brandy
1 tsp. Dijon mustard
2/3–1 cup Béchamel Sauce
   (chap. 13)

1 lb. crab meat (white or claw),
   picked over
Salt and white pepper to taste
6 cleaned crab shells*
1 cup bread crumbs,
   seasoned with salt and pepper

*Serves 6*

Heat 4 Tbs. of the butter and cook the shallots until transparent. Remove the pan from the fire and swirl in the brandy. Add the Dijon mustard a little at a time.

Add the béchamel sauce a little at a time and finally combine the crab meat with this mixture. Should more béchamel sauce be needed to bind the crab, add a bit more at a time.

Season with salt and white pepper to taste.

Fill the crab shells with this mixture and cover each with the seasoned bread crumbs. Dot each shell with remaining butter and place under the broiler until bread crumbs are brown—about 5 minutes.

*If fresh shells are not available, you can purchase shells made of plastic or foil, but these are not very elegant.

## SOFT-SHELL CRABS 1840

12 soft-shell crabs*                1 Tbs. chopped chives
2 sticks butter                     2 cups dry white wine
6 shallots, chopped                 ½ cup Chicken Stock (p. 183)
¾ lb. fresh mushrooms, sliced       1 cup heavy cream, scalded
1 Tbs. chopped parsley              ½ pint absinthe or Abisante

*Serves 4–6*

Rinse the crabs in salt water. Cut off the heads about ½″ behind the eyes and discard the green bubble. Lift the soft shell where it comes to a point at each side and cut off the white gills. Peel back the apron and cut it off.

You can buy soft-shell crabs already cleaned, in which case you can omit the above step.

Butter a large casserole generously with about 6 Tbs. of the butter. Put in the crabs, shallots, mushrooms, parsley and chives. Using another 6 Tbs. of the butter, dot each crab. Add the white wine and chicken stock.

Bring to a boil, cover the casserole and cook over a brisk fire for 10 minutes. Transfer the crabs to another casserole and keep them warm.

Reduce the sauce in the first casserole to about a generous cup, bring to a boil and add the crabs. Boil up twice and remove from the fire. Remove the crabs and set to one side.

Into the sauce, beat the remaining 4 Tbs. butter, the heavy cream a little bit at a time and finally the absinthe a little at a time. Just use enough for personal taste; you may not want the full amount. Be sure that sauce is well blended.

Pour this sauce back over the crabs, cover the casserole and set in a low oven (250°) for 10–12 minutes.

* Soft-shell crabs are seasonal in New Orleans from April until about early September. However, you can now purchase them frozen year-round, and these are acceptable although not recommended.

# SOFT-SHELL CRABS NEW ORLEANS

12 soft-shell crabs,
   cleaned and ready for use*
2 Tbs. chopped parsley
2 Tbs. chopped chives
2 Tbs. chopped celery leaves
2 Tbs. chopped onion
2 Tbs. leeks, chopped
1 small clove garlic, chopped
½ tsp. Tabasco pepper sauce

1 quart milk
4 egg yolks, well beaten and
   highly seasoned with a pinch
   of salt, pepper, thyme,
   tarragon and nutmeg
2 cups flour, seasoned
   with salt and pepper
2 cups cooking oil or 2 sticks
   butter

*Serves 6*

Place crabs in a deep bowl.

In a separate bowl, mix together the next 7 ingredients. Add this mixture to the milk, combined with the egg yolks, and pour over the crabs.

Place a board or plastic wrap over the bowl and let stand for 30 minutes. The crabs will absorb much of the milk mixture and its flavor.

When ready to serve, lift out the crabs, roll them in the seasoned flour and sauté them in the butter or fresh cooking oil until golden brown on both sides— about 15–20 minutes.

* Buy the crabs already cleaned, or clean them yourself as directed for Soft-Shell Crabs 1840.

# CRAYFISH

## BAKED CRAYFISH CANAPÉS

¾ cup cream cheese
¾ cup Roquefort cheese
½ cup olive oil
2 large black olives, chopped
2 pimientos, chopped
1 tsp. lemon juice
¼ tsp. Tabasco pepper sauce

12 thin rounds Melba Toast
  (chap. 13)
1 lb. crayfish tails or shrimp
  or lobster, cooked (p. 247)
12 thin slices of American cheese
  cut to fit the Melba Toast

*Serves 6*

Cream together the cream cheese, Roquefort cheese, olive oil, olives and pimientos and season with the lemon juice and Tabasco. Spread generously on each round of toast.

Divide the crayfish among the rounds of toast. Top with a thin round of American cheese.

Bake in a moderate oven (350°) until cheese just begins to melt and the canapé is hot—about 5 minutes.

This dish can be prepared in advance and heated at the last minute.

Serve these canapés with a small plate for each person.

## CRAYFISH IN GARLIC SAUCE

½ cup olive oil
3 lbs. shelled crayfish tails
Salt and pepper to taste
4 cloves garlic, finely minced

½ cup finely chopped parsley
1 large ripe tomato,
  peeled, seeded and chopped
Lemon wedges

*Serves 6*

Fill the bottom of a heavy skillet with olive oil to a depth of about ¼". Sauté the crayfish tails in the oil for about 5 minutes. Season with salt and pepper. With a slotted spoon, remove them to a heated platter.

To the oil remaining in the pan, add the garlic, parsley and tomato. Cook for 5 minutes, stirring from time to time.

Pour the sauce over the crayfish and serve immediately with wedges of lemon.

# CRAYFISH VIEUX CARRÉ

2 Tbs. butter
1 carrot, diced
1 onion, diced
¼ cup shallots, chopped
1 clove garlic, chopped
¼ cup parsley, chopped
1 bay leaf, crushed
4 tomatoes, peeled, seeded and
  chopped
½ tsp. salt

½ tsp. Tabasco pepper sauce
4 dozen crayfish tails
  or small shrimp, cooked
  (p. 247)
4 Tbs. cognac, warmed
2 cups dry white wine
1 Tbs. *Beurre Manié* (chap. 13)
⅛ tsp. black pepper
1 tsp. lemon juice
Extra chopped parsley

*Serves 4*

Melt butter in a heavy skillet and add the carrot, onion, shallots, garlic and parsley as well as the bay leaf. Cook very slowly for about 15 minutes or until the vegetables are soft.

Add the tomatoes, salt and Tabasco. Add the crayfish. Add the warm cognac and ignite. When the flame burns out, add the white wine and cook for about 12 minutes longer.

With a slotted spoon, remove the crayfish. Cook the liquid until it is reduced by about half and thicken with the *beurre manié*. Correct the seasoning with a little freshly ground black pepper and lemon juice.

Pour the sauce over the crayfish and sprinkle with freshly chopped parsley. Serve on toast.

# FLOUNDER

## BAKED FLOUNDER

6 small flounder
Salt and pepper to taste
1 bunch shallots, chopped
½ cup parsley, chopped
2 cups dry white wine

2 cups coarse bread crumbs
1 stick butter
Chopped parsley
Lemon wedges

*Serves 6*

Clean the fish and cut 4 shallow slits on each side of the bone with the point of a knife.

Place the fish in a buttered baking dish. Sprinkle with the salt and pepper, shallots and parsley; pour in enough of the dry wine so that it is level with the fish. Sprinkle with coarse bread crumbs and generous dabs of butter.

Bake in a very hot oven (450°) until the fish is thoroughly cooked and the top is browned—about 20–25 minutes.

Serve very hot, sprinkled with parsley and garnished with lemon wedges.

NOTE: Filets of flounder may also be prepared in this manner, but cut the cooking time in half.

## BROILED STUFFED FLOUNDER

½ cup butter
2 tbs. green pepper,
    finely chopped
1 medium onion, finely chopped
2 tsp. parsley, chopped
1 clove garlic, chopped
½ cup celery, chopped
1–2 pimientos, chopped
Salt and pepper to taste
½ tsp. Tabasco pepper sauce

3 cups crab meat,
    cleaned and picked over
6 small flounder, cleaned and
    split, backbone removed
    without separating top
    from bottom
Juice of 1 lemon
½ cup dry vermouth
Chopped parsley and lemon
    wedges

*Serves 6*

In a heavy sauce pan, melt butter, reserving 2 Tbs., and sauté the next 6 vegetable ingredients. Add some of the salt and pepper and the Tabasco sauce. Cook until vegetables are tender and the onion takes on color.

Remove, cool and add the crab meat. Mix thoroughly.

Stuff the flounder with the crab meat mixture. Fasten the halves together with skewers and arrange the stuffed fish on a buttered baking dish.

Sprinkle with salt and white pepper and broil slowly, basting frequently with a mixture of the remaining butter, lemon juice and dry vermouth, until the fish are golden brown, first on one side and then the other—about 20 minutes. Garnish with parsley and lemon wedges and serve with a bowl of Hollandaise Sauce (chap. 13), passed separately.

## FILET OF FLOUNDER VIEUX CARRÉ

4 medium filets of flounder, each
  cut down the middle,
  making 8 pieces
1 cup flour, seasoned
  with salt and pepper
2 eggs, beaten with a little olive
  oil
1½ cups Italian seasoned bread
  crumbs

½ cup Clarified Butter (chap. 13)
4 small or 2 large zucchini,
  sliced and sautéed in butter
2 tomatoes,
  halved and sautéed in butter
8 black olives
8 Tbs. Maître d'Hôtel Butter
  (chap. 13)
Paprika

*Serves 4*

Dry the fish filets. Dip them in the seasoned flour, the egg wash and then the bread crumbs. Refrigerate for about 1 hour or until ready to fry.

Fry them lightly in the clarified butter. Place them on individual heated dinner plates and lay a row of the zucchini on each filet. On top of this place a tomato half and on top of this some black olive slices.

Moisten with a little maître d'hôtel butter seasoned with paprika and serve.

## GARDEN DISTRICT FILET OF FLOUNDER

¼ cup butter
1 Tbs. tomato paste
½ cup dry vermouth
4 filets of flounder, each cut
  down the middle, making
  8 pieces
Salt and white pepper to taste

1–2 Tbs. sour cream
1–2 Tbs. heavy cream
1 Tbs. finely chopped black
  olives
Finely chopped parsley
Lemon wedges
4 slices toasted bread

*Serves 4*

In a heavy skillet, heat the butter and then add the tomato paste and vermouth. Lay filets of flounder on this; add salt and pepper to taste. Cook over high heat and then reduce until the filets are cooked—about 10 minutes.

Combine the sour and heavy creams. Remove filets to a heated platter. Add creams to the sauce remaining in the pan and stir. Heat, but do not boil.

Place filets on individual heated plates. Pour suace over them and garnish each with some of the black chopped olives.

Sprinkle with chopped parsley and serve with lemon wedges and toast points.

# FROGS' LEGS

## FROGS' LEGS AND CRAB MEAT

| | |
|---|---|
| 18 pairs frogs' legs | 1½ cups heavy cream |
| 2 cups white wine | 1½ Tbs. chopped chives |
| 1 large bay leaf | 1–2 Tbs. *Beurre Manié* (chap. 13) |
| 2 whole cloves | 2 egg yolks |
| ½ lb. lump crab meat, picked over | Dash of cayenne |
| | Salt and white pepper to taste |
| 8 Tbs. butter | 1 Tbs. brandy or cognac |
| ½ cup dry sherry | 6 rounds toasted French bread |
| 1 cup mushrooms, chopped | |

*Serves 6*

Trim the meat from the frogs' legs. Place in a saucepan and cover with white wine. Add the bay leaf and cloves and cook over medium heat for about 8 minutes.

Drain and add crab meat. Add 4 Tbs. of the butter and the sherry and let stand for 40 minutes.

Transfer the mixture to a shallow casserole and cook over a gentle flame for about 10 minutes, stirring occasionally.

Drain off half the liquid and add the mushrooms, which have been sautéed for 5 minutes in the remaining 4 Tbs. butter and then drained.

Heat the cream with the chives and thicken with 1–2 Tbs. *beurre manié*. Blend this into the frogs'-legs mixture, cover and simmer for 20 minutes.

When ready to serve, stir in the egg yolks beaten with the cayenne and salt and pepper to taste. Lastly, add the brandy.

Serve at once on the bread rounds.

# FROGS' LEGS CREOLE

3 lbs. frogs' legs
Salt and pepper to taste
½ cup butter
1 Tbs. onion, finely chopped
1 green pepper,
   cut into thin julienne strips
6 ripe tomatoes,
   peeled and cut into eighths
1 cup mushrooms, finely chopped

3 shallots, tops and bottoms,
   minced
2 cloves garlic, minced
½ tsp. Tabasco pepper sauce
1 cup tomato sauce
½ cup Chicken Stock (p. 183)
Chopped parsley
Lemon wedges

*Serves 6*

Season the frogs' legs with salt and pepper and sauté them over a brisk flame in the hot butter until they are golden brown on both sides. Transfer the frogs' legs to a heated casserole.

To the butter in the skillet, add the onion, green pepper, tomatoes, mushrooms, shallots and garlic. Add Tabasco and cook all the vegetables for about 10 minutes, stirring constantly.

Add vegetable mixture to the frogs' legs in the casserole. Combine tomato sauce and chicken stock and add. Toss well and bake in a hot oven (450°) for about 15–20 minutes or until the legs are tender but not falling apart. Depending on the size of the legs, more time may be required.

Serve the frogs' legs from the casserole generously sprinkled with chopped parsley and garnished with lemon wedges.

# FROGS' LEGS PROVENÇALE

18 pairs frogs' legs
Salt and pepper to taste
12 Tbs. butter

Juice of 2 lemons
½ cup chopped parsley
2–3 tsp. garlic, chopped

*Serves 6*

Soak frogs' legs in cold water for 2 hours. Drain.

Dry the frogs' legs and season with salt and pepper. Sauté the legs in 6 Tbs. of hot butter until they are golden brown on each side and tender—about 20 minutes.

Arrange them on a heated platter and sprinkle with lemon juice and parsley.

Add the garlic and the remaining butter to the saucepan. When the butter is nut brown, pour it quickly over the frogs' legs.

Serve with the garlic butter still foaming.

## FROGS' LEGS VINAIGRETTE

*Frogs' legs:*
    3 lbs. frogs' legs, preferably small      1 cup wine vinegar
    1½ cups dry white wine      1 clove garlic, chopped
    1½ cups water      ½ cup parsley, chopped
    Salt and pepper to taste      ½ cup green onions, chopped
    1 cup olive oil

*Garnish:*
    6 hard-boiled eggs, quartered
    Green olives
    Gherkins

*Serves 6*

Poach the frogs' legs in a mixture of the wine and water for 5–10 minutes or until tender.

Make a vinaigrette sauce by combining all other ingredients and mixing well.

Chill frogs' legs in the water-wine mixture and then remove with a slotted spoon.

When ready to serve, arrange individual portions of lettuce leaves and divide the frogs' legs among them. Over each portion pour some of the well-mixed vinaigrette sauce.

Garnish with quarters of hard-boiled eggs, green olives and gherkins.

# LOBSTER

## PAPRIKA LOBSTER

    2 Tbs. butter      Salt and pepper to taste
    1 medium red onion, grated      1 Tbs. flour
    2 tsp. Hungarian sweet paprika      ½ cup Fish Stock (p. 184)
    2 lbs. cooked lobster meat,      ½ cup sour cream
      cut into bite-size pieces
      (p. 247)

*Serves 4*

In a frying pan, heat the butter and sauté the grated onion until almost golden—about 5 minutes. Blend in the paprika and toss in the lobster pieces. Add salt and pepper to taste.

Blend in the flour and moisten with the stock. Stir gently and cook for about 5 minutes.

Remove from the fire and carefully fold in the sour cream a little at a time until well blended and thoroughly heated.

Serve with green noodles.

# OYSTERS

## ANGELS ON HORSEBACK

16 very thin slices of bacon           16 toothpicks
16 large, plump oysters, shucked       Dash of Tabasco pepper sauce

*Serves 4*

Wrap bacon around oysters and secure with a toothpick. These may be wrapped in advance and refrigerated.

When ready to use, place on a cookie sheet or in a broiler pan and broil for 10 minutes, until bacon is cooked but not so crisp that it will crumble.

Serve as hot hors d'oeuvres.

*VARIATION:* Arrange 4–6 wrapped oysters on a skewer and then broil. To serve, remove from skewer and arrange on triangles of toast which have been sprinkled with minced parsley and a few drops of lemon juice. Add a dash of Tabasco to each serving.

## DEVILS ON HORSEBACK

2 dozen large, plump oysters          Grating of nutmeg
3 Tbs. butter                         ¼ tsp. paprika
3 Tbs. flour                          1 cup fried bread crumbs
1 cup heavy cream                     Sprigs of parsley
Salt and white pepper to taste        Lemon wedges

*Serves 6*

Shuck oysters; reserve and clean 12 shells.

Poach oysters in their own liquid until they just begin to curl—about 5–10 minutes. Remove oysters and reserve the liquid.

Heat the butter and blend in the flour to make a roux. Combine the heavy cream with the oyster liquid and add little by little to the roux, stirring continuously until you have a smooth, thick sauce—about 5–10 minutes.

Season the sauce with salt and white pepper, nutmeg and paprika.

Toss the oysters in this sauce and divide into the well-cleaned oyster shells.

Sprinkle each shell with a little of the fried bread crumbs. Arrange shells on a baking sheet and place in a hot oven (400°) for 5 minutes before serving.

Garnish with parsley and lemon wedges.

## OYSTERS EDWARD E. BENEDICT

16 large, plump raw oysters,
   shucked
1 cup flour, seasoned
   with salt and pepper
1 cup cooking oil, more or less
4 slices Canadian bacon, lightly
   fried

2 English muffins, lightly toasted
1 cup Hollandaise Sauce
   (chap. 13)
16 drops Tabasco pepper sauce
Paprika

*Serves 4*

Dredge the oysters in flour and then fry lightly in a pan filled about halfway with cooking oil. Fry for about 5 minutes, only, so that the oysters are not hard.

Prepare the Canadian bacon and English muffins.

Hollandaise sauce can be prepared in advance and kept hot in a double boiler.

To assemble each serving, place 1 slice Canadian bacon on ½ English muffin. Arrange 4 fried oysters on top. Put a drop of Tabasco on each oyster and cover with a portion of the warm hollandaise sauce.

Sprinkle a little paprika on top of the sauce for color and serve immediately.

## OYSTER PIE

2 Tbs. butter, for baking dish
1 quart fresh oysters, shucked
1 large onion, minced
2 Tbs. minced parsley
3 Tbs. minced green pepper
2 slices bacon,
   diced and fried until crisp
2 tsp. salt

½ tsp. black pepper
Pinch of cayenne pepper
Juice of 1 lemon
Basic Pie Crust recipe,
   top only (p. 382), to cover a
   deep, round 9″ baking dish
½ tsp. paprika

*Serves 6*

Butter the baking dish and place a layer of oysters in it.

Mix together the onion, parsley and green pepper. Sprinkle half this mixture over the oysters. Add another layer of oysters and sprinkle with the remaining vegetable mixture. Add the rest of the ingredients except pie crust and paprika.

Cover with the dough and make several slits with a knife to let out the steam. Sprinkle dough with paprika for color.

Bake in a 350° oven for about 30 minutes or until dough is cooked and deliciously brown.

# POMPANO

## FILET OF POMPANO CARIBBEAN

4  8-oz. pompano filets
Salt and white pepper to taste
1½ Tbs. shallots, minced
2 cups dry white wine
1 cup Fish Stock (p. 184)
¾ cup lime juice

2 tsp. curry powder
1½ cups heavy cream
2 egg yolks
2 cups cooked white rice
2 firm bananas, sliced

*Serves 4*

Sprinkle the pompano filets with salt and pepper. Sprinkle the shallots in a shallow saucepan just large enough to hold the filets. Add the white wine and the fish stock. Now add the lime juice.

Cover the filets with buttered waxed paper and simmer over moderately high heat for about 8 minutes or until they are just done. Transfer the filets with a slotted spoon to a heated platter to keep warm.

Stir the curry powder into the cooking liquid and reduce the liquid over heat until about ½ cup remains. Add 1 cup of the heavy cream and reduce this liquid to ½ cup. Stir in the 2 egg yolks, beaten with the remaining ½ cup heavy cream, and cook for 2–3 minutes longer, being careful not to boil.

Divide 2 cups of fluffy rice among 4 shallow ovenproof dishes. Top the rice in each dish with slices of banana. Arrange a filet on each dish. Pour the hot sauce over each fish filet and place the dishes under a preheated broiler for 3 minutes or until the sauce is lightly browned.

# SALMON

## BARBECUED SALMON STEAK

6 fresh salmon steaks,
   about 1½" thick
2 cups dry white wine
½ cup water
½ cup olive oil
4 sprigs parsley, chopped
Juice of 2 lemons

Salt and pepper to taste
½ tsp. Tabasco pepper sauce
2 bay leaves
2 stalks celery, chopped
1 green pepper, chopped
3 green onions, chopped
2 cloves garlic, minced

*Serves 6*

In a deep, flat pan, marinate salmon steaks in a mixture of all the ingredients for 1 hour on each side.

When ready to barbecue, have your coals hot. Lay a sheet of aluminum foil on top of the grill and poke holes throughout.

Place the salmon steaks on this and baste frequently with the marinade until done—if the fire is right, about 3–5 minutes on each side.

Strain the rest of the marinade, heat, adjust seasonings and pour over steaks.

## CROQUETTES SALMONETTE

1 lb. fresh young salmon
1 cup water
1 cup white wine
3 Tbs. butter
3 Tbs. flour
1 cup light cream
3 green onions,
   tops and bottoms, minced
½ cup parsley, chopped

½ tsp. Tabasco pepper sauce
Salt and pepper to taste
1 cup flour, seasoned
   with salt and pepper
2 whole eggs, beaten
   with a little water
2 cups bread crumbs
2 cups cooking oil

*Serves 6*

Poach salmon in water and wine for 8–10 minutes and cool. Pick over salmon meat; you should have 3 cups.

Melt butter, add flour and blend well. Gradually add the light cream and continue cooking until you have a smooth white sauce—about 10 minutes. Remove from heat and cool.

In a mixing bowl, stir together the salmon, green onions, parsley and Tabasco;

blend well. Add the cooled white sauce and taste for salt and pepper. Place in refrigerator overnight.

When ready to use, shape salmon croquettes and roll first in seasoned flour, then the egg wash and finally the bread crumbs. Place on a platter and return to refrigerator for a couple of hours or until ready to fry. Fry in cooking oil until golden brown, being careful not to overcrowd the pan.

Serve with tartar sauce or white sauce mixed with sautéed onions or tomato sauce. Macaroni and cheese is an excellent accompaniment.

These croquettes may be prepared entirely in advance and simply heated in an oven on a cookie sheet.

## POACHED LUMMI COHO YEARLING SALMON

*Poached salmon:*

1 cup dry white wine
3 cups water
1 large carrot, peeled and sliced
3 sprigs parsley
3 green onions,
    tops and bottoms, sliced
1 medium onion,
    studded with a few cloves

1 Tbs. salt
½ tsp. white pepper
½ tsp. Tabasco pepper sauce
2 stalks celery,
    tops and bottoms, chopped
6 Lummi coho yearling salmon
    (or a 6–8-lb. fresh salmon of a
    different variety)

*Lummi sauce:*

¼ cup green onions, minced
½ cup fresh mushrooms, minced
¼ cup green pepper, minced
7–9 Tbs. butter
3 Tbs. flour

2 cups strained liquid in which
    the fish has been poached
Juice of 2 lemons
Salt and white pepper to taste

*Garnish:*

Chopped parsley

*Serves 6*

Place white wine, water and all other ingredients except salmon in a fish poacher or a shallow pan and bring to a slow boil on top of the stove.

When water-wine mixture has come to a boil, reduce heat and poach as many of the salmon at a time as will fit in your pan, using the same liquid throughout. Cook the salmon complete with head and tail. Cover with lid or foil and allow to cook for a bare 8–10 minutes, turning only once.

Remove cover or foil and test with a sharp paring knife. If skin comes off easily, remove from heat.

Allow to cool for a few minutes and carefully skin both sides of the salmon, leaving the head and tail intact. (If the head offends you, then cut it off.) Remove to a heated platter.

*To make the sauce:* Sauté all the vegetables in a saucepan in 4–6 Tbs. butter. Drain and keep hot.

Melt 3 Tbs. butter and gradually stir in the 3 Tbs. flour until well blended. Add fish liquid and the juice of the lemons. Continue to stir and cook for about 10 minutes or until sauce has the consistency of light cream. Correct seasonings for salt and white pepper.

Pour sauce over each individual salmon, garnish with chopped parsley and serve with boiled potatoes.

# SCALLOPS

## FRIED SCALLOPS VIEUX CARRÉ

2 lbs. scallops
Juice of 1 lemon
1 Tbs. olive oil
½ tsp. finely chopped parsley
Salt and pepper to taste
Dash of cayenne
2–3 eggs beaten with a little
   water
3 Tbs. finely chopped ham
1–1½ cups bread crumbs

2 Tbs. grated Parmesan cheese
1 Tbs. finely chopped chives
2 cups cooking oil, more or less
2 green tomatoes, thickly sliced
1 cup fresh mushrooms, thinly
   sliced
1 stick butter
2–3 hard-boiled eggs, quartered
Tartar sauce

*Serves 6*

Wash and drain the scallops and let stand for 30 minutes in a mixture of the lemon juice, olive oil, parsley, salt, pepper and cayenne.

Drain the scallops well and dip them first in the beaten eggs and then in a mixture you have made of the chopped ham, bread crumbs, Parmesan cheese and chives.

Place the scallops in a wire basket and fry them in hot, deep fat (385°) until they are crisply brown—about 5–10 minutes.

In the meanwhile, sauté the tomatoes and mushrooms in the butter, using 2 separate pans.

Drain the scallops and pile them on a heated round platter. Garnish with the hard-boiled egg wedges and the tomatoes and mushrooms.

Serve with tartar sauce.

# HORS D'OEUVRE SCALLOPS

| | |
|---|---|
| 1 lb. tiny bay scallops | Juice of 2 lemons |
| 1 pint dry white wine | 1 tsp. Tabasco pepper sauce |
| 1 Bouquet Garni (chap. 13) | Seasoned salt |
| Salt and white pepper to taste | Watercress |

*Serves 4*

If you are fortunate enough to get the tiny bay scallops, no bigger than the top of your finger, this is a treat. If you have to use sea scallops, use the same amount, but they must be quartered.

Cook the scallops in the white wine with the bouquet garni for 5–10 minutes, depending on which scallops you use. Drain and toss the scallops in a mixture of the salt, pepper, lemon juice and Tabasco. Dip each scallop in seasoned salt.

Arrange on a platter, refrigerate and serve as a cold hors d'oeuvre with a garnish of watercress.

# SCALLOPS MORNAY

| | |
|---|---|
| 1 lb. sea scallops | 1½ cups Mornay Sauce |
| ½ stick butter | (chap. 13) |
| ½ cup sliced fresh mushrooms | 1 cup buttered bread crumbs |
| 3 tsp. finely chopped green | ½ cup grated Swiss cheese |
| onions | Paprika |

*Serves 4*

Coarsely cut scallops and cook them in their own liquor for 10 minutes. Drain.

Heat butter and lightly sauté mushroom slices and green onions. Combine scallops, mushrooms and green onions with the hot Mornay sauce.

Spoon into ovenproof ramekins or shells; sprinkle with the crumbs combined with the cheese. Dust with paprika.

Place under broiler until lightly browned—about 5 minutes.

## SCALLOPS WITH MAYONNAISE

1 lb. scallops
1 pint dry white wine
1 Bouquet Garni (chap. 13)
½ cup olive oil
¼ cup wine vinegar
Salt and white pepper to taste
¼ tsp. Tabasco pepper sauce

½ head lettuce, shredded,
  blanched (chap. 13) and
  cooled
4 scallop shells
1 cup mayonnaise
4 anchovy fillets
1 Tbs. capers
4 hard-boiled eggs, quartered

*Serves 4*

Like all shellfish, scallops may be prepared as a cold dish.

Cook the scallops in white wine with the bouquet garni until tender—about 5–10 minutes. Cool and slice them. Marinate them in the oil, vinegar, salt, pepper and Tabasco for about 1 hour.

Lay some shredded lettuce on each shell. Distribute the scallop slices evenly on the shells. Cover with mayonnaise. Decorate each with a fillet of anchovy and some of the capers.

Garnish the shells with quarters of hard-boiled eggs.

# SHRIMP

## BAKED AVOCADO WITH SHRIMP

2 avocados
Juice of ½ lemon
3 Tbs. water
¾ cup mayonnaise
½ tsp. curry powder

1½ lbs. small cooked shrimp
  (p. 247), cleaned and deveined
1 Tbs. capers
2 hard-boiled eggs, quartered
½ cup buttered bread crumbs
Paprika

*Serves 4*

Brush avocado halves with a little of the lemon juice. Blend together water, remaining lemon juice and mayonnaise. Simmer over low heat. Stir in curry powder. Add shrimp, capers and eggs; mix well.

Fill avocado halves with this mixture. Top with buttered bread crumbs and dust with paprika.

Bake in a 325° oven for 10 minutes.

The shrimp mixture may be made in advance.

# CHRISTOPHER BLAKE'S SHRIMP STEW

4 Tbs. butter
4 Tbs. flour
1 cup Swamp Water
    (Fish Stock, p. 184)
1 cup dry white wine
6 very ripe tomatoes,
    peeled and quartered
2 green peppers, sliced in slivers
1 large onion, chopped

2 large cucumbers,
    peeled and diced
1 medium can tomato sauce
1 clove garlic, minced
½ tsp. Worcestershire sauce
¼ tsp. Tabasco pepper sauce
Salt and pepper to taste
4 lbs. medium to large shrimp,
    cooked (p. 247), cleaned and
    deveined

*Serves 6*

Melt the butter and add the flour; stir to make a light roux. Cook for 10 minutes.

Add the swamp water and the wine and cook until the sauce gets thick—about 10 minutes.

Now add the tomatoes and other vegetables and the next 5 seasoning ingredients. Cook over medium heat, uncovered, for about 1 hour.

Add cooked shrimp and continue to cook for another 10 minutes, uncovered.

Serve immediately with fluffy rice and garlic bread.

# JUMBO SHRIMP AND ASPARAGUS

2 bunches fresh asparagus,
    cleaned and cut into 1"
    lengths, using only the tender
    top parts of the stalks
2 cups water
2 Tbs. cooking oil

24 large shrimp, cleaned and sliced
    lengthwise in half
1 tsp. chopped fresh ginger
2 Tbs. soy sauce
1 tsp. sugar
1 tsp. sherry
⅛ tsp. salt

*Serves 6*

Add the asparagus pieces to the water. Bring to a boil and continue to cook for 3 minutes. Drain and save 2 Tbs. of the cooking liquid.

Heat the cooking oil in a heavy skillet. Add shrimp pieces and cook until the color changes—about 5 minutes.

Add the asparagus, ginger, soy sauce, sugar, sherry and salt. Finally, stir in the 2 Tbs. asparagus water and continue to cook for 5 minutes.

Serve hot with fluffy rice.

## HUNGARIAN PAPRIKA SHRIMP

8 Tbs. butter
2 lbs. shrimp, shelled and
    deveined
¼ cup shallots, minced
½ lb. small mushrooms, sliced
1 green pepper, cut into thin
    strips
1 heaping Tbs. Hungarian
    sweet paprika

Salt and pepper to taste
1 tsp. tomato paste
1 cup light beer
¾ cup heavy cream
¼ cup sour cream
Slivered almonds or
    chopped walnuts

*Serves 4*

Melt 6 Tbs. of the butter in a saucepan. Cook shrimp in this, tossing until
they are just pink—about 5–10 minutes. Transfer the shrimp and the pan juices
to a bowl. Cover with a buttered round of waxed paper.

Add the remaining 2 Tbs. butter to the pan and sauté the shallots, mushrooms
and green pepper until they are softened—about 10 minutes. Add the Hungarian
paprika and the salt and pepper.

Stir in the tomato paste, the beer and the reserved shrimp juices and reduce
this mixture over high heat to ½ cup.

Reduce the heat to low, add the combined heavy and sour creams and the
reserved shrimp, and simmer the mixture for 5–10 minutes, until it is hot.

Arrange the mixture on a heated platter with fluffy rice and garnish with
slivered almonds or chopped walnuts.

## SHRIMP AND APPLE SALAD

1 lb. small cooked shrimp
    (p. 247), cleaned and deveined
2 medium apples, diced
1 medium green pepper,
    cut into narrow strips

8 pimiento-stuffed green olives,
    sliced
½ cup mayonnaise
1 Tbs. lime juice
Salad greens of your choice
1 grapefruit, sectioned,
    membranes removed

*Serves 4*

Combine shrimp, apples, pepper and olives in a large bowl. Blend mayonnaise
with lime juice. Add to the shrimp mixture and toss. Chill.

Serve on salad greens, garnished with grapefruit sections.

# SNAILS

## CREOLE SNAILS

¼ lb. lean salt pork, finely diced
18 tiny white onions
2 cloves garlic, minced
2 Tbs. parsley, finely chopped
1 Tbs. celery leaves, chopped
Pinch of fresh or dried thyme
Salt and pepper to taste
4 dozen canned snails drained

1 cup dry red wine
18 button mushrooms
1 large tomato,
   peeled, seeded and chopped
2 Tbs. *Beurre Manié* (chap. 13)
2 Tbs. cognac or brandy
6 slices French bread
Chopped parsley

*Serves 8*

In a casserole, blend the salt pork, onions, garlic, parsley, celery leaves, thyme, salt and pepper. Place the drained snails over the mixture. Add the red wine.

Cover the casserole and place in a very slow oven (250°) for 1 hour.

Uncover and add mushrooms and tomatoes. Cover and cook for another 15 minutes. Uncover, thicken with 2 Tbs. *beurre manié* and continue to cook for another 5 minutes.

Flame cognac and add to the snails.

Hollow out the 6 slices of French bread to form a shell and toast.

Divide the snail mixture into these shells. Sprinkle with finely chopped parsley and serve hot.

# TROUT

## RIVERFRONT FILET OF TROUT

¼ cup butter
3–4 shallots, minced
1 lb. fresh tomatoes,
    peeled, seeded and chopped
⅓ cup parsley, chopped
6 medium filets of trout
1 cup dry white wine
1–2 cups Fish Stock (p. 184)
    or water

⅓ cup mayonnaise
Salt to taste
1 Tbs. ketchup
1 Tbs. Worcestershire sauce
¼ tsp. Tabasco pepper sauce
6 lemon wedges dipped in
    finely chopped parsley

*Serves 6*

Preheat oven to 350°.

Butter a baking dish generously. Spread with shallots, tomatoes and parsley. Lay filets on top of mixture. Add all of the wine and 1 cup of the fish stock or water.

Cover with buttered waxed paper and bake for 10 minutes or until the fish flakes easily with a fork. Never overcook fish.

Carefully place cooked filets flat on a serving platter and cool to room temperature until ready to serve.

Return baking dish to a high heat and cook the liquid down until most of it has evaporated and a thick tomato concentrate remains.

When cool, mix in ⅓ cup mayonnaise to ⅔ cup of the tomato concentrate. (You'll probably have extra concentrate left over, and this is excellent for stuffing hard-boiled eggs or garnishing an omelet.) If sauce seems too thick, thin with a little of the fish stock, water or wine. Season with salt, ketchup, Worcestershire sauce and Tabasco. Blend well.

Smooth sauce over cooled filets and garnish with lemon wedges dipped in finely chopped parsley.

## STUFFED TROUT IN CHABLIS

4 medium trout  
½ cup bread crumbs  
¼ cup mushrooms, finely chopped  
2 Tbs. sour cream  
2 Tbs. heavy cream  

3 Tbs. shallots, chopped  
1 cup Chablis wine  
1 Tbs. *Beurre Manié* (chap. 13)  
Juice of 1 lemon  
Finely chopped parsley  

*Serves 4*

Have fish dealer clean trout by making an opening under the head, but leave them uncut otherwise.

Mix together bread crumbs, mushrooms, 1 Tbs. each of the sour cream and the heavy cream and 1½ Tbs. of the shallots.

Force this stuffing into fish.

Place fish individually on buttered waxed paper and sprinkle with remaining shallots. Wrap fish loosely in this paper and place in buttered baking pan. Add the wine.

Bake in a 425° oven for 10–12 minutes, basting occasionally. Remove fish and keep warm.

Strain cooking liquids into saucepan; boil 2 minutes. Blend together remaining sour cream and heavy cream and add to the liquid, along with the *beurre manié*, until sauce is smooth. Gradually add lemon juice.

Pour sauce over fish and sprinkle with finely chopped parsley.

## TROUT IN RED WINE

4 medium trout, whole  
1½ cups dry red wine  
1 bay leaf  
½ cup pickled walnuts, chopped  
¼ tsp. Tabasco pepper sauce  

1 dozen peppercorns  
Salt to taste  
1½ Tbs. flour  
1½ Tbs. butter  
Juice of 1 lemon  

*Serves 4*

Clean trout but do not remove head or tail.

In a saucepan place the wine, bay leaf, chopped walnuts and other seasonings. Bring to a boil and let it reduce to almost half its original quantity.

Brown the flour in butter, stirring for 10 minutes until you have a good roux; carefully dilute with the wine mixture, stirring all the time. Keep the sauce barely simmering.

Poach the fish in this sauce for 8–10 minutes or until done. Keep the heat very gentle. If necessary, thin the sauce down with a little more red wine mixed with equal parts water.

Taste for seasonings, and just before serving, add the lemon juice.

Remove the fish to a platter and spoon sauce over each fish.

NOTE: It is not true that one may not drink red wine with fish. Here is a recipe that cooks fish in red wine.

## TROUT MEUNIÈRE

6 filets of trout
1 cup plain flour more or less
  depending on size of trout,
  seasoned with salt and white
  pepper

1 cup Clarified Butter
  (chap. 13)
½ cup parsley, finely chopped
Juice of 2 lemons

*Serves 6*

Wipe the trout well. Roll them in the seasoned flour. Heat clarified butter in the frying pan and cook the fish over medium heat. Turn once or twice until trout filets are golden brown—about 10 minutes in all.

Arrange them on a serving dish. Sprinkle with chopped parsley and then with lemon juice, and serve.

NOTE: This is a simple and classic method of preparing fresh trout. If you would like to cook the trout whole you may use the same method. It can also be applied to other small, firm fish in this book. The method can even be used for shellfish such as soft-shell crabs and jumbo shrimp.

# TURTLE

## TURTLE FRICASSEE

2 Tbs. lard
2 lbs. turtle meat, cut into
   3″ pieces
2 Tbs. all-purpose flour
Salt and black pepper to taste
4 cloves
Sprig of fresh thyme
   (or ½ tsp. dried thyme)

1 medium tomato, peeled and
  chopped
1 cup water
1 cup dry sherry
2 hard-boiled eggs, sliced
4 thin slices lemon

*Serves 4*

In a heavy skillet, heat the lard and add the turtle meat a little at a time. Stir and dry out the meat for 15–20 minutes. When brown, sprinkle in the flour. Add the next 3 seasonings and lastly the tomato.

Cover and boil gently for a good 3 hours or until meat is tender, adding 1 cup water a Tbs. at a time as necessary. The sauce should be thick.

Half an hour before the meat is done, add the sherry. When ready to serve, slice the hard-boiled eggs on top and garnish with the lemon slices.

# 9
# POULTRY & GAME BIRDS

NOT ONLY POLITICIANS want a chicken in every pot. Food economists like to say that ground meat is the best bargain. I disagree. There's no telling what has been added to ground meat, and you can always water down ham. However, it's rather difficult to do anything to a chicken except pluck the feathers. For the gourmet table, I think chicken is king, and the best buy.

In Europe, especially in France and England, the chicken is still treated with great respect. I don't know why it is not so in this country. Perhaps it's because of the endless signs for fried chicken we see everywhere. While fried chicken done well is a masterpiece of Southern cuisine, there are many, many more ways to prepare chicken.

Some of the greatest dishes, peasant or classic gourmet, are based upon the use of chicken. After one of his battles, Napoleon ordered a new dish and his chef created the famous Chicken Marengo because all he could find were some scrawny chickens running around. Though chickens do not have a monopoly on the poultry line, they are certainly a basic in our cuisine today. In New Orleans the chicken has even made its way into gumbos.

In addition to chicken, many people enjoy ducks, geese and turkey. Since we can also now buy domesticated quail and pheasant, I have included a few choice recipes from our New Orleans area. These recipes were designed for wild birds but can be used for those found in commercial markets today.

# CHICKEN

## ALBERTA'S FRIED CHICKEN

2–3 small fryers, cut up
  in about 8 pieces each with
  giblets, neck, backs, wings
Salt and pepper
1 cup all-purpose flour

2 cups fresh cooking oil
2 cloves minced garlic (optional)
½ tsp. Tabasco pepper sauce
  (optional)

*Serves 4–6*

Wipe chicken pieces and generously salt and pepper them. Put flour in a brown paper bag and shake the chicken pieces a few at a time until each piece is well coated.

Heat cooking oil in either a deep fryer or an iron skillet. Oil should be hot but not boiling. (As a variation, add garlic and Tabasco to the oil.)

Place the chicken pieces in the skillet a few at a time. Part of each piece should protrude from the cooking oil. The pieces should not be completely submerged in the oil. This is important.

Cover the pan at once. (Contrary to some thinking, this will not make the chickens soggy—only moist on the inside.)

Look in on the chicken pieces once or twice. They will float to the top and begin to brown. At this point, turn them over and return the cover. Repeat this once more. Allow about 30 minutes cooking time in all.

When chicken pieces are brown, tender and crisp, drain on paper toweling. They are good cold as well as hot and crisp . . . and great with honey and biscuits.

NOTE: This is fried chicken done simply—Southern and at its best. It is for those gourmets who like the whole thing.

## ARROZ CON POLLO

2 fryers, about 2½ lbs. each,
  cut into pieces
1 cup flour, seasoned with
  salt and white pepper
4 Tbs. olive oil
6 shallots, minced
2 medium onions, thinly sliced
6 fresh tomatoes, peeled,
  seeded and cut into wedges

2 Tbs. minced parsley
1 large bay leaf
½ tsp. saffron
2 cups Chicken Stock (p. 183),
  heated
1 lb. raw rice
2 medium green peppers, sliced
1–2 jiggers dry sherry

*Serves 6*

Dredge the chicken pieces in seasoned flour. In a heavy dutch oven, heat the oil and sauté the shallots and onions until they soften—about 5–10 minutes.

In the same oil sauté the chicken pieces a few at a time, turning frequently to prevent from burning. They should be a delicate golden brown.

Now add the tomatoes, minced parsley, bay leaf, saffron and hot chicken stock and mix well with the chicken. Cover and simmer for 25–30 minutes.

Wash the rice in several washes of water and drain well. Add the rice and green pepper to the chicken mixture and cook for 20 minutes longer, or until the rice absorbs all the liquid and the mixture is on the dry side.

When rice and chicken are done, finish off by adding the dry sherry and serve.

## BRAISED CHICKEN RUE ROYALE

1 fat chicken (4–5 lbs.), with
  giblets
Salt and pepper to taste
1 bunch fresh tarragon*
  (or 1 tsp. dried tarragon)

2 Tbs. butter
5 Tbs. Chicken Stock (p. 183)
6 Tbs. heavy cream
Extra tarragon, finely chopped,
  for garnish

*Serves 4*

Season cavity of chicken with salt and pepper and stuff tarragon and giblets inside. Melt butter in a deep flameproof casserole and brown chicken until lightly golden.

Add the chicken stock. Cover and simmer over low heat for 40–60 minutes or until chicken is tender.

Remove tarragon from cavity and discard. Allow chicken to cool for a few minutes before carving. Carve and arrange pieces on a heated serving platter.

Stir cream into pan juices and heat. Strain over chicken pieces. Sprinkle a little more tarragon over the chicken pieces and serve hot.

*This dish was created with fresh tarragon but will work with dried.

## BREAST OF CHICKEN BELLE AURORE

3 large chicken breasts,
   skinned, boned and cut in half
Salt and white pepper to taste
2 Tbs. olive oil
½ stick butter
1 medium onion, finely chopped
4 medium tomatoes,
   peeled, seeded and chopped

1½ cups Moselle wine
1 tsp. each fresh tarragon and
   chervil (or ½ tsp. dried)
1 cup heavy cream
2 Tbs. flour
Chopped parsley

*Serves 6*

Flatten chicken breasts between pieces of waxed paper. Salt and pepper them. Sauté them in olive oil and butter for 3 minutes on each side.

Stir in onion and sauté for 3 more minutes. Stir in tomatoes, white wine, tarragon and chervil.

Simmer the chicken breasts in this mixture, tightly covered, for 20 minutes or until tender and plump.

Transfer chicken breasts to a heated platter. Stir the heavy cream, which has been mixed with the flour, into the pan juices and continue to cook until thick and smooth.

Correct for salt and pepper. Do not strain. Pour sauce over the chicken breasts and garnish with chopped parsley.

Serve with buttered white noodles.

# BREAST OF CHICKEN CABILDO

2 whole chicken breasts,
  boned, skinned and cut in half
Salt and white pepper to taste
8 Tbs. butter
1 cup long grain rice, raw
½ cup chopped onion
¼ tsp. crumbled saffron

¼ cup each sliced red
  and green peppers
½ cup frozen green peas,
  defrosted
1 large ripe tomato,
  peeled, seeded and chopped
1½ cups Chicken Stock (p. 183)
2 Tbs. flour

*Serves 4–6*

Rub chicken breast with salt and pepper. Melt 3 Tbs. of the butter in a baking dish and brush some of it over the chicken breasts. Bake in a moderate oven (350°), basting frequently, for 30 minutes or until chicken breasts are tender.

Cook rice. Melt 2 Tbs. of the butter, add rice and sauté until rice is dry and begins to stick to the pan. Add 2 more Tbs. of butter. Add the chopped onion and cook until the onion is limp. Add saffron, salt, pepper, red and green peppers, peas, tomatoes and 1 cup of the chicken stock. Cover and cook for 12–15 minutes.

Melt the remaining butter in the chicken pan drippings. Blend in the flour and add the remaining ½ cup chicken stock. Cook, stirring constantly, until thick and well blended.

Slice chicken breasts into 6 servings. Place chicken slices over rice mixture and spoon sauce over the chicken slices. Serve hot from the casserole.

*NOTE:* The Cabildo, formerly the government building, faces Jackson Square in New Orleans and now houses part of the Louisiana state museum.

# BREAST OF CHICKEN SARAH PROCTOR

½ lb. butter
6 medium potatoes, diced
3 white onions, diced
1 lb. fresh mushrooms, diced
Salt and white pepper to taste
3 large chicken breasts,
  skinned, boned and cut in half

1½ cups dry white wine
2 cups cooking oil
1½ cups Hollandaise Sauce
  (chap. 13)
Paprika

*Batter:*

2 egg yolks
²/₃ cup milk
1 Tbs. olive oil
   (or 2 Tbs. melted butter)
1 tsp. lemon juice
   (or ½ Tbs. brandy)

1 cup flour
½ tsp. salt
2 egg whites, beaten
   until stiff but not dry

*Serves 6*

In a large frying pan, melt butter. Begin by sautéing the potatoes for 10–15 minutes. Next add the onions and finally the mushrooms. Cook until all are evenly done—about another 10–15 minutes. Season with salt and white pepper to taste. The sautéed vegetables may be prepared in advance, reserved and reheated at serving time.

Poach the boned and skinned chicken breasts in the white wine until plump and tender—depending on the size of the breasts, about 15–20 minutes. Remove and drain well.

Meanwhile, prepare a batter: Beat the egg yolks until they are thick and lemon in color. Add the milk, olive oil or melted butter, and lemon juice or brandy; blend well.

Sift the flour with the ½ tsp. salt and stir into the egg-yolk mixture until well blended. Fold in the 2 egg whites beaten until stiff but not dry.

Dip each chicken breast in the batter and fry in cooking oil until golden brown—10–15 minutes.

On individiual plates, surround each breast with some of the sautéed potatoes, onions and mushrooms.

Cover each chicken breast with hollandaise sauce and sprinkle with paprika.

## CHICKEN AMARETTO À LA CARMEN

4 large chicken breasts,
   boned, skinned and cut in half
¼ lb. crumbled blue cheese
½ lb. ground ham
2 eggs, beaten
2 sticks butter

1 cup mushrooms, thinly sliced
¼ cup green onions, chopped
¼ cup parsley, chopped
1 clove garlic
White pepper to taste
¾ cup Amaretto

*Serves 8*

Flatten chicken breasts until very thin. Spread each breast with the combined blue cheese and ground ham. Roll chicken breasts and pin together with tooth-picks. Dip in beaten egg.

Melt 1 stick of the butter in a frying pan and brown 1 or 2 chicken breasts at a time. Remove from pan to a casserole.

In another pan, melt the remaining stick of butter and in this sauté the mushrooms, green onions, parsley and garlic until done. Season with white pepper to taste.

Pour mixture over chicken breasts in casserole. Over this pour the Amaretto.

Cover casserole and bake in a moderate oven (350°) for about 20–25 minutes, until chicken breasts are tender and done.

Serve immediately with fluffy white rice.

## CHICKEN BIENVILLE

| | |
|---|---|
| ½ cup olive oil | 1 lb. tomatoes, |
| 4 oz. salt pork, diced | peeled, seeded and chopped |
| 1 3-lb. roasting chicken | ¼ cup brandy |
| ½ lb. fresh button mushrooms, | 1 lb. new potatoes, unpeeled |
| left whole | ½ tsp. sugar |
| 4 pitted black olives | Pepper to taste |

*Serves 4*

Heat ¼ cup of the olive oil and brown the diced salt pork. In this mixture brown the chicken on all sides. Add mushrooms, olives and tomatoes and flame with the brandy. Cover tightly and simmer for 1 hour or until chicken is tender.

Meanwhile, brown the new potatoes in the remaining ¼ cup olive oil and add to the pot halfway through the cooking time for the chicken.

Remove the chicken and the potatoes to a serving platter. Taste the sauce and add sugar and pepper.

Carve the chicken into serving pieces and pour the sauce over it.

*NOTE:* Jean Baptiste le Moyne, sieur de Bienville, was a colonizer and governor of Louisiana. He founded New Orleans in 1718.

## CHICKEN CONGO SQUARE

*Marinated chicken:*

| | |
|---|---|
| 3 Tbs. soy sauce | 2 Tbs. water |
| 1 Tbs. molasses | 1 Tbs. lemon or lime juice |
| 1 Tbs. dark brown sugar | 4 whole chicken breasts, skinned, |
| 2 cloves garlic, crushed | boned and cut into 1″ cubes |

*Sauce:*

    6 Tbs. crunchy peanut butter      1 Tbs. soy sauce
    1 garlic clove, crushed           1 tsp. brown sugar
    1 cup coconut milk              1 bay leaf
    1 tsp. cayenne pepper

*Serves 6*

    Combine all marinade ingredients and marinate the chicken cubes in this mixture for 30 minutes, stirring frequently.

    Thread chicken cubes on skewers and broil over hot charcoal, under the broiler or in a rotisserie for about 10 minutes, turning until chicken pieces are crisp and golden brown.

    While chicken pieces are cooking, make sauce by combining all ingredients. Heat in a small saucepan.

    Remove bay leaf, and serve sauce with chicken.

# CHICKEN CURRY SALAD

*Salad:*

    2 Tbs. lemon juice            2½ cups cooked, diced chicken
    ²/₃ cup mayonnaise             (dark and light meat
    1 tsp. salt                    combined)
    1 tsp. curry powder,          1 cup celery, diced
       or more to taste         ¼ cup slivered blanched almonds
                            Salad greens

*Garnish:*

    1 avocado, cut in wedges     1 cup canned pineapple chunks,
    ½ cantaloupe, cut in wedges    drained
    1 cup seedless grapes        Paprika

*Serves 6*

    Blend lemon juice, mayonnaise, salt and curry powder until smooth. Pour over diced chicken and celery and toss lightly. Chill thoroughly.

    Just before serving, mound salad in the center of a serving platter. Sprinkle with almonds and surround with salad greens.

    Arrange small mounds of fruit on the salad greens. Dust with paprika.

## CHICKEN CUTLETS

3 large whole chicken breasts,  
   skinned and boned  
1 cup fresh bread crumbs  
½ cup milk  
½ cup butter  

¼ cup heavy cream  
1 tsp. salt  
½ tsp. white pepper  
½ cup flour  
½ cup Clarified Butter (chap. 13)  

*Serves 6*

Grind the breasts or have your butcher do it. You should have enough to make 3 cups.

Soak the bread crumbs in the milk for 15 minutes. Drain and press to remove excess liquid.

Combine with the raw chicken and all other ingredients except flour and clarified butter.

Divide the mixture into 6 portions and shape to resemble breasts of chicken. Flour them lightly and sauté gently in clarified butter until nicely browned and cooked through—about 10–15 minutes.

Dust with paprika and serve hot.

## CHICKEN FRICASSEE

1 large hen, disjointed into pieces  
1 large onion, stuck with 1 clove  
1 medium carrot, sliced  
1 Bouquet Garni (chap. 13)  
1 tsp. salt  
6 peppercorns  
4 cups hot water  

3 Tbs. butter  
3 Tbs. flour  
3 egg yolks  
3 Tbs. heavy cream  
1 dozen small white onions  
½ lb. fresh mushrooms, sliced  
Juice of ½ lemon  

*Serves 4–6*

In a large saucepan, place the pieces of chicken, the onion stuck with a clove, the sliced carrot, the bouquet garni, salt and peppercorns.

Pour over this the 4 cups hot water. Bring to a boil and skim. Cover the saucepan, leaving a small opening, and simmer gently for 1 hour or until the chicken pieces are just tender. Skim again if necessary.

Strain off all the stock. Reserve chicken pieces and keep warm.

In another saucepan, melt the butter and mix in the flour until you have a smooth roux—about 10 minutes. Keep over a low flame and gradually add 1 cup of the hot stock. Cook, stirring, until the sauce is smooth and thick—about

15 minutes. Add the egg yolks and cream, which you have mixed thoroughly and diluted with a little of the warm stock.

Shortly before serving, parboil the onions for 10 minutes and sauté the mushrooms in butter for 5 minutes without browning. Add them to the sauce, along with the lemon juice.

To serve, put the chicken pieces on a hot dish and garnish with the onion and mushroom sauce.

Serve with parsley potatoes.

## CHICKEN LIVER CANAPÉS

| | |
|---|---|
| 1 quart Chicken Stock (p. 183) | 2 Tbs. chicken fat or butter |
| 1 lb. chicken livers | Salt and pepper to taste |
| 2 hard-boiled eggs | Toast fingers |
| 1 medium onion, finely chopped | Finely chopped parsley |

*Serves 4*

In a heavy saucepan, bring chicken stock to a boil. Reduce heat, add chicken livers and cook until they have lost their pink color—about 10–15 minutes.

Remove, drain and put through a food chopper along with the hard-boiled eggs. Use a blender if necessary, because the mixture must be of a spreadable consistency.

Cook onion in chicken fat or butter until soft—about 10 minutes. Add to the liver mixture. Mix well and season for salt and pepper.

Spread the mixture on toast fingers. Sprinkle with finely chopped parsley and serve cold.

## CHICKEN LIVERS JEAN LAFFITE

| | |
|---|---|
| 4 Tbs. butter | 1 Tbs. grated onion |
| 4 lamb kidneys, | 1 clove garlic, crushed |
|   skinned, cored and sliced thin | Salt and pepper to taste |
| 8 chicken livers, cut into thirds | ¼ tsp. Tabasco pepper sauce |
| 1 Tbs. flour | Grating of nutmeg |
| 1½ cups Beef Stock (p. 183) | 3 Tbs. Madeira wine |
| 1 bay leaf | 6 slices toasted French bread |

*Serves 6*

In a shallow saucepan, melt butter. Fry the kidney slices briskly over a high flame. Add the chicken liver pieces and continue to cook until both are tender—about 15–20 minutes.

Add flour and mix well.

Gradually stir in the beef stock and all other ingredients except the bread. Bring to a boil and remove from heat.

Discard the bay leaf. Serve hot on the slices of toasted French bread.


## CHICKEN MARENGO

| | |
|---|---|
| 2 2-lb. broilers, cut into pieces | 1 cup dry white wine |
| Salt and pepper to taste | 2 large tomatoes, |
| ¾ cup flour | peeled and cut into wedges |
| 4 Tbs. olive oil | 1 jigger brandy or cognac |
| ½ stick butter | 12 mushroom caps, quartered |
| 2 garlic cloves, minced | ¼ cup finely chopped parsley |
| 1 Bouquet Garni (chap. 13) | Garnish (optional) |

*Serves 6*

Rub each piece of chicken with a damp cloth, season with salt and pepper and sprinkle with flour.

In a heavy skillet heat 4 Tbs. olive oil and ½ stick butter and brown the chicken pieces a few at a time over a high flame until golden—about 5–8 minutes. Turn them frequently.

Transfer the chicken pieces to a casserole; add garlic and the bouquet garni. Add the white wine and the tomatoes.

Warm the brandy or cognac, add to chicken and ignite.

Cover the casserole tightly, reduce heat and cook gently until the chicken pieces are almost tender—about 30 minutes. Turn pieces with a wooden spoon several times during cooking.

After 30 minutes, taste for seasoning and add the quartered mushroom caps. Cook for 10 minutes longer or until the chicken pieces are tender but not falling apart.*

Serve from the casserole, sprinkled with finely chopped parsley.

The garnishes for Chicken Marengo vary and are optional. The casserole may be sprinkled with finely chopped truffles, a slice of French bread fried in olive oil per serving, an egg fried in olive oil per serving or even cooked crayfish or shrimp.

This dish may be prepared the night before and heated when ready to serve.


*If a thicker sauce is desired remove 1 cup of the sauce and combine with 1 Tbs. *beurre manié* (chap. 13). Then blend back into casserole sauce.

# CHICKEN MOUSSE

2 medium chickens,
   light and dark meat
1 lb. Philadelphia cream cheese
1 cup mayonnaise
2 cups sour cream
½ cup chili sauce
1 green pepper, minced

6 green onions,
   tops and bottoms, minced
Grating of nutmeg
Salt and pepper to taste
1½ Tbs. Knox gelatine
Juice of 2 lemons
¼ cup cold water

*Serves 8–12*

Precook chickens by boiling in salted water for 1–1½ hours. Place in a blender in small quantities and chop finely.

Cream together the cream cheese, mayonnaise and sour cream. Work in the chili sauce, green pepper, green onions, nutmeg, salt and pepper. Then add the chopped chicken. Blend well.

Soften the gelatine in lemon juice and water. Melt in a double boiler or over low direct heat until completely dissolved. Add the gelatine mixture to the other ingredients and blend well. Pour into a chilled 9″ ring mold and refrigerate until firm—4–5 hours.

Unmold by dipping in hot but not boiling water for a few seconds and inverting onto a cold platter.

Slice and serve with mayonnaise. Top with parsley.

# CHICKEN ORLEANS

2 medium chickens, cut into
   pieces but reserving breasts
   whole
3 cups Chicken Stock (p. 183)
1 cup dry white wine
1 lb. fresh mushrooms, sliced
1½ sticks butter
4 Tbs. flour

2 egg yolks
1 cup heavy cream
Juice of 1 lemon
Salt and white pepper to taste
½ cup Parmesan cheese, grated
2 bunches fresh broccoli
   (fresh asparagus may be used)
Paprika

*Serves 4–6*

Cook all chicken pieces except breasts in 3 cups stock. Cool, skin and remove the meat from the bones in large pieces; reserve.

Combine stock and white wine. Poach the breasts, which have been skinned, boned and cut in half, in the wine-stock mixture for about 20 minutes. Set to one side.

Sauté the mushrooms in 6 Tbs. of the butter and set to one side.

In the same sauté pan, add the remaining 6 Tbs. butter and stir in the flour to make a smooth roux. Add 2 cups of the chicken-wine mixture a little at a time and cook until sauce is smooth—about 10 minutes.

Stir egg yolks into the cream, blend well and then gradually add to the hot sauce. Add lemon juice a little at a time and correct seasonings with salt and white pepper. Add mushrooms, chicken chunks and ¼ cup of the Parmesan cheese and set to one side.

In the meantime cook broccoli for 15 minutes and drain. Place the drained broccoli in a buttered casserole and cover with most of the chicken-sauce mixture. Lay pieces of sliced chicken breasts over this. (You may reheat the breasts in the remaining wine-stock mixture before adding.) Top with the remaining sauce and garnish with Parmesan cheese and paprika.

Just before serving, pass under the broiler and brown for a few minutes until sauce begins to bubble.


## CHICKEN WINGS CREOLE

| | |
|---|---|
| 2 lbs. chicken wings | 1 green pepper, |
| Pepper to taste | cut into julienne strips |
| 4 oz. salt pork, diced | 1½ cups ripe tomatoes, |
| ¼ tsp. saffron threads | peeled, seeded and chopped |
| 3 cups plus 1 Tbs. Chicken Stock | 1 Tbs. Creole seasonings |
| (p. 183) | 1½ cups raw long grain rice |
| 2 medium onions, | 1 cup frozen peas, thawed |
| chopped to make 1 cup | ¼ cup pimiento, diced |
| 2 cloves garlic, minced | ¼ tsp. Tabasco pepper sauce |

*Serves 4–6*

Preheat oven to 350°.

Pat chicken wings dry with a paper towel and season with pepper. Do not add salt because the salt pork will provide enough.

In a large ovenproof skillet, sauté the salt pork pieces until crisp. With a slotted spoon, remove the pieces to a dish and reserve.

In the fat remaining in the pan, sauté the wings, turning them until they are slightly brown—about 10 minutes. Remove wings and keep warm.

In a small dish, soak the saffron threads in 1 Tbs. chicken stock.

In the fat remaining in the pan, sauté the chopped onion and garlic over moderate heat until the onion is soft. Add the green pepper and sauté the mixture for another 10 minutes. Stir in the tomatoes, add the Creole seasonings and cook the mixture over moderate heat for another 5–10 minutes or until liquid is reduced by half.

Return wings to the pan, stir in the 3 cups chicken stock, heated, and the saffron. Add the raw rice. Bring liquid to a boil.

Transfer the mixture to the preheated moderate oven and bake, covered, for 40 minutes or until rice and wings are tender.

With a fork, stir in lightly the thawed peas, the reserved pieces of salt pork and the pimiento. Test for seasonings, add the Tabasco and bake for an additional 10 minutes.

## CHICKEN WITH APPLE BRANDY

¼ lb. unsalted butter
2 fryers, cut into serving pieces
Salt and pepper to taste
4 Tbs. warm Calvados
   or applejack
6 shallots, finely chopped
1 Tbs. chopped parsley

1 sprig fresh thyme
   (or ¼ tsp. dried thyme)
½ cup good apple cider
   or dry white wine
½ cup heavy cream (whipping
   cream)

*Serves 6*

In a heavy casserole, melt butter. Season chicken pieces with salt and pepper and sauté in butter over low heat for about 15 minutes, turning frequently until chicken pieces are brown.

Warm the Calvados, light and pour over the chicken, shaking the pan until the flame dies. Add the shallots, parsley and thyme and pour in the cider or wine. Blend well, cover and cook until chicken pieces are tender—about 15–20 minutes.

Arrange the chicken on a heated platter. Add heavy cream to the casserole juices and heat without boiling. Pour the sauce over the chicken just before serving.

Serve with peeled apple slices that have been poached in a little white wine for about 5 minutes.

## CHICKEN WITH VINEGAR SAUCE

1 chicken (4–5 lbs.),
   cut into serving pieces
½ cup flour,
   seasoned with salt and pepper
½ cup butter
4 cloves garlic, finely chopped
1 onion, chopped

½ cup wine vinegar,
   flavored with tarragon
½ cup dry white wine
½ cup Chicken Stock (p. 183)
1 Tbs. tomato purée
Salt and pepper
1 Tbs. Dijon mustard

*Serves 6*

Coat chicken pieces with seasoned flour. In a deep frying pan, melt the butter. Add chicken pieces, turning frequently until lightly browned.

Add garlic, onion and vinegar. Mix well and add wine, chicken stock, tomato purée, salt and pepper. The liquid should barely cover the chicken pieces. If it does not, add a little more wine or water.

Cover and simmer for 30 minutes or until chicken is done.

Transfer chicken pieces to a serving dish and keep warm.

Skim fat from cooking liquid. If flavor is weak, boil liquid to concentrate and reduce. Add more tomato purée if necessary.

Remove from heat and whisk in 2 Tbs. of the skimmed fat and the mustard. Strain over chicken pieces and serve.

## CHOPPED CHICKEN LIVERS FANNY-MAE

| | |
|---|---|
| 4 Tbs. chicken fat | 1 stalk celery, finely minced |
| ½ lb. chicken livers | 1 hard-boiled egg, finely chopped |
| 1 onion, finely minced | Salt and pepper to taste |
| ½ slice stale French bread | ¼ cup cognac |

*Serves 6*

Melt chicken fat in a skillet. Cook chicken livers and onion in this until tender—about 15–20 minutes.

Purée mixture in a blender with the stale bread.

Mix with the finely minced celery and egg. Season with salt and pepper to taste. Gradually moisten with the cognac.

Refrigerate and serve on rounds of toast as an hors d'oeuvre.

## CREOLE CHICKEN BALLS

| | |
|---|---|
| 1 lb. chicken breasts (2 large chicken breasts), boned and skinned | ¼ tsp. turmeric |
| | ¼ tsp. Tabasco pepper sauce |
| | Salt and white pepper to taste |
| 1 thick slice French bread, trimmed of crust | 1 cup cooking oil |
| | Juice of 1 lemon |
| 1 egg | Sprigs of watercress |
| 2 Tbs. chopped parsley | |

*Serves 6*

Poach chicken breasts in salted water to cover for 20 minutes. Cool and grind in a meat grinder.

Moisten the bread slice with a little water and squeeze until dry. Mix with the ground chicken meat.

Add egg, parsley, turmeric, Tabasco pepper sauce, salt and white pepper to taste and mix well. Shape into balls the size of a walnut.

Fry in hot oil until golden brown—about 5–8 minutes. Drain on paper toweling and sprinkle with lemon juice.

Serve hot and garnish with watercress.

# DEEP SOUTH CHICKEN PIE

Basic Pie Crust, top and
  bottom, (p. 382)
2 Tbs. melted butter
4 cups cooked chicken meat,
  dark and white, cubed
3 eggs, slightly beaten
Salt and pepper to taste
1 cup dry white wine,
  preferably Moselle

Grating of nutmeg
6 artichoke bottoms,
  coarsely chopped
4 hard-boiled eggs,
  coarsely chopped
1 cup Chicken Stock (p. 183)
1 Tbs. light cream
3 Tbs. dry sherry

*Serves 6*

Line a deep-dish pie plate with the pastry dough and brush with the melted butter.

Mix chicken cubes with eggs. Salt and pepper to taste. Add white wine and a grating of nutmeg. Add artichoke bottoms and hard-boiled eggs. Mix well and stir in the chicken stock a little at a time.

Pour this into the deep-dish pie shell and top with a crust.

With a sharp knife, cut 3 or 4 openings in the crust to allow steam to escape. Bake in a hot oven (450°) for 8–10 minutes.

Open the oven door and brush the top crust with some light cream. Shut the door and bake for 25–30 minutes more in a moderate oven (350°).

Remove pie from oven and, using a small funnel, pour in the dry sherry through one of the slits. Shake gently to mix well.

Serve warm or cold.

## GIBLETS AND MUSHROOMS BAYOU TECHE

¼ cup butter
1 medium onion, sliced
24 medium mushrooms, sliced
½ lb. raw chicken livers
¼ lb. chicken gizzards,
  precooked in water for ½ hour
¼ lb. chicken hearts,
  precooked in water for ½ hour

Salt and pepper to taste
½ tsp. Tabasco pepper sauce
½ cup dry white wine
6 thick slices toasted French
  bread
¼ cup finely chopped parsley

*Serves 6*

In a heavy skillet, heat butter and sauté onion and mushrooms until tender, stirring frequently.

Cut livers in half and add, cooking and stirring until livers are almost done—about 5–10 minutes.

Slice cooked gizzards and hearts and add to the liver mixture. Continue to cook for 5–10 minutes longer.

Season to taste with salt and pepper and add Tabasco. Add wine and cook for another 5 minutes.

Serve hot over toasted French bread and sprinkle with finely chopped parsley.

## GYPSY CHICKEN LIVERS

3 onions, thinly sliced
3 Tbs. butter
1 lb. chicken livers
Salt and pepper to taste
1 Tbs. Hungarian sweet paprika

1 cup sour cream
Pinch of thyme
1 bay leaf
3 egg yolks

*Serves 6*

Cook onions in butter until limp and slightly golden. Add chicken livers, salt, pepper and paprika. Cook over a low flame until the blood runs out of the livers, which means they are almost done—about 20 minutes.

Scald sour cream with thyme and bay leaf. Stir in the egg yolks and heat until thick.

Remove bay leaf. Combine sour cream mixture with chicken livers and serve with white noodles.

# KENTUCKY BURGOO

1¼ cups okra, sliced
1¼ cups uncooked peas, fresh,
   or frozen and defrosted
1¼ cups corn
1¼ cups green beans, sliced
¼ lb. dried lima beans
3 large raw potatoes, diced
2 large carrots, diced
½ Tbs. powdered allspice
1 stalk celery, diced
2 large green peppers,
   coarsely chopped

2 onions, coarsely chopped
1 lb. green cabbage, shredded
2 cloves garlic
6 cups tomatoes, chopped
2 Tbs. Worcestershire sauce
1 Tbs. chili sauce
5 quarts water
1 Tbs. salt
1 tsp. pepper
1 5-lb. hen,
   cut up into small pieces
1½ lbs. shredded tripe

*Serves 6*

Place all the ingredients except for the chicken and tripe in a large kettle. Cover with 2 quarts of the water. Bring to a boil. Cover, reduce heat and simmer gently for 1 hour, stirring occasionally.

Place the remaining 3 quarts water in another kettle. Add the salt, pepper and cut-up chicken pieces. Bring to a boil.

Now turn the chicken and its liquid into the kettle with the vegetable mixture. Add the shredded tripe and simmer gently for 3½–4 hours or until the chicken and tripe are done.

# MARDI GRAS BREAST OF CHICKEN

1 quart water
1 tsp. salt
3 whole chicken breasts,
   skinned, boned and cut in half
4 cups Jellied Mayonnaise
   (chap. 13)
4 cups Aspic (chap. 13)

1 truffle or 2 large black olives,
   sliced
6 very thin slices eggplant,
   unpeeled
6 thick slices cucumber, unpeeled
6 hard-boiled egg yolks, chopped
Tomato wedges

*Serves 6*

In the simmering, salted water, poach the chicken breasts, covered, for 20–30 minutes or until plump and tender. Remove, cool and refrigerate.

When the chicken breasts are cold and ready to handle, trim well so that they are almost oval in shape. Coat with half-set jellied mayonnaise and refrigerate until set. Then glaze with half-set white chicken aspic. Refrigerate again until set.

When ready, arrange chicken breasts in the center of a large platter on a bed of chopped aspic. Decorate each breast with truffle or black olive slices.

Surround the chicken breasts with alternate slices of raw eggplant and cucumber topped with a sprinkling of chopped egg yolk.* Arrange wedges of tomato on the same platter.

* Purple, green and yellow are the Mardi Gras colors.

## MRS. GEE'S CHICKEN LIVERS

| | |
|---|---|
| 1½ lbs. chicken livers | 3 Tbs. cornstarch |
| ¼ cup soy sauce | ⅓ cup wine vinegar |
| ⅓ cup peanut oil | 1⅔ cups pineapple juice |
| 1 cup pineapple chunks | ½ tsp. salt |
| ¾ cup almonds, | ⅛ tsp. black pepper |
|    blanched and slivered | ⅓ cup sugar |

*Serves 6*

Marinate chicken livers in soy sauce for 15 minutes. Drain. Reserve soy sauce.

Brown the livers lightly in peanut oil for about 10–15 minutes. Remove and keep warm.

Place soy sauce in a skillet or saucepan and add pineapple chunks and almonds. Stir over low heat for about 5 minutes.

Stir the cornstarch to a paste with the vinegar, and combine with pineapple juice, salt, pepper and sugar. Cook the sauce until thick and clear. Add chicken livers and soy sauce mixture and reheat.

Serve hot with white rice.

## ORIENTAL ORANGE CHICKEN

| | |
|---|---|
| 2 scallions, cut in ¼" pieces | Vegetable oil, for deep frying |
| 2½ Tbs. soy sauce | 2 Tbs. sesame oil |
| 2 tsp. sugar | 2 tsp. peppercorns |
| 1 Tbs. white wine vinegar | 2 tsp. fresh ginger, shredded |
| 1½ Tbs. Chicken Stock (p. 183) | ½ tsp. chili pepper flakes |
| 2 Tbs. dry sherry | Salt to taste |
| 3 lbs. chicken, | 2 or 3 slices dried orange peel, |
|    cut into about 20 pieces |    broken into pieces |

*Serves 4*

In a small bowl, combine scallions, soy sauce, sugar, vinegar, stock and sherry. Marinate chicken pieces in this mixture for ½–1 hour.

Heat the vegetable oil; when hot, fry the drained chicken pieces a few at a time for about 8–10 minutes, or until they are brown and done but still moist.

Heat the sesame oil in a skillet. Add the peppercorns, ginger, chili, salt and orange peel and fry for about 3 minutes, stirring constantly. Add the scallion-sherry mixture and stir-fry for another 3 minutes.

Combine everything, heat thoroughly and serve hot with white rice.

## PAPRIKA-BUTTER CANAPÉS

| | |
|---|---|
| 1 large chicken breast, skinned and boned | 12 rounds of white bread, cut with a small cookie cutter |
| ¾ stick softened, unsalted butter or margarine | Salt and white pepper to taste |
| 1 Tbs. sweet Hungarian paprika | ¼–½ cup mayonnaise |
| | 12 julienne slices green pepper |
| | 12 julienne slices red pepper |

*Serves 4*

Poach chicken breast in water or stock to cover for 20–25 minutes. When done, cool and chop very, very fine, using a blender if necessary.

Combine softened butter with paprika until you have an even pinkish color. Spread rounds of white bread with this mixture.

Season chopped chicken with salt and pepper. Add enough mayonnaise to make a spreadable consistency. Spread this on the buttered bread rounds.

Arrange an evenly fitted slice of green and red pepper on each round.

Arrange on a platter, cover with foil and refrigerate for 2 hours.

## POULET MADEMOISELLE DAUPHINE

| | |
|---|---|
| 3 Tbs. butter | 6 canned artichoke bottoms, quartered |
| 3½ oz. salt pork, cubed and blanched | ½ tsp. Tabasco pepper sauce |
| 12 small white onions | 5 Tbs. Veal Stock (p. 185) or Chicken Stock (p. 183) thickened with 1 Tbs. *Beurre Manié* (chap. 13) |
| 1 large fryer | |
| 1½ lbs. potatoes, diced | |

*Serves 4*

In a casserole, brown the butter. Add the salt pork and cook the onions in this for a few minutes.

Remove the onions and the pork fat and brown the chicken on all sides in the same casserole for about 10 minutes.

Replace the onions and the pork fat. Cover and cook in a low oven (250°) for about 1 hour.

About 20 minutes before the chicken is cooked, add the potatoes. Add the quartered artichoke bottoms for the last 5 minutes of cooking time.

Carve the chicken and arrange it on a heated platter surrounded with potatoes and artichoke bottoms.

To the pan juices, add the Tabasco and the thickened veal or chicken stock. Cook, stirring, for several minutes, and pour over the chicken.

## POULET MONSIEUR CHARTRES

| | |
|---|---|
| 10 Tbs. butter | 24 pitted, blanched black olives |
| 1 large fryer, cut into serving pieces | 1 large Creole tomato, peeled, seeded and chopped |
| Salt and pepper to taste | ½ cup dry white wine |
| 4 oz. salt pork, cut into strips and blanched | 5 Tbs. Chicken Stock (p. 183) or Veal Stock (p. 185) thickened with 1 Tbs. *Beurre Manié* (chap. 13) |
| 12 small white onions, parboiled | |
| 12 small carrots, parboiled and cut into thick slices | ¼ cup finely chopped parsley |

*Serves 4*

Heat the butter in a casserole. Lay in the pieces of chicken seasoned with a little salt and pepper, the strips of salt pork, the parboiled onions and carrots.

Cover and cook slowly in a moderate oven (350°) until the chicken is just barely done—about 35–40 minutes.

The last 15 minutes of cooking time, add the olives, the tomato and the white wine. Simmer for about 10 minutes.

Finally add the thickened veal or chicken stock. Mix well and sprinkle with finely chopped parsley.

Serve in the same casserole.

# POULET PRESBYTÈRE

| | |
|---|---|
| ¼ stick butter | Salt and pepper to taste |
| 4 slices bacon, diced | Pinch of fresh (or dried) basil |
| 2 cloves garlic, crushed | 2 Tbs. flour |
| 1 stewing hen, cut into 8 pieces | 1 cup Chicken Stock (p. 183) |
| 1 lb. tomatoes, | 1 tsp. sugar |
|    peeled, seeded and quartered | Juice of ½ lemon |

*Serves 4*

In a heavy casserole, melt butter and fry bacon. Add garlic and then the chicken pieces. Reduce heat, cover and allow to cook without any additional liquid for about 15 minutes.

Now add tomatoes, salt, pepper and basil. Continue cooking until tender—about 1 hour.

Remove chicken to a heated platter. Stir the flour into the tomato mixture and blend well. Add the chicken stock and continue to cook until sauce is thick and well blended—about 15 minutes. Add sugar.

Strain the gravy and combine with the chicken pieces. Reheat until hot. Stir in the lemon juice and serve immediately.

*NOTE:* The Presbytère is a government building facing Jackson Square in New Orleans.

# ROAST CHICKEN WITH OYSTER DRESSING

| | |
|---|---|
| 1 roasting chicken (4–5 lbs.) | ½ tsp. dried thyme |
| Salt and pepper | ¼ cup finely diced celery |
| 2 Tbs. minced onion | 1 cup well-drained oysters, |
| 2 cups toasted bread, diced |    coarsely chopped |
| 1 tsp. salt | ¼ cup Chicken Stock (p. 183) |
| ¼ tsp. ground black pepper | ½ stick softened butter |
| ¼ tsp. Tabasco pepper sauce | ¼ cup melted butter |

*Serves 4–6*

Wash and towel-dry chicken. Sprinkle inside and out with salt and pepper.

Combine onion, toasted bread, salt, ground pepper, Tabasco pepper sauce, thyme and celery and mix well. Add chopped oysters and chicken stock.

Stuff chicken with this mixture and truss well. Rub with softened butter.

Place in a slow (250°) oven and bake for 3½ hours, basting with the ¼ cup melted butter and the pan drippings from time to time.

## ROC'S CHICKEN KORNILOFF

8 large mushrooms, sliced
3 Tbs. butter
¾ cup Béchamel Sauce (chap. 13)
3 Tbs. purée of foie gras
3 large chicken breasts,
   skinned, boned and halved

1–2 whole eggs
1 tsp. cold water
2 cups commercially seasoned
   bread crumbs
Fat or butter, for frying

*Serves 6*

Sauté mushrooms in butter for about 10 minutes or until soft and tender. Add béchamel sauce and purée of foie gras. Heat mixture slightly.

Flatten each chicken-breast half between 2 pieces of waxed paper until paper-thin but manageable.

Distribute the mushroom mixture onto the chicken halves. Fold each evenly and shape into the form of cutlets.

Slightly beat an egg with water. Dip cutlets in this egg wash. If 1 egg is not enough, add another. Then dip the chicken breasts into the bread crumbs. Refrigerate for at least an hour or until ready to use.

When ready to serve, fry in deep fat or in a skillet with butter until delicately browned—about 10 minutes.

## VIENNESE SPRING CHICKEN

2 small fryers,
   cut into 8 pieces each
½ cup flour, seasoned
   with salt and pepper

1 or 2 eggs, beaten slightly
   with a little cold water
2 cups bread crumbs
Cooking oil, for frying
Paprika

*Serves 6*

Dry the pieces of chicken thoroughly with a towel. Dredge in seasoned flour. Dip quickly into the egg wash and lastly roll in the bread crumbs. (Commercial seasoned bread crumbs may be used.)

Refrigerate for at least 2 hours.

Heat cooking oil and fry chicken pieces a few at a time until done and golden brown—about 15 minutes. Drain on brown paper.

Sprinkle with paprika just before serving.

# WATERFRONT CHICKEN

*Casserole:*

4 whole chicken breasts
    (8 halves)
2 cups Chicken Stock (p. 183)

1 large onion, chopped
8 oz. grated Cheddar cheese
12 tortillas

*Sauce:*

1 8-oz. carton sour cream
1¼ cups Chicken Stock (p. 183)
2 Tbs. *Beurre Manié* (chap. 13)
1 4-oz. can taco sauce

1 4-oz. can green chilies
Salt and pepper to taste
8 oz. Monterey Jack cheese,
    sliced

*Serves 4–6*

Simmer chicken in stock until tender—about 20 minutes. Dice.

Mix chicken, onion and cheese.

Soften the tortillas in the warm chicken stock. Fill them with the chicken mixture and roll up. Place seam side down in a greased baking dish.

To make the sauce, blend all ingredients except cheese and heat in a saucepan for 3–5 minutes. Pour over casserole and top with the slices of Monterey cheese.

Bake at 375° for 30–40 minutes or until the casserole is bubbly and the cheese is browned.

# DUCK

## CURRIED DUCK

| | |
|---|---|
| 2 sticks butter | Salt and pepper to taste |
| 4 cups cooked duck meat | 1–2 Tbs. good Indian curry |
| from a large Long Island duck,* | powder |
| coarsely chopped | 1 cup plain yogurt |
| 1 lb. mushrooms, | 3 Tbs. Madeira wine |
| caps only, thinly sliced | ½ cup duck or Chicken Stock |
| 1 medium onion, grated | (p. 183) |
| 2 small apples, | 1 large bowl fluffy white rice |
| peeled, cored and diced | 2 bananas, diced and sautéed in |
| 3 Tbs. flour | 3 Tbs. butter |

*Serves 6*

In a skillet, melt 12 Tbs. (¾ cup) of the butter and sauté the chopped duck and mushroom slices until mushrooms are tender and duck pieces slightly browned—about 15 minutes. Remove and keep warm.

Add the remaining 3 Tbs. butter to the pan and in it cook the onion and apples until soft—about 10–15 minutes. Remove from heat and sprinkle in the flour, salt, pepper and curry powder, blending thoroughly.

Return pan to fire and stir in the yogurt, which has been mixed with the Madeira and the duck or chicken stock. Stir constantly until sauce is thick and creamy.

Stir in the duck and mushroom pieces. Heat well and taste for seasonings.

Serve at once with the hot white rice, which has been mixed with the sautéed bananas.

* You may use duck that has been cooked in any fashion. However, I prefer duck that has been boiled in water or stock for 2–3 hours.

## DUCKLING WITH RED CABBAGE

1 duckling, about 3 lbs.
1 tart green apple,
    peeled, cored and quartered
1 small orange, peeled and sliced
2 slices raw bacon, chopped
Salt and pepper to taste

1 small head red cabbage,
    finely shredded, white core
    removed
2–3 Tbs. bacon drippings
1 bay leaf
6 peppercorns

*Serves 4*

Fill the cavity of the duck with the apple, orange and chopped bacon. Truss. Salt and pepper the duck.

Roast in a moderate oven (350°), basting frequently in its own fat, for 1–2 hours. When meat is tender, increase oven temperature to hot (425°) to crisp the skin.

Sprinkle the shredded red cabbage with salt and let it stand for a few hours. Drain and press dry.

Heat the bacon drippings in a heavy pot. Put in the cabbage, bay leaf and peppercorns and a little water. Cover tightly and steam over *gentle* heat for about 45 minutes.

Carve the duckling and serve with red cabbage.

## DUCK WITH SWEET CREAM

3 slices stale French bread,
    soaked in milk
1 can sweet corn
Salt and pepper to taste

3 slices raw bacon, chopped
Liver of the duck, chopped
1 cup heavy cream
1 duck (4–5 lbs.)

*Serves 4*

Drain bread. Mix with corn, salt, pepper, chopped bacon, duck liver and heavy cream.

Stuff cavity of duck and truss well.

Roast in a moderately hot oven (350°) for 1–2 hours or until duck is tender. Baste duck frequently with its own fat and juices. If necessary add 1 Tbs. or so of hot water.

When duck is done, carve and surround with corn stuffing. Skim excess fat from pan juices and pour over duck and stuffing.

# WILD DUCK WITH LOUISIANA ORANGE WINE

1½ sticks butter
2 cloves garlic, crushed
½ tsp. black pepper
²/₃ cup soy sauce
6 mallard or teal ducks
2 cups Wild Rice Dressing (below)
½ cup candied ginger, slivered

6 mandarin or satsuman oranges,
   or tangerines, peeled and
   sectioned
1 bottle Louisiana orange wine
   (or ¼ cup Triple Sec mixed
   with 3 cups dry white wine)

*Serves 6–12*

In a heavy skillet, melt butter and then add garlic and pepper. Do not use salt, as the soy sauce has enough. Add soy sauce.

In this mixture, brown each duck, being careful not to crowd the skillet. Remove ducks. Reserve pan juices.

Fill each duck cavity with the dressing. Truss well. Place remaining dressing in foil and leave a small opening.

In a heavy casserole, arrange the ducks evenly, placing the extra dressing in the center. Around the ducks place the candied ginger and the mandarin, satsuman or tangerine sections.

Over all this pour the juices from the skillet plus most of the bottle of Louisiana orange wine, or the Triple Sec and white wine mixture—enough to almost cover.

Cover the casserole tightly and cook in a moderate oven (350°) for about 1–2 hours, depending on the size of the ducks.

When ready to serve, split the ducks in half and serve with the unstrained sauce spooned over each duck.

Everyone can have an extra spoonful of dressing, or you can save it for your next bird!

# WILD RICE DRESSING

1 stick butter
½ cup green onions,
   tops and bottoms, chopped
½ cup diced celery
1 can bean sprouts, drained

1 small can bamboo shoots,
   drained and chopped
1 small can water chestnuts,
   drained and chopped
2 cups cooked wild rice
Salt and pepper to taste

*Yields 4 cups*

In a heavy skillet, melt butter and sauté the green onions and celery for about

10 minutes or until tender. Add bean sprouts, bamboo shoots and water chestnuts and cook for another 5 minutes.

Add all this to the hot, cooked wild rice and toss well. Season with salt and pepper and add pan juices if any. Use for stuffing wild ducks.

This dressing may be used for other game as well as Rock Cornish hens or chicken.

# PHEASANT, QUAIL AND SQUAB

## AVERY ISLAND QUAIL IN WINE

6 quail, ready for cooking
Salt and pepper to taste
3 Tbs. butter
½ cup diced carrots
2 Tbs. diced onion
2 Tbs. diced green pepper
½ cup diced fresh mushrooms

2 medium pieces orange peel,
   blanched and thinly sliced
1 Tbs. flour
1 cup Chicken Stock (p. 183)
½ cup dry white wine
¼ tsp. Tabasco pepper sauce

*Serves 3*

Sprinkle quail with salt and pepper and brown lightly in butter in a skillet. Transfer to a buttered casserole and arrange evenly.

To the skillet, add the carrots, onion, green pepper, mushrooms and orange peel. Cook slowly for 5–6 minutes. Add flour and mix well. Gradually stir in stock and cook until thickened.

Pour the wine over the quail and cook in a moderate oven (350°) for 15–20 minutes.

Add the vegetable sauce and the Tabasco, cover and cook for 25 minutes longer or until the birds are done.

## BRAISED PHEASANT WITH WILD RICE

1 ready-to-cook pheasant
   (2–3 lbs.)
Salt and pepper to taste
⅓ cup sliced celery
1 medium onion, chopped
1 cup Chicken Stock (p. 183)

1 whole celery heart,
   cut into 4 pieces
1 cup cooked wild rice,
   seasoned with salt and black
   pepper

*Serves 4*

Rub pheasant inside and out with salt and pepper. Stuff bird with celery and onion. Truss.

Place in a large saucepan and add chicken stock. Cover and simmer for 45 minutes or until bird is tender.

Add celery hearts to saucepan 10 minutes before cooking time is up.

Carve bird and serve with celery hearts and mounds of wild rice.


## PHEASANT BAYOU DES ALLEMANDS

1 pheasant
10 thin slices bacon
Salt and pepper to taste
8–10 peppercorns

1 bay leaf
1½ lbs. sauerkraut
½ can stale beer

*Serves 4*

Clean pheasant and wrap with bacon slices. Truss. Place in a deep saucepan and cook over high heat, turning frequently until bacon has been rendered.

Add salt and pepper, peppercorns and bay leaf. Cover and simmer for 1 hour or until the bird is almost tender.

Add the sauerkraut, correct seasonings and pour in the stale beer.

Cover and stew for 25 more minutes.


## SQUAB BUTTE DE MONTMARTRE

6 small squab (Rock Cornish
   hens may be used)
Salt and pepper to taste
3 sticks butter
½ cup dried mushrooms,
   soaked in hot water for ½ hour,
   then thinly sliced

2 cups light Scotch
2 cups Chicken Stock
   (p. 183)
1 Bouquet Garni (chap. 13)
½ cup flour
1 tsp. Dijon mustard
6 slices cured country ham*

*Serves 6*

Sprinkle squab with salt and pepper. In a heavy skillet, melt 2 sticks of the butter and lightly sauté the squab. When they are delicately browned, remove to a dutch oven.

In the same skillet, brown the mushroom slices.

Remove mushroom slices to the dutch oven and pour 1½ cups of the Scotch and the 2 cups chicken stock over the squab and mushrooms. Add the bouquet garni.

Cover, place in a moderate oven (350°) and baste at 20-minute intervals for about 1 hour. Squab should be tender but not falling apart.

When squab are done, remove to a heated platter to keep warm, reserving liquid. Reserve mushroom slices separately.

In another skillet make a roux by combining the remaining butter and the flour. Add the mustard. Gradually add the hot chicken-Scotch liquid and the remaining Scotch and cook, stirring constantly until sauce has the consistency of heavy cream. Add mushroom slices. Remove the bouquet garni and keep the sauce warm.

In the same skillet in which the mushroom slices were browned, lightly fry the slices of country ham. When ready to serve, place an individual squab on each slice of country ham and ladle the hot sauce over the squab.

*Smithfield and Talmadge hams are now sold in slices in many supermarkets. Be sure to soak the slices for at least 1 hour to remove any excess salt. If you can't obtain either of these, any Virginia ham, sliced in medium-thick slices, will do.

# ROCK CORNISH HENS

## FRENCH MARKET ROCK CORNISH HENS

| | |
|---|---|
| 4 thick slices bacon, cut into ½″ pieces | 4 cups hot Chicken Stock (p. 183) |
| 24 small white onions, peeled | 3 whole celery hearts, split lengthwise |
| 6 Tbs. butter | 1 Bouquet Garni (chap. 13) |
| 6 small Rock Cornish hens, trussed | Pinch of sugar |
| Salt and pepper to taste | 3 cups frozen peas, thawed |
| ¼ cup flour | |

*Serves 6*

Preheat oven to 350°.

In a heavy skillet, sauté the bacon pieces and the small onions until lightly browned. Transfer the bacon and onions with a slotted spoon to a casserole. Add 4 Tbs. of the butter to the casserole.

In the fat remaining in the skillet, brown the trussed Rock Cornish hens, seasoned with salt and pepper. Arrange them in the casserole over the butter, onions and bacon pieces in a single layer.

Sprinkle the flour over the remaining bacon fat in the skillet and stir this roux over moderately low heat for about 10 minutes.

Remove the skillet from the heat and stir in the hot chicken stock. Cook the mixture, stirring in the brown bits clinging to the bottom and sides of the pan, until it comes to a boil.

Pour this mixture over the Rock Cornish hens; add the split celery hearts, bouquet garni, sugar, salt and pepper to taste.

Transfer the casserole to the preheated oven and braise the dish, uncovered, for 30 minutes. Add the thawed peas and the remaining 2 Tbs. butter. Continue to braise the dish, covered, for another 30 minutes or until the Rock Cornish hens are tender.

Remove the bouquet garni and serve with the sauce.


## ROCK CORNISH HENS WITH GRAPES

| | |
|---|---|
| 4 dozen muscat grapes, peeled and seeded | ¼ cup water |
| | ¾ cup port wine |
| ½ cup fine bread crumbs | 1 Tbs. butter |
| 3 Tbs. brandy | ½ Tbs. flour |
| Salt and pepper to taste | Watercress |
| 6 small Rock Cornish hens | |

*Serves 6*

Mix half the grapes with the bread crumbs; moisten with 1 Tbs. of the brandy and season with salt and pepper.

Divide the grape mixture among the 6 birds and stuff cavities.

Arrange the birds in a buttered baking pan and sprinkle them with salt and pepper. Pour the remaining 2 Tbs. brandy over them and allow them to mellow for 1 hour before roasting.

Add the water and ½ cup of the port to the pan and roast the birds in a hot oven (425°) for 30–40 minutes, basting often.

Place the birds on a warm serving platter.

Add the remaining ¼ cup port and the rest of the grapes to the pan juices. Mix the flour and butter into a paste and add to the pan, bringing the sauce to a boil and stirring constantly until thick.

Correct seasonings and pour over the birds.

Serve with watercress.

# TURKEY

## BREAST OF TURKEY DUMAINE

2 lbs. cherries, pitted
2 Tbs. sugar
2 Tbs. water
1 tsp. allspice

12 thin slices cooked turkey
   from a large breast
Salt and pepper to taste
1 stick unsalted butter
3 oz. Madeira

*Serves 4–6*

Place the cherries in a saucepan with the sugar, water and allspice. Cook very slowly until they are reduced to a pulp—about 20–25 minutes. Then put them in a blender or through a sieve.

Season the turkey slices with salt and pepper. Heat them a few at a time in a frying pan with butter and Madeira. Turn them only once.

To serve, put the cherry sauce in the center of a hot dish and place the turkey slices around the dish.

## CREOLE TURKEY HASH

3 Tbs. butter
3 Tbs. shallots, finely chopped
½ green pepper, finely chopped
3 cups cooked turkey meat, diced
¼ cup black olives, sliced
   (about 6)
1 large ripe tomato,
   peeled, seeded and chopped

¼ cup turkey or Chicken Stock
   (p. 183)
½ tsp. Tabasco pepper sauce
2 egg yolks
½ cup heavy cream
Salt and white pepper to taste
Chopped parsley, for garnish

*Serves 4–6*

Melt butter in a chafing dish or skillet. Add shallots and green pepper and cook until soft—10–15 minutes.

Add turkey meat, black olives and tomato. Continue to cook for another 10 minutes. Add the stock and Tabasco. Cook until liquid is reduced by half—about 10 minutes.

Combine egg yolks and cream; add gradually and cook for about 5 minutes, being careful not to let the cream-egg mixture boil. Stir in salt and white pepper to taste.

Serve on toast or in patty shells and sprinkle with finely chopped parsley.

## FRENCH MARKET TURKEY SANDWICH

24 large, thin slices
   breast of cooked turkey,
   trimmed so they are even
12 thin slices prosciutto ham,
   each cut in half
12 slices mozzarella cheese,
   cut to fit the turkey slices
2 eggs, beaten with
   2 Tbs. cold water

2 cups seasoned Italian bread
   crumbs
2 cups cooking oil
1½ cups Béchamel Sauce
   (chap. 13), colored and
   flavored with 1 tsp. paprika
12 large black olives pitted

*Serves 6*

On each of 12 slices of turkey breast, lay 2 halves of prosciutto ham and on top of this a slice of mozzarella cheese. Close each sandwich with another piece of turkey and trim again if necessary.

Dip each sandwich in the egg wash and then in the seasoned bread crumbs. Lay on a platter and refrigerate for at least 1 hour or until ready to fry.

When ready to serve, heat cooking oil and fry 1 or 2 turkey sandwiches at a time, turning once, until they are golden brown—about 5 minutes. Place a sandwich on each plate. Cover each with some of the hot béchamel sauce and top with a whole black olive.

# 10
# MEATS

I WOULD NOT call New Orleans a meat-and-potatoes town. Although the New Orleans table frequently caters to the classic steak, its cuisine often looks for more sauce-conscious methods of preparing a cut of meat.

There was a time when the numerous open butcher stalls in the French Market attracted everyone. Even today, New Orleans has many interesting meat markets, and a shopper need not depend solely on prepackaged items. A New Orleanian still has the advantage of small talk with his butcher while watching him cut and prepare the meat of his choice.

There is no waste in New Orleans with regard to meat and its by-products. Innards are acceptable in the market, on the table and on menus in restaurants. Many a visitor to New Orleans has eaten sweetbreads or boudin (blood sausage) for the first time and come to like it. Of course, this is a culinary throwback to Old World tradition, but in New Orleans, respect for all cuts of meat is a way of life. Almost nothing is wasted. The local hog's head cheese is a treat for anyone and ranges from mild to fiery hot. It can grace a gourmet table as an hors d'oeuvre or serve as the makings of a Po Boy sandwich.

Whether it is panned veal of daube glacé, veal shanks or ham hocks, or grillades and grits . . . I have learned from the cooks of New Orleans to let no meat pass me by.

# BEEF

## BRISKET OF BEEF BELLE CREOLE

*Sauce Belle Creole:*

½ bunch watercress
½ bunch parsley
8 blades fresh chives (or ½ tsp.
  dried or frozen chives)

1 large ripe tomato, peeled,
  seeded and coarsely chopped
2 cups mayonnaise
Whites of 2 hard-boiled eggs

*Meat and vegetables:*

3–4 lbs. corned beef
1 Tbs. salt
1 tsp. black pepper
6 medium carrots, quartered
3 turnips, quartered
6 medium potatoes, quartered

1 head cabbage, quartered
3 lbs. green beans
1 lb. andouille sausage or boudin,
  parboiled for 10 minutes
½ cup chopped parsley

*Serves 6–8*

*To make sauce:* Blanch the watercress, parsley and chives in hot water for 2–3 minutes. Drain well and purée in a blender, adding the tomato for the last few seconds. Combine purée with mayonnaise and add the whites of the hard-boiled eggs.

*To prepare meat and vegetables:* Place beef, with cold water to cover, in a dutch oven. Add salt and pepper. Bring to a boil and skim. Reduce heat, cover and simmer for 4 hours or until the meat is tender. Do not boil.

Add carrots and turnips to the liquid 30–40 minutes before cooking time is up, potatoes 20 minutes before and cabbage 10 minutes before.

Meanwhile, cook green beans in a separate saucepan of salted water for 20 minutes.

*To serve:* Remove meat and vegetables from liquid. Slice corned beef on a hot platter, arranging the vegetables and hot slices of sausage around the meat. Sprinkle the vegetables with chopped parsley and serve with Sauce Belle Creole.

## CAJUN CHOPPED BEEF AND EGGPLANT

1 medium eggplant, quartered
    and cut into 1" thick slices
¼ cup cooking oil
1½ lbs. ground beef
2 Tbs. grated onion
1 clove garlic, minced
2 Tbs. chopped parsley
2 Tbs. chopped celery leaves
Salt and pepper to taste

½ tsp. Tabasco pepper sauce
1 tsp. Creole seasonings
5 Creole tomatoes, peeled,
    seeded, chopped and cooked
    down to a purée for 20 minutes
1–2 Tbs. white wine, if needed
6 Tbs. butter
1 cup cooked fluffy white rice
Paprika

*Serves 6*

Fry the eggplant slices in the cooking oil for about 5 minutes or until tender, stirring frequently with a wooden spoon.

Mix the ground beef with the next 7 seasoning ingredients and moisten with the tomato purée. If mixture seems too thick, add some white wine.

Grease a deep pie dish with 2 Tbs. of the butter, fill with a layer of eggplant, and then the meat mixture, and repeat until all is used.

Cover the surface of the pie with a thin layer of cooked rice. Dot with remaining butter and sprinkle with paprika. Bake in a moderate oven (350°) for about 40 minutes.

## CREOLE POT ROAST

6 slices bacon
A 2-lb. flank steak
    or top round steak
Salt to taste
6 peppercorns
1 red onion, sliced
1 large carrot, sliced

1 bay leaf
2–3 cups Beef Stock (p. 183)
1 tsp. sugar
Juice of 1 lemon
½ tsp. Tabasco pepper sauce
¼ cup dry red wine
½ cup sour cream

*Serves 6*

Line the bottom of a large, heavy skillet with the bacon. Put the roast on top and add salt, peppercorns, onion, carrot and bay leaf. Moisten with very little of the stock—about 1 cup.

Cover and steam on top of the stove for about 2 hours or until meat is tender. Add a little more stock from time to time as necessary.

When done, slice the meat and keep warm.

Put the gravy through a sieve and flavor with sugar, lemon juice, Tabasco and red wine. Correct for salt.

Bring to a boil once, remove from the flame, cool slightly and gradually blend in the sour cream.

Return meat slices to this sauce and heat thoroughly.

## CREOLE STUFFED PEPPERS

6 medium green peppers
3/4 lb. pickled pork sausage or
   regular Italian sausage mixed
   with 1 Tbs. vinegar
1 lb. ground beef
Salt and pepper to taste

1 clove garlic, crushed
1½ cups uncooked rice
1½ cups Beef Stock (p. 183)
3 Tbs. bacon fat
2 Tbs. flour
1 can (1 lb.) tomatoes

*Serves 6*

Cut tops off each pepper and carefully remove seeds. Wash and dry inside and out.

In a mixing bowl, combine the sausage and the ground beef. Add salt, pepper and crushed garlic. Add the uncooked rice. Work to a paste with 1–2 Tbs. of the stock.

Fill each green pepper 3/4 full with this mixture. Never fill the peppers completely, because the rice swells while cooking. If any mixture remains, roll into medium-size balls and cook at the same time.

In a large saucepan melt the bacon fat and fry the flour for 2–3 minutes. Add the canned tomatoes, which you have rubbed through a sieve, and the remaining beef stock. Correct for seasonings.

In this sauce, put the stuffed peppers and any meatballs you may have. Bring carefully to a boil, cover, reduce heat and cook very slowly for 1 hour. If more liquid is required, add a little water.

When done, remove peppers and any extra meatballs with a slotted spoon.

Pour sauce over each individual serving.

## FILET ST. FERDINAND

1 cup boiled water, cooled
½ cup white wine vinegar
Juice and rind of 1 lemon
2 Tbs. olive oil
5 cloves
2 bay leaves
8 peppercorns

½ large onion, preferably red,
  sliced
4 filet steaks
4 Tbs. butter
Salt to taste
1 Tbs. flour

*Serves 4*

Make a marinade by combining the cooled water with the wine vinegar. Add the juice and rind of the lemon, the oil, cloves, bay leaves, peppercorns and onion slices.

Place filets in this marinade; cover and keep in a cool place (not refrigerated) for 24 hours. Heat 2 Tbs. of the butter in a frying pan and cook each steak, drained from the marinade, until done as you like it—4 minutes on each side for rare, 5–6 minutes for medium and more for well done. Correct for salt, remove and keep hot.

Blend the flour with the remaining butter and pan juices and add 1–1½ cups of the marinade. Bring to a boil, reduce heat and cook for 5 minutes.

Pour the sauce over the filets and serve hot. Accompany with parsley potatoes.

## FRENCH QUARTER GROUND MEAT PIE

2 Tbs. lard
1 large onion, chopped
2 lbs. lean ground meat
1 tsp. Tabasco pepper sauce
1 Tbs. Creole seasonings

1 tsp. salt
1 stick butter
4 cups mashed potatoes
½ cup grated Parmesan cheese
1 Tbs. paprika

*Serves 6*

In a heavy skillet, melt lard and fry onion for 5–10 minutes. When onion pieces are tender, break up meat and add gradually, stirring constantly with a fork until the meat is well browned but not cooked—about 5–10 minutes. Add Tabasco, Creole seasonings and salt and mix well.

Use some of the butter to grease a deep ovenproof casserole. Alternately layer mashed potatoes with the meat and onion mixture, ending with a layer of mashed potatoes. Cover with Parmesan cheese. Dust with paprika and dot with the rest of the butter.

Bake in a moderate oven (350°) for 30 minutes or until potatoes are nicely browned on top.

# GRILLED SALISBURY STEAK CABILDO

*Salisbury steak:*

1³/₄ lbs. ground chuck
¼ lb. ground Italian hot sausage
1 small red onion, grated
½ green pepper, grated
1 clove garlic, mashed
1½ Tbs. finely chopped green
   onion

1 Tbs. finely chopped parsley
1 tsp. Creole seasonings
¼ tsp. Tabasco pepper sauce
2 Tbs. flour, seasoned with
   salt and pepper
4 Tbs. olive oil
Extra parsley, finely chopped

*Cabildo Sauce:*

4 Tbs. butter
¹/₃ cup tomato ketchup
1 Tbs. lemon juice
1 tsp. Creole seasonings
1 tsp. Worcestershire sauce

1 tsp. Creole mustard
½ tsp. Tabasco pepper sauce
Salt and pepper to taste
3 Tbs. dry sherry

*Serves 6*

*To cook steaks:* To the ground meats, add all the steak ingredients except the flour, olive oil and extra parsley. Mix well.

Shape into 6 individual steaks. Sprinkle lightly with flour and brush with olive oil. Broil to the desired degree—about 5 minutes on each side for rare, 8 minutes for medium.

*To make sauce and serve:* Blend all the sauce ingredients well, stir in the sherry and bring almost to the boiling point.

Pour sauce over each steak and sprinkle with the extra parsley.

## LAFAYETTE STREET CORNED BEEF HASH

1 stick butter
3 potatoes, diced
2 medium onions, chopped
1 lb. canned corned beef,
  coarsely chopped

1 Tbs. Worcestershire sauce
½ tsp. Tabasco pepper sauce
½ tsp. salt
1 cup heavy cream
4 poached eggs

*Serves 4*

In a skillet, melt butter. Sauté potatoes for about 10 minutes, stirring frequently to prevent sticking, and add more butter if needed.

Add onions and continue to cook until potatoes are done and onions are lemon-colored—about another 10 minutes. During this process, you may cover the skillet.

Add corned beef and cook ingredients together until potatoes are soft—about 10 more minutes. Add the next 3 seasonings and finally blend in the heavy cream, mixing well. Heat thoroughly.

Serve in individual servings with a poached egg on top of each.

## LAFAYETTE STREET LONDON BROIL

*London broil:*
  1 beef flank steak, about 2 lbs.
  Salt and pepper to taste

1½ cups Christopher Blake's
  French Dressing (chap. 13)
Finely chopped parsley

*Lafayette Sauce:*
  ½ cup unsalted butter
  ½ tsp. Tabasco pepper sauce
  1 Tbs. Worcestershire sauce

About ¼ cup pan juices
  from steak
Juice of ½ lemon

*Serves 4–6*

*To cook steak:* Sprinkle the flank steak with salt and pepper and marinate in the French dressing for about 1 hour.

Broil on a greased grill about 3″ below the flame, allowing 5–8 minutes for each side, or less if you like it very rare. Reserve the juices for the sauce and the parsley for garnish.

*To make sauce and serve:* Combine all the sauce ingredients and heat to the boiling point. Carve the steak diagonally against the grain and pour the sauce over it.

Garnish with parsley and serve.

# NEW ORLEANS SPOON BEEF

3 lbs. round steak,
   cut into pieces 1″ thick
Salt and freshly ground
   black pepper to taste
1 cup all-purpose flour
2–3 Tbs. cooking oil
½–1 cup dry white wine

1 cup diced carrots
¼ cup chopped onion
½ green pepper, chopped
½ tsp. minced garlic
½ tsp. Tabasco pepper sauce
1 Tbs. tomato paste

*Serves 6*

Rub the steak lightly on both sides with salt and pepper. Dredge the meat lightly in flour and brown slowly for 5 minutes on each side in cooking oil.

Add wine, vegetables, garlic and Tabasco. Cover the skillet.

Cook over low heat or in a 350° oven for 1–1½ hours or until the meat is so well done that it will fall apart when you slice it.

Transfer the meat to a heated platter. Add tomato paste to the gravy, adjust seasonings and pour over the meat.

Serve with corn bread.

# SHREDDED STEAK

A 2-lb. skirt or flank steak
2 cups Beef Stock (p. 183)
1 medium onion, finely chopped
1 clove garlic, minced
1 cup olive oil

4 medium Creole tomatoes,
   blanched, peeled and chopped
Salt and freshly ground
   black pepper to taste
½ tsp. Tabasco pepper sauce

*Serves 6*

Put the steak in a heavy saucepan or casserole with stock to cover. Simmer, covered, for 1½–2 hours or until tender. Leave the meat in the stock until it is cool enough to handle.

Lift out the meat and reserve the stock for some other recipe. Cut the meat into pieces about ¼″ wide and 1″ long.

In a large, heavy frying pan, fry the onion and garlic in the oil until the onion is limp but not browned—about 5 minutes. Add the tomatoes, season with salt and black pepper and cook for 5 more minutes. Season with Tabasco.

Add the steak and simmer in the sauce until it is heated through.

Heap the beef in the center of a heated platter and surround it with a ring of fluffy white rice or mounds of red beans or both.

## STEAK AND KIDNEY PIE

3 veal kidneys or 6 lamb kidneys
5 Tbs. flour
1½ tsp. salt
⅛ tsp. ground black pepper
¼ tsp. ground ginger
1 Tbs. butter
3 Tbs. shortening
1 tsp. prepared mustard

4 medium onions, sliced
1¼ cups Beef Stock (p. 183)
2 cups water
1 lb. round steak,
   cut into 1" cubes
Basic Pie Crust, top only (p. 382)
1 egg yolk mixed with
   1 Tbs. water

*Serves 6*

Wash kidneys and remove membranes, fat and tubes. Cut kidneys into quarters. Combine flour and the next 3 seasonings and dredge kidneys, reserving the flour that is left.

Brown kidneys in the combined butter and shortening for about 10 minutes.

Remove from heat and blend in the reserved flour, mustard, onions, beef stock and water.

Cover, bring to the boiling point, reduce heat and simmer for 1 hour.

Add the cubed steak ½ hour before the kidneys are done.

When done, remove beef and kidney pieces with a slotted spoon. Put them into a 10" x 6" x 2" baking dish. Spoon enough of the gravy over the meat to just cover.

Cover this with Basic Pie Crust. Trim, turn the edges under and decorate with the end of a fork. Cut 2 or 3 gashes on top of crust to allow steam to escape. Brush the top with beaten egg yolk mixed with a little water.

Bake in a hot oven (425°) for 40 minutes or until browned.

## STEAK AU POIVRE

2 thick steaks
Enough freshly ground
   coarse black pepper
   to coat both sides of the steaks

1 stick unsalted butter
Salt to taste
2 jiggers good brandy
2 jiggers dry white wine

*Serves 2*

Into each side of the steaks pound freshly ground black pepper until they are well coated.

Cook in 4 Tbs. of the butter until they are done the way you like them—4 minutes on each side for rare, 5–6 minutes for medium and more for well done.

Remove steaks to a heated platter and salt.

Pour brandy into same skillet and ignite. Add the remaining butter and the white wine. Swirl the butter, scraping the skillet constantly until sauce is thoroughly heated—about 3–5 minutes.

Pour sauce over the hot steaks and serve at once.


# STEAK DIANE

| | |
|---|---|
| 5 Tbs. butter | ½ tsp. Tabasco pepper sauce |
| 2 Tbs. chopped shallots | 1 Tbs. A-1 sauce |
| 2 individual filets, each cut in 3 round pieces, pounded | Salt and freshly ground black pepper |
| 2 Tbs. chopped parsley | Lemon juice (optional) |
| 1 Tbs. Worcestershire sauce | |

*Serves 2*

In a heavy skillet, melt 3 Tbs. of the butter and gently sauté the chopped shallots until they are golden—about 5 minutes.

Add the steak slices and sear them on both sides, cooking them until they are done the way you like them—about 2 minutes on each side for rare and up to 5 minutes on each side for well done.

Add the parsley, Worcestershire sauce, Tabasco and A-1 sauce and season with salt and freshly ground black pepper to taste. Finally, swirl in the remaining 2 Tbs. butter and a little lemon juice if you like.

Remove the steak slices to a heated platter and pour the sauce over them.

# LAMB

## BAKED LAMB FERRARA

1 leg of spring lamb (3–3½ lbs.)  
2 rosemary sprigs  
   (or ½ tsp. dried rosemary)  
Salt and pepper to taste  

¼ cup butter or lard  
4 large potatoes,  
   peeled and cut into cubes  
4 Tbs. dry white wine  

*Serves 4*

Preheat the oven to 450°.

Sprinkle the lamb with rosemary, or make small incisions all over the lamb and push a few rosemary leaves in each slit. Season with salt and pepper.

In a heavy ovenproof casserole, brown the lamb on all sides in the butter for about 15–20 minutes. Surround with the potatoes.

Bake for 1 hour or until tender. Turn the lamb and potatoes occasionally so that they brown evenly. If necessary, baste the lamb with a little white wine to prevent it from browning too quickly.

Transfer the lamb to a heated serving platter and surround with the potatoes.

## BRAISED LAMB SHANKS

6 young lamb shanks  
½ cup bacon or ham drippings  
   or lard  
2 cups boiling water  
12 small white onions  
2 whole cloves  
1½ cups chopped celery  
1½ cups thinly sliced carrots  
1 turnip, peeled and quartered  

1½ cups green beans,  
   cut into ¼" pieces  
1 cup fresh green peas or frozen,  
   large green peas, thawed  
1 Bouquet Garni (chap. 13)  
2 cloves garlic  
Salt and freshly ground  
   black pepper to taste  
4 Tbs. flour  
1 cup dry red wine  

*Serves 6*

Wash the lamb shanks, and if there is any thin parchmentlike covering, remove it. Heat the fat in a braising kettle and brown the shanks on all sides. Stir in the boiling water and thoroughly scrape the bottom of the pan.

Stud 2 of the onions with a clove each; add them and the other onions, the celery, carrots, turnips and green beans. If fresh peas are used, they may be added at this point as well. Add the bouquet garni and the garlic and season with salt and pepper.

Cover the kettle and braise in a moderate oven (350°) for 1 hour or until shanks are tender but not falling away from the bone.

Dilute the flour with red wine and add to the kettle, stirring well. Add the frozen peas if frozen peas are used, cover again and cook for another 15 minutes.

Discard the bouquet garni, taste for seasonings and serve shanks cut up into serving pieces or whole.

Garnish with the cooked vegetables and sauce. Serve with boiled rice or noodles.

## BRETON-STYLE LEG OF LAMB

*Lamb:*

| | |
|---|---|
| 1 young leg of lamb (not more than 5 lbs.) | 2 carrots, peeled and thinly sliced |
| 4 cloves garlic, cut into slivers | 2 large onions, thinly sliced |
| 3 Tbs. lard | ¼ bunch parsley |
| Salt and freshly ground black pepper to taste | ½ bunch celery tops |
| | 1½ cups boiling water |

*White beans:* *

| | |
|---|---|
| 2 lbs. Great Northern white beans | 1 onion, quartered |
| 1 carrot, sliced | Salt to taste |
| | ½ tsp. black pepper |

*Serves 8*

*To cook lamb:* With a sharp knife, make tiny slits over the surface of the lamb. Fill each cavity with a sliver of garlic. The frequency of placement will depend on your taste for garlic.

Rub the lamb with the lard, salt and pepper. In a skillet over high heat, brown the surface of the lamb on all sides.

Place in a roasting pan and distribute carrots, onions, parsley and celery around it. Pour the boiling water over this and place in a hot oven (450°) for 15 minutes. Reduce heat to moderate (350°) and baste lamb every 20 minutes. If juices evaporate, add more water. When lamb is finished, at least 2 cups of the juice should be available after the fat is skimmed off.

Lamb should be served "pink," and for this, cooking time is a little more than

1 hour after the initial 15 minutes at high heat. You may wish to cook for an additional period of time, according to your taste.

*To prepare beans:* While the lamb is cooking, thoroughly wash and clean the white beans. Place in a heavy pot with the carrot and onion. Add salt and black pepper and cover with cold water.

Bring to a boil, reduce heat and cook for 1 hour or more until beans are tender but not falling apart. Drain the beans of all liquid.

*To serve:* When the lamb is cooked, remove the leg and strain the juices to remove vegetable pulp. Scrape any bits that may be clinging to the pan, mix with additional hot water and add to the juices. Combine the juices with the white beans and serve beans and lamb together.

*Flageolets, the green beans of Brittany, are now available in cans at gourmet shops. If you wish, you may substitute these for the white beans. Simply drain 1 can of flageolets, combine with the lamb juices and heat thoroughly before serving.

## CREOLE STUFFED LEG OF LAMB

*Stuffing:*

½ cup cooked ham, chopped
2 oz. suet
6 slices day-old French bread, crumbled
2 Tbs. chopped onion
1 Tbs. finely chopped green pepper
1 Tbs. finely chopped parsley

1 Tbs. finely chopped celery leaves
3 cooked chicken livers, chopped
1 tsp. salt
1 tsp. Creole seasonings
¼ tsp. Tabasco pepper sauce
⅛ tsp. nutmeg
2 Creole tomatoes, peeled, seeded and chopped

*Roast lamb:*

1 leg of lamb (6–7 lbs.), boned for stuffing
½ cup sliced carrots
½ cup sliced white turnips
½ cup sliced celery

1 Bouquet Garni (chap. 13)
1 clove garlic, mashed
1 medium onion, sliced
1 cup red wine

*Gravy:*

Pan juices from lamb
1 Tbs. *Beurre Manié* (chap. 13)

*Serves 8*

*To make stuffing:* Combine all stuffing ingredients and mix well.

*To cook and serve lamb:* Stuff the lamb and sew or skewer it together. Surround with all roasting ingredients and pour in the red wine. Roast in a 450° oven for 25 minutes. Reduce heat to 350° and roast for 2 hours.

Remove roast from pan. Strain juices into a saucepan and thicken with *beurre manié* to make the gravy.

Pour over the roast lamb and serve.

## GARDEN DISTRICT LEG OF LAMB

1 leg of lamb (4–5 lbs.)  
3 Tbs. goose fat or butter  
15 cloves garlic,  
  peeled and halved*  

3 Tbs. Armagnac  
1 cup Sauterne, Chateau d'Yquem  
  or Louisiana orange wine  
Salt and pepper to taste  

*Serves 8*

Blanch the lamb by putting it in boiling salted water for 15 minutes. Drain and dry well with paper towels or a clean cloth.

Melt the fat or butter in a large, deep casserole. Add the lamb and brown it all over.

Put the halved garlic cloves around the lamb. (You may want to add even more, as you'll want a good garlic flavor.) Pour in the Armagnac and ignite. When the flames die down, add the wine and season with salt and pepper.

Cover the casserole tightly, using foil to make a perfect seal. Cook over very low heat for 5–6 hours, turning the leg once every 2 hours.

Serve the lamb with its cooking juices on a large platter, surrounded by the cooked garlic pieces. Accompany with a purée of your favorite vegetable.

*Don't let the number of garlic pieces frighten you. Remember, these are boiled, and so the end result is quite different. Matter of fact, you can even whisper to your elegant partner.

## JASON'S SKEWERED LAMB

1 leg of lamb (5–6 lbs.), boned
   and cut into large, even chunks
1 tsp. salt
1 tsp. coarsely ground
   black pepper
1 Tbs. Creole seasonings
1 Tbs. Creole mustard
2 Tbs. chopped parsley
1 bay leaf

2 cloves garlic, minced
3/4 cup olive oil
3/4 cup Chianti wine
2 small eggplants, cubed
1 green pepper,
   cut into bite-size pieces
1 lb. mushrooms, caps only
1 lb. tomatoes, quartered

*Serves 6*

Place meat in a large bowl and sprinkle with all the seasonings, mixing well before adding the olive oil and Chianti. Marinate overnight at room temperature.

When ready to cook, arrange the meat on skewers, alternating with pieces of eggplant, green peppers, mushroom caps and tomato quarters.

Grill over hot coals, turning frequently and basting with the marinade until the lamb is done—about 10–15 minutes.

## LAMB KORMA

2 lbs. raw lamb meat from a leg
3/4 cup yogurt
2½ tsp. salt
1 tsp. ground cumin
1½ tsp. ground turmeric
¼ tsp. ground cardamom
1½ cups chopped onion
1 clove garlic, crushed
¼ cup peanut oil

1 tsp. powdered mustard
1 tsp. ground ginger
½ tsp. ground black pepper
¼–½ tsp. cayenne pepper
⅛ tsp. ground cloves
1 cup water
1 tsp. lemon juice
2 Tbs. fresh or packaged
   grated coconut

*Serves 4–6*

Trim off and discard excess fat from lamb. Cut meat into 1″ pieces. Mix well with the yogurt, salt, cumin, turmeric and cardamom and marinate for 2 hours or more.

In a skillet, cook onion and garlic in peanut oil until golden—about 5–10 minutes. Add the mustard, ginger, black pepper, cayenne and cloves. Stir well and cook for 2 minutes. Pour off any excess fat.

Add the lamb, cover tightly and simmer for 20 minutes. Pour in 1 cup water, mix well and cover again. Simmer for 30 minutes or until the lamb is tender, adding a little more water if needed.

Stir in the lemon juice and coconut just before serving.

## LANCASHIRE HOT POT

| | |
|---|---|
| 2 lbs. mutton, cubed | 18–20 oysters, shucked |
| 2 Tbs. butter or fat drippings | 2 lbs. potatoes, thickly sliced |
| Salt and pepper to taste | 3/4 cup Beef Stock (p. 183), |
| Pinch of sugar | heated |
| 3 lamb kidneys, sliced | Chopped parsley |
| 6 fresh mushrooms, sliced | |

*Serves 4–6*

Neatly trim meat of skin and fat. Brown in butter and place in a deep casserole. Season with salt and pepper and a pinch of sugar.

Over the meat place the kidneys, mushrooms and oysters in layers. Arrange the potatoes neatly on top to completely cover the meats.

Pour the hot beef stock over all, cover and bake in a moderate oven (350°) for 2 hours. About 15 minutes before done, remove the lid so that the potatoes can brown.

Serve from the casserole and garnish with chopped parsley.

## STEWED LAMB WITH PEAS

| | |
|---|---|
| 2½ lbs. boneless shoulder of | 2 stalks celery, chopped |
| lamb, cut in 1¼" cubes | 2 sprigs parsley |
| 3 Tbs. flour | 2 Tbs. tomato purée |
| 6 Tbs. butter | 12 small white onions |
| 2–3 cups Beef Stock (p. 183) | 1 cup cooked green peas |
| 1 tsp. salt | ¼ tsp. ground black pepper |

*Serves 6*

Preheat oven to 350°.

Trim off and discard fat from lamb. Dust with flour and brown on all sides in 3 Tbs. of the butter in a dutch oven. Add enough of the stock to come halfway to the top of the meat. Add salt, celery, parsley and tomato purée. Cover and cook in the oven for 1 hour.

Brown onions in the remaining 3 Tbs. butter and add to the meat. Cover and cook for another ½ hour or until the meat and onions are tender.

Remove and discard parsley. Strain sauce and return to meat. Add cooked peas and season with black pepper.


# PORK AND HAM


## BURAS ORANGE PORK

1 center-cut loin of pork
  (5–6 lbs.), boned
Salt and black pepper to taste
1 onion, sliced
3 tangerines,
  peeled and sectioned
¼ cup chopped celery

½ tsp. Creole seasonings
1 cup Louisiana orange wine
  (or ¼ cup Triple Sec mixed
  with ¾ cup dry white wine)
2 Tbs. wine vinegar
1 cup fresh orange juice
2 Tbs. *Beurre Manié* (chap. 13)

*Serves 6–8*

Sprinkle the loin with salt and black pepper and place on a rack in a roasting pan, fat side up. Add onion, tangerine sections, chopped celery, Creole seasonings, wine, vinegar and orange juice. Roast in a moderate oven (350°), 25–30 minutes to the pound, until pork is well done. Baste frequently with the pan juices.

Remove the pork and slice. Skim off any excess fat. Thicken the juices remaining in the pan with the *beurre manié* to make a nice sauce. Serve hot with the pork.


## GARNISHED SAUERKRAUT

1 cup bacon rinds
2½ lbs. sauerkraut
6 slices bacon
6 frankfurters
1½ lbs. pickled spareribs
  or ham hocks

1½ lbs. cooked ham, cubed
1 sprig parsley
2 medium carrots, sliced
2 whole medium onions
2 whole cloves
1 cup dry white wine

*Serves 6*

Preheat oven to 325°.

Line a 2-quart casserole with bacon rinds. Wash the sauerkraut and squeeze well by hand. Place half of it in the casserole.

Blanch bacon and frankfurters for 10 minutes in boiling water, drain and place over the sauerkraut. Put the remaining sauerkraut on top.

Cut spareribs and place over the sauerkraut along with the ham, parsley and carrots. Stud each onion with a clove and add. Pour in the wine. Do not add any salt.

Cover and cook in the preheated oven for 1½ hours.

To serve, place sauerkraut mixture in the center of a dish and arrange spareribs around it. Serve with boiled potatoes and a good hot mustard.

## HAM FRITTERS

| | |
|---|---|
| ½ cup butter | 1 Tbs. Creole seasonings |
| 1 cup boiling water | 2 cups lean cooked ham, ground |
| 1 cup sifted flour | Pinch of white pepper |
| 4 eggs | 2 cups cooking oil |

*Serves 4–6*

Add the butter to the boiling water, and when it has melted, add the flour all at once. Stir until the dough comes away from the sides of the pan.

Add the eggs one at a time, beating well after each addition. Stir in the Creole seasonings and the ham. Correct the seasonings for a little white pepper. Salt will not be necessary. Refrigerate.

When ready to use, drop by the tablespoon into hot deep fat (390°) and cook the fritters until they are golden brown—about 10–15 minutes. Drain well on paper toweling and serve with Louisiana fig preserves.

## HAM MOUSSE CREOLE

3 egg yolks
2 lbs. finely ground cooked ham
1 cup heavy cream
1 lb. cooked spinach
  (fresh or frozen), chopped

½ tsp. Tabasco pepper sauce
3 egg whites, stiffly beaten
2 cups *Sauce Velouté* (chap. 13)

*Serves 8*

Work the egg yolks into the ground ham; then mix in the cream and chopped spinach. Add the Tabasco and fold in the stiffly beaten egg whites.

Pour into a buttered 9″ ring mold, a loaf pan or individual molds. Bake in a moderate oven (350°) for about 45–60 minutes or until set and firm.

To serve, unmold by running a knife around the edge and inverting. If baked in a ring mold or loaf pan, cut into serving pieces. Top with hot *sauce velouté.*

The mousse and sauce may be prepared in advance and refrigerated. Reheat by placing serving pieces on a baking tray and warming in the oven. The mousse is also good cold without the sauce.

## HAM WITH CREAM SAUCE

8 slices cooked ham
4 shallots, finely chopped
3 juniper berries, crushed
6 Tbs. white wine vinegar
4 Tbs. butter
2 Tbs. flour

1 cup Beef Stock (p. 183),
  heated
8 Tbs. white wine
Salt and pepper to taste
1 scant cup heavy cream
³/₄–1 cup bread crumbs

*Serves 4*

Arrange the ham slices in a shallow baking dish.

In a small saucepan cook the shallots and juniper berries in the wine vinegar until all the liquid has evaporated. Reserve.

Meanwhile, melt 2 Tbs. of the butter in another saucepan, stir in the flour and cook gently until the roux is a pale coffee color. Gradually pour in the beef stock, stirring constantly. Add the wine, the shallot-berry mixture, salt and pepper and cook over low heat for 30 minutes, stirring constantly.

Preheat the oven to 425°.

Bring the cream to the boiling point in a small saucepan and then stir into the sauce. Remove the pan from the heat and stir in the remaining butter.

Pour the sauce over the ham slices, sprinkle with bread crumbs and place in the oven for 20 minutes or until slightly browned on top.

# PORK KORNILOFF

1 loin of pork (4–5 lbs.), boned
1 cup all-purpose flour,
  seasoned with salt and pepper
1 egg beaten with 1 Tbs. water
1 cup bread crumbs
1 stick butter, melted
2 cups Veal Stock (p. 185) or
  Chicken Stock (p. 183)

2 Tbs. apple jam
2 Tbs. plum jam
2 Tbs. cherry jam
2 Tbs. honey
½ tsp. finely grated lemon rind
½ tsp. cinnamon
5 cloves, pounded

*Serves 4–6*

Cut the meat into pieces about 3″ long and boil in salted water. Remove when tender—about 10 minutes. Drain.

Roll the pieces first in seasoned flour, then in egg wash and finally in bread crumbs. Refrigerate for at least an hour.

Lay pork pieces in a pan, drizzle with melted butter and cook in the oven for 20 minutes. Remove to a heated platter and keep warm.

In a heavy skillet, heat the stock; when warm, stir in the jams and honey. Add the lemon rind, cinnamon and cloves. Stir and simmer for a few minutes before pouring over the meat slices.

## PORK MANDARIN À LA CHRIS

2 5-oz. bottles soy sauce
1 large can pineapple chunks,
  with juices
1 tsp. dry mustard
2 cloves garlic, mashed
Salt and pepper to taste
Grated rind of 3 oranges
Juice of 3 oranges
Juice of 1 lemon

1 cup dark brown sugar
¼ cup candied ginger,
  cut in julienne strips
1 bunch green onions,
  tops and bottoms, chopped
5 lbs. lean center-cut loin of
  pork, boned
¼–½ cup cornstarch,
  mixed with cold water

*Serves 8–10*

Make a marinade by thoroughly combining all ingredients except pork and cornstarch. Marinate the pork roast overnight, refrigerated.

Roast the pork in a moderate oven (350°), 25–30 minutes to the pound, and baste from time to time with the marinade. If sauce reduces too much, add an extra cup of liquid—half water, half a mixture of orange juice and soy sauce.

When pork is tender, remove from the oven. Drain off all the sauce and strain, reserving pineapple chunks, ginger and other bits and pieces. Thicken sauce with some of the cornstarch paste. Stir constantly until sauce gets thick and is dark in color. Combine pineapple chunks and other ingredients with the sauce.

Slice the pork on a heated platter and cover with the sauce.

Serve with Chris's Unorthodox Fried Rice (p. 374).

## POTTED PORK

3 lbs. boneless shoulder butt
  of pork
1 cup boiling water
1 bay leaf
3 whole cloves
½ tsp. marjoram

½ tsp. dried sage
¼ tsp. rosemary
1½ tsp. salt
1 tsp. coarsely ground
  black pepper

*Yields 2 lbs.*

Cut pork, both lean and fat, into ½″ cubes. Place in a saucepan with the boiling water, bay leaf and cloves. Cook slowly, stirring occasionally, until water has evaporated. Continue to cook until the fat cubes begin to brown, but not until the meat is dry.

Remove from the heat and transfer the meat to a strainer. Set the strainer over the saucepan in which the meat was cooked until most of the fat has drained out. Reserve the liquid fat. Remove and discard bay leaf and cloves.

Put the meat through a food chopper, using the finest blade, and chop until very fine. Finish by pounding in a mortar or wooden bowl. Gradually blend in the reserved fat, saving 1 cup. Add the herbs, salt and pepper and mix well.

Divide meat mixture into small jars or crocks. Pour a ½″ layer of the remaining fat on top. Cover the jars with lids.

Store in the refrigerator until ready to use. To serve, remove fat layer from top and spread the mixture on toast.

## ROAST LOIN OF PORK NEW ORLEANS STYLE

1 whole loin of pork
  (about 5–6 lbs.)
2–3 white onions, thinly sliced
2 cloves garlic, sliced
½ cup flour, seasoned
  with salt and pepper
½ cup cold milk
3 onions, finely chopped

2 Creole tomatoes, peeled, seeded
  and chopped
1 green pepper, diced
½ cup celery leaves, chopped
1 Bouquet Garni (chap. 13)
½ tsp. Tabasco pepper sauce
2 cups boiling water
4–5 Tbs. brown sugar
2 Tbs. *Beurre Manié* (chap. 13)

*Serves 8*

Saw the bone through in several places to make carving simple.

Wipe the loin of pork with a damp cloth. Place a thin slice of onion in the openings of the bone. Rub the bones, fat and meat well with garlic and then coat with a mixture of the seasoned flour and milk. Make sure all the fat part is well coated.

Arrange the meat, fat side up, on the rack of an open roasting pan. In the bottom of the pan put the chopped onions, tomatoes, pepper, celery and bouquet garni. Add the Tabasco to the boiling water and pour this over the vegetables. Roast in a moderate oven (350°), 25–30 minutes to the pound, basting frequently with the juices from the pan.

About 15 minutes before the meat is done, remove from the oven and increase oven temperature to 400°–425°. Remove the slices of onion from the meat and bone, and the bouquet garni from the vegetables. Sprinkle the meat with brown sugar and return to the hot oven to glaze.

Pour off all excess fat, strain the vegetables and thicken the remaining sauce with the *beurre manié*. Correct the seasonings and serve with the carved roast.

# VEAL

## BLANQUETTE DE VEAU

3 lbs. lean veal stew meat,
  cut into 1½" cubes
1 lb. brisket of veal,
  cut into squares
½ tsp. each salt and white pepper
1 Bouquet Garni (chap. 13)
2 cups dry white wine
1 cup Veal Stock (p. 185)
  or Chicken Stock (p. 183)

24 small white onions
1¼ sticks butter
4 Tbs. flour
1 cup light cream
3 egg yolks
Juice of 2 lemons, strained
1 lb. mushrooms, caps only

*Serves 6*

Place veal, seasoned with salt, pepper and a bouquet garni, in a dutch oven. Cover with white wine and stock. Bring to a boil, skim for impurities and reduce heat.

Cover and simmer for 1 hour or until the meat is tender but not falling apart.

In the meantime, boil the onions in a separate pan with water until tender—about ½ hour—and set to one side.

When meat is done but not falling apart, strain off the liquid and reserve.

Melt 4 Tbs. of the butter and add the flour to make a light roux. Add the cream and finally the egg yolks; blend well. Add about ½ cup of the hot stock from the veal. Now gradually add the lemon juice and blend well. Combine with about another cup of the cooking stock to make a good thick sauce. Add sauce and onions to the veal pieces and combine very carefully.

Lightly sauté the mushrooms in the remaining butter and add to the veal. Correct for salt and pepper.

This is a good provincial dish, but it is bland. It should not have heavy seasoning, so concentrate on a well-seasoned vegetable or starch such as String Beans Lyonnaise (p. 367) or Risotto Araujo (p. 138).

*NOTE:* Peasants traditionally make this dish with brisket only, but try serving a bunch of bones at a posh buffet! I have added the veal stew for meatiness while retaining the brisket for flavor.

# BREAST OF VEAL CREOLE

1 onion, minced
3/4 lb. mild Italian sausage,
   chopped
4 Tbs. fat*
3 cups fresh, cooked spinach,
   finely chopped
1 cup French-bread crumbs
4 eggs

1 tsp. salt
½ tsp. freshly ground
   black pepper
Juice of 1 lemon
A 4-lb. veal pocket
   (have your butcher prepare)
1 or 2 cloves garlic, halved

*Serves 6–8*

Sauté the onion and the sausage meat in the fat until well browned—about 10 minutes.

Drain off the fat and put the onions and sausage in a large mixing bowl. Add the spinach and bread crumbs and beat in the eggs one by one. Add the salt, pepper and lemon juice. Mix well.

Rub the veal pocket inside and out with garlic and season with salt and pepper. Discard garlic. Stuff the pocket with the spinach forcemeat. Secure by sewing or with skewers.

Place the veal, fat side up, in an open roasting pan. Roast in a moderately slow oven (325°) for about 2½ hours.

When done, remove skewers or threads and garnish with small broiled tomatoes.

*Ask your butcher for some veal fat and trimmings and melt it down. Otherwise, any fat will do.

## FRENCH QUARTER VEAL LOAF

½ lb. calves' liver
1 cup Veal Stock (p. 185) or
   Beef Stock (p. 183)
1 lb. raw shoulder of veal
1 lb. hot Italian sausage
1–2 cups French-bread crumbs,
   crumbled
½ stick butter
½ lb. fresh mushrooms, chopped
1 onion, chopped

½ green pepper, chopped
1 whole pimiento, sliced
1½ Tbs. chopped parsley
1½ Tbs. chopped celery leaves
1 clove garlic, chopped
3 eggs
Salt and pepper to taste
1 Tbs. Creole seasonings
½ cup dry Marsala wine

*Serves 6–8*

Parboil calves' liver in stock for 10 minutes and chop.

Grind the veal and sausage 2–3 times. Brown the bread crumbs in butter; add them, the liver and the next 7 ingredients and grind once more with the veal and sausage. Blend in the eggs one by one and mix thoroughly.

Place the mixture in a large bowl; season with salt, pepper and Creole seasonings. Add enough dry Marsala to make the mixture rather soft. Mix thoroughly and allow to stand in a cool place for 1–2 hours.

Grease a 9" x 5" x 2³/4" loaf pan and fill ²/3 full with the mixture. Place loaf pan in a shallow pan filled with hot but not boiling water, and bake in a moderate oven (350°) for about 1 hour.

Remove and allow to cool completely in the refrigerator.

Unmold by running a sharp knife around the edges. Dip pan in hot water for several seconds and invert loaf onto a plate. Slice, place on a baking sheet, heat in a 300° oven for about 20 minutes and serve. Or slice and serve cold.

## GERMANTOWN VEAL ROAST

Salt and pepper to taste
1 loin of veal (about 4–5 lbs.)
2 Tbs. lard
3 carrots, sliced
3 onions, sliced

½ stick butter, melted
1½ cups dark beer
1 bay leaf
2 cloves
1 Tbs. flour

*Serves 6–8*

Salt and pepper the meat and rub with lard. Place in a deep casserole. Add the sliced carrots and onions and pour melted butter over all. Cook for ½ hour until the meat is evenly browned on all sides.

Pour the beer over the meat, add the bay leaf and cloves and cook until the meat is tender, basting frequently—about 1½ hours.

When meat is done, slice on a heated platter.

Strain the sauce; stir in the flour to make it smooth and thick. Cook for 5 minutes. Strain again and pour sauce over the meat slices.

## ITALIAN VEAL STEW

3 lbs. veal knuckles,
    sawed in 2½" pieces*
1 cup flour, seasoned
    with salt and pepper
6 Tbs. butter
1 clove garlic, finely chopped
1 carrot, thinly sliced
Grated rind of ½ lemon

¾ cup finely chopped parsley
1 cup fresh tomato pulp
    (about 2 large tomatoes)
1 cup dry white wine
2–3 cups Veal Stock (p. 185)
Salt and freshly ground
    black pepper to taste

*Serves 6*

Roll the veal pieces in seasoned flour. Sauté them in the butter in a dutch oven for 20–25 minutes.

When they are well browned on all sides, add the garlic, carrot, lemon rind, ¼ cup of the parsley and all the tomato pulp. Add the white wine and veal stock. Season with salt and black pepper.

Bring the mixture to a boil, reduce the heat and simmer gently, covered, for about 1 hour or until the meat is tender but not falling off the bones. Turn the pieces occasionally while cooking.

Remove the lid for the last 10 minutes of cooking to allow the sauce to simmer and become slightly thickened.

Taste for seasoning, garnish with the remaining chopped parsley and serve with little new potatoes or green noodles.

*Veal knuckles must be sawed, not chopped, as the marrow must remain in the bone.

# MARIGNY VEAL RAMEKINS

1 Tbs. finely chopped green
    onion, tops only
½ green pepper, finely minced
½ cup fresh mushrooms, chopped
1 bay leaf
2 Tbs. butter
2 cups finely chopped, cooked
    lean veal from a roast
1 cup andouille sausage, chopped
¾ Tbs. paprika blended with
    ¾ Tbs. unsalted butter

Salt and pepper to taste
Pinch of powdered thyme
½ tsp. Tabasco pepper sauce
¼ tsp. Creole mustard
½ cup heavy cream, scalded with
    a bay leaf and cooled
3 egg whites, stiffly beaten with
    a little salt
6 slices Creole tomato

*Serves 6*

Sauté green onion, green pepper, mushrooms and the bay leaf in the butter for 5–10 minutes. Drain and reserve.

Mix the veal and sausage in a bowl with the paprika butter. Add the sautéed vegetables and season to taste with salt, pepper, thyme, Tabasco and mustard. Mix again and at the same time gradually add the cooled cream. Remove the bay leaves.

Make sure the mixture is cool and then fold in the stiffly beaten egg whites; mix well.

Divide the mixture into 6 buttered ramekins and set in a shallow pan of hot water. Bake in a hot oven (400°) for 15–20 minutes. During the last 5 minutes, place a tomato slice on each ramekin.

Serve immediately.

# PAPRIKA SCHNITZEL

2 lbs. veal scallops
6 Tbs. unsalted butter
3 green onions, finely chopped
1 Tbs. flour, seasoned with a
    little salt, white pepper and
    1 Tbs. Hungarian sweet paprika

1 cup Veal Stock (p. 185),
    heated
1 cup dry white wine
¼ cup thick sour cream
2 Tbs. capers

*Serves 4–6*

In a heavy skillet, sauté the veal scallops in the butter until tender—about 10 minutes. Transfer them to a heated platter.

Add the green onions to the butter and juices remaining in the skillet and sauté until they are golden—about 10 minutes. Stir in the seasoned flour and gradually add the hot stock and white wine.

Stir constantly and continue to cook for 5 minutes until sauce begins to thicken. Lower the flame and simmer for another 10 minutes.

Gradually stir in the thick sour cream, and heat but do not boil. Add the capers and a little of the caper juice.

Mix well and pour over the heated veal schnitzels.


## VEAL CHOPS WITH CHEESE

| | |
|---|---|
| 4 veal chops, with bone | 1½ cups fine bread crumbs |
| 1 cup flour, seasoned | ¾ stick butter |
|   with salt and pepper | 4 slices fontina cheese |
| 1 egg, beaten with 1 Tbs. water | |

*Serves 4*

Pound the chops out to twice their original size without separating them from the bone. (If you're really into easy elegance, you'll have your butcher do this for you.) Dust them with seasoned flour and dip them in the egg wash. Then coat them with the bread crumbs. Refrigerate for at least an hour.

Fry the chops in foaming butter until they are cooked through and golden brown on both sides—about 15 minutes.

Meanwhile, preheat the broiler to high.

Put the chops on a heatproof serving platter. Cover each with a slice of fontina and place under the broiler just long enough to melt the cheese—about 5 minutes.

# VEAL PAPRIKA

1½–2 lbs. veal stew, boneless     Salt and white pepper to taste
3 Tbs. bacon fat or lard          1 cup Veal Stock (p. 185)
1 small red onion, finely chopped 2 Tbs. flour
1–2 Tbs. Hungarian sweet paprika

*Serves 4*

Cut the veal into small pieces.

Heat the bacon fat in a heavy saucepan and fry the onion until golden—about 5–10 minutes.

Sprinkle with the paprika and add the meat. Fry over brisk heat, stirring constantly, until meat is well coated and only lightly fried. Season with salt and pepper.

Stew the meat gently in the covered pan for about 30 minutes, depending on the age of the veal. If necessary, moisten from time to time with a spoonful or so of the stock.

When done, remove meat with a slotted spoon. Blend flour into pan juices and cook until smooth—about 5 minutes. Add the stock gradually, reduce heat and cook without boiling for about 10 minutes or until sauce is thickened.

Return meat to sauce and serve with buttered green noodles.

# INNARDS

## BRAINS AND EGGS BONNE CREOLE

1 lemon, halved                     ½ cup chopped parsley
1 tsp. salt                         ½ cup chopped black olives
4 calves' brains                    ½ tsp. Tabasco pepper sauce
1½ sticks butter                    Salt and black pepper to taste
8 eggs                              1 Tbs. Hungarian sweet paprika

*Serves 4*

Add lemon and salt to a saucepan of boiling water. Reduce heat and gently simmer the brains for 15 minutes. Remove, drain well and place in a bowl with ice and a little cold water. Refrigerate for about ½ hour until they are thoroughly chilled. When brains are cool, cut into small cubes.

Melt half the butter in a large iron skillet and fry the brains until they are thoroughly cooked and almost crisp—about 20 minutes. Remove brains with a slotted spoon and keep warm.

Add a little more butter if needed and scramble the eggs. When they begin to lose their liquid texture, add the chopped parsley, black olives, Tabasco, salt and pepper. Now add the hot cubes of brains and continue to scramble until brains and eggs are thoroughly heated. Sprinkle with paprika and serve immediately.

## CALVES' BRAINS WITH BLACK BUTTER

6 calves' brains,
   cleaned and halved
1 lemon, halved
1 tsp. salt

1 cup flour, seasoned
   with salt and pepper
1½ sticks butter
2 Tbs. wine vinegar
Capers and chopped parsley

*Serves 6*

Soak the brains in cold water for 1 hour. Drain, rinse and place in boiling water with the lemon and salt. Simmer gently for 15 minutes.

Drain again and cover with ice cubes and a little cold water for about 30 minutes.

Dry with a towel and dip each brain half in seasoned flour.

Sauté the brains a few at a time in 1 stick of the butter until they are done and nicely browned—about 15 minutes. Remove the brains to a heated platter.

Put the rest of the butter in the pan in which brains have been sautéed. When butter begins to brown, remove from fire, add vinegar and shake the pan to mix butter and vinegar. Heat the mixture to the foaming point and pour it sizzling hot over the warm brains. Serve at once, garnished with finely chopped parsley and capers.

## CALVES' LIVER HAMMOND STYLE

1 lb. calves' liver
1 Tbs. bacon fat

1 small red onion, chopped
1 Tbs. Hungarian sweet paprika

*Serves 4*

Cut liver into strips ½" wide and 2" long. Do not wash or salt the liver.

Heat the fat in a frying pan and fry the chopped red onion until golden—about 5 minutes. Sprinkle with the paprika, increase heat and add liver, stirring all the time until the liver changes color. Cook for about 5 minutes in all.

Serve at once with salt and pepper on the table and hot buttered noodles.

## CALVES' LIVER WITH AVOCADO

2 avocados, not too ripe
Juice of 2½ lemons
12 very thin slices calves' liver
¾ cup flour, seasoned
  with salt and pepper
1½ sticks butter

½ cup Beef Stock (p. 183)
Pinch of fresh thyme
  (or ½ tsp. dried thyme)
¼ cup dry sherry
Chopped parsley

*Serves 4*

Cut avocados into thin strips and sprinkle with the juice of ½ lemon. Dip slices of liver in seasoned flour and reserve. Dip avocado strips in seasoned flour and reserve.

Melt half the butter in a heavy skillet. When it stops foaming, sauté the slices of liver for 2 minutes on each side and remove to a heated platter. Now sauté the avocado slices for about 5 minutes. Arrange alternate slices of liver and avocado on the platter.

In another skillet, melt the rest of the butter and heat until it just begins to brown. Add the remaining lemon juice and the beef stock and thyme. Cook for 3–5 minutes so that the sauce is thoroughly heated. Add the sherry. Continue to cook for a minute or so and pour over the hot liver and avocado slices. Sprinkle with chopped parsley.

## COLD CALVES' BRAINS VINAIGRETTE

6 calves' brains,
  cleaned and halved
2 Tbs. vinegar
1 tsp. salt
5 peppercorns

1 onion, sliced
1 small carrot, sliced
4 sprigs parsley
1 bay leaf
Pinch of fresh or dried thyme

*Serves 6*

Wash brains and soak in cold water for 1 hour.

Place in a saucepan with enough water to cover. Add remaining ingredients. Bring to a boil and simmer gently for 25 minutes.

Allow the brains to cool in their own cooking liquid. Refrigerate in the cooled liquor. When cold, drain well, slice and serve wtih C.B.'s Vinaigrette Sauce (chap. 13).

## CREOLE TONGUE VINAIGRETTE

*Tongue:*
  4 small calves' tongues
  1 lemon, halved
  1 Tbs. salt

*Marinade:*

½ cup chopped green onions, tops and bottoms
1 large carrot, peeled and finely chopped
1 green pepper, finely diced
½ cup chopped parsley
Pinch of thyme

3 cloves garlic, minced
1 Tbs. Creole mustard
½ tsp. Tabasco pepper sauce
1 Tbs. salt
1 cup chopped celery, with leaves
1¼ cups olive oil
½ cup wine vinegar

*Serves 8*

*To cook tongue:* Clean, wash and pat the tongues dry. Place in a deep saucepan and cover with water. Add lemon and salt. Bring to a boil, skim off any impurities, reduce heat and simmer for about 2 hours or until tongues are tender but not falling apart. Cool enough to handle and then remove tough outer skin. Refrigerate.

*To marinate and serve:* Combine all ingredients to make the marinade. Mix well.

When tongues are very cold, cut into thick slices. In a shallow glass dish, alternate layers of tongue and marinade until all are used up. Cover and allow to sit, unrefrigerated, for about 24 hours, tossing from time to time.

Chill slightly just before serving.

## FRENCH QUARTER FRIED SWEETBREADS

4 large pieces of sweetbreads
1 lemon, halved
1 cup flour, seasoned with salt and pepper
2 eggs beaten with 1 Tbs. cold water
2 cups fine bread crumbs mixed with 1 Tbs. Creole seasonings

1 stick butter
Juice of 1 lemon
½ tsp. Tabasco pepper sauce
Salt and pepper to taste
Chopped parsley
Lemon wedges

*Serves 4*

Clean sweetbreads. Bring water and lemon to a boil in a saucepan. Reduce heat and parboil sweetbreads for 15 minutes.

Remove sweetbreads, cool them in ice and clean of any excess matter and membranes. Refrigerate for a couple of hours until cold enough to slice.

When cold, slice sweetbreads thickly and then flatten them between pieces of waxed paper with the flat side of a meat cleaver. Dip them in seasoned flour, then in the egg wash and finally in the seasoned bread crumbs. Refrigerate once more until ready to use.

Melt butter and gently fry the sweetbread slices a few at a time for 10 minutes on each side, until they are done and golden in color.

Sprinkle with lemon juice, a few drops of Tabasco and salt and pepper. Garnish with chopped parsley and lemon wedges.


# LAMB KIDNEYS WITH CHAMPAGNE

| | |
|---|---|
| 1 stick butter | 1 Tbs. flour |
| ½ lb. mushrooms, sliced | ½ cup champagne *nature* |
| 12 lamb kidneys, thinly sliced |   or any other dry white wine |
| Salt and pepper to taste | 3 Tbs. Beef Stock (p. 183) |
| Grating of nutmeg | Juice of ½ lemon |
| 2 Tbs. chopped parsley | 12 bread triangles fried in butter |

*Serves 6*

Melt 1 Tbs. of the butter in a small pan. Add the mushrooms, cook them lightly for 5–10 minutes and reserve.

Melt 5 Tbs. butter in another pan and fry the kidney slices very quickly until they are lightly browned on both sides—about 4–8 minutes.

Season with salt and pepper to taste; add a pinch of grated nutmeg and the parsley. Sprinkle with the flour. Stir in the champagne or wine, the beef stock and the mushrooms. Cook gently for 5 minutes.

Correct the seasonings, add the lemon juice and mix in the remaining 2 Tbs. butter.

Turn the kidneys onto a heated serving dish, surround with the fried bread triangles and serve immediately.

# SAUTÉED KIDNEYS CREOLE

5 veal kidneys,                      1 large Creole tomato,
  soaked in cold water          peeled, seeded and chopped
½ stick butter                       1 tsp. Creole mustard
½ cup Veal Stock (p. 185)            Salt and pepper to taste
½ cup dry white wine                 1 Tbs. *Beurre Manié* (chap. 13)
¾ cup sliced fresh mushrooms         2 Tbs. chopped parsley

*Serves 6*

Trim and thinly slice the kidneys. Sear them in a little butter over high heat for 4–8 minutes. Shake the pan constantly to prevent sticking. Transfer the kidneys and keep warm.

Lower the flame and add the stock and wine, along with the mushroom slices and tomato. Add the mustard and season with salt and pepper. Cover the pan and cook for 5 minutes. Thicken the gravy with the *beurre manié*. Stir and cook for another 5 minutes or until the sauce is very thick and smooth.

Add the parsley and the kidney slices. Heat thoroughly but do not boil after kidneys have been added.

# TONGUE WITH ORANGE SAUCE

3 Tbs. butter                        ½ tsp. grated lemon peel
3 Tbs. flour                         2 Tbs. dry sherry
1 cup stock from cooking tongue      1 tsp. currant jelly
1 cup orange juice                   Salt and pepper to taste
1 Tbs. grated orange peel            3 lbs. cooked beef tongue*

*Serves 6–8*

Melt 2 Tbs. of the butter in a 1-quart saucepan. Remove from heat and blend in flour. Stir and cook for 1 minute. Remove from heat again and add tongue stock and orange juice.

Mix well and simmer until the sauce has reduced to 1½ cups, stirring frequently. Add orange and lemon peels, sherry and jelly. Stir and cook for another minute or so. Strain and stir in remaining butter. Season with salt and pepper.

Serve over hot slices of tongue.

*Tongue should be cooked with lemon and salt in same manner as Creole Tongue Vinaigrette (p. 346).

# 11
# VEGETABLES & SALADS

ALTHOUGH the French Market in the Vieux Carré is changing, there are some remnants of a farmers' market. One can still go down near the Mississippi River and find stall after stall of fresh produce brought to the market daily in season— and sometimes even out of season, when it is shipped in.

The word *Creole* does not only mean a haughty combination of French and Spanish aristocratic ancestry, as some romantic historians would have us believe. *Creole* can be applied to anything grown in the soil of Louisiana when it was a colony. So it is quite proper to refer to Creole tomatoes, Creole corn, Creole eggplant and Creole string beans. Nothing creates quite such a stir in New Orleans gourmet circles as the appearance of Creole tomatoes in season. These funny-looking, odd-shaped tomatoes give a wonderful flavor to everything but are best eaten by themselves.

What with traditional canning and contemporary freezing, you can now pick your method of storing these fresh products for those days when their original taste and fragrance have become only a memory.

# VEGETABLES

## ACADIAN MUSHROOMS

4 Tbs. olive oil
1 lb. fresh mushrooms,
    washed, caps whole and
    stems finely chopped
1 clove garlic, minced
3 shallots, minced
1 Tbs. flour

1 cup dry white wine
1 Tbs. chopped parsley
½ tsp. fresh thyme
    (or a pinch of dried thyme)
1 Tbs. tomato paste
Salt and black pepper to taste
½ tsp. Tabasco pepper sauce

*Serves 4*

In a skillet heat 3 Tbs. of the olive oil and sauté the mushroom caps until they are tender. Remove and keep warm.

In the same skillet, blend the remaining olive oil with the cooking juices; add the chopped mushroom stems, garlic and shallots and cook for 3 minutes. Stir in the flour and gradually add the white wine, stirring constantly until the sauce thickens.

Add parsley, thyme, tomato paste, salt, black pepper and Tabasco and cook for another 10 minutes, stirring occasionally.

Reheat the mushroom caps in the sauce and serve on fried French bread.

## ASPARAGUS POLISH STYLE

2½ lbs. asparagus,
    cleaned and peeled
2 hard-boiled eggs, chopped
½ cup chopped parsley

6 Tbs. butter
½ cup coarse bread crumbs
Salt and pepper to taste

*Serves 6*

Cook asparagus standing up in an asparagus cooker or a deep pot, with enough salt water to cover the stalks but not the tips, for about 20 minutes.

Arrange the cooked asparagus in overlapping rows in a shallow baking dish, leaving the tips visible. Sprinkle with chopped egg and parsley.

Melt butter in a small saucepan, add bread crumbs and, stirring constantly, fry until they have browned. Season with salt and pepper.

Sprinkle bread crumbs over the hot asparagus and serve immediately.

## BASIC OKRA

2 lbs. medium okra                    4 Tbs. butter
½ tsp. salt                           Black pepper to taste

*Serves 4*

Wash okra and cut off stems. Be careful not to cut too close to the pod, or they will ooze.

Place in a saucepan with salt and pour in boiling water to a depth of ½". Bring to the boiling point and cook for 5 minutes. Cover and cook for 5 more minutes or until okra is tender. Drain off and discard water.

Add butter to the saucepan. Simmer for 2–3 minutes. Sprinkle with black pepper. Serve hot.

## BAVARIAN CABBAGE

1 medium white cabbage                1 tsp. caraway seed
½ lb. salt pork, diced small and      ½ cup dry white wine
   parboiled for 10 minutes           2 Tbs. sugar
2–3 Tbs. water                        1 Tbs. flour
2–3 Tbs. vinegar                      ½ tsp. white pepper

*Serves 4–6*

Remove the outer leaves of the cabbage and the coarse ribs; shred finely. Cook for 10 minutes in salted boiling water.

Remove and drain thoroughly. Put the cabbage in a casserole with the salt pork, water, vinegar and caraway seed. Cover and simmer for 1 hour.

Add the white wine and sugar and cover again. Cook for almost 1 hour more.

Before serving, stir in the flour and blend well. Sprinkle with the white pepper and serve. Excellent with game.

# BAYOU BEAN CASSEROLE

| | |
|---|---|
| 4 Tbs. butter | 1 Bouquet Garni (chap. 13) |
| 18 small white onions, peeled | Salt and pepper to taste |
| 1 Tbs. flour | 2 cups fresh lima beans* |
| 1 cup water | Fresh parsley and lemon juice |

*Serves 4–6*

In a heavy casserole, melt butter and sauté the onions gently until golden in color—about 5 minutes. Sprinkle with the flour and mix well. Add the water and the bouquet garni. Season with salt and pepper and simmer gently, tightly covered, for about 20–25 minutes.

Add the fresh lima beans and continue simmering until the beans are tender—another 20–25 minutes.

Shake the casserole frequently to prevent the vegetables from sticking to the bottom of the pan.

Sprinkle with freshly chopped parsley and a little lemon juice.

*Frozen or canned beans may be used, in which case the cooking time for the beans should be halved.

# BLACK OLIVE SPINACH

| | |
|---|---|
| 2 lbs. fresh spinach | 10 ripe black olives, |
| 1 clove garlic, crushed | pitted and minced |
| ½ cup unsalted butter | Salt and pepper to taste |
| | 1 tsp. lemon juice |

*Serves 4*

Wash spinach in several washes of water to remove all sand. Cook spinach over moderate heat for about 15 minutes with just the water that clings to it, leaving the leaves whole.

In a heavy saucepan, fry the garlic in hot butter for about 3 minutes. Discard the garlic and stir in the ripe olives. Add salt and pepper to taste. Add the lemon juice, mix well and pour over the well-drained spinach leaves.

# BOILED LEEKS

4 bunches leeks                        Ground black pepper to taste
¼ tsp. salt                            ¼ cup chopped parsley
3 Tbs. butter                          Juice of ½ lemon

*Serves 8*

Cut off and discard the green tops and the whiskers from the root ends of the leeks. Remove 1 or 2 layers of their white skin. Wash them in lukewarm water and rinse under cold running water to make sure all sand is removed. Drain.

Place leeks in a saucepan with salt and boiling water to barely cover. Cover and cook for 15–20 minutes or until just tender.

Drain well. Add butter and pepper. Cover and let stand for 2–3 minutes or until the butter melts. Transfer to a serving dish, sprinkle with chopped parsley and lemon and serve.

*VARIATION*: Omit the butter. Allow the leeks to get cold and cut in half lengthwise. Lay on a lettuce leaf and cover with Christopher Blake's French Dressing (chap. 13).

# BRAISED CELERY

6 fresh, small, whole hearts           Salt and white pepper to taste
   of celery, cleaned                  2 cups Chicken Stock (p. 183)
1 tsp. chicken fat                     2 Tbs. *Beurre Manié* (chap. 13)
1 large carrot, sliced                 Lemon juice (optional)
1 white onion, sliced

*Serves 6*

Parboil the celery hearts for 6–10 minutes and drain. Grease a baking dish with chicken fat and lay the slices of carrot and onion on the bottom. Lay the celery hearts on top. Season with salt and white pepper. Add enough chicken stock to barely cover.

Bring the liquid to a boil and cover. Braise the celery hearts in a 375° oven for about ³/₄ hour or until the hearts are fork tender but not overcooked. Cooking time will depend on the size of the hearts and may be less, so it's best to check.

Remove the celery and keep warm. Blend the *beurre manié* into the celery liquid to thicken the sauce. Strain and pour over the celery hearts. Add a dash of lemon juice at the last minute, if you like.

# BRAISED ENDIVES JOHN BUDDINGH

6 fresh Belgian endives
¼ cup melted butter
Juice of 1 lemon
Salt and white pepper to taste

1 Tbs. sugar
½ cup Chicken Stock (p. 183)
½ cup finely chopped parsley
Paprika

*Serves 6*

Wash and drain the endives. Cut them in half lengthwise and arrange them in an ovenproof dish.

Pour the melted butter, lemon juice, salt, pepper and sugar over them. Add the chicken stock.

Cover and cook in a moderate oven for 35–40 minutes or until endives are tender.

Remove cover and brown slightly under the broiler. Sprinkle with parsley and paprika and serve from the baking dish.

# BRUSSELS SPROUTS SOUBISE

*Soubise Sauce:*
3 Tbs. butter
4 large onions, grated
½ tsp. salt

4 Tbs. rice
½ cup boiling water
½ cup Béchamel Sauce (chap. 13)

*Sprouts and topping:*
1 quart Brussels sprouts, cooked
⅓ cup grated Gruyère or
Parmesan cheese

*Serves 4–6*

In a saucepan, heat butter and cook the onions, covered, for about 15 minutes, until tender.

Add the salt, rice and boiling water. Mix well and cover. Simmer gently for 20–30 minutes or until the water has virtually disappeared. Purée in a blender and combine with the béchamel sauce.

Mix with the sprouts, place in an ovenproof dish and sprinkle with cheese. Brown under a broiler flame for 3–5 minutes.

# CARROTS VICHY

2 dozen very small new carrots,       ½ tsp. salt
   scraped                              1 tsp. white pepper
1 stick butter                        1 cup finely chopped parsley

*Serves 4*

Cook carrots for 15–20 minutes in salted water until just barely tender but not overcooked. Drain. If baby carrots are not available, use regular carrots cut into thick slices. Or use canned Belgian carrots; these need no cooking, just heating.

In a saucepan, melt the butter until hot and foamy. Gently toss in the carrots to coat them with butter and just heat through. Season with salt and white pepper and add the chopped parsley, shaking the pan vigorously.

# CASHAW*

*Method 1:*
   1 cashaw                            ½ cup white sugar
   1 stick butter                      Salt and white pepper to taste

*Method 2:*
   1 cashaw                            1 cup white sugar
   1–1½ cups boiling water             Grating of nutmeg
   3/4 stick butter                    ⅛ tsp. cinnamon
   Salt and white pepper to taste

*Serves 6–8*

*Method 1:* Cut cashaw into sections, quarter each section and remove seeds; leave in the rind. Place quartered sections on a baking sheet and bake in a moderate oven (350°) for 1 hour or until they can be pierced with a fork. Serve in the rind with butter that has been previously melted and mixed with sugar, salt and white pepper.

*Method 2:* Peel away the rind and cut cashaw into small pieces. Cook in water in a heavy covered pot until tender enough to mash—about 1 hour. Drain and mash with the butter. Add salt, pepper, sugar, nutmeg and cinnamon. Blend well and serve.

*This recipe is equally good with pumpkin or acorn squash.

# CAULIFLOWER POLONNAISE

3 quarts salted water
2 small heads fresh cauliflower,
    left whole but cleaned
3/4 lb. butter

3 cups coarsely ground bread
    crumbs
Salt and pepper to taste

*Serves 8*

Bring water to a boil and put in the cauliflower. Cook until just fork tender—about 15–20 minutes. Remove, drain and cool. When cooled, divide cauliflower into flowerettes and reserve.

In a heavy skillet, melt the butter, toss in the bread crumbs and cook for about 10 minutes until they begin to brown. Add the flowerettes and keep tossing until thoroughly heated. Correct for seasonings with salt and pepper and serve.

# CHRIS'S ORANGED BEETS

18 small beets,* peeled
3 Tbs. unsalted butter
2 Tbs. cornstarch
1/2 cup lemon juice
Grated rind of 1/2 lemon

2 cups orange juice
Grated rind of 1 large orange
1/4 cup sugar
Salt and white pepper to taste

*Serves 6*

Cook the beets for 20–30 minutes in water to cover. Slice and cool.

In a saucepan, blend the butter, cornstarch, lemon juice and rind, orange juice and rind, and the sugar. Cook until the sauce thickens. Season with salt and white pepper.

Gently combine sliced beets with this mixture, heat thoroughly and serve.

*Frozen or canned may be used, but the cooking time will be 5–10 minutes.

## CREOLE CORN PUDDING

| | |
|---|---|
| 1 dozen ears of corn | A grating of nutmeg |
| 1 green pepper, finely diced | 3 egg yolks, beaten |
| 6 Tbs. butter | 3 egg whites, stiffly beaten |
| 1 cup heavy cream | Paprika |
| Salt and white pepper to taste | |

*Serves 4–6*

Scrape kernels off cobs and reserve. Cook the green pepper in 4 Tbs. of the butter until tender—about 15 minutes. Add the corn, cream, salt, pepper and nutmeg.

Add the beaten egg yolks and mix well. Now fold in the stiffly beaten egg whites and blend well. Grease a baking dish generously with the remaining butter and pour in the corn mixture.

Bake for 35–40 minutes in a very low oven (275°). Raise the heat to 375° and bake for another 10–15 minutes or until brown on top. Dust with paprika and serve.

## CREOLE MINTED PEAS

| | |
|---|---|
| 3 lbs. green peas, shelled and washed | 1½ quarts boiling water (more, if needed) |
| 2 Tbs. minced fresh mint leaves | 2 Tbs. butter |
| 1 Tbs. salt | Freshly ground black pepper to taste |
| 1 tsp. sugar | 6 whole fresh mint leaves |

*Serves 6*

Place peas in a heavy saucepan with the minced mint leaves, salt and sugar. Pour in the boiling water, to barely cover.

Bring to the boiling point and cover. Boil briskly for 5 minutes or until peas are almost done.

Drain off water, add butter, cover and simmer for 3–4 minutes longer or until peas are tender. Add pepper and toss lightly.

Turn into a serving dish, add a little more sugar if needed and garnish with the whole fresh mint leaves.

# CREOLE STUFFED CABBAGE

1 large white cabbage
½ stick butter
1 large onion, finely chopped
1 clove garlic, chopped
1 or 2 Creole tomatoes,
    peeled, seeded and chopped
¾ lb. Italian sausage meat,
    finely diced
Pinch of thyme

½ cup parsley, chopped
1 bay leaf
½ tsp. Tabasco pepper sauce
Salt and white pepper to taste
6 slices streaky bacon
2 carrots, sliced
1 turnip, sliced
6 small white onions

*Serves 6*

Remove the coarse outer leaves of the cabbage and set them to one side. Blanch the cabbage in salted boiling water for 8–10 minutes and then drain thoroughly.

Heat the butter and brown the onions and garlic; add the chopped tomatoes and stir well. Add the sausage meat, thyme, parsley, bay leaf, Tabasco, salt and pepper. Mix well and cook for 20 minutes over a slow fire.

Open the cabbage carefully and spread a thin layer of the sausage meat mixture between the leaves, pressing them together again. Put the large outer leaves of the cabbage around the outside, cover the top of the cabbage with a few slices of the bacon and tie with a string.

Line a large saucepan with a few more slices of the bacon and lay the cabbage on this. Add a few Tbs. water along with the carrot and turnip slices and the onions. Simmer very gently, covered, for 1½ hours.

To serve, remove the string, the bacon and the outer leaves of the cabbage and strain the sauce over it.

Plain boiled rice is a good accompaniment.

## EDITORS' EGGPLANT

2 medium eggplants
4 small tomatoes,
   peeled and seeded
2 onions, chopped
2 cups cooked chicken,
   dark and light meat

½ cup olive oil
Salt and pepper to taste
4 thin slices Monterey cheese
Chopped parsley
4 black olives

*Serves 4*

Cut eggplants in half lengthwise and blanch them in boiling water for 10 minutes. Cool and remove the pulp, being careful not to break the skins. Reserve the skins.

Chop the tomatoes, onions and chicken pieces very finely. Cook in heated olive oil for 10 minutes. Add the mashed eggplant pulp and cook for 10 minutes longer. Season with salt and pepper.

Stuff each eggplant shell with the mixture, top with a thin slice of cheese and put in a moderate oven (350°) for 5–10 minutes or until cheese melts.

Before serving, sprinkle with chopped parsley and top with a black olive each.

## EGGPLANT PUGLIA

6 mild Italian sausages
3 medium eggplants, halved
Salt and freshly ground black
   pepper

3 white onions, thinly sliced
½ cup olive oil
½ cup grated Romano cheese

*Serves 6*

Cook sausages in simmering water to barely cover for about 20 minutes. Drain and slice thinly lengthwise.

Cut the eggplant flesh away from the skin, remove and cut into slices ½" wide. Sprinkle with salt and pepper.

In a skillet sauté the white onions in olive oil until they are transparent—about 10 minutes. Add the eggplant slices and sauté them quickly for about 5 minutes on each side. Return the mixture to the eggplant shells.

Cover with the slices of Italian sausage. Sprinkle generously with the Romano cheese and bake in a moderate oven (350°) for about 10 minutes.

# FRENCH FRIED ONION RINGS

2 cups milk
3 eggs, well beaten
2 Tbs. melted butter
2 cups flour,
  sifted with 1 tsp. salt

4 large onions, thickly sliced
  and separated into rings
1 cup cooking oil

*Serves 4–6*

Mix 1 cup of the milk, the eggs and the melted butter with the sifted flour to form a batter.

Soak the onion rings in the remaining milk for 1 hour.

Drain well. Dip them into the batter one at a time and then drop them one at a time into hot, deep fat. Do not crowd them in the pan.

The rings will come to the surface as they brown. When golden brown, remove and drain on absorbent toweling. Sprinkle with salt and serve at once.

# FRENCH MARKET EGGPLANT

2 medium eggplants
1 cup flour, seasoned
  with salt and pepper
6 Tbs. olive oil
5 Creole tomatoes,
  peeled, seeded and chopped

2 cloves garlic, crushed
¼ cup chopped parsley
Salt and pepper to taste
6 rounds French bread
¼ cup grated Parmesan cheese

*Serves 6*

Peel the eggplants and cut them into large dice. Dredge in seasoned flour.

Heat 3 Tbs. of the olive oil in a heavy saucepan and sauté eggplant dice until golden brown—10–15 minutes.

In another pan, heat the remaining 3 Tbs. olive oil and sauté the tomatoes for about 5–10 minutes.

Combine the 2 vegetables, add the garlic and parsley and cook for 5 minutes. Season with salt and freshly ground black pepper.

Meanwhile, crisp French bread in a 350° oven for 10 minutes. Top with eggplant mixture and sprinkle with grated Parmesan cheese.

# FRIED BRUSSELS SPROUTS

1½ lbs. Brussels sprouts
Salt to taste
Ground black pepper to taste

6 Tbs. butter
Chopped parsley

*Serves 6*

Cook Brussels sprouts in salted water until barely tender—about 15–20 minutes.

Drain and sprinkle cooked Brussels sprouts with a little salt and black pepper. Fry in hot butter, turning frequently with a wooden spoon, until brown on all sides—about 10 minutes. Sprinkle with chopped parsley.

Serve immediately.

# FRIED OKRA CREOLE

1 lb. okra with large pods
Salt and freshly ground black
   pepper to taste
2 eggs, slightly beaten
   with 1 Tbs. water

1 cup flour, seasoned
   with salt and pepper
1 cup fine bread crumbs
1½ cups cooking oil

*Serves 4*

Wash the okra several times and trim stems. Be careful not to cut too close to the pod, or they will ooze. Cover with slightly salted water, bring to a boil and cook until tender—about 10 minutes. Drain and season with salt and black pepper.

Roll the okra first in the egg wash, then in flour and finally in bread crumbs. Lay flat on a sheet and refrigerate.

When ready to use, fry a few at a time in hot, deep fat until they are delicately browned—about 5–10 minutes.

Drain on paper toweling and serve hot.

# LENTILS WITH HAM

1 lb. dried lentils, soaked
   overnight in cold water
1 large onion, chopped
2 Tbs. butter
2 tomatoes,
   peeled, seeded and chopped

1 clove garlic, cut into 4 pieces
1 carrot, whole
½ lb. ham, cut in large dice
Salt and black pepper to taste
¼ cup chopped parsley
1 Tbs. wine vinegar

*Serves 4–6*

Place lentils in a pot of cold salted water. Bring to a boil and cook until tender—about 30–40 minutes. Drain thoroughly.

Meanwhile, fry the onion in butter until golden brown—about 10–15 minutes. Add the lentils, tomatoes, garlic, carrot and ham. Mix thoroughly, season with salt and pepper and cook for 15–20 minutes.

Sprinkle with chopped parsley, add a dash or so of wine vinegar and serve immediately.

# MUSHROOMS ON TOAST

½ stick butter
1 lb. fresh mushrooms, cleaned,
   washed and thinly sliced
1 cup finely chopped parsley
2 cloves garlic, minced

Salt and pepper to taste
1 tsp. lemon juice
2 Tbs. *Beurre Manié* (chap. 13)
6 slices hot buttered toast,
   trimmed and cut in half

*Serves 6*

Melt butter in a heavy skillet. Add sliced mushrooms and cook for about 10 minutes. Remove mushrooms with a slotted spoon.

Add parsley and garlic to the mushroom juices and cook 5 minutes longer. Season with salt and pepper. Add the lemon juice.

Gradually add the *beurre manié* and cook until the sauce thickens. As it thickens, return mushrooms and continue to cook until thoroughly heated.

Divide mushrooms onto the toast and spoon the remaining sauce over them.

## PURÉE OF JERUSALEM ARTICHOKE CREOLE

2 lbs. Jerusalem artichokes
1 stick butter
4 Creole tomatoes,
    peeled, seeded and chopped

½ cup heavy cream
Salt and white pepper to taste

*Serves 4–6*

Cook the scrubbed Jerusalem artichokes in boiling salted water to cover for about 30 minutes or until tender. Drain, peel and put through a ricer.

In a saucepan with a little of the butter, cook the chopped tomatoes until all liquid has evaporated and you are left with a mushy pulp. Add to the artichokes and whip the combination smooth with the remaining butter and the cream. Season with salt and pepper and serve hot.

## RED CABBAGE IN WINE

1 large head red cabbage
1 tsp. salt
White pepper to taste
Pinch of nutmeg
2 Tbs. unsalted butter

1 white onion, finely chopped
1 Tbs. white vinegar
2 cups red wine
2 cups water
2 apples, peeled,
    cored and chopped

*Serves 4–6*

Clean the cabbage, cut in quarters and remove the hard core. Cut into fine julienne strips and parboil in boiling water for 10 minutes. Cool in cold water and drain well. Season with salt, pepper and nutmeg.

In a saucepan, melt the butter, add the onion and cook until soft—about 5 minutes. Add the vinegar, wine and water. Add the drained cabbage and cook very gently for 20 minutes. Add the apples and cook for 25–30 minutes longer, using a little more water if necessary.

When done, drain of any excess liquid and serve on a heated platter.

# RIVERFRONT BROCCOLI

1 large bunch broccoli
1 Tbs. olive oil
1 large white onion, thinly sliced
2 medium Creole tomatoes,
　thinly sliced

½ cup pitted, sliced black olives
1 anchovy fillet,
　cut up into pieces
½ cup grated Romano cheese
1 cup dry red wine

*Serves 4*

Wash broccoli and cut the stalks lengthwise into thin pieces. In a heavy skillet, heat the olive oil and add a layer of sliced onion, tomato, black olives and anchovy. Top with a layer of the broccoli and sprinkle with Romano cheese. Repeat the process until all is used up, reserving a few pieces of anchovy. Pour in the red wine.

Cover the skillet and cook over low heat for 20–30 minutes or until broccoli is just tender. Finish with the remaining pieces of anchovy.

# ROC'S HONEY-GLAZED ONIONS

1 dozen small white onions
¼ cup honey
4 Tbs. butter

*Serves 4*

Peel and parboil onions in boiling water until they are fork tender. Drain well.

Melt butter in a saucepan and add honey. Stir until mixture is well blended. Add onions and cook slowly, stirring, until they are glazed.

# SAUERKRAUT PAPRIKA

1½ lbs. sauerkraut, washed
4 large tomatoes,
   peeled, seeded and chopped
Salt to taste

1–1½ Tbs. Hungarian sweet
   paprika
½ cup raw rice
½ cup Tomato juice, if needed

*Serves 6*

Combine sauerkraut and tomatoes in a heavy saucepan. Add salt and Hungarian sweet paprika. Bring to a boil and reduce heat. Add raw rice and blend well. If more liquid is needed, add the tomato juice.

Cover tightly and continue to cook until the rice begins to swell—about 20 minutes. Unlike most rice dishes of this kind, it is not necessary that the rice absorb all the liquid.

When finished, stir several times and serve from the pot with a slotted spoon.

# STEWED CUCUMBERS

3 large cucumbers,
   peeled and sliced
3 Tbs. butter
2 Tbs. flour
1½ cups Chicken Stock (p. 183),
   heated

½ cup sour cream
1 clove garlic, minced
Juice of ½ lemon
Salt and white pepper to taste
Paprika

*Serves 4–6*

Parboil cucumbers in boiling salted water to cover for 10 minutes and drain.

Melt the butter in a saucepan. Sprinkle in the flour and blend well. Gradually add the hot chicken stock and cook until sauce is thick and smooth—about 5–10 minutes.

Stirring constantly, gradually add the sour cream, garlic, lemon juice, salt and pepper. When sauce is well mixed, add the cucumber slices and cook until they are tender—about 20 minutes.

Remove cucumber slices to a heated casserole and strain sauce over them. Sprinkle with paprika and serve.

# STRING BEANS LYONNAISE

| | |
|---|---|
| 1 lb. tender string beans | Salt and black pepper to taste |
| 1 medium onion, chopped | ½ Tbs. wine vinegar |
| 3 Tbs. butter | ½ cup finely chopped parsley |

*Serves 4*

Wash the string beans. Leave them whole, merely snapping off the ends. Cook in boiling water until tender but still crisp—about 15–20 minutes. Drain and dry in a cloth.

Chop the onion and sauté in 2 Tbs. of the butter until soft and slightly yellow—about 10 minutes. Season with salt and black pepper.

Add the string beans and remaining butter and sauté all together until beans begin to brown a little. Add wine vinegar.

Sprinkle with finely chopped parsley and serve.

# STUFFED MUSHROOMS

| | |
|---|---|
| 12 large mushrooms | 3 Tbs. flour |
| 4 Tbs. butter | 3 Tbs. dry sherry |
| ¼ cup finely chopped green onions, tops and bottoms | 12 rounds white bread, cut the size of a half-dollar |
| ¼ cup finely chopped parsley | ½ stick melted butter |
| Salt and black pepper to taste | Lemon juice |

*Serves 4*

Remove stems from mushrooms and chop. Reserve caps.

Melt the butter in a heavy saucepan and cook the green onions and parsley until tender—about 5 minutes. Add the mushroom stems and cook for another 5 minutes. Add the salt, pepper and flour and blend very well, stirring for about 10 minutes, to get a good light roux. Gradually add the sherry. Sauce should be thick enough to fill the mushroom caps. If too thick, add a little water.

Brush the rounds of white bread with a little of the melted butter. Fill each mushroom cap and place face down on each round of bread. Brush each cap with a little melted butter, a few drops of lemon juice and salt and pepper.

Bake in a moderate oven for 15 minutes or until tender.

## STUFFED TOMATOES PARISIAN

6 tomatoes
½ lb. fresh mushrooms, chopped
1 onion, chopped
2 Tbs. butter

Salt and black pepper to taste
1 tsp. chopped parsley
2 Tbs. tomato purée
2 Tbs. olive oil

*Serves 6*

Cut tops off tomatoes. Scoop out flesh, drain and reserve. Gently cook the chopped mushrooms and onion in butter until all moisture is cooked away—about 10–15 minutes. Add salt and pepper, parsley and the tomato flesh. Now add the tomato purée.

Stuff tomatoes with this mixture. Sprinkle a little olive oil on top and bake them in a moderate oven (350°) until cooked but not mushy—about 15 minutes.

## TOMATO CHUTNEY

1 lb. tomatoes,
   blanched, peeled and chopped
1 medium onion, finely chopped
1″ piece fresh ginger,
   finely chopped
¾ cup pitted dates

²/₃ cup raisins
²/₃ cup currants
1 tsp. cayenne pepper
1 tsp. salt
4 Tbs. vegetable oil
1 tsp. mustard seeds

*Serves 4–6*

Place all ingredients except oil and mustard seeds in a heavy saucepan and bring to a boil, stirring occasionally. Reduce heat and simmer, uncovered, for 1½–2 hours or until chutney is thick.

Meanwhile, heat oil in a small frying pan. Add mustard seeds and fry, covered, until they stop popping—about 5–10 minutes. Remove pan from heat and tip contents into saucepan with chutney. Stir well.

Serve cold.

# TOMATOES À LA ROC

6 large green tomatoes,
   cut into thick slices
3/4 cup flour,
   seasoned with salt and pepper

4 Tbs. unsalted butter, melted
½ cup dark brown sugar
1 cup heavy cream
¼ cup chopped parsley

*Serves 6*

Dip tomatoes in the seasoned flour and arrange the slices in a large skillet in the melted butter. Sprinkle with some of the brown sugar and cook over a moderate flame until the slices are brown underneath—about 5 minutes.

Turn the slices with a spatula and sprinkle again with brown sugar. Cook slowly so that the sugar and butter blend but do not burn—about another 5 minutes.

Add the heavy cream and cook until the cream begins to bubble—about 3–5 minutes. Arrange the tomato slices on a warm serving dish, cover with the sauce, sprinkle with chopped parsley and serve with filet mignon, veal chop or a thick slice of fish.

# YELLOW SQUASH

12 small yellow squash
1 stick butter

Salt and pepper to taste
½ cup granulated sugar

*Serves 6*

Parboil squash until almost fork tender—about 15 minutes. Cut in half lengthwise.

Lay in a buttered baking dish. Season with salt and pepper and thin pats of butter. Sprinkle with sugar.

Bake in a moderate oven (350°) for about 15 minutes.

## ZUCCHINI CREOLE

1 stick butter (more, if needed)
2 medium white onions,
   halved and thinly sliced
6 medium zucchini squash,
   unpeeled and thinly sliced

Salt and white pepper to taste
½ tsp. Tabasco pepper sauce
½ cup Romano cheese, grated

*Serves 6*

In a heavy skillet, melt butter and fry onions until tender—about 10 minutes. Remove onion, add more butter if needed and add zucchini slices; cover and cook until almost tender—about 10 minutes. Remove cover, add onions and finish cooking for about another 15 minutes. Correct seasonings with salt, pepper and Tabasco. Sprinkle with grated Romano cheese at the last minute.

# SALADS

## BIRD OF PARADISE SALAD

*Salad:*
   3 oranges
   3 avocados

18 canned beet slices
Lettuce leaves

*Poppy Seed Dressing:*
   ¼ cup lemon juice
   ½ cup good light salad oil

½ cup honey
2 Tbs. poppy seeds

*Serves 6*

Peel oranges and slice crosswise. Peel avocado and cut into wedges. Drain beets.

Allowing ½ orange, ½ avocado and 3 beet slices per person, arrange alternate slices of each in an attractive pattern on lettuce leaves.

Make the dressing by putting all ingredients into a blender and mixing well. Pour only enough dressing over each salad to coat well.

# GUACAMOLE

2 large, ripe avocados
1 medium tomato, blanched,
    peeled, seeded and chopped
½ small white onion,
    finely chopped
2 canned or fresh hot serrano
    (green) chili peppers,
    or more to taste

2–3 sprigs fresh coriander or
    flat-leaf parsley, finely chopped
1 strip bacon,
    fried crisp and crumbled
Salt to taste

*Serves 2–4*

Halve the avocados and remove the pits. Scoop out the flesh with a spoon and mash it with a fork. Add the rest of the ingredients, mixing well. Cover tightly with plastic wrap and refrigerate.

Use as soon as possible so color does not turn. (Leave the avocado seed in the center of the guacamole dip, and discoloration will be delayed.)

Serve with Fritos.

# HUNGARIAN CUCUMBER SALAD

4 medium cucumbers
Salt and white pepper to taste
2 medium white onions,
    thinly sliced
1 cup olive oil
⅓ cup white wine vinegar

3 Tbs. sweet Hungarian paprika
1 tsp. salt
¼ tsp. white pepper
1 Tbs. granulated sugar,
    dissolved in 2 Tbs. water

*Serves 8*

Peel and slice cucumbers. Sprinkle with salt and pepper and drain on paper towels for about 30 minutes. Press tops of cucumbers with additional towels in order to remove as much moisture as possible.

Toss the cucumbers with the onion slices, separated into individual rings. Mix remaining ingredients to make a dressing and pour over the cucumber-onion mixture. Toss again and marinate, unrefrigerated, overnight.

Chill for 1 hour before serving. Drain with a slotted spoon just before serving and then pour a little of the juice over the cucumber and onion slices.

## LEEK SALAD

8 firm leeks, 1"–1½" in diameter
½ cup cooking liquid
  from the leeks
½ cup sour cream
½ cup cider vinegar

½ tsp. Creole mustard
1 tsp. bottled horseradish,
  drained and squeezed dry
½ tsp. salt
¼ tsp. Tabasco pepper sauce

*Serves 4*

With a sharp knife, cut off the roots of the leeks and strip away any withered leaves. Trim until they are about 6"–7" long. Wash the leeks under cold water to get rid of all sand.

Lay the leeks in 2 layers in a heavy skillet with water to cover. Bring to a boil, reduce heat and cook for 10–15 minutes or until they are just barely tender.

With a slotted spoon, remove leeks to paper toweling and let drain. Arrange on a cold serving platter and refrigerate for about an hour.

In the meantime make the sauce. In a bowl, combine the leek cooking liquid, sour cream, vinegar, mustard, horseradish, salt and Tabasco. Beat the dressing with a wooden spoon or a whisk.

Pour dressing over the leeks and serve chilled.

## SALADE À LA RUSSE

2 cups cooked diced carrots
2 cups raw diced celery
2 cups canned beets, diced
2 cups cooked string beans, diced
1 package frozen lima beans,
  cooked

1 package frozen green peas,
  cooked
Salt and freshly ground black
  pepper to taste
1 cup mayonnaise
½ cup Christopher Blake's
  French Dressing (chap. 13)

*Serves 6–8*

Drain vegetables well and refrigerate for at least an hour. Place in a large mixing bowl and add salt and pepper. Fold in mayonnaise and at the last minute gently add the French dressing.

Allow to chill, and serve on a lettuce leaf or fill an avocado or a tomato.

# SPINACH SALAD

1½ lbs. young, fresh spinach  
½ lb. lean bacon  
2 hard-boiled eggs, separated

¼ cup red wine vinegar, warmed  
Salt and pepper to taste

*Serves 4*

Clean and wash spinach in several changes of water to remove all sand. Pat very dry with paper toweling. Wrap in fresh paper towels and refrigerate.

Fry bacon until crisp. Remove bacon pieces, drain dry and crumble. Reserve hot bacon fat. Chop egg yolks and whites separately.

Pour hot bacon grease in a bowl and add warm vinegar, salt and pepper. Add chopped eggs. Add spinach leaves, which have been torn in pieces, and lastly the bacon bits.

Toss well and serve immediately.

# POTATOES AND RICE

## CANDIED SWEET POTATOES

6 sweet potatoes  
3 Tbs. unsalted butter  
Salt and white pepper to taste

1½ tsp. lemon juice  
¾ cup dark brown sugar  
½ tsp. grated lemon peel

*Serves 6*

Boil the potatoes in salted water to cover until they are fork tender—about 35–40 minutes. Peel and cut lengthwise in ½" slices.

Arrange in a shallow baking dish greased with 1 Tbs. of the butter. Season with salt and pepper. Sprinkle with lemon juice, then brown sugar and lemon peel. Dot with the remaining butter.

Bake, uncovered, in a moderate oven (350°) for 20–35 minutes, basting often until the potatoes are well glazed.

## CHRIS'S UNORTHODOX CHINESE FRIED RICE

½ lb. bacon*                          Salt and pepper to taste
1 can bean sprouts, drained          3 eggs, beaten
1 cup thinly sliced green onions     2 Tbs. butter
1 small can bamboo shoots,           2 cups cold cooked rice
  drained and minced                 ½ cup soy sauce
1 small can water chestnuts,
  drained and diced

*Serves 6*

Fry bacon until crisp and reserve the fat. Crumble bacon and add the bean sprouts, green onions, bamboo shoots, water chestnuts, and salt and pepper to taste (go easy on the salt).

Fry eggs in butter until well done and browned. It should look like a pancake. Shred and add to the above ingredients.

In the hot bacon fat, toss the rice until it is thoroughly heated. Mix with all other ingredients and add enough soy sauce to give it a rich brown color. Mix well.

Pack tightly into a large bowl and unmold immediately by inverting onto a plate.

*Shrimp, ham or chicken may be substituted for the bacon. However, you will need ham or bacon fat.

## CLASSIC FRENCH FRIED POTATOES

1 large potato, peeled and           3/4–1 cup fresh cooking oil
  cut in pieces about as             Salt to taste
  long as your little finger

*Serves 2*

Dry the potato pieces thoroughly in paper toweling.

Heat oil to about 375° on a deep frying thermometer. Cook the potatoes, adding a few at a time, for just 7–8 minutes, until they are soft but only starting to brown.

Remove potatoes from fat and drain well on absorbent towel. Let fat get hotter (about 390°–400°) and return potatoes to the fat. Cook for another minute or so until they are golden brown and crisp.

Drain, sprinkle with salt and serve at once.

# DUCHESS POTATOES

| | |
|---|---|
| 2 lbs. potatoes | Grating of nutmeg |
| 2 Tbs. butter | 2 whole eggs |
| 1 tsp. salt | 2 egg yolks |
| White pepper to taste | |

*Serves 6*

Peel the potatoes and cut them in small pieces. Cook in boiling salted water to cover until soft but not mushy—about 10 minutes. Drain and dry well by shaking them in the pan over the fire until all moisture has evaporated.

Rub the potatoes through a sieve or put them through a ricer. Work them with a wooden spoon until they are very smooth. Add butter, salt, white pepper and a little nutmeg. Add the whole eggs, which have been beaten with the egg yolks. Beat the mixture briskly until it is very fluffy and serve.

These potatoes may be made in advance and kept ready by brushing a little melted butter over the top to prevent a crust from forming. Reheat over a very low flame, stirring constantly.

# FRENCH MARKET PARSLEY POTATOES

| | |
|---|---|
| 2 lbs. small new potatoes | Salt and white pepper to taste |
| 1 stick butter | 1 cup very finely chopped parsley |

*Serves 6–8*

In boiling salted water, cook the potatoes in their skins until fork tender but not overdone—about 20 minutes. With a sharp knife, make a gash in each potato.

In a very heavy skillet, melt the butter and toss the potatoes in it until they are all well coated.

Season with salt and white pepper. Add parsley, shake well and serve immediately.

NOTE: These potatoes were the standard accompaniment for entrées at my restaurant—far more elegant than baked.

## MASHED SOUFFLÉ POTATOES

1 cup water or milk
2 Tbs. butter
½ tsp. salt
1 cup flour

4 eggs
2 cups Duchess Potatoes (p. 375)
2 cups cooking oil

*Serves 8*

Combine the water or milk, butter and salt. Bring mixture to a boil and add flour all at once, stirring well until the mixture leaves the sides of the pan.

Remove from the fire and add the eggs one at a time, stirring well after each addition.

Blend the mixture with the potatoes. Refrigerate until ready to use.

Drop a teaspoon at a time into hot, deep fat (350°) until they puff and rise to the surface. Turn once, and when golden brown, drain and serve hot.

## PATATE ALLA VENEZIANA

1 lb. potatoes
½ cup olive oil, mixed with
   ½ cup melted butter

2 or 3 medium onions
Salt and black pepper to taste
About ¼ cup chopped parsley

*Serves 4*

Parboil the potatoes in their skins in salted water, being careful not to overcook—about 10–15 minutes.

When done, peel, cut in thick round slices and cook to a light golden color in a little more than half the oil-butter mixture—about 15–20 minutes.

Slice the onions thinly and evenly, and fry to a light golden color in another saucepan with the remaining olive oil and butter—about 10 minutes. If more olive oil and butter is necessary, simply increase quantity.

When the onions are done, add them to the potatoes; mix gently and sprinkle with salt and pepper and chopped parsley.

## POTATO BALLS BAYOU DES ALLEMANDES

3 potatoes, boiled
½ cup milk
2 Tbs. butter
2 egg yolks
Salt and pepper to taste
Dash of nutmeg

1 cup flour, seasoned
   with salt and pepper
1 egg, beaten
   with a little cold water
1 cup fine bread crumbs
1½ cups cooking oil for frying

*Serves 4–6*

Mash the potatoes with milk and butter. Bind with the egg yolks. Season with salt, pepper and nutmeg. Refrigerate for at least 1 hour.

When cold, shape into small balls; roll in flour, then in egg wash and finally in bread crumbs. Refrigerate once again for at least 1 hour.

When ready to use, either bake in a preheated 350° oven for about 20 minutes or fry in very hot fat for about 5 minutes.

## VIEUX CARRÉ SAUSAGE POTATOES

6 large potatoes in their skins
1 lb. mild Italian sausage
3 slices French bread, soaked in
   milk and squeezed dry
2 Tbs. butter
2 Tbs. chopped parsley

1 Tbs. chopped basil
½ tsp. Creole mustard
1 egg yolk
2 Tbs. Chicken Stock (p. 183)
Salt and pepper to taste
¼ stick melted butter

*Serves 6*

Boil potatoes in their skins for about 15 minutes. With a tablespoon, scoop out a deep hole in the center of each.

Cook the Italian sausages in simmering water to cover for about 20 minutes, until tender. Remove from their casings and mash. Add the bread, butter, parsley, basil, mustard, egg yolk and chicken stock. Mix well.

Stuff the potatoes with this mixture and place in a hot buttered baking dish. Sprinkle with salt, pepper and melted butter.

Bake in a hot oven (400°) for 30 minutes or until the potatoes are tender.

## WILD RICE STUFFING

1 cup wild rice
4 cups Chicken Stock (p. 183)
1 medium onion, chopped
½ cup chopped celery
½ green pepper, chopped
4 Tbs. butter

½ lb. fresh mushrooms, sliced (or
   1 4-oz. can mushrooms, sliced)
¾ tsp. dried marjoram
⅛ tsp. dried thyme
Salt and pepper to taste

*Yields 6 cups*

Wash the wild rice thoroughly in several changes of cold water until water runs clean.

Bring the chicken stock to a boil. Add the rice, and when the stock returns to a boil, cover the pan and simmer for 35–40 minutes or until the rice is tender, the grains have opened and the stock has for the most part been absorbed.

While the rice cooks, fry the onion, celery and green pepper in the butter for about 10 minutes, until soft but not brown. If you use fresh mushrooms, cook them with the vegetables. If you use canned mushrooms, drain them well and stir into the vegetable mixture after it is cooked. Combine the vegetable mixture and seasonings with the cooked rice.

Cool before using to stuff game. Also good to stuff tomatoes as a garnish for fish or fowl.

# 12
# DESSERTS

DESSERTS were the high point of my youth. For those of you who are still sweet in the tooth—dig in! As for me, pass me a brandy. . . .

# BASICS

## BASIC BEER CRÊPES

1 cup all-purpose flour
1 Tbs. powdered sugar
1 tsp. baking powder
½ tsp. salt

1 Tbs. melted butter
1 egg
1 10-oz. can warm beer

*Yields 10–12 crêpes*

Sift dry ingredients together and mix in melted butter and egg. Work well until completely blended. Batter should be in pea-size lumps.

Slowly beat in the beer. The batter should now be smooth and have the consistency of heavy cream.

Coat a hot, greased flat griddle as thinly as possible with the batter, and cook until the top is dry. Turn the crêpe and cook for about ½ minute on the other side.

Stack on a plate, the side that was cooked first down.

These crêpes may be prepared in advance, wrapped well and stored in the refrigerator. Reheat for serving by stacking on a pie tin, covering with foil and heating in a 200° oven for 10–15 minutes.

Serve these crêpes with French Provincial Crêpe Sauce (p. 410) or filled with any savory or sweet stuffing of your choice.

## BASIC CHOCOLATE CUPS

6 squares semisweet chocolate
2 Tbs. unsalted butter

6 paper baking cups, as for cupcakes

*Yields 6*

Heat the chocolate with the butter in the top of a double boiler over hot but not boiling water until the chocolate is almost melted.

Remove from the heat and stir rapidly until chocolate is completely melted and well blended with the butter.

With a teaspoon swirl the mixture around the insides of 6 paper baking cups, covering the entire surface and all crevices with a thin layer.

Place the cups in muffin tins and chill until the coating hardens. When hard, carefully remove the paper, leaving a complete chocolate cup.

For dessert, fill with your favorite custard or ice cream and serve.


## BASIC CRUMB CRUST

2–2½ cups finely crushed crumbs,      ¼ cup melted butter
   graham cracker or vanilla wafer      2 Tbs. sugar

*Yields 1 crust*

Combine crumbs, butter and sugar and press firmly into a lightly buttered 9″ pie plate. Bake in a 300° oven for 15 minutes. If shell buckles, press it down again with your hands.


## BASIC FRITTER BATTER

1 cup flour                                1 egg, slightly beaten
½ tsp. salt                                ¾ cup milk
2 Tbs. sugar                               1 Tbs. melted butter
1 tsp. baking powder

*Yields 2 cups*

Mix dry ingredients together. Combine egg, milk and melted butter and stir into the dry ingredients. Batter will be lumpy.


## BASIC PIE CRUST

3 cups all-purpose flour                   ¾ cup softened butter
5 egg yolks                                ½ tsp. salt
1 Tbs. olive oil                           ¼–½ cup cold water

*Yields 2 crusts*

Place flour in a mixing bowl and make a well. Place egg yolks, olive oil, butter and salt in the well. Mix thoroughly.

Add enough cold water to moisten and make a good dough, ready to roll out. If time permits, form pastry into a ball, place in a towel and refrigerate for 1 hour.

When ready to use, return to room temperature before rolling out.

Some recipes call for a cooked pie shell. For these, proceed in the following manner.

Roll out the dough and line 2 9" pie pans. Lightly prick the bottom in several places with a fork. Bake in a 300° oven for 15–20 minutes or until golden.

Cool and fill as desired or wrap in foil and freeze for later use. If frozen, thaw completely before using.

## BASIC TART SHELLS

| | |
|---|---|
| 2 cups flour | 10 Tbs. unsalted butter, creamed |
| 1 tsp. salt | 2 Tbs. fine sugar |
| 2 tsp. sugar | for sprinkling shells |
| 1 egg yolk | Dried beans or raw rice |

*Yields 12*

Sift all dry ingredients in a bowl. Make a well and add egg yolk and creamed butter. Work in from the sides with your fingers until dough is completely mixed. Wrap ball in a towel and refrigerate for an hour or so.

Return to room temperature and roll out ready to line tart shells.

Butter a dozen tart tins and fit a piece of pastry in each, cutting them evenly. Prick a few holes in the bottom. Sprinkle each shell with a little fine sugar. Cover with waxed paper the size of the shell and fill with dried beans or raw rice to keep them from buckling or rising.

Bake in a 450° oven for 15 minutes or until golden brown.

Remove and cool, discarding waxed paper, beans and rice, and keep ready for any filling.

# CAKES AND PIES

## APPLE JASON

6–8 green cooking apples
4 Tbs. maple syrup
3 Tbs. unsalted butter
½ cup sugar

1 egg, beaten
1 cup flour
2 tsp. baking powder
½ tsp. salt

*Serves 6*

Peel, core and thinly slice the apples. Layer them in a shallow baking dish and pour the maple syrup over them, letting it seep between the layers.

Cream the butter and sugar and mix in the beaten egg. Mix in the flour, baking powder and salt to make a thick batter. Spread this over the apples and let stand for 5–10 minutes to settle.

Bake in the center of a moderately hot oven (400°) for 35–40 minutes or until a toothpick inserted in the center comes out clean.

Serve hot or at room temperature with fresh cream or whipped cream.

## BLACK POUND CAKE

12 2½" rounds from ¼"-thick
slices of day-old pound cake*
or New Orleans French bread
½ cup Myers's Jamaican rum
8 oz. semisweet chocolate

½ cup Louisiana strawberry
preserves
½ cup New Orleans Whipped
Cream (chap. 13)

*Serves 6*

Preheat oven to 350°.

Toast the rounds of pound cake or bread on a baking sheet in the oven. Transfer the rounds to a rack, let them cool, and sprinkle them with some of the rum, reserving at least ¼ cup.

In the top of a double boiler, melt the chocolate and flavor with the rest of the rum.

Spread 6 of the rounds thinly with some of the strawberry preserves and top them with the remaining rounds.

Place the rounds in a shallow dessert dish and ladle the hot chocolate-rum sauce over them.

Garnish with New Orleans Whipped Cream.

*Bogie's Pound Cake (below).

## BOGIE'S POUND CAKE

| | |
|---|---|
| 1 lb. (4½ cups) flour | 1 lb. (2⅓ cups) sugar |
| ½ tsp. salt | 6–8 eggs |
| ½ tsp. nutmeg | ½ tsp. almond extract |
| 1 lb. butter | 1 tsp. vanilla |

*Serves 6–8*

Sift flour once. Measure it to make sure you have 4½ cups and sift twice more with salt and nutmeg.

Cream butter and sugar together until light and fluffy. Add eggs one at a time, beating well after each addition.

Gradually add sifted dry ingredients, beating until smooth after each addition. Add almond and vanilla extracts and blend.

Grease a 9" x 5" x 3" pan and line with greased waxed paper. Pour in the batter and bake in a 325° oven for 1 hour.

## CHERRY BATTER CAKE

| | |
|---|---|
| ½ cup sugar | 2 Tbs. kirsch |
| 4 eggs | Pinch of salt |
| 1 cup flour | 1 lb. ripe black cherries, pitted |
| 2 Tbs. melted butter | 2 Tbs. unsalted butter |
| 1½ cups milk | Whipped cream |

*Serves 6–8*

Preheat oven to 450°.

In a bowl, beat the sugar and eggs until thick and lemon-colored. Add the flour slowly while beating, then the melted butter, milk, kirsch and salt.

Grease and lightly flour a 7″ x 11″ x 1¼″ pan. Pour a ¼″ layer of batter into the pan.

Bake for 5 minutes or until batter just sets. Cover with the cherries and the remaining batter. Dot with the unsalted butter and bake for another 30 minutes.

If it browns too fast, cover with aluminum foil and continue to bake.

Serve hot or cold with whipped cream.

## CHOCOLATE POTATO CAKE

| | |
|---|---|
| ¾ cup shortening | 1 tsp. allspice |
| 2 cups sugar | 1 tsp. nutmeg |
| 1 cup mashed potatoes | ½ cup milk |
| 4 eggs | ½ cup dark corn syrup |
| 3 cups sifted cake flour | 1½ oz. unsweetened chocolate, |
| 1 Tbs. baking powder | grated |
| Dash of salt | 1 tsp. vanilla |
| 1 tsp. cinnamon | 1 cup chopped pecans |
| 1 tsp. ground cloves | Confectioners' sugar |

*Serves 8–10*

Cream shortening and sugar. Add potatoes and blend for 5 minutes with an electric beater. Add eggs one at a time, beating after each addition.

Sift together flour, baking powder, salt and spices. Blend alternately into egg mixture with milk and syrup. Stir in chocolate, vanilla and pecans and blend thoroughly. Pour into a greased and lightly floured 10" tube pan. Bake at 350° for 1–1¼ hours.

Cool in pan for 10 minutes. Remove and finish cooling on a wire rack. Dust with confectioners' sugar.

This is an old mountain recipe, and it keeps very well.

## FRENCH CHEESECAKE

| | |
|---|---|
| 18 slices zwieback, finely crushed | 1 tsp. salt |
| ¼ cup melted butter | ½ pint heavy cream |
| ½ cup sugar | 4 eggs, separated |
| 1 lb. cream cheese, softened | 1 Tbs. lemon juice |
| ½ tsp. vanilla | 1 Tbs. grated orange rind |
| 4 Tbs. flour | Sliced strawberries (optional) |

*Serves 8–10*

Combine zwieback with melted butter and 2 Tbs. of the sugar and press firmly into a well-buttered 9" springform pan.

Cream the cream cheese with the vanilla. Add 2 Tbs. of the sugar, the flour, salt and heavy cream and stir until fluffy. Add egg yolks and beat thoroughly. Stir in lemon juice and orange rind.

Beat the egg whites until almost stiff. Gradually add the remaining sugar and beat until stiff and glossy. Fold the meringue into the cheese mixture lightly but thoroughly and pour into the prepared crust.

Bake in a moderate oven (350°) until set in the center—about 1½ hours. Chill the cheesecake before removing it from the pan.

Serve chilled but not ice cold. Sliced strawberries may be used as a garnish on top.

## LIME MERINGUE PIE

1 ¾ cups sugar
7 Tbs. cornstarch
2 cups boiling water
5 eggs, separated
½ cup unstrained fresh lime juice

2 drops green food coloring
¼ tsp. salt
Basic Pie Crust, bottom only
    (p. 382)
8 Tbs. granulated sugar

*Serves 8*

Combine the 1 ¾ cups sugar with the cornstarch and blend in boiling water. Cook over low heat or in a double boiler, stirring constantly, until mixture thickens and bubbles—about 10 minutes.

Very carefully and gradually stir in the egg yolks, which have been beaten slightly. Blend in the lime juice, the green food coloring and half the salt. Stir constantly until smooth and thick—about another 10 minutes.

Cool but do not chill. Pour the filling into the cooked pie shell.

Make a meringue by beating the egg whites with the rest of the salt. When they begin to get stiff, gradually add the 8 Tbs. sugar and beat until thick.

Cover the pie with this meringue. Place in a moderate oven (325°) and bake until the meringue is delicately browned—about 15 minutes. More sugar may be sprinkled on the meringue before baking. Cool before refrigerating.

## MYERS'S JAMAICAN RUM PIE

¾ stick softened unsalted butter
4 cups finely ground graham
    crackers
5 egg yolks
¾ cup granulated sugar
2 envelopes Knox gelatine

¼ cup cold water
¾ cup Myers's Jamaican rum
2 cups cream, stiffly whipped
Gratings of chocolate or
    sprinklings of dark brown sugar

*Serves 12–16*

Prepare pie shells by working the butter into the graham cracker crumbs with your fingers. Divide them into 2 8″ pie pans. Press the crumbs to fit the pans and bake in a moderate oven (350°) for 10–15 minutes. Allow to cool.

In a mixing bowl, blend the egg yolks and sugar until thick and lemon-colored. Dissolve the gelatine in the cold water and ½ cup of the rum and heat in a double boiler for 5 minutes, stirring briskly. Cool slightly and gradually add to the egg-sugar mixture. Allow to cool.

Fold in the whipped cream, which has been allowed to refrigerate for 3 or 4 hours before using. When well blended, mix in the remaining rum.

Fill pie shells with this mixture and refrigerate for at least 3 hours until set. When ready to serve, sprinkle with gratings of chocolate or some brown sugar.

## NEW ORLEANS LEMON CREAM TARTS

½ cup unsalted butter              3 whole eggs beaten with
Juice of 3 lemons                    3 egg yolks
Grated rind of 1 lemon           12 Basic Tart Shells (p. 383)
Pinch of salt                         1 cup stiffly whipped cream or
1 cup sugar                            sour cream

*Serves 12*

Melt butter in the top of a double boiler and stir in the lemon juice, lemon rind, salt, sugar and eggs. Cook, stirring constantly until mixture thickens— about 10 minutes. Allow to cool slightly.

Fill tart shells and serve immediately or refrigerate. When ready to serve, top with whipped cream or sour cream.

*VARIATION* (Strawberry Tarts): Melt 2 squares semisweet chocolate in the top of a double boiler. Coat shells thinly with chocolate. Allow to cool and set. Fill shells about halfway with lemon cream. Cover with sliced fresh strawberries or strawberry halves. Refrigerate and then serve at room temperature.

## POUND CAKE À LA ROC

1 cup Vanilla Custard (p. 396)     2 cups shredded coconut
1 cup sweetened condensed milk   6 canned peach or pear halves
6 slices pound cake*

*Serves 6*

Combine the custard with the condensed milk. Dip the pound cake slices in the mixture and roll them in the coconut.

Place on a buttered baking dish, top with one peach half each and place in a moderate oven (300°). Bake until the coconut begins to brown—about 15 minutes.

*Bogie's Pound Cake (p. 385).

# COOKIES AND CANDIES

## CHARLOTTE BLAKE'S COOKIES

½ lb. plus 1 Tbs. butter, softened
1 lb. flour
1 Tbs. sugar
2 eggs

Pinch of baking soda
Grated rind of 1 lemon
¼–½ cup water

*Yields 2 dozen*

Mix together all ingredients except the 1 Tbs. butter and place dough in the refrigerator for 1½–2 hours. Return dough to room temperature, add the 1 Tbs. butter and roll out to about ¼″ thick on a lightly floured board.

With a heavy glass or a small cookie cutter, cut rounds the size of a quarter or half-dollar and bake in a low oven (250°) on an ungreased cookie sheet until lightly brown and done—about 20–25 minutes.

Cool and store in a tin box.

Serve plain or top each cookie with your favorite homemade jams or savories.

## CHINATOWN ALMOND COOKIES

3 cups flour
1 tsp. baking soda
1 tsp. salt
1 egg
1 tsp. almond extract

1 cup sugar
1⅓ cups shortening
Blanched almonds (54 halves) or
    red food coloring

*Yields 54 cookies*

Sift flour, baking soda and salt together.

Beat egg with fork until lemon-colored. Add almond extract. Cream together sugar and shortening, blending well. Combine with beaten egg and mix thoroughly. Gradually blend in dry ingredients.

Roll into balls about 1″ in diameter and place 1″ apart on a greased cookie sheet. Press thumb gently into each ball. Fill center with a blanched almond half or touch it with the end of a chopstick dipped in red food coloring.

Bake for 12 minutes at 350°.

## LEROUX CHOCOLATE AMARETTO KISSES

1 6-oz. package semisweet
   chocolate chips
½ cup granulated sugar
3 Tbs. light corn syrup
½ cup Leroux Chocolate
   Amaretto liqueur

2½ cups finely crushed vanilla
   wafers
1 cup finely chopped pecans or
   walnuts
Sifted powdered sugar

*Yields 36 kisses*

Melt chocolate in the top of a double boiler over simmering water. Stir constantly until chocolate is melted. Remove from heat and stir in sugar and corn syrup. Add Leroux Chocolate Amaretto and blend well.

Combine vanilla wafer crumbs and chopped nuts in a large bowl. Add chocolate mixture and mix well. Form into 1″ balls and roll in powdered sugar. Place in an airtight can and allow to sit for several days.

## NEW ORLEANS TRUFFLES

8 oz. semisweet chocolate
4 egg yolks
¼ cup unsalted butter

2 tsp. light cream
   or evaporated milk
2 Tbs. Myers's Jamaican rum
½ cup unsweetened cocoa

*Serves 6–8*

Melt chocolate over very low heat and beat in the egg yolks one at a time, beating well after each addition. Beat in the butter, light cream and rum.

Form into uneven truffle shapes. Roll in cocoa and set aside to dry.

Refrigerate and serve as a candy.

# CREAMS AND MOUSSES

## BISCUIT TORTONI

1 cup heavy cream                1 cup finely crumbled macaroons
¼ cup powdered sugar             2 tsp. sweet sherry
1 egg white, stiffly beaten

*Serves 6*

Whip the cream until stiff and gradually fold in the powdered sugar, the stiffly beaten egg white, ½ cup of the sieved macaroons and the sweet sherry.

Pack the mixture in individual paper baking cups or ramekins and sprinkle with the remaining macaroons.

Freeze without stirring.

## IRISH CHANNEL CREAM

4 eggs, separated                1 cup heavy cream,
2 Tbs. honey                        lightly whipped
2 cups milk, scalded             2 oz. Irish Mist liqueur
2 envelopes Knox gelatine        Whipped cream
4 Tbs. water                     Mint leaves

*Serves 6*

Lightly beat the egg yolks with the honey. Combine with the scalded milk and stir over medium heat until thick—about 10 minutes. Be careful not to let the mixture boil.

Soften the gelatine in water, dissolve over low heat and add to the egg-milk mixture.

Add the lightly whipped cream and Irish Mist and mix well. Beat egg whites stiffly and add. Combine thoroughly and pour into a 1-quart mold to set.

Unmold* onto a plate, decorate the base with whipped cream and garnish with a few fresh or candied mint leaves.

*Unmold by running a knife around the edges, dipping into hot but not boiling water for a few seconds and inverting onto a plate.

# MARQUISE AU CHOCOLAT

| | |
|---|---|
| ⅓ lb. unsalted butter or margarine | 3⅓ cups heavy cream |
| 6 egg yolks | 1 lb. grated semisweet chocolate |
| | ½ cup Myers's Jamaican rum |

*Serves 8–10*

Melt the butter in a heavy saucepan over low heat or in the top of a double boiler. While butter is melting, beat the egg yolks with ⅓ cup of the heavy cream and reserve.

To the hot melted butter, add the grated chocolate, stirring constantly until it has all melted. Add 1 cup of the heavy cream, continuing to stir until thick.

Add the yolk-cream mixture and cook, stirring constantly until thick again—about 15 minutes.

Pour immediately into a 9″ x 5″ x 2¾″ loaf pan and place in either freezer or refrigerator until firm and set—at least 4 hours or overnight. If placed in freezer, allow to thaw slightly before unmolding.* Slice into individual servings.

Stiffly beat the remaining cream, gradually add the rum and blend well. Spoon over each serving of the Marquise. This is a very rich dessert and should be served in small quantities.

*Unmold by running a sharp knife around the edges, dipping pan into hot but not boiling water and inverting onto a plate.

# MISSISSIPPI STRAWBERRY BREEZE

| | |
|---|---|
| 2 cups heavy cream | ¼ cup fresh strawberries, puréed in a blender |
| 1 tsp. vanilla extract | Crystallized violets |
| ½ cup powdered sugar | |

*Serves 6*

Whip cream until stiff. Add vanilla and gradually add powdered sugar, beating until very stiff.

Fold in the purée of strawberries and pipe into wineglasses with a pastry bag that has been fitted with a fluted tip.

Decorate with a few crystallized violets. Refrigerate until ready to serve.

## NEW ORLEANS COFFEE BAVARIAN CREAM

| | |
|---|---|
| 1 envelope Knox gelatine | 4 egg yolks |
| 2 Tbs. cold water | ½ cup sugar |
| 2 Tbs. cold, very strong | 1 cup milk, scalded |
| New Orleans coffee | 1 cup heavy cream, |
| 2 Tbs. Coffee Amaretto | stiffly whipped |

*Serves 4*

Soften gelatine in a mixture of the cold water, coffee and Amaretto.

Beat the egg yolks with the sugar until smooth and creamy. Combine with the scalded milk and cook over low heat, stirring constantly, until smooth and thick—about 10 minutes.

Add the softened gelatine and continue to stir until the gelatine is completely dissolved.

Cool, stirring from time to time to prevent a crust from forming. Fold in the stiffly whipped cream.

Serve in stemmed glasses or small bowls and add a dash of Coffee Amaretto for garnish.

## NEW ORLEANS 18TH-CENTURY CHOCOLATE

| | |
|---|---|
| 6 oz. semisweet chocolate | Pinch of salt |
| 6 egg yolks, slightly beaten | 6 egg whites, stiffly beaten |

*Serves 6*

In the top of a double boiler, melt chocolate until smooth. Add egg yolks and a pinch of salt. Continue to cook for 5 minutes, stirring continuously.

Remove from heat, cool slightly and quickly fold in the stiffly beaten egg whites.

Fill small glasses, such as the classic martini glass, with the mixture and leave in refrigerator overnight to set.

*VARIATION:* After the egg whites have been folded in, ¼ cup of Myers's Jamaican rum may be added.

# SABRA MILK AND HONEY

6 egg yolks
6 Tbs. sugar
12 Tbs. Sabra orange liqueur
  from Israel

½ pint cream, stiffly whipped
Orange peel or tangerine sections

*Serves 6*

In a heavy saucepan, combine the egg yolks, sugar and the Sabra orange liqueur. Cook over a very low flame or in a double boiler and stir constantly with a wire whisk or a wooden spoon until the custard is smooth, thick and rich—about 15 minutes.

Allow to cool, fold in the stiffly whipped cream and pour into small chilled wineglasses. Refrigerate and serve with a garnish of orange peel or a small section of tangerine.

This is a very rich dessert, and small servings are suggested.

# STRAWBERRY BAVARIAN CREAM

1 quart fresh strawberries, cleaned
  and puréed in a blender
1 Tbs. lemon juice
¾ cup granulated sugar
2 Tbs. Knox gelatine

½ cup cold water
2 cups heavy cream,
  stiffly whipped
8 whole strawberries
Extra whipped cream for garnish

*Serves 8*

To the puréed strawberries, add the lemon juice and sugar and stir until the sugar is completely dissolved.

Soften the gelatine in the water and cook over low heat until the gelatine is completely dissolved. Add to the strawberry mixture.

Stir the mixture over a bowl filled with cracked ice and continue to stir until it begins to thicken. Fold in the 2 cups whipped cream. Divide into individual glasses and refrigerate for 3 or 4 hours.

Garnish with a whole strawberry and whipped cream that has been flavored with any fruit liqueur.

## STRAWBERRIES SINGAPORE

¾ cups rice
1 quart milk
½ tsp. salt
¾ cup sugar
1 tsp. vanilla extract
2 envelopes Knox gelatine

¼ cup cold water
1 cup cream, whipped
3 cups strawberries
2 oz. kirsch or Triple Sec
½ cup sugar

*Serves 6*

Cook rice in milk with salt and sugar for about ½ hour. When soft and creamy, force through a sieve or purée in a blender.

Add vanilla. Soften gelatine in cold water and dissolve in the hot rice. Cool to lukewarm and fold in the whipped cream.

Turn into a greased 6″ ring mold and chill for 2 hours or until well set.

Unmold* on a cold platter and fill center with strawberries, which have been marinated in the liqueur and sugar. Save a few of the best berries for garnish. A sprig of mint makes it New Orleans.

*Unmold by running a knife around the edges, dipping into hot but not boiling water for a few seconds and inverting onto a platter.

## VANILLA CUSTARD

4 egg yolks
¼ cup sugar
1/3 tsp. salt

2 cups scalded Half n' Half
½ tsp. vanilla

*Yields 2 cups*

Beat egg yolks and add sugar and salt. Slowly add the Half n' Half. Place on very low heat and stir constantly until it begins to thicken—about 15 minutes. Strain and cool slightly. Add the vanilla.

This custard may be used in many different desserts or with fresh fruit.

# ZABAGLIONE

6 Tbs. sugar
6 egg yolks
12 Tbs. good Italian sweet Marsala

*Serves 5*

Blend the sugar and egg yolks in a heavy saucepan, using a wire whisk. Add the Marsala 1 Tbs. at a time and blend well.

Over low heat or in a double boiler, cook and stir the mixture constantly until it begins to foam and then take on the consistency of heavy cream—about 15 minutes.

Be very careful not to leave the mixture for one moment, or you will have sweet scrambled eggs.

Serve immediately in a thin wineglass.

This dessert may be chilled, then combined with equal parts whipped cream and served cold with your favorite fruit in season.

# FRUITS

## APPLE FRITTERS

3 large, tart apples                    1 cup Basic Fritter Batter
3 Tbs. sugar                                 (p. 382)
½ tsp. ground cinnamon          1 cup cooking oil
1 Tbs. Myers's Jamaican rum
   or kirsch

*Serves 4*

Peel and core apples. Cut into cartwheel slices about ¼″ thick.

Combine the sugar and cinnamon and sprinkle 1 Tbs. over the apple slices. Sprinkle with the rum and allow to marinate for 1 hour.

Drain the juices into the fritter batter and stir well. Coat each apple slice with the batter and deep fry in preheated cooking oil (375°) until golden brown—about 5 minutes.

Drain on paper toweling, sprinkle with the remaining cinnamon-sugar mixture and place in a hot oven (450°) for 5 minutes to glaze.

Serve hot.

## BANANA FRITTERS

3–4 bananas, not too ripe  
½ cup Myers's Jamaican rum  
3 Tbs. flour

1 cup Basic Fritter Batter  
  (p. 382)  
2 cups cooking oil

*Serves 6–8*

Peel bananas and cut each on the diagonal into 4 or 6 pieces, depending on size of the banana. Soak in rum for 20 minutes.

Remove pieces with a slotted spoon and reserve rum for sauce. Dredge bananas in flour and then dip into fritter batter.

Fry in hot, deep oil until fritters are brown, turning over once—about 5 minutes.

Drain on paper toweling and serve with Lemon Sauce (p. 411) mixed with the reserved rum.

## BASIN STREET GRAPEFRUIT

4 grapefruits  
½ cup granulated sugar  
½ cup 100-proof bourbon  
6 egg whites  
Pinch of salt

1 cup powdered sugar  
1 quart hard French vanilla  
  ice cream  
8 Maraschino cherries

*Serves 8*

Cut grapefruits in half and remove sections. Clean membranes from the half shells and place shells in a freezer until ready to use.

Sprinkle grapefruit sections with granulated sugar, cover with bourbon and chill.

Combine egg whites with salt and beat until soft peaks appear. Slowly add ¾ cup powdered sugar and beat until stiff to make a meringue.

To serve, fill the frozen shells with the marinated grapefruit sections. Over this spoon vanilla ice cream. Top with the meringue, spreading the edges to seal the ice cream. Dust with remaining powdered sugar.

Bake in a very hot oven (450°) until the meringue turns a light brown.

Serve at once, garnished with a Maraschino cherry.

# BEN'S BANANAS

1 stick unsalted butter
Juice and grated rind of 1 lemon
Juice and grated rind of 2 oranges

1 cup dark brown sugar,
  firmly packed
½ cup Myers's Jamaican rum
6 firm plantains or 6 bananas

*Serves 6*

In a heavy skillet, melt butter with lemon and orange rinds over very low heat, stirring frequently to blend well. Add the brown sugar and stir until mixture is smooth.

Add the lemon and orange juices and continue cooking further until the sugar is completely melted and blended with the other ingredients—about 5 minutes. Add the Myers's Jamaican rum a little at a time and bring to a slow boil. Reduce heat.

Peel plantains or bananas. Either slice them in half lengthwise or in cartwheels. Poach the banana pieces in the rum sauce, turning them, for about 10 minutes or until they are tender but not mushy.

Serve with hard vanilla ice cream or just as they are for a bruncheon dessert.

# CAMILLE'S PEACHES

*Crème Camille:*
1½ cups milk
1 3″ stick vanilla bean,
  cut in half
½ cup sugar

4 egg yolks
¼ cup flour
¼ cup Maraschino liqueur

*Peaches:*
6 fresh peaches
  (white, if available)
½ cup white wine
½ cup water

1 3″ stick vanilla bean,
  cut in half
12 Maraschino cherries

*Serves 6*

*To make Crème Camille:* Scald the milk with the vanilla bean. In a separate saucepan mix the sugar with the egg yolks until creamy and light-colored. Add the flour and mix until blended.

Add the scalded milk gradually, stirring vigorously until the mixture thickens. Do not boil.

Remove vanilla bean, strain, add Maraschino liqueur and cool until ready to use.

*To prepare peaches:* Blanch peaches in boiling water for 5–10 minutes and remove skins. Cut in half and remove pits.

In a heavy saucepan, bring wine, water and vanilla bean to a boil and reduce heat. Poach peach halves in this mixture for 5 minutes. Drain well and cool.

Fill an attractive glass dish with *Crème Camille* and arrange peach halves on top. Place 1 Maraschino cherry in each peach half.

## CHERRIES JUBILEE

1 pint jar Bing cherries
1 tsp. cornstarch
¼ cup kirsch

1 quart hard French vanilla
ice cream

*Serves 6*

Drain cherries and reserve juice.

In a saucepan or the top of a chafing dish, blend the cornstarch with 1 Tbs. cherry juice, add the rest of the cherry juice and cook until slightly thickened— about 5–10 minutes.

Add the cherries and continue cooking until they are thoroughly heated. Add the kirsch and ignite.

Serve the flaming sauce over hard French vanilla ice cream.

## KEITH'S GINGER PEARS

8 fresh pears
2 cups water
2 cups sugar
1 stick cinnamon

2 strips lemon peel
1 tsp. whole cloves
1 thick slice fresh ginger
   (or 3 slices candied ginger)

*Serves 6–8*

Peel and core pears. Make a syrup of remaining ingredients. Bring syrup to a boil and cook slowly for 5 minutes.

Add pears to the syrup and simmer gently for about 30 minutes or until they are just transparent and tender.

When tender, remove from liquid and serve with New Orleans Whipped Cream (chap. 13). They may also be served cold with ice cream.

## PEACHES WITH NEW ORLEANS WHIPPED CREAM

| | |
|---|---|
| 6 medium fresh peaches | 1 cup New Orleans Whipped |
| 6 whole cloves | Cream (chap. 13) |
| | 6 sprigs fresh mint |

*Serves 6*

Parboil peaches in boiling water along with the cloves for about 10 minutes until skin removes easily with sharp knife. Remove skins and cool peaches in their liquid. Cut in half and remove pits.

Lay 2 halves per person in a glass plate and top each half with New Orleans Whipped Cream. Garnish with a sprig of fresh mint.

## STRAWBERRIES ROMANOFF

| | |
|---|---|
| 1 pint French vanilla ice cream | 6 Tbs. Triple Sec or Cointreau |
| 1 cup heavy cream, stiffly beaten | 2 quarts fresh strawberries, |
| Juice of 1 lemon | hulled, sugared and chilled |

*Serves 6*

Whip the ice cream slightly. Quickly fold in the whipped cream and lemon juice. Add the Triple Sec or Cointreau.

Quickly blend in the cold strawberries and serve immediately in chilled champagne glasses.

## STUFFED PLANTAIN

| | |
|---|---|
| 2 Tbs. seedless white raisins | ½ cup unsalted butter |
| 4 Tbs. Myers's Jamaican rum | ½ cup powdered sugar |
| 3 large, ripe plantains | 3 Tbs. chopped toasted pecans |
| 4 Tbs. lemon or lime juice | 12 Maraschino cherries |

*Serves 6*

Put the raisins in a bowl with half the rum to marinate while you prepare the other ingredients.

Peel plantains; slice in half lengthwise and then crosswise. Place in a buttered baking dish, sprinkle with the lemon juice and bake in a 350° oven until soft—about 15–20 minutes. Allow to cool.

Cream butter and sugar together until smooth and creamy. Beat in the rest of the rum and add the nuts. Scoop out half a boat from the plantains and fill with the butter mixture.

Garnish with the raisins and any rum they have not absorbed, as well as with the cherries.

Refrigerate before serving. Ice cream may be served with this dessert.

# ICES

## BURAS ORANGE ICE CUPS

2 cups sugar
4 cups water
2 cups orange juice
¼ cup lemon juice
Finely grated rind
    of 2 large oranges

6 small orange shells,* scooped
    out and frozen
6 tsp. Louisiana orange wine (or
    a mixture of 2 tsp. Triple Sec
    and 4 tsp. white wine)
6 slivers candied ginger

*Serves 6*

Combine sugar and water in a saucepan. Bring to a boil and boil for 5 minutes. Remove from heat and add the orange juice, lemon juice and orange rind. Allow to cool. Strain and freeze in ice trays or something similar.

Scoop out by scraping with a spoon; fill each orange shell and return to freezer. Just before serving add 1 tsp. Louisiana orange wine to each shell and garnish with a sliver of candied ginger.

*Cut a third off the top of the oranges.

# INGRID'S LEMON ICE CUPS

4 cups water
2 cups sugar
1 Tbs. grated lemon rind
1 cup fresh lemon juice

6 lemon shells,*
   scooped out and frozen
6 sprigs fresh mint or
   6 pieces candied lemon peel

*Serves 6*

Combine water and sugar in a saucepan. Bring to a boil and boil gently for 5 minutes. Remove from heat and stir in the lemon rind and juice. Let cool and freeze in ice trays or something similar.

Scoop out by scraping with a spoon; fill lemon shells and return to freezer until ready to serve.

Garnish with a sprig of fresh mint or a piece of candied lemon peel.

*Cut a third off the top of the lemons.

# LIME SHERBET

¾ cup sugar
1 cup water
1 envelope Knox gelatine
2 cups white wine,
   preferably Sauterne

2 Tbs. green crème de menthe
1 cup freshly squeezed lime juice,
   unstrained
1 egg white, stiffly beaten with
   ¼ tsp. salt

*Serves 6–8*

Boil the sugar and water together for 10 minutes, stirring. Soften gelatine in a little cold water. Pour the boiling syrup over this and stir until the gelatine is dissolved. Add wine, 1 Tbs. of the crème de menthe and the cup of lime juice.

Freeze the sherbet to a mush—about 1 hour. Remove from freezer and fold in the stiffly beaten egg white.

Return to freezer and finish freezing. Serve in frosted sherbet glasses, each brushed with a little of the remaining crème de menthe.

## STRAWBERRY ICE

| | |
|---|---|
| 3½ cups water | 2 cups strained strawberry juice |
| 1½ cups sugar | 2 Tbs. strained lemon juice |
| ½ cup apricot brandy | ½ tsp. grated orange rind |
| Pinch of salt | 6–8 whole fresh strawberries |

*Serves 6–8*

Make a syrup of the water, sugar and brandy and boil for 5–6 minutes.

Cool a bit and add the remaining ingredients, except the whole strawberries. Mix well and chill. Freeze in ice trays or something similar overnight.

When ready to use, scoop out by scraping with a spoon and serve in small wineglasses, each topped with a whole fresh strawberry.

# PUDDINGS AND SOUFFLÉS

## BREAD PUDDING WITH WHISKEY OR RUM SAUCE

*Bread pudding:*

| | |
|---|---|
| 6 slices bread, preferably French | 1 Tbs. vanilla |
| 3½ cups milk | 1 cup seedless raisins |
| 10 Tbs. sugar | Pinch of salt |
| 4 eggs, separated | |

*Whiskey or rum sauce:*

| | |
|---|---|
| ½ cup sugar | ¼ cup 100-proof bourbon (or |
| ¼ cup water | ½ cup Myers's Jamaican rum) |
| ¼ stick unsalted butter | |

*Serves 4–6*

*To make pudding:* Break bread into small pieces and soften with a small amount of the milk in an ovenproof dish. Beat 6 Tbs. of the sugar with the egg yolks. Add the rest of the milk and stir well. Add vanilla and raisins. Pour mixture over the bread.

Place dish in a pan of water and bake in a 300° oven for 40–50 minutes or until a silver knife comes out clean.

Make a meringue by beating the egg whites until stiff and adding 2 Tbs. sugar and a pinch of salt. Spread meringue over bread pudding, sprinkle with remaining sugar and return to a 350° oven until meringue is brown—about 10 minutes.

*To make sauce:* Cook the sugar, water and butter, stirring constantly until butter is melted and well combined—about 5 minutes. Add the bourbon or rum and cook for another 2–3 minutes.

Serve warm over the bread pudding.

## CHOCOLATE SOUFFLÉ

3 Tbs. unsalted butter
2 Tbs. flour
1 cup milk, scalded
¼ tsp. salt
½ cup sugar

3″ piece of vanilla bean
2 squares semisweet chocolate
4 egg yolks, slightly beaten
5 egg whites

*Serves 6*

In a saucepan, melt butter and blend well with the flour until golden—about 10–15 minutes over a very low flame. Stir constantly. Gradually add the scalded milk, stirring constantly. Mix in the salt, sugar, vanilla bean and chocolate. Over low heat, still stirring constantly, cook for about 10 minutes, until chocolate is completely melted.

When the sauce is thick and smooth, remove from heat and cool. Remove vanilla bean. Add the egg yolks and beat well.

Stiffly beat the egg whites until they stand in peaks, and gently fold them into the mixture.

Butter a 1½-quart soufflé dish, sprinkle with sugar and pour in the batter. Bake in a hot oven (400°) for 15 minutes, reduce heat to moderate (350°) and cook for 20–30 minutes longer.

Serve with warm Blueberry Sauce (p. 410).

## HAMMOND STRAWBERRY SOUFFLÉ

3 Tbs. unsalted butter
2 Tbs. flour
½ cup hot milk
5 egg yolks
5 Tbs. powdered sugar

1 cup fresh strawberries, chopped
1 Tbs. Triple Sec, brandy
  or any fruit liqueur
6 egg whites
Whole strawberries

*Serves 6*

Melt butter in a double boiler. Add the flour and cook, stirring constantly, until it turns golden—about 15–20 minutes. Add the hot milk and continue to cook, stirring constantly with a wire whisk for 3–5 minutes. Add the egg yolks, beaten with 2 Tbs. of the sugar. Add the chopped strawberries, mixed with 2 Tbs. sugar and the liqueur.

Beat the egg whites until stiff, adding the remaining 1 Tbs. sugar, and fold lightly into the first mixture. Pour into a buttered and sugared 1½-quart soufflé dish and add a few berries on top for decoration.

Bake in a moderate oven (350°) for 35–40 minutes. Sprinkle powdered sugar over the top before serving.

## ICED LEMON SOUFFLÉ

Grated rind of 4 lemons
½ cup strained lemon juice
1 cup superfine sugar
1 envelope Knox gelatine
2 Tbs. cold water

7–8 egg whites
1 cup heavy cream
Extra whipped cream for garnish
8 lemon slices
About 8 fresh mint leaves

*Serves 6*

In a saucepan, combine the lemon rind, lemon juice and sugar. Dissolve the gelatine in the water and add to the mixture. Stir over low heat until gelatine is completely dissolved. Chill to a syrupy consistency.

Beat egg whites until very stiff and fold into the lemon-gelatine mixture. Whip the heavy cream until stiff and fold into the lemon mixture until thoroughly mixed.

Tie a double band of waxed paper around the top of a 1½-quart soufflé dish. Pour in the lemon soufflé and chill thoroughly.

Remove waxed-paper collar before serving. Decorate top of soufflé with extra whipped cream and garnish with paper-thin lemon slices and fresh mint.

# IRISH CHANNEL TRIFLE

18 finger-size pieces stale pound
  cake,* about 1″ thick
1 can apricots,
  drained and liquid reserved
1 can fruit salad, drained
½ cup sweet sherry

2 cups Vanilla Custard (p. 396),
  at room temperature
1 cup whipped cream
Maraschino cherries
Crystallized fruit

*Serves 6*

Line the bottom of a glass dish with the cake fingers. Top with a layer of the canned apricots and fruit salad. Repeat the process until all the pound cake, apricots and fruit salad are used, finishing with the cake.

Mix the apricot liquid with the sherry and pour over the cake and fruit so that the cake absorbs it all. Pour the custard over this; it will seep through the entire cake.

Chill for several hours, and when set, decorate with whipped cream and garnish with Maraschino cherries and crystallized fruit.

*Bogie's Pound Cake (p. 385).

# OLD FRENCH BREAD PUDDING

4 eggs, separated
½ cup powdered sugar
1 tsp. vanilla extract
2 cups cold Half n' Half

18 thick slices white bread,
  trimmed and cut in half
½ cup jam, marmalade or jelly
Pinch of salt
4 Tbs. granulated sugar

*Serves 6–8*

Beat egg yolks until fluffy and lemon-colored. Add ¼ cup of the powdered sugar a little at a time, beating all the time. Continue to beat and add ½ tsp. of the vanilla and all the Half n' Half.

Arrange the bread slices on the bottom of a flat, deep dish and pour the egg mixture over them. Cover with waxed paper and allow to soak for 15 minutes. Drain off excess liquid and reserve 3 Tbs.

With a spatula, transfer the bread slices to another deep baking dish lined with unglazed white paper. Spread each piece of bread with a thin coating of whatever jam or jelly you are using and set to one side.

Beat the egg whites and add the remaining powdered sugar a little at a time, beating until stiff. Add a pinch of salt. Put the meringue in a saucepan over low heat. Blend in the granulated sugar, the 3 Tbs. reserved egg-milk mixture and the rest of the vanilla. Beat vigorously from the bottom of the pan until well blended, with no granular appearance. Spread over the bread slices and bake in a very low oven (250°) for about 40 minutes or until browned.

## SUMMER SNOW EGGS

4 eggs, separated
1 cup sugar
Pinch of salt
2 cups Half n' Half, scalded

1 tsp. vanilla
1¼ cups sliced fresh fruit or
   berries in season
¼ cup toasted slivered almonds

*Serves 6*

Beat the egg whites and gradually add ¾ cup of the sugar, beating until very stiff.

With 2 large, wet, oval spoons, divide the meringue into 12 egg shapes and slide them one at a time into simmering water in a shallow pan.

Poach for 2 minutes on one side, turn them over and poach for 2 minutes on the other side. Remove from the water and dry on paper towels.

Beat the egg yolks slightly with the remaining ¼ cup sugar and add a pinch of salt. Add the scalded Half n' Half. Cook over low heat, stirring constantly until thick—about 10–15 minutes. Be careful not to overcook. Remove from the heat, stir in the vanilla and allow to cool.

Put the slices of fresh fruit or berries on the bottom of a deep dish, arrange the poached meringues over the fruit, cover with the cooled custard and sprinkle with the toasted almonds.

# TWELFTH NIGHT SOUFFLÉ

*Soufflé:*

4 Tbs. butter
2 Tbs. flour
1 cup light cream, scalded

5 egg yolks, beaten with
    4 Tbs. sugar
1 jar Nesselrode
6 egg whites, stiffly beaten

*Sauce:*

5 Tbs. sugar
5 egg yolks

5 Tbs. Myers's Jamaican rum
½ pint heavy cream, whipped

*Serves 6*

*To make the soufflé:* Melt butter, add flour and cook until the mixture starts to color. Gradually add the cream, stirring constantly, and cook for about 5 minutes. Stir in the egg yolks beaten with the sugar. Flavor with the jar of Nesselrode and fold in the stiffly beaten egg whites.

Pour into a buttered 1½-quart soufflé dish that has also been sugared and bake in a moderate oven (350°) for 35–40 minutes.

*To make the sauce:* Blend sugar, egg yolks and rum and cook in a double boiler for about 10 minutes, until thick and creamy. Allow to cool and fold in the whipped cream. The sauce should be a little on the runny side.

Pour over each soufflé serving.

# SAUCES

## BLUEBERRY SAUCE

| | |
|---|---|
| 1/3 cup granulated sugar | 1 scant cup hot water |
| 1½ Tbs. cornstarch | 1 cup fresh blueberries |
| ¼ tsp. salt | 2 tsp. unsalted butter |
| 1 Tbs. lemon juice | 2 Tbs. Myers's Jamaican rum |

*Yields 2 cups*

In the top of a double boiler or in a saucepan over low heat, mix the sugar, cornstarch and salt. Stir in the lemon juice and gradually add the hot water. Stir until the mixture is smooth and begins to thicken—about 5–10 minutes.

Add the blueberries, mash them and continue to cook, stirring constantly, until mixture is thick—about another 10–15 minutes.

Remove from heat and beat in the butter and rum.

Serve hot with any soufflé, except cheese of course.

*VARIATION:* Triple the amount of blueberries, add a little more rum and fill a Basic Crumb Crust (p. 382) to make elegant blueberry pie. Garnish with whipped cream and berries on top.

## FRENCH PROVINCIAL CRÊPE SAUCE

| | |
|---|---|
| 1 stick unsalted butter or | 1 cup orange juice |
| margarine | ½ cup brandy |
| Grated rind of 1 large orange | ½ cup Triple Sec |
| 1 cup confectioners' sugar | |

*Yields 2 cups*

Melt butter, add orange gratings and simmer for 1 minute. Stir in the sugar; add the orange juice, brandy and Triple Sec.

Bring to a boil and remove from heat. Serve hot over folded crêpes.

This sauce turns the Basic Beer Crêpes (p. 381) into a dessert.

# LEMON SAUCE

½ cup butter
1 cup sugar
3 egg yolks

¾ cup boiling water
3 Tbs. lemon juice

*Yields 2 cups*

In the top of a double boiler, cream butter. Slowly add sugar. Add 1 egg yolk at a time and beat until thoroughly blended.

Gradually pour in the boiling water. Cook in the top of a double boiler over low heat, stirring constantly, until the sauce thickens slightly. Add the lemon juice, mix well and cook for another 5 minutes.

Serve with Banana Fritters (p. 398).

This sauce can be prepared in advance and reheated in the top of a double boiler.

# 13
# SAUCES, ETC.

# HINTS

## SPECIAL INGREDIENTS

*Creole tomatoes:* All vegetables grown in Louisiana are generally called Creole—thus, Creole tomatoes. We think they are some of the best. However, if you're in another part of the country, be sure you choose a good juicy one for a substitute.

*Other ingredients:* These can be found in most gourmet and specialty shops around the country. Of course, if you're in New Orleans, I suggest you stock up.

Crab boil, dry or liquid
Creole mustard
Creole seasonings
Gumbo filé
New Orleans coffee and chicory
Pechaud bitters (Sazerac bitters)

## HOW TO BLANCH

For fruits, vegetables and nuts: Dip in boiling water for a minute or two to loosen skins for peeling or to prepare for use in salads.

## HOW TO PARBOIL

Boil for about 5–10 minutes or as directed in preparation for further cooking.

# BASICS

## ASPIC

1 envelope Knox gelatine
1 can jellied consommé madrilene
   or white chicken consommé
Juice of ½ lemon
Salt and white pepper to taste

*Yields 1½ cups*

Dissolve gelatine in consommé at room temperature. Add lemon juice. Heat over hot but not boiling water for 5 minutes. Cool and chill slightly. Mixture must be fluid enough to spoon as necessary.
Use in recipes as called for.

# BEURRE MANIÉ

2 Tbs. butter
2 Tbs. flour

*Yields 2 Tbs.*

Cream butter and flour together until well mixed.
*Beurre manié* is a thickening agent for sauces. Use it a little at a time, being careful to keep the sauce hot but not boiling.

# BOUQUET GARNI

1 stalk celery with leaves          2 sprigs parsley
1 carrot, peeled                    1 bay leaf
½ onion

Tie all ingredients together with a string or place in a piece of cheesecloth and tie with a string. For large quantities of soups and stock, you may double or triple the ingredients. Use as called for in recipes.

# ROUX

While the roux does belong to French cuisine, the Creole and Cajun cuisines have taken it over and made it their own. It is no idle statement when a Creole or Cajun cook tells you, "First you make a roux."

A roux is a combination of flour and butter or cooking oils. There are white roux and dark roux, depending on the dish. In this book, there are many recipes which call for a roux, from the light, white roux in a soufflé to the dark roux in a gumbo.

The classic roux takes time and should be cooked *very* slowly. Many cooks will tell you that you need anywhere from ½–1 hour of constant stirring. To save time, the directions for some of the roux in this book have been reduced to 10 minutes, but don't be afraid to cook longer, and be sure to keep stirring. Your soufflés will be lighter if you cook your roux longer.

# BUTTERS

## CLARIFIED BUTTER

1 stick butter
Hot water

*Yields ½ cup*

Place the stick of butter in a cup. Stand the cup in hot water. When the butter has melted, strain through a tea strainer or some cheesecloth to remove the milky sediment. The remaining pure yellow liquid is clarified butter. Many sauces call for it.

## MAÎTRE D'HÔTEL BUTTER

8 Tbs. butter
1 Tbs. chopped parsley
1 tsp. salt

Pinch of white pepper
Juice of ½ lemon

*Yields 8 Tbs.*

Knead the butter until soft and mix with the remaining ingredients. Use with fish and vegetables.

## ROC'S BUTTER

1 lb. butter or margarine
4 Tbs. seasoned salt
4 Tbs. Worcestershire sauce

1 tsp. garlic powder
2 Tbs. fines herbes
1 tsp. Tabasco pepper sauce

*Yields 2 cups*

Allow butter to reach room temperature and whip in all other ingredients to make a seasoned butter.

This delicious butter was created for grits but may be used with any of your favorite vegetables.

# DRESSINGS

## C.B.'S VINAIGRETTE SAUCE

½ cup olive oil
½ cup red wine vinegar
½ tsp. Dijon mustard
¼ cup chopped green onions
1 clove garlic, minced

1 Tbs. chopped capers
1 pimiento, finely chopped
Salt and fresh black pepper to
    taste

*Yields 1 cup*

Thoroughly blend all ingredients in a mason jar and refrigerate.

## CHRIS'S COCKTAIL SAUCE

1 bottle ketchup (14-oz. size)
Juice of 1 large lemon or lime
1 Tbs. Creole mustard or
    a horseradish-type mustard

½–²/₃ tsp. Tabasco pepper sauce
1 tsp. salt
¼ cup chopped capers

*Yields 1½ cups*

Mix all ingredients in a mason jar and store refrigerated until ready to use.

## CHRISTOPHER BLAKE'S FRENCH DRESSING

1 cup olive oil
¹/₃ cup wine vinegar
1 tsp. salt
½ tsp. freshly ground black
    pepper

1 clove garlic, minced
1 tsp. Creole mustard or
    a good horseradish mustard
1 tsp. dried tarragon leaves

*Yields 1½ cups*

Place ingredients in a jar and shake well before using. Quantities may be multiplied and dressing stored unrefrigerated.

# GREEN MAYONNAISE

2 cups mayonnaise                2 Tbs. chopped parsley
1 Tbs. chopped chives            1 tsp. chopped chervil
1 Tbs. chopped tarragon          1 tsp. chopped dill

*Yields 2 cups*

Into the mayonnaise, fold all the green herbs, which have been finely chopped.

Let stand in a cool place for 2 hours and use with cold fish, especially salmon.
I do not recommend dried herbs for this dish.

# JELLIED MAYONNAISE

2 envelopes Knox gelatine
½ cup cold water
2 cups mayonnaise

*Yields 2 cups*

Soften the gelatine in the cold water for about 5 minutes. Stir over hot water until the gelatine is dissolved. Add 2 cups mayonnaise to this mixture and mix well and rapidly.

Use immediately, before it sets.

Use to bind salads as well as to coat cold dishes such as chicken breasts, tongue, eggs or lobster.

# MAYONNAISE

2 egg yolks                      ½ tsp. dry mustard
½ tsp. salt                      2 tsp. vinegar or lemon juice
⅛ tsp. white pepper              1 cup olive oil*

*Yields 1 ½ cups*

Rinse a wooden mixing bowl with hot water and dry it well. In this bowl, beat the egg yolks with a wire whisk. Add the salt, pepper, dry mustard and 1 tsp. of the vinegar. Mix well.

Add the olive oil, drop by drop and very slowly, beating constantly, until a little more than half the olive oil has been added.

Add another ½ tsp. vinegar and then pour in the rest of the oil in a thin stream. Beat continuously and stop from time to time to make sure that the mixture is well combined.

When all the oil has been added, finish with a final ½ tsp. vinegar.

*Half salad and half olive oil may be used, or all vegetable oil.

# SAUCES

## AVOGLEMONO
### A Popular Greek Sauce

2 Tbs. butter
2 Tbs. flour
1¼ cups hot Fish Stock (p. 184)
   or Chicken Stock (p. 183)*

2 egg yolks
3 Tbs. lemon juice
1 Tbs. cold water
1 Tbs. chopped parsley

*Yields 1½ cups*

In the top of a double boiler, melt the butter. Stir in the flour and cook for 1 minute. Gradually pour in the hot fish or chicken stock, stirring constantly, and bring to just under the boiling point. Keep the sauce hot.

Beat 2 egg yolks with 3 Tbs. lemon juice and 1 Tbs. cold water. Add the hot sauce to the egg mixture, a spoonful at a time, stirring constantly.

Return the mixture to the double boiler and cook, stirring, over simmering water until the sauce is thick and smooth. Lastly, stir in the chopped parsley.

Serve with fish and vegetables or use to flavor stews and soups.

*Depending on the dish the sauce will accompany.

# BASIC BROWN SAUCE

4 Tbs. butter                     1 tsp. Kitchen Bouquet
4 Tbs. flour                      Salt and black pepper to taste
2 cups Beef Stock (p. 183),
    heated

*Yields 2 cups*

Melt butter in a heavy saucepan. Add flour and cook very slowly, stirring constantly, for about 10 minutes. Stir in Kitchen Bouquet.

Gradually add the hot beef stock and continue to cook, stirring, for another 15 minutes or until sauce is thick and well blended. Finally season with salt and black pepper.

This is a good quick basic brown sauce. If too thick, it may be thinned out with a little more beef stock.

# BÉCHAMEL SAUCE

4 Tbs. butter                     2 cups milk or Half n' Half,
4 Tbs. flour                          heated
                                  Salt and white pepper to taste

*Yields 2 cups*

Melt butter in a heavy saucepan. Add flour and cook very slowly, stirring constantly for about 10 minutes. Gradually add hot milk or Half n' Half and continue to cook for another 15 minutes or until sauce is thick and well blended. Finally season with salt and white pepper.

This sauce may be refrigerated for several days, but do not freeze.

# HOLLANDAISE SAUCE

1 stick butter                    Pinch of white pepper
4 egg yolks                       Pinch of salt
2 tsp. lemon juice

*Yields 1 cup*

Divide the stick of butter into 3 equal parts. Into the top of a double boiler place the 4 egg yolks with 1 part of the butter. Over hot but not boiling water, stir rapidly and constantly with a wooden spoon until butter is melted.

Add the second piece of butter. As the mixture thickens and the butter melts, add the third piece, stirring constantly. Do not allow the water over which the sauce is cooking ever to come to a boil.

When the butter is melted and the sauce is well mixed, remove pan from heat and continue beating for at least 2 minutes. Add the lemon juice and a pinch of white pepper and salt.

Replace the double-boiler top over the hot but not boiling water for 1–2 minutes longer, beating constantly with a wooden spoon. Remove from the heat at once and use. (Or reserve until ready to use and then heat slowly over hot but not boiling water.)

Should the mixture curdle, as sometimes happens, immediately add 1–2 Tbs. boiling water, beating constantly, in order to rebind the emulsion.

## MADEIRA SAUCE

1 cup Basic Brown Sauce (p. 421)
2 Tbs. Madeira wine

*Yields 1 cup*

In a heavy saucepan, heat the brown sauce. Add the Madeira and blend well. Use as directed.

## MORNAY SAUCE

1 cup Béchamel Sauce (p. 421)          1 Tbs. grated Swiss cheese
¾ cup dry white wine                    1 Tbs. butter
1 Tbs. grated Parmesan cheese

*Yields 1¾ cups*

Put béchamel sauce and wine in a saucepan. Reduce to approximately ⅓ the volume over high heat, stirring constantly—about 8–10 minutes. Add cheeses. Remove from heat and stir well. Add butter just before serving.

# SAUCE VELOUTÉ

3 Tbs. butter  
2 Tbs. flour  
1 onion, finely chopped  
2 cups hot Chicken Stock  
  (p. 183)

Salt to taste  
White pepper to taste  
¼ tsp. Tabasco pepper sauce  
½ lb. raw veal, finely chopped

*Yields 2 cups*

In a saucepan, melt butter and add flour, stirring together to make a light roux. Add the onion and continue to cook for 5 minutes. Gradually add the hot chicken stock, salt, pepper and Tabasco. Blend well.

Add the raw veal and cook over low heat, stirring occasionally, for about 1 hour. If sauce gets too thick, it may be thinned out with a little more chicken stock.

When sauce is cooked, correct seasoning for salt and white pepper and strain to remove veal and onion pieces. The finished sauce should have the consistency of heavy cream.

# ETC.

## FRIED CROUTONS

1 cup olive oil  
2 cloves garlic, crushed  
  (or less, if desired)

4–6 slices bread, preferably ends,  
  cubed (enough to make 2 cups)

*Yields 2 cups*

In a heavy skillet, heat the olive oil until hot but not boiling—about 3–5 minutes.

Add the crushed garlic and fry for a few minutes. Add bread cubes and stir frequently with a slotted spoon.

When the bread cubes have absorbed most of the olive oil and have become golden brown, remove with a slotted spoon. Drain on absorbent paper and remove the garlic pieces.

A delicious garnish for many soups and salads.

## MELBA TOAST

Remove crusts from thin slices of bread. Cut each slice into small rounds or into 4 squares. Place on a cookie sheet, leaving space between the rounds or squares. Bake slowly in a 250° oven for about ½ hour, until light and yellow, turning once.

## NEW ORLEANS WHIPPED CREAM

| | |
|---|---|
| 1 cup cream | 4 Tbs. strained lemon juice |
| 4 Tbs. sugar | 1 lemon rind, grated |

*Yields 1 cup*

Whip the cream and fold in the remaining ingredients. Blend well. Use with fruits and desserts.

# TABLE OF
# COMPARATIVE MEASUREMENTS AND CONVERSIONS

**OVEN TEMPERATURES**

| FAHRENHEIT | | CENTIGRADE |
|---|---|---|
| 500° F. | Extremely Hot | 260° C. |
| 450° F. | Very Hot | 235° C. |
| 400° F. | Hot | 215° C. |
| 350° F. | Moderate | 175° C. |
| 325° F. | Slow | 160° C. |
| 275° F. | Very Slow | 135° C. |
| 225° F. | Cool | 105° C. |

**COMMON MEASUREMENTS**

3 teaspoons = 1 tablespoon = 1/2 fluid ounce
2 tablespoons = 1/8 cup = 1 fluid ounce
8 tablespoons = 1/2 cup = 1/4 pint = 4 fluid ounces
1 cup = 1/2 pint
2 cups = 1 pint
4 cups = 1 quart
2 quarts = 1/2 gallon

**VOLUME**

1 teaspoon = 5 grams (.5 deciliter)
1 tablespoon = 15 grams (1.5 deciliters)
1 fluid ounce = 30 grams (3 deciliters)
1 quart = 900 grams (.95 liter)
1 gallon = 3.60 kilograms (3.8 liters)
1 liter = 1.06 quarts = 954 grams
1 cup = 200 grams (237 milliliters)

**CONVERSION TABLE**

*Centigrade into Fahrenheit:* multiply centigrade temperature by 9, divide by 5, and add 32

*Fahrenheit into centigrade:* subtract 32 from the Fahrenheit temperature, multiply by 5, then divide by 9

*Ounces to grams:* multiply ounces by 28.35

*Grams to ounces:* multiply grams by .035

*Centimeters to inches:* multiply centimeters by .39

*Inches to centimeters:* multiply inches by 2.54

**DRY OR SOLID INGREDIENTS**

| INGREDIENT | AMERICAN/ENGLISH | | METRIC |
|---|---|---|---|
| Rice | 1 teaspoon | 1/6 ounce | 5 grams |
| Salt | 1 tablespoon | 1/2 ounce | 15 grams |
| Margarine | 1 cup | 8 ounces (1/2 pound) | 240 grams |
| Dried fruit | 2 cups | 16 ounces (1 pound) | 500 grams |

## DRY OR SOLID INGREDIENTS

| INGREDIENT | AMERICAN/ENGLISH | | METRIC |
|---|---|---|---|
| Spices | 1 teaspoon | 1/12 ounce | 2-1/2 grams |
| Grated cheese | 1 cup | 4 ounces | 100 grams |
| Rice flour | 1 tablespoon | 1/2 ounce | 15 grams |
| | 1 cup | 4 ounces | 120 grams |
| | 2 cups | 8 ounces (1/2 pound) | 240 grams |
| | 4 cups | 16 ounces (1 pound) | 500 grams |
| | 8-1/2 cups | 2 pounds, 3 ounces | 1 kilogram |

## STANDARD CAN SIZES

| CAN SIZE | WEIGHT | CONTENTS |
|---|---|---|
| 6-ounce | 6 ounces | 3/4 cup |
| 8-ounce, or buffet | 8 ounces | 1 cup |
| No. 1, flat | 9 ounces | 1 cup |
| No. 1, picnic | 10-1/2 to 12 ounces | 1-1/4 cups |
| No. 300 | 14 to 16 ounces | 1-3/4 cups |
| No. 303 | 16 to 17 ounces | 2 cups |
| No. 2 | 20 ounces | 2-1/2 cups |
| No. 2-1/2 | 1 pound, 13 ounces | 3-1/2 cups |
| No. 3 cylinder (46 ounces) | 3 pounds, 4 ounces | 5-3/4 cups |
| No. 10 | About 7 pounds | 12 to 13 cups |

## COMPARATIVE MEASURES

| AMERICAN/ENGLISH | | METRIC |
|---|---|---|
| 1 ounce | — | 32 grams, or .035 kilogram |
| 1 pound | 16 ounces | 454 grams |
| 2.2 pounds | — | 1000 grams, or 1 kilogram |
| — | 3-1/2 ounces | 100 grams |
| 1 teaspoon | 1/6 ounce | 5 grams (5 milliliters) |
| 1 tablespoon | 1 dessertspoon, or 1/2 ounce | 15 grams (15 milliliters) |
| 4 ounces | 1/5 pint | 1/10 liter |
| 8 ounces | 2/5 pint | 1/4 liter |
| 16 ounces | — | 1/2 liter |
| 20 ounces | 1 pint | — |
| 32 ounces | — | 1 liter |
| 34 ounces | 1-3/4 pints | — |
| 64 ounces | — | — |
| 68 ounces | — | 2 liters |